TEACHING IN SOCIAL WORK

TEACHING IN SOCIAL WORK

AN EDUCATORS' GUIDE TO THEORY AND PRACTICE

Jeane W. Anastas

COLUMBIA UNIVERSITY PRESS   NEW YORK

COLUMBIA UNIVERSITY PRESS
Publishers Since 1893
New York   Chichester, West Sussex

Library of Congress Cataloging-in-Publication Data
Anastas, Jeane W.
  Teaching in social work : an educators' guide to theory and practice /
Jeane W. Anastas
     p.   cm.
  Includes bibliographical references and index.
  ISBN 978-0-231-11524-7 (cloth : alk. paper)
  ISBN 978-0-231-11525-4 (pbk. : alk. paper)
  ISBN 978-0-231-52093-5 (e-book)
  1. Social work education. I. Title.
  HV11.A56 2010
  361.3071—dc22
                                                    2009041189

Columbia University Press books are printed on permanent and durable
   acid-free paper.
This book is printed on paper with recycled content.
Printed in the United States of America

*This book is dedicated to a gifted teacher and a lifelong friend,
Jennifer Rochow, who first introduced me to the literature on
teaching and learning in higher education from which I have
learned so much. I make this dedication with thanks for the
inspiration I have drawn from her life and work and for
the loving support she has provided in all aspects of mine.*

CONTENTS

Acknowledgments ix

1. Teachers and Learners in Social Work: A Framework 1
2. How Adults Think and Learn 13
3. Teaching Courses: Methods and Modalities 33
4. Affirming Diversity in the Classroom 61
5. Field Education in Social Work:
   Teaching Roles amid Old and New Challenges 93
   K. Jean Peterson
6. Technology in Social Work Education 115
   James W. Drisko
7. Assessing Learning and Teaching 151
8. Academic Jobs and Faculty Work 187
9. Ethical Issues in Teaching 223
10. Conclusion 255

References 263
Index 293

ACKNOWLEDGMENTS

YEARS AGO, THE LATE John Michel, a senior editor at Columbia University Press, encouraged me to develop a proposal for a book like this one. John was not only "my editor"; he was an intelligent, discerning, witty, and always encouraging friend. Sadly, I did not fully realize until after his passing the scope and value of his gifts to me over the years. I thank him for his role in the genesis of this work, and I hope I honor his memory by bringing this project to a conclusion.

Also important to the origin of this book have been the scores of doctoral students I have had the privilege of "teaching about teaching" in two different doctoral programs in social work, Smith College's School for Social Work and New York University's Silver School of Social Work. What I have learned from these experienced and successful learners who are or are aspiring to be teachers has been immeasurable. The doctoral students in these seminars provide new and useful insights every time I give the course, so I have been a learner as much as a teacher. Teaching about teaching is not easy. In addition, I know that my students are observing what I do, and I am humbled at how often I have to fall back on the motto of the hypocrite and the error prone: "Do as I say, not as I do." I thank all these students—past, present, and future—for how much they have contributed, often unwittingly, to my own teaching and the thinking that informs this book.

A few other people deserve special mention and thanks. Over the years, Dr. Starr Wood has read and commented helpfully on parts of this manuscript. When I came to New York University in late 1999, my colleagues Dr. Gary Holden and Dean Emeritus Thomas Meenaghan generously included me in their research on educational outcomes in the MSW program, a very valuable opportunity for me. Dean Suzanne England, a great supporter of the scholarship of teaching and learning, authorized a sabbatical leave for me in

2006/2007, much of which I spent working on this manuscript. Matt McGuirk, who works in information technology at the Silver School, generously helped in the final preparation of the illustration that presents the book's conceptual framework. Anonymous reviewers provided by Columbia University Press both at the prospectus stage and for the completed manuscript provided valuable feedback that has improved the final product. Now it is Lauren Dockett at Columbia University Press who has provided the patience and encouragement that enabled me to complete this long-term project. While all these people have contributed much, the flaws and limitations of this work cannot be attributed to anyone but me.

Finally, I thank my life partner and now spouse, Janice Gibeau, for her encouragement and forbearance during this long, drawn-out project. At the very least, she has endured too many hours of, as she would say, "looking at the back of my head." My gratitude for her enduring love and support is beyond measure.

TEACHING IN SOCIAL WORK

1

TEACHERS AND LEARNERS IN SOCIAL WORK:

A FRAMEWORK

JUST AS SOCIAL WORK EDUCATION has been growing in recent years, so has our knowledge about teaching effectively. In 2007, the Council on Social Work Education (CSWE) counted more than 180 accredited master's programs and more than 450 accredited baccalaureate programs in the United States, with more being developed (CSWE 2007b). Total student enrollment in these programs was estimated at about 32,000 in baccalaureate programs and 39,000 in master's programs in 2006/2007, all the students learning in either the classroom and/or the field. The Council on Social Work Education estimated that there were more than 8,000 faculty members in social work schools and departments in 2006/2007, 74 percent of them full time. These teachers and these learners are part of a profession that is predicted to grow in the coming years, in an increasingly multicultural society. These teachers and learners share the conviction that their clients need and deserve the services of social workers who are well prepared for this varied, complex, and demanding work.

In higher education generally, knowledge about how to teach effectively is expanding rapidly and is growing in sophistication. Social work educators traditionally have used a range of teaching methods. But even though many doctoral graduates in social work become full-time faculty in social work, only about one-third (Valentine et al. 1998) to one-half (Hesselbrock 2006) of social work doctoral programs require or make available courses on teaching. Because many doctoral students in social work decide to obtain a doctorate in order to enter academia, many would like better or more systematic preparation for teaching.

This book links the "practice wisdom" of today's social work educators with current theories and knowledge about students' learning and effective teaching methods. It is designed for newcomers to teaching in social work, for those who want to refresh their approach to their work, and for those in social work doctoral programs and educational administration to enhance their students' education.

This book, which grew out of teaching aspiring social work educators, summarizes the existing literature on teaching and learning in social work. It also draws selectively on the literature in the field of higher education more generally to show how teaching can be applied to social work education specifically. However, the literature on teaching in higher education is typically addressed to teaching in the academic disciplines, and not to the professions. Thus, we must consider how this knowledge can best be applied to social work education, whose goal of nurturing student growth must be combined with ensuring that graduates will be effective and ethical service providers. In some ways, I have tried to write the book I wished I had when I began to teach the teachers.

The framework I am using could be characterized as a "person-in-environment" perspective. Davis (1993), for example, described those factors that affect teaching and learning: the *teacher*, the *learner*, the *subject matter*, and the *setting*, meaning the educational institution, that is, the department or school and the university or college. Social work education has two settings for education: the classroom that is part of an *educational institution* and the *social service agency* in which field learning takes place. For a *profession* like social work, we also must consider the general social context, that is, the *society* in which the educational process takes place and in which the students will practice and apply what they have learned. A schematic representing this constellation might look something like figure 1.1.

The arrows at the center of the figure represent the processes of teaching and learning that place the teacher, the learner, and what is to be learned in a specific context. This book emphasizes the teacher, the learner, the settings in which they interact, and especially the processes and kinds of interactions they are engaged in. Among the several excellent recent books on field instruction and field learning in social work, now considered the "signature pedagogy" of the field (CSWE 2008), are those by Bogo and Vayda (1998) and Ortiz Hendricks, Finch, and Franks (2005). With the exception of a chapter on field learning by guest author K. Jean Peterson, the book concentrates on classroom teaching.

In the past, the literature in social work education predominantly addressed the subject matter of social work education, which is what the U.S. curricular standards focused on and what both beginning and experienced teachers tend to think about most. This is not surprising, since content is

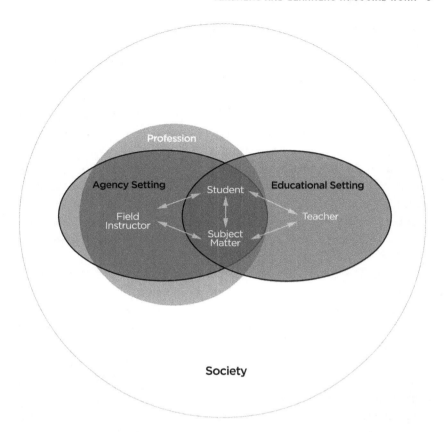

FIGURE 1.1 Model of teaching and learning in social work context.

important, and determining what a social worker should know and be able to do is especially important to a relatively new field or profession. In addition, people are generally recruited to teach social work because of what they already know and know how to do. Because social work curricula differ and because curriculum content is addressed elsewhere, this book concentrates on teaching and learning and the contributions to them of teacher, learner, subject matter, and setting. My aim is to draw attention to aspects of teaching that may not be considered when preparing to teach.

Bertha Reynolds (1942/1985) began her classic book on learning and teaching in social work by defining the subject of social work. Although I will not attempt to do the same, I agree with her that much content is generic to all social work. Reynolds, however, wrote only about graduate (and in-service) education, whereas this book intends to address teaching and learning in both BSW and MSW programs. Although the continuing education of professional social workers is thriving, continuing education and doctoral teaching each are sufficiently different from teaching in professional degree-granting programs to deserve separate treatment elsewhere.

Writing in the middle of World War II, Reynolds was acutely aware of how much social change and social challenges affect professional practice and social work education. Thus, while the influence of contemporary society—its problems and needs, ideas and ideologies, and resource issues—is never far from higher education in general, it is especially felt in social work education. Much of our discourse about curriculum is addressed to ensuring that what we teach is relevant to the changing world in which graduates will practice. This connection now includes bringing a global perspective to our work (CSWE 2008), which is a new emphasis in social work education in the United States.

The social work profession itself—its purpose, mission, and ethics—is intrinsically related to social aspirations and social needs, whatever the specific form of social work practice being taught. The subjects of social work programs must include the knowledge, values, and skills that define the scope and tradition of social work. Those who teach must be able to socialize students into the profession, and social work students must demonstrate that they can function as professionals with the requisite knowledge, values, and skills. Thus teachers, students, and learning environments must respond to professional norms in addition to the usual academic ones, which can lead to some predictable tensions.

Education in the professions means doing as well as knowing. There is a long tradition in social work of educating in the field as well as in the classroom. Social work education takes place in a variety of settings over which we, as teachers, have differing degrees of influence. While the traditional academy is in the process of discovering the value of real-world, doing-related, and community-based service learning, social work education has always made practicum learning intrinsic to its operations. Social work educators and social work students must contend with at least three kinds of settings: the college or university as a whole, the school or department and its classrooms, and the field agency. Tensions between school and university and between school and agency can affect students, teachers (their careers and their roles), and the curriculum.

Social work education takes place both inside and outside the academy, in world of the *social agency*. Field learning settings are part of the larger health and social service delivery systems to which human needs and current social problems are presented every day. Even though learning in the agency is not the main focus of this book, social work students are challenged to function in and transfer learning between both settings, meaning that classroom teachers must make what they do relevant to their practice. In addition, educators and academic administrators in social work must deal with two different teaching and learning contexts, and they have much more control over one of them than the other.

In part because we educate our students in both the classroom and the field setting, we use a variety of *teaching modalities*. Because we have defined social work education as including knowledge, values, and skills, we need different modes of teaching and learning to address them. Faculty must teach effectively, and students must learn effectively in both the classroom and the field, in classes and groups, and in dyadic supervisory and advisory relationships. We may require that students demonstrate their learning behaviorally, through examination, and/or through scholarly work. Much in the general literature on teaching and learning in higher education can help us choose among and improve on our teaching in all these modalities. In addition, many departments and school of social work are considering how best to incorporate new technologies, especially those that support distance learning. In figure 1.1, the complex, bidirectional set of lines that join teacher, student, and subject represent the teaching modalities used and the factors that must be considered when using them.

The literature has sometimes addressed who our students are, their motivations, values, and skills (or lack of them). We may be interested in what their personal histories contribute to or detract from their capacities to become effective social workers or clinical social workers. In addition, most schools try to recruit and retain students who reflect the diversity of contemporary society in race, ethnicity, language, religion, (dis)ability, and the like. In both undergraduate and graduate social work education, we are familiar with teaching what the higher education community calls "nontraditional" students, that is, those who are older and have significant life and work experiences. In fact, in graduate education, we tend to prefer to teach nontraditional students. This, in turn, has led to discussion of how adult education theory and models—androgogy instead of pedagogy—can be used to enhance teaching and learning in social work. We also have tried to identify students' differing learning styles and professional developmental issues (see, e.g., Saari 1989). Finally, our current accreditation standards (EPAS), like most others, are challenging schools to examine our students' educational outcomes more rigorously than in the past.

We know something (but not a lot) about the teachers who are currently working in social work education. We debate the importance and role of their post-MSW practice experience when hiring them and when admitting them to and preparing them in doctoral social work programs. We also know that as in other parts of the academy, women, minority faculty members, and teachers who concentrate on scholarly work, traditionally underrepresented groups may not fare as well in work assignments, teaching loads, publication, promotion, and other indicators of success in the academic workplace (LeDoux 1996). Even though the situation in social work is better than that in many other fields and disciplines, it is not yet a level playing field, despite our ideological commitment to make it so. Finally, we can do more to develop our faculty as teachers and as scholars and to help them succeed in their academic careers.

CONTENTS OF THIS BOOK

In each aspect of preparing to teach, many factors must be considered: teacher, learner, subject matter, setting, the profession, and society. This book looks at the aspirations, controversies, and tensions pertaining to diversity issues, which affect all aspects of the teaching and learning enterprise. Each chapter of the book highlights a different facet of being a social work educator.

Whatever the context, learning in the end is a personal enterprise, and any significant educational experience is always, to some extent, transformative for the learner. Chapter 2 compares some of the major theories of adult psychosocial and cognitive development that are commonly used in thinking about how students in higher education learn. These theories emphasize that social work education is *adult education* and that our teaching should be aimed at helping students think about more complex ideas. Learning styles also are important to what they say about effective teaching styles. In fact, enabling students to use a wider range of ways of knowing and styles of learning is itself an important educational outcome.

Chapter 3 considers the range of teaching modalities that can be used in social work education. Social work education, like other forms of professional education, requires knowledge, values, and skills. Teaching social work includes not only classroom instruction but also field instruction and advising. In addition, I describe the advantages and disadvantages of classroom teaching techniques, such as lecturing, discussion leading, using group and individual projects, and coaching and mentoring, with an emphasis on the teacher's ability to expand his or her repertoire of teaching techniques and to match the teaching modality to content and to students' learning goals and styles.

One way in which social work education has responded to the changing social context has been to address diversity issues, the topic of chapter 4. We speak about how the increasing diversity in U.S. society influences (or should influence) what we teach, that is, the curriculum. But our changing ways of understanding and dealing with diversity also influence who are students are, who our teachers are, and how the settings in which we teach—both the university and the social agency—respond to multicultural and other diversity issues. The tensions arising from these interactions are often points of anxiety or crisis but also opportunities for growth for students, faculty, and institutions. The ethics of the social work profession have helped sustain our collective and individual commitments to addressing diversity issues even when social forces tend to diminish them or render them invisible. Chapter 4 addresses the many challenges that remain in order to include diversity in what we teach, who we teach, and who teaches. We also review racial identity theory, especially in regard to teaching and learning and to understanding and overcoming some of the tensions in teaching about diversity in the current social context.

Chapter 5, by guest author K. Jean Peterson, covers teaching and learning in the field setting. Field learning must take into account the complexities of teaching and learning across the organizational boundaries of both schools and agencies. Peterson reviews the various models that social work education has used to frame this part of students' education, common issues in student learning in the field, and the roles of the field instructor and the faculty–field liaison in supporting student learning. The chapter concludes with a discussion of the current pressures on field education and some ideas about what will be needed in future.

Chapter 6, by guest author James Drisko, discusses the use of electronic technologies in teaching and learning. From the complexities of distance learning to computer-aided classroom instruction, electronic technologies are a hot topic in the academy today. While some people may see these tools as a welcome revolution, others worry about the possible negative effects on the teaching/learning relationship. This chapter gives an overview of the common technologies being used in social work education today in various areas, along with an assessment of the strengths and weaknesses of each. It includes tips on how and when they may best be applied from the perspective of someone who has considered them in relation to both teaching and practice.

These six chapters cover the key actors, settings, tools, and techniques in social work education. The next three examine other topics essential to understanding teaching in higher education. Chapter 7 looks at assessment and evaluation in social work education. One of the most worrisome tasks facing a beginning teacher is evaluating students' learning. In addition, the gatekeeping function of social work education typically competes with the helping impulse that faculty feel toward students, rooted in their identity as practitioners. Although this chapter follows those on learning, teaching modes, field education, and technology, its premise is that in planning a course or curriculum, student assessments provide important opportunities for learning beyond what happens each day in the classroom. The more that learning outcomes are emphasized in higher education, the more important it is that student assignments not depend solely on tradition and prior practice but also on opportunities for students to demonstrate that they have achieved specific learning goals. How faculty are evaluated in their teaching by students and others also is a great concern. While there has been much creative work in higher education generally on evaluation issues, little seems to have entered the mainstream of social work education, although that is beginning to change. This chapter considers evaluation techniques related to both teaching and learning and how they can be used to enhance social work education.

Because of the many and far-reaching missions of institutions of higher education in today's society, demands on faculty time and standards of excellence in job performance are limitless (Kennedy 1997). Chapter 8 describes faculty work, including classroom preparation, student advising and mentoring, committee work and other departmental and institutional service, professional and community service, and the scholarly work that is necessary to keep one's job and enrich one's teaching. All make demands on a faculty member's time. Building on this analysis of faculty work, the chapter summarizes what is known about those who are already employed in social work education. New data on the job market are presented to help in career planning, and the special obstacles that race, ethnicity, gender, sexual orientation, and other issues of difference may present to career development are discussed.

All professions are characterized by ethical commitments. In social work in the United States, the Code of Ethics of the National Association of Social Workers (1999), designed for practitioners, is the one most often named by social work programs for students to follow. The code discusses only briefly ethical issues in teaching and learning. Special ethical dilemmas arise in teaching and the academic setting. Chapter 9 covers theses ethical issues in greater depth as they apply to both students and teachers. As in all areas of professional ethics, awareness of the issues and the common pitfalls and dilemmas provides the best safeguard against ethical problems, and the chapter tries to alert teachers to potential problems and common ways of preventing or resolving them. Its placement toward the end of the book does not reflect its lack of importance; rather, I thought it better to describe all the major aspects of faculty work first—including those related to student assessment, teaching, and scholarship—in order to understand the many aspects of faculty work that have important ethical dimensions. Finally, the concluding chapter summarizes some main points of the book and suggests areas in which social work education needs further study and development.

LIMITATIONS

Some important areas are not covered in this book. Technologies for research and teaching are rapidly expanding, and an obvious omission is an extensive discussion of online education. Although chapter 6 talks about online learning, it is in comparing this kind of teaching with a "bricks and mortar" education. Some online programs do offer social work, and human service programs are available, at the BSW, MSW, and PhD levels. To date, however, only one such program has obtained CSWE accreditation, so this book addresses the most common teaching environment, which has at least some face-to-face and place-based teaching.

Continuing education—education and training that takes place after a degree is awarded—is another area important to the profession that is not addressed here. As in such professions as medicine and nursing, many states require continuing education credits for relicensing in social work. Accreditation standards require that students conduct themselves as social workers, which includes "engag[ing] in lifelong learning" (CSWE 2008:3). Schools and departments of social work (and other professional and service delivery organizations) often offer continuing education courses to graduate practitioners and field instructors, as well as development opportunities for their own faculty and/or adjunct and full-time teachers. As with supervision, however, this is a topic that merits its own discussion and analysis.

Another area not covered is international or global education in social work, which is being emphasized in higher education generally and in social work education specifically (see, e.g., Abram and Cruce 2007; Askeland and Payne 2006; Drucker 2003). Global and international issues are presented in higher education by students from overseas studying in U.S. institutions of higher learning and U.S. students going abroad for some portion of their studies. For social work programs, global issues also come up in the practice settings where social workers serve many migrant groups, those who are here voluntarily as well as displaced populations fleeing war, torture, and other disasters. The social work curriculum must prepare students for these contingencies. Finally, many schools and departments of social work have relationships with service programs and social work education programs abroad. There are both uncritical ("export") and critical (e.g., "reverse mission" and anticolonial) models for them, meaning that they deserve attention and new scholarship of their own. Their omission here does not represent lack of interest or importance but, instead, my lack of specialized knowledge.

Perhaps the most important limitation of this volume is that it surveys many topics rather than dealing in depth with a few. For example, chapter 2 presents several different models of adult learning and cognitive development rather than exploring in detail any one of them and its implications. Similarly, chapter 8 covers common job responsibilities for full-time faculty, some features of the tenure process, and a bit about searching for faculty jobs. Entire books have been written about the many topics covered in each of these (and the other) chapters. The hope is to entice readers to learn more about specific topics of interest to them from the books and articles on the reference list and on their own.

The social work profession itself continues to evolve and change, and discussion of how these changes may, should, or should not drive changes in social work education is also beyond the scope of this book. Social work educators of the future must craft creative new ways of meeting these challenges and bringing out the best in our students. Only in this way can we ensure that those who need social work services now and in the future will get the excellent service that they deserve. However, it is my hope that readers will find in this volume information that will help them begin, renew, or foster in others an effective and fulfilling approach to being a social work educator.

BECOMING AND RENEWING

Like responsible professional practitioners, all of us who teach should engage in self-reflection and continuing professional development and renewal. This and other books on how to teach may help in that effort. New challenges are always arising; for example, I now often hear stairwell conversations about managing the presence of electronic devices (cell phones, PDAs, laptop computers, and live Internet connections) in the classroom, keeping them available for the legitimate enhancement of learning while effectively proscribing their use for texting, game playing, and/or personal e-mail, all of which distract the student involved and others as well.

A Chinese proverb that a student told me is "To teach is to learn twice." I began work on this book many years ago because I had begun teaching seminars on teaching to doctoral students in social work and was challenged to develop content for those courses, which I continue to teach today. At the time, more information on how to teach, as opposed to what to teach, was available in the higher education literature than in social work, which has changed a great deal for the better since then. The reason I developed the broad "teacher-in-situation" conceptual framework for this book (and in my teaching), however, is that my experience has convinced me that taking context into account at all levels produces the best teaching and makes career development in academia more understandable for beginning professors. Like every industry/occupation, higher education has its mores and unwritten rules, and whether or not one is critical of the current arrangements, it is important to explain them.

Beginning a career as a social work educator, which is most commonly done during doctoral studies, is intellectually, professionally, and personally challenging (McGranahan 2008; Sussman, Stoddart, and Gorman 2004). Stresses may arise from being simultaneously a student and a teacher. Other stresses may be specific to adapting to a research university setting in which the doctoral program is located and can be seen as devaluing the practice experience that in fact may qualify one to teach (Mendenhall 2007; Sussman, Stoddart, and Gorman 2004). McGranahan's article emphasizes what she wished she had known in conducting her first class, which she learned from a mentor and later in a course on teaching. Both Sussman and colleagues (2004) and McGranahan (2008) emphasize the importance of self-reflection in becoming a teacher. Only McGranahan speaks about the joys of teaching and the passion for the material that got her through the tough times and that keep her motivated to improve her teaching skills. Perhaps the most important thing we can do in mentoring new faculty is to help them get in touch with the rewards of the work and to emphasize the assets, from both their practice experience and their continuing education, they bring to their work.

To use Bertha Reynolds's terminology, becoming a social work educator, as in the rest of academia, used to be a matter of "sink or swim." Fortunately, there is much more available now in the literature of social work and of higher education more generally, in campus-based centers and in social work doctoral programs to help the new or renewing teacher. As a beginning, some recommended journals are *Journal of Baccalaureate Education in Social Work*, *Journal of Social Work Education*, *Journal of Teaching in Social Work*, and *Social Work Education*. There is much to admire in the current state of teaching in social work, but there is also much we could improve, individually and collectively. If this book helps in this endeavor, I will have achieved my goal.

2

HOW ADULTS THINK AND LEARN

Just as living involves the whole person, so does learning, especially learning to practice an art which is intimately the person, using sensitivity and judgment in relation to adapting knowledge and skills to a real situation.

B. C. REYNOLDS, *LEARNING AND TEACHING IN THE PRACTICE OF SOCIAL WORK*

THE BEST TEACHING IS BASED on a sound understanding of learning. In addition, the kinds of skills needed to practice social work effectively require complex learning and thinking skills that are characteristic of advanced levels of cognitive development in adulthood. Adult development is, of course, a vast field that cannot be adequately summarized in one short chapter. In recent decades, we have changed our understanding of adulthood and now think of it as a time of dynamic development and continued learning. In particular, we now know much about how adults develop their thinking and learning in both education and professional development.

Adults do not function and learn in the same ways that children do, so we must examine our assumptions about how to support, nurture, and enhance growth and learning in adults. Whether we teach undergraduate or graduate students, we should be aware that the greatest growth in higher education enrollments in the United States in recent years has been in *nontraditional* students, that is, those who are older than 18 or so and are returning to school often many years after completing high school or college. Many of these students are not studying full time but are simultaneously holding jobs or rearing families or both. We therefore must consider their ages, life situations, and work experiences when we help them learn to be professional social workers.

This chapter focuses on the individual student, as shown in figure 1.1. Our understanding of the individual learner must include the society and culture in which he or she has developed and is currently functioning (figure 2.1). In addition, the particular demands of professional practice affect the kinds of thinking and learning that we must be educating *for*, so we discuss how key traditions in social work education relate to current conceptions of learning in adulthood. Finally, what we know about adult thinking and learning has

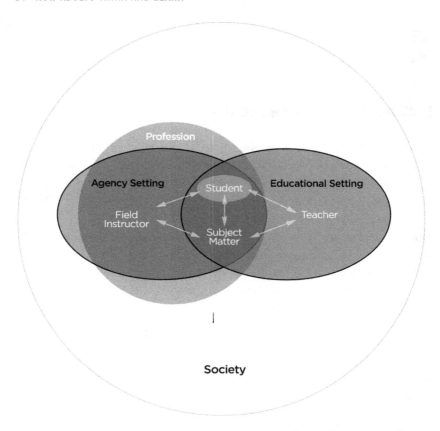

FIGURE 2.1 Model of teaching and learning that highlights student development.

implications for our teaching, for the arrow in figure 2.1 representing the interaction or relationship between learner and teacher.

Besides the many theories explaining cognitive development in childhood, we have developed many models to understand thinking and learning
in adults. While theories are always imperfect models for a particular person, they can be useful in drawing our attention to common characteristics
that may be helpful in identifying an individual's learning needs. Understanding how adults learn and know can help us teach effectively, whether
it is one on one, when advising or supervising, or in groups, when in the
classroom. As Mentkowski and associates (2000) put it, understanding learning, understanding the learner, and envisioning the learner as a mature,
motivated, and self-directed person will help create learning that lasts in the
postgraduate environment.

INDIVIDUAL DEVELOPMENT IN ADULTHOOD

Much of our understanding of development in adulthood is based on stage theories that were developed from mid-twentieth century onward. Erik Erikson (1963) was the first to write about developmental stages that extended into late adolescence and beyond. He also showed that working on such life tasks as choosing and preparing oneself for a specific vocation were essential to forming a psychological identity. Accordingly, social work educators may encounter students in late adolescence and early adulthood, like traditional students in undergraduate social work programs, who, for the first time, are establishing an identity separate from that of their family. Other students may be entering the field later in life, perhaps looking for a greater sense of "generativity." Understanding *who* is learning is essential (Mentkowski and associates 2000).

Levinson's (1978) longitudinal research on college-educated men also has influenced our thinking about the education of adults (Tennant and Pogson 1995). Of Levinson's major eras in life, each lasting about twenty-five years, the two that most often concern social work educators are early adulthood (ages 17 to 45) and middle adulthood (ages 40 to 65). The educational experience is generally quite different for people at these two stages because of their different developmental tasks and challenges. Early adulthood is concerned with "entering the adult world" and building a life structure that includes both work and intimate or family life. Following Erikson, Levinson's theory states that working on *preparing oneself for an occupation or profession* proceeds at the same time as work on other major life tasks. Therefore, when students' reactions to feedback on their educational performance seem extreme, it may be helpful to remember that a great deal may be at stake psychologically for them, in what appears to the teacher to be only a simple educational matter. In addition to the psychological sense of identity, what is at stake in Levinson's view is "the dream" that is providing the road map to an adult life course.

In contrast, midlife may be a time when people try to find "a better balance between the needs of the self and the needs of society" (Tennant and Pogson 1995:73). This may be the point at which a person decides to change careers to one that seems more rewarding or meaningful or the time when a woman who has been largely engaged in child rearing reenters school to prepare to enter or reenter the workforce. People at this stage of life begin their educational process with a psychological identity and life and work experiences quite different from those of a young adult. In addition, these students, at different phases of life, must study and work together, respecting one another while still meeting their differing learning needs. Their teacher also will be challenged to teach students from these different starting points.

Levinson speaks of "normative disequilibrium," during which people are negotiating changes in life eras and the stages within them. Often at such times, people choose to enter a degree-granting program or to change occupations or professions. At such times, people may be psychologically fragile but may also have the potential for rapid growth and change.

Erikson's and Levinson's theories, however, do not take into account important contextual and social factors. Neugarten (1976) was one of the first critics to point out that the meaning of being a certain age is profoundly affected by the historical epoch in which one is living. For example, in the United States, being 40 in the latter decades of the twentieth century, when the average life expectancy was in the eighties, and being 40 at the beginning of the century, when the average life expectancy was in the forties, suggested quite different life chances and developmental tasks.

Cultural and social context also affect all development, including adult development. For example, at age 40, an immigrant may have to repeat tasks associated with a different age, like choosing and preparing for employment in a new context, tasks already negotiated in a different linguistic, cultural, and social context. Some people lose their previous professional status or legitimacy, which can be psychologically stressful. Depending on the circumstances of migration and the differences between the old and new situations, choosing a new occupation may be either a welcome or unwelcome challenge.

In addition, Levinson's original research was done only on men, and there is still controversy about how well his and other theories of adult development fit the realities of women's lives or patterns of learning (see, e.g., Belenky et al. 1986; Gilligan 1982; Miller 1976). In particular, Gilligan (1982) and Belenky and her colleagues (1986) raised issues that influenced educational practice. Gilligan, as well as Miller and her colleagues, pointed out that these models of personal and developmental achievement and cognitive development are based on a male assumption of separateness, independence, and competition as the goals and signs of healthy adult development, norms that may also apply best to Western industrialized societies.

ADULT THINKING AND LEARNING

The work of Belenky and her colleagues (1986) is especially relevant to education. Noting that ideas about cognitive development in adulthood, such as those of Perry (1970), were also based on research on male undergraduate students in an elite university, Belenky and her colleagues studied a group of poor, rural women who were nontraditional students enrolled in a college program to examine how they approached learning and how their ways of thinking developed and changed. What they discovered was different from the earlier findings on young men, and their findings have influenced the social work education literature. They described many of the women as beginning from a position of "silence," of having no "voice" or placing little value on anything they might think, know, or say (see figure 2.1). Belenky and her colleagues (1986) argued that this position was found more often in women than in men because of women's many experiences of disadvantage, even oppression. From this position, many women then moved to a position of "received knowledge," of placing value on what expert others, such as teachers or books, might have to say. They thus equated learning with listening, with "hearing, understanding, and remembering" (45). This position resembles what students and the educational process look like in the traditional "empty vessel" model of teaching and learning and also reflects dualism, or the idea that every question has a right and a wrong answer. The position of "subjective knowing" was the most common among the women that Belenky and her colleagues (1986) studied. As they observed, "the move away from silence and an externally oriented perspective on knowledge and truth eventuates in a new conception of truth as personal, private, and subjectively known or intuited" (54). The shift to this position often reflected experiences with "failed authority," that is, with traumatic or invalidating family, interpersonal, or social experiences. The shift out of dualism is regarded as important to all models of adult cognitive development because it involves "the inward watching and listening" needed for the development of an authentic self. For educational purposes, however, like preparing people to be professional practitioners, scholars, or critical thinkers, this is a necessary achievement for doing the work.

A more complex epistemological position that Belenky and her colleagues (1986) found among the women they studied was what they called "procedural knowledge." That is, the women believed that "intuitions may deceive; that gut reactions can be irresponsible and no one's gut feeling is infallible; that some truths are truer than others; that they can know things they have never seen or touched; that truth can be shared; and that expertise can be respected" (93). This is called procedural knowledge because one of its important features is evaluating *how* a given piece of knowledge was derived. It may be characterized by an emphasis on the impersonal rules of method ("separate knowing," emphasizing doubt, skepticism, and objectivity) or on empathic connection, the ability to suspend judgment and to take another's perspective even when it is different from one's own ("connected knowing"). The final position described is termed "constructed knowledge," in which women tried to "reclaim the self by attempting to *integrate* knowledge that they felt intuitively was personally important with knowledge they had learned from others . . . of weaving together the strands of rational and emotive thought and of integrating objective and subjective knowing" (134, italics in original). Here, people are "challenged, not daunted" by conflict and ambiguity and are actively concerned with the moral and spiritual as well as the pragmatic dimensions of their actions. As the epigraph at the beginning of the chapter illustrates, these more complex ways of knowing are what is required in reconciling the specifics of a case or situation with general knowledge, in keeping the value dimension of professional practice in view, and in dealing with complex psychological, interpersonal, organizational, cultural, and social realities that must be taken into account in all social work practice.

Merdinger (1991) pointed out that for women and others from nondominant groups in the society, the simple but profound act of finding "voice," of developing confidence in the value of one's own perceptions and experiences in a situation and of being able to describe those perceptions to others, must be a goal of learning. In fact, traditional reflective techniques often used in the classroom and the field, such as keeping a journal and process recording, require students to record their personal observations, perceptions and subjective reactions to the practice encounters, readings, or classroom events. While students may regard these exercises as a way for the teacher to "find them out" as "right" or "wrong" in their perceptions or actions, they are in fact exercises in identifying and giving voice to their own experiences. This approach maintains that only from a firm anchoring in the self can one move to the multiple meanings of an interaction as various clients and practitioners (and learners) might experience them, and hence to enlarge the possibilities for actions and responses. It is important to remember that culture influences what is regarded as appropriate behavior for a learner and that silences in the classroom may have multiple and unexpected meanings (Holley and Steiner 2005; Zhou, Knoke, and Sakamoto 2005).

Drawing on this and other research, Davis (1993), Tennant and Pogson (1995), and others summarized what these conceptions of learning and knowing say about cognitive development in adulthood. These ideas, along with those of Belenky and colleagues (1986), are summarized in table 2.1. In part because they based their ideas on the early work of Perry (1970), these mod-

TABLE 2.1 Conceptions of Learning and Knowing for Adult Cognitive Development

WOMEN'S WAYS OF KNOWING (BELENKY ET AL. 1986)		STAGES OF REFLECTIVE JUDGMENT (KING AND KITCHENER 1994)		EPISTEMOLOGIES (PARTIAL) (KEGAN 2000)	
Epistemological position	Learning goal	Stage	View of knowledge	Epistemology	
Silence	Finding voice; identifying and valuing one's own feelings, perceptions, and thoughts.	1	(Childhood) Knowledge is absolute, concrete, and self-evident; single-category belief system.		
Received knowledge	Feeling capable of hearing, understanding, and remembering. Knowledge is "right" or "wrong" as determined by expert others. Dualistic thinking.	2	(Adolescence) Dualism: knowledge is either right or wrong. Correct knowledge is accessible with recourse to the correct source, such as an expert		
Subjective knowledge	A belief in multiple, personal truths. When there is disagreement, final reference is to the "inner voice" (rather than expert others) and what "feels right." Experience is the best source of knowledge. Self-reflection is key.	3	Sometimes even experts do not have access to the truth at the time. When there is no concrete evidence or expertise available, recourse is to what feels right at the moment.	Socialized mind	Cognitively concerned with ideals, values, hypotheses, inference, and hypotheses, inference, and generalization. Interpersonally concerned with role consciousness, mutual reciprocity, fairness, and point of view. Self-consciousness about one's own dispositions, needs, and preferences. (Traditionalism)
		4	Knowledge is uncertain because of inadequacies in the knower. There is skepticism about authority and experts. Well-structured (solvable) and ill-structured problems can be distinguished		

(continued on next page)

TABLE 2.1 Conceptions of Learning and Knowing for Adult Cognitive Development *(continued)*

WOMEN'S WAYS OF KNOWING (BELENKY ET AL. 1986)		STAGES OF REFLECTIVE JUDGMENT (KING AND KITCHENER 1994)		EPISTEMOLOGIES (PARTIAL) (KEGAN 2000)
Epistemological position	Learning goal	Stage	View of knowledge	Epistemology
Procedural knowledge *	How knowledge was generated is key to evaluating it. Doubting, listening to reason, perspective taking, suspending judgment, and striving to acknowledge but suspend the personal are characteristic.	5	Knowledge must be placed in a context because interpretation plays a role in perception. Hence it is not possible to evaluate the worth of differing interpretations from different perspectives	
		6	Although knowing is seen as interpretive and contextual, knowing also involves evaluating different points of view by comparing evidence and opinions across contexts.	Self-authoring mind — Cognitively concerned with the relationships among abstractions, the formulation of problems. Mutuality is a goal. Self-regulation, self-formation, and autonomy are emphasized. Systemic thinking. (Modernism)
		7	Although knowledge is interpretive and contextual, one can make justifiable claims about the better or best solution to a problem through critical inquiry and by synthesizing existing evidence.	
Constructed knowledge	"All knowledge is constructed, and the knower is an intimate part of the known." Integration of inner and outer voices. Listening and talking are essential. Tolerance of ambiguity.			Self-transforming mind — Cognitively trans- or post-ideological. Exploration of paradox and contradiction. Complexity accepted. Interpersonally recognizes interpenetration of self and other. (Postmodernism)

* In this position, Belenky and colleagues (1986) distinguish between separate and connected knowers, which, for space reasons, is not described here (see Belenky and Stanton 2000).

els share certain features. Truth goes from being seen as unitary to dualistic (right versus wrong) to potentially multiple. The way that personal experience is viewed and used also changes from being irrelevant compared with the knowledge of experts to being a source of knowledge by being able to reflect on and contextualize it.

At first, subjectivity does not seem relevant, then is overly valued in the face of ambiguity or uncertainty, and finally is integrated into a multidimensional approach to knowing.

While each of the theories outlined differs in the specific stages or phases it addresses, all describe a progression from simpler to more complex ideas of truth; from a focus on *what* is known to *how* knowledge is developed and by whom; from reliance on expert others to the ability to evaluate truth claims oneself; and from universalistic to contextual perspectives on knowledge. Tolerance of uncertainties and ambiguities is emphasized as well.

In teaching, we often overestimate our students' cognitive level of development (Davis 1993). Wherever they actually are according to these schemes, they have the potential to advance their cognitive development, since each phase contains valuable components of the next ones. In addition, especially when meeting a new challenge, in a new situation, or at other times of stress, any of us can revert to earlier ways of knowing because they all remain part of us.

Students often come to school expecting access to a dualistic truth and are disappointed to be encouraged to see the world as more complex. These theories about knowledge also suggest that our students will start at different points and differ in how far they are likely to progress in their ways of knowing as we are teaching them. For example, Belenky and her colleagues (1986) and Kegan (2000) explicitly relate their highest-level epistemologies (constructed knowledge and the self-transforming mind) with postmodernism, which is not currently the dominant paradigm in many fields of study.

Competent social work practice requires that general knowledge be applied to specific clients and situations in the context of the complexity of the helping relationship. Because lifelong learning is necessary in any professional career, we must find ways to help our students become self-reflective and conscious of their own learning needs. We also must help them understand that knowledge depends on context and standpoint and how to understand and tolerate the ambiguities and uncertainties of this recognition. While not all our students will fully achieve these goals, this must be the vision we hold out to them.

Many traditions and practices in social work education are already well adapted to these goals. Field instruction represents learning through experience and reflection on that experience, as do teaching from cases and using techniques like role-playing to learn interviewing techniques in the class-room. The reflective judgment model (King and Kitchener 1994) is based on an analysis of how adults think about "ill-defined problems." In fact, there may be no better way to describe the practice situations that students (and graduate social workers) face and are asked to analyze and act on every day. Adult learning theory has caught up with tacit knowledge in the field of so-cial work education. Revisiting these educational practices in light of adult learning theory, however, can help us use them in the ways that will best help students learn.

CRITICAL THINKING

Critical thinking, which is increasingly viewed as central to undergraduate and graduate education, is now also a mandated area of curricular content in social work education (CSWE 2008). According to Scriven and Paul (2008), "Critical thinking is that mode of thinking—about any subject, content, or problem—in which the thinker improves the quality of his or her thinking by skillfully taking charge of the structures inherent in thinking and imposing intellectual standards upon them." Although some social work educators have begun to assess critical thinking skills formally as a measure of educational outcome (see, e.g., Clark 2002), developing feasible social work–specific mea-sures remains a challenge (Gibbs et al. 1995).

At their highest levels, all these models of cognitive development describe a complex consideration of knowledge, its sources, and its limitations. To the extent that these highest levels of cognitive functioning encompass *thinking about thinking*, they can be thought of as critical thinking (box 2.1). Teaching critical thinking skills includes identifying the common errors in thinking, as Gambrill (2006) does, to which all humans are prone, a feature *not* in these developmental models. As Scriven and Paul (2008) state, "Critical thinking of any kind is never universal in any individual; everyone is subject to episodes of undisciplined or irrational thought." This belief is based on both logic and cognitive science (see, e.g., Gambrill 2006; Tavris and Aronson 2007). Recog-nizing common errors in thinking is vital to self-monitoring and improving one's thinking and judgment.

Potter and East (2000) argued that the reflective judgment model is use-ful for fostering critical thinking. Levels of reflective judgment have not yet been used as an outcome measure in social work education, in part because the accepted protocol for assessing them is an intensive interview (King and Kitchener 1994; Potter and East 2000). Earlier research showed, though, that the level of reflective judgment usually rises with the level of education. Thus it is reasonable to assume that a social work education program could improve thinking skills in general and reflective judgment in particular. Potter and East (2000) suggest several attitudes and behaviors that instructors can use to enhance students' reflective judgment, including framing their course contents as a series of solutions to ill-structured problems rather than as a collection of immutable facts; modeling comfort with ambiguity; refusing to oversimplify complex concepts and content; and accepting students' varying levels of thinking skills while expecting improvement in them. Most important, Potter and East emphasize that it is the opportunity to share thoughts and to be exposed to multiple perspectives on issues and situations that best supports the development of higher levels of reflective judgment.

CRITICAL CONSCIOUSNESS

The pursuit of social justice is considered a defining characteristic of the social work profession (CSWE 2008). Some social work educators use Freire's (2000) work to direct their teaching toward "conscientization," using participatory teaching and learning processes to raise consciousness about oppressions, reduce power hierarchies in the classroom, and enhance students' commitment to antioppressive and social change activities (see, e.g., hooks 1994). Unlike developmental models of adult thinking and learning that recommend that individuals achieve specific levels of thinking, the process of consciousness raising must be continuous because the dominant social discourses tend to obscure or "mystify" (a Marxist term) the oppressions inherent in society. Consciousness raising also is a group or collective process in which "teachers" and "students" educate each other equally. This model contrasts with the standard view of social work (or any professional) education in which students must demonstrate an acceptable level of expertise in the field in order to be credentialed to graduate and to practice, with the "gatekeeping" responsibility falling to the teacher and to the educational institution as a whole, meaning that a power imbalance is part of teaching.

Freire's original critique of the "banking model" of education, in which expert teachers "deposit" knowledge into passive students, has had broad influence on adult education, in promoting active learning and in educational efforts described as "progressive" (the work of Belenky and colleagues is an example). In its original form, however, this model, as exemplified in the subtitle of hooks's widely read 1994 work, is about "teaching to transgress." As such, it also requires critiquing and transforming the institutions and societies in which both students and teachers live and do their work. In this way it is revolutionary and is identified most closely with radicals and radical critiques of the profession and society. Feminists and others committed to ideas of "critical consciousness" (see, e.g., Sakamoto and Pitner 2005) are those most likely to use this theory of learning in their teaching.

LEARNING STYLES

Another perspective on adult thinking and learning pertains to the ways in which people seem to learn best. This framework differs from those presented in table 2.1 because it also does not use a developmental hierarchy of skills in thinking but simply describes variations in approaches that individuals seem to prefer when solving problems. Kolb (1984) devised a system for thinking about styles of learning that has been used in social work. It contains four ways of interacting with the world, through *active experimentation, concrete experience, reflective observation,* and *abstract conceptualization.* Although everyone uses each of these learning modes, often in a cycle, most people learn using one of these styles more often than the others. Kolb also developed a nine-item inventory to assess these preferred learning styles. Based on this self-assessment, the modes on which the highest scores are obtained (active experimentation, concrete experience, reflective observation, or abstract conceptualization) determine the learning style with which an individual is most comfortable. *Assimilative learners* prefer reasoning, theoretical models, explanations, and working with ideas, concepts, and precise theories, that is, using a combination of abstract conceptualization and reflective observation. *Convergent learners* prefer problem-solving, decision-making models, the practical application of ideas, and technical or skill-based tasks. Those who like to learn through *accommodation* prefer doing and acting, carrying out plans, fitting theory to facts, and relying on other people for information. Those who are *divergent* in their thinking and learning gravitate toward inductive reasoning (generating concepts from observations), generating alternative ideas and implications, and using brainstorming and imagination in their work (Davis 1993). For example, some students in social work come with a history of success in working with people, based largely on intuition. Consequently, they sometimes find the more conceptual approaches to the work that they encounter in school both a threat and a challenge to their former ways of functioning. Such students need to have their earlier ways of learning affirmed while seeing the advantages of more conceptual approaches as well.

Traditional systems of higher education tend to use the assimilative mode of learning, which emphasizes abstract conceptualization and reflective observation, but the assumption in Kolb's model is that there is no single best way to learn. Unlike the traditional system, Kolb's model suggests that an educational goal might be helping each learner broaden his or her repertoire of ways to learn. For example, a student (an assimilative learner) in a doctoral seminar in which the participants were asked to discuss the progress of their dissertations and to provide consultation to one another (a group exercise in convergent learning) was angry that the professor did not lecture more, which she said was what she most enjoyed in an educational encounter. She was not as comfortable with the practical application of ideas and with problem solving with others, as she did not see how they could advance her own learning. She needed help in seeing this process as a legitimate form of learning, even if it was not her preferred one, which in turn would help her value and use such an approach with her own future students, some of whom probably will favor learning by reflecting on experience over learning in other ways. In fact, Kolb (1991/1998) pointed out that these different styles of learning form a *cycle* of learning, in which one moves from concrete experience to observation and reflection to abstract generalization and then to active experimentation, that is, testing out new ideas in action. Enhancing the number of ways in which students can learn is thus an important goal in itself.

Social work education has used Kolb's theory. One study (Van Soest and Kruzich 1994) showed that students at different educational levels (BSW versus MSW), field faculty, and classroom faculty all preferred different learning styles. Field faculty scored highest in concrete experience, and students' satisfaction with their relationship with the field instructor was highest when their preference scores for concrete experience were most like that of their supervisor. Raschick, Maypole, and Day (1998) also found that field students, and especially field faculty, tended to be concrete rather than abstract and active rather than reflective in their learning styles (the accommodator constellation). They also found that the degree of similarity between student and supervisor on the active experimentation / reflective observation continuum was related to the students' satisfaction with the learning experience in placement. All these studies recommended that field instructors learn how to modify their teaching techniques when needed to suit their supervisees' preferred learning styles.

Teachers, like learners, tend to prefer the styles of learning that come most easily to them (Cranton 1996). In fact, teachers tend to expect that students will learn in the same style that they do and therefore tailor their teaching methods to that style of learning. For example, if a teacher is most comfortable learning conceptually and reflectively, he or she, like the doctoral student in the preceding example, tends to think that lecturing and assigning readings are the best ways to convey knowledge. In fact, a mismatch in learning style between teacher and student is a common source of impasse in the teaching/learning situation. The challenge for teachers, then, is to determine students' differing learning styles and to develop teaching methods that can reach students with differing learning styles. The challenge for students is to be able to use a wider range of learning styles in the different learning situations they will encounter.

TRANSFORMATIONAL LEARNING

Teachers, of course, wish for students who can already use complex ways of thinking and learning in their work. But using complex ways of learning and thinking should be considered an achievement, not an expectation of where students will begin. In fact, the highest levels of conceptual development are considered to be rare even in middle adulthood (Davis 1993).

As we think about teaching, we must think about not only *what* our students think but also helping them transform *how* they think: "Transformative learning occurs when an individual has reflected on assumptions and expectations about what will occur, has found these assumptions to be faulty, and has revised them . . . it has the potential to lead to transformed meaning perspectives or changed ways of seeing the world" (Cranton 1996:2).

Focusing on theories and their underlying premises is one way of becoming aware of different "meaning perspectives." Appreciating that many perspectives can be useful in understanding an event or an interaction is another strategy that can encourage transformative learning. In fact, all teaching should be aimed at helping students move beyond their current levels of thinking and knowing to higher ones (Davis 1993). Hence, teaching about cultural diversity is not just an end in itself; it also can be a means of encouraging more complex perspectives on thinking and knowing. Because transformational learning refers to changes in how people think and learn, education that addresses ways of knowing can result in a "developmental shift (a new world view) rather than simply developmental progress" (Tennant and Pogson 1995:119).

Beginning teachers, especially, tend to think much more about content than about changes in perspective on meaning, or changes in thinking itself. In social work education, changes in thinking is sometimes referred to as the "development of critical thinking skills," although with some exceptions (Gibbs and Gambrill 1996), little that is specific to social work has been written about it.

The idea of transformative learning contains, explicitly or implicitly, the concepts of liberation from received and preconceived ideas and of critical reflection. That is, transformative learning is connected to a kind of critical thinking that can lead to social action and social change as well as personal transformation. Although not so radical, this view of transformative learning has its roots in the work of Freire (2000) as well as that of Mezirow and others who have made the term common usage in the adult education literature (Brookfield 2000). As Mezirow (2000) observed, new ways of thinking must lead to action, to reengagement with the world in new ways. Daloz (2000) found that socially responsible people can be understood as having transformed themselves and their original views of the world in profound ways. According to him, such a transformation in perspective that leads to a constructive engagement with the world for positive social change requires "constructive engagement with otherness" (110), an opportunity for reflective discourse about these experiences, a mentoring community of supportive others to nurture these new ideas and understandings, and "opportunities for committed action," for testing and grounding in action these ideas and commitments. Social work education uses some of these approaches to help students think critically about common or unexamined beliefs about social problems and the solutions to them and to adopt a different, professionally informed view of them instead.

A SOCIAL WORK THEORY OF STUDENT LEARNING

Although not as comprehensive or well researched as the general theories of adult learning just outlined, a model of student learning was developed for social work education, specifically clinical social work education (Reynolds 1942/1985), which Saari (1989) reworked for clinical supervision. This model rests essentially on "practice wisdom." In addition, although Saari (1989) suggested links between the stages and specific phases of a two-year MSW course of study, she found that students take varying amounts of time to reach each stage of development, especially considering the variation in program structures, which has only increased over time, and in the students' earlier experiences. While the original theory sees a fixed series of progressive stages, learners may instead cycle in and out of the various stages or stances at different points in or in different aspects of their work. That said, however, the stages are presented here for their heuristic value in understanding and connecting with how students think about their work.

Reynolds's (1942/1985) five stages of learning are based on how students view the work they are doing and thus how they view themselves as professional helpers. The first stage, *acute self-consciousness*, is reflected in students' view that *caring helps* (Saari 1989). In this stage, in a fashion reminiscent of Belenky and colleagues' (1986) position of "received knowledge," the teacher or field instructor is often perceived as "omnipotent and omniscient" (Saari 1989:39). Thus, any criticism or suggestion by a teacher may be seen as an attack on the student's motivations or goodness as a person. In addition, at this stage, students may unwittingly regard the clients they work with in their field placements "as need-fulfilling . . . since they provide students with the opportunity to demonstrate their caring" (Saari 1989:38). Students therefore tend to be reassuring to clients and take an action-oriented approach to their work in order to demonstrate their caring. The best teaching strategy for students at this stage is to be *security giving* (Reynolds 1942/1985:76), to affirm their positive motivations and evident abilities.

The second stage, *sink-or-swim adaptation*, reflects the practice idea that *talking helps* (Saari 1989). It is a stage of "barely keeping up with what the situation demands from moment to moment" (Reynolds 1942/1985:77), but also one in which the student can do less and listen more. Because the student at this stage is learning the language of the profession without being able to understand entirely what it may mean, the teacher may become frustrated having to deal with someone who "talks so well and does so poorly" (Reynolds 1942/1985:77). A combination of patience, support, and reassurance, along with the gradual introduction of new ideas, is needed to help students move beyond this stage.

In the third stage, students learn to *understand the situation without being able to control their own activity in it,* viewing practice from the conviction that *understanding helps* (Saari 1989). They no longer are so absorbed in the survival of the self in the helping situation but now are focused almost exclusively on helping the "other" feel heard and understood. At this stage, students' ability to understand the complexity of the client's situation is better developed than the ability to translate these understandings effectively into specific interventions. The role of the teacher is to help students think about what worked and what did not and why, and to extend new understandings of the client to the client's experience of the worker and then to the worker and her or his actions and interventions.

The fourth stage of this model is one of relative "mastery," *in which one can both understand and control one's own activity.* At this stage, students concentrate on the client, the practitioner, and their interaction, as well as on the conscious and unconscious, the psychological and social, and the unique and more universal factors in the interaction. As Reynolds (1942/1985) stated,

> The person can . . . see himself working as he might see another person in the situation working. He can criticize and change his approach as the situation demands something different. He has become professional in that he can apply knowledge to the solving of practical problems, using himself as an instrument, with all his acquired skills and his emotional responses disciplined and integrated to the professional purpose. (81)

This capacity to be self-observant and hence self-regulating, to contextualize, and to integrate the subjective and the objective reflects some of the higher levels of cognitive development described in figure 2.1. Reynolds (1942/1985) points out, however, that even at this advanced stage of professional learning, there is always a need for further stimulation and growth, even though a high level of self-regulation and autonomy in practice is possible.

Not every professional social worker reaches the fifth stage, *learning to teach what one has mastered.* Saari (1989) says little about this stage except that it is poorly understood. Reynolds (1942/1985) talks about being freed up enough from subject matter to consider also the complexities of learner, teacher, and learning context. Although Reynolds suggests that many social workers may not reach this stage of development, for those with graduate degrees as well as for many with a BSW, the supervision of others, a form of teaching, is an extremely common part of the work they will do, sooner rather than later in their professional careers.

Ortiz Hendricks, Finch and French (2005) applied Reynolds's model to students' learning about cultural competence in practice. Deal (2002) then combined Saari's (1989) adaptation of Reynolds's model with several other stage theories of clinical learning in order to give supervisors of MSW students a map of students' expected stages of learning about direct or clinical practice during the two years of an MSW program. Although some evidence supports the idea that clinical MSW students typically reach Reynolds's (1942/1985) or Saari's (1989) third stage of learning at the end of the second year field placement (Deal 2000; Platt 1993), there are other ways to conceptualize the observed changes and some evidence that skill and confidence can regress sometimes, too (Deal 2000, 2002).

THE REFLECTIVE PRACTITIONER

Schön's (1983, 1987) theory of how professional practitioners function has in- fluenced social work educators, especially those who teach practice and/or are involved in field learning. Unlike the models of adult learning presented in figure 1.1, this theory is not specifically developmental. Rather, it describes a complex way of functioning, sharing many features of these models' higher levels of cognitive functioning.

Schön's theory offers the idea of "reflection-in-action" to capture how all professions must deal not just with thinking but also with taking action. His theory rejects technocratic views of professional functioning. The steps in this process are (re)framing a problem, holding both the uniqueness of each practice encounter and prior (general) knowledge in kind, making a tenta- tive "experiment" in action in the practice situation, and evaluating what was learned from each practice "move." This process is intended to be iterative and continually evaluative. It uses both science and artistry to apply the general to the specific case. It engages both inner and outer sources of knowledge and insight, acknowledges complexity and ambiguity, and considers the contributions of both the self and others to the problem and any solutions tried. Self-awareness is central. Functioning in this way may be thought of as manifesting a high level of complexity in cognitive functioning. Whatever the professional field, Schön (1987) sees the practicum experience as central to educating the reflective practitioner, but classroom activities like role-playing can also be used to teach students how to practice in this way. Classroom teachers, like practitioners, must address both content and process in real time as they unfold in interaction with others. Mishna and Bogo (2007) suggest that reflection-in-action following the Schön model (1983, 1987) can be useful for social work educators in the classroom, especially when conflict occurs.

"BORN OR MADE?"

I often ask the doctoral students in my classes on teaching what the characteristics of an ideal social work student might be. Box 2.2 shows some common answers to my question. Obviously, admissions processes are designed to select students for undergraduate and graduate degree programs who seem capable and motivated to become social work practitioners. But academic screening and selection processes are inherently imperfect, and students arrive with differing educational backgrounds, life experiences, and personal characteristics. While my students (and most teachers) wish that all their students had these characteristics, current theories of adult learning suggest that with the correct teaching approaches, these virtues can be drawn out or enhanced in students.

BOX 2.2

Sensitive	Open to learning
Flexible	Curious/inquisitive
Committed	Critical thinker
Nonjudgmental	Motivated
Self-aware	Reflective
Thoughtful	Insightful
Compassionate	Caring
Able to work individually and in groups	

UNDERSTANDING HOW LEARNING INFORMS TEACHING

The principles informing each teaching situation are derived from understanding adult thinking and learning. Many different teaching skills are needed to work effectively with a variety of learners in different situations. Thus the highest levels of thinking and learning described in figure 1.1 drive the best-informed teaching, which takes account of both what is being taught and how it is taught. Reynolds's (1942/1985) model of learning and the others discussed have the following implications for teaching:

■ *Start where the learner is.* When working with students in groups, varying the teaching techniques offers learners of different styles and stages easier access to the material. When working with students individually, take into account their developmental issues and cognitive and learning styles and capacities.

■ *Engage the student in the learning process.* Adult learners enjoy learning by doing and integrating their experiences into the learning process, in short, by being active learners (Dore 1994). In addition, all the models of cognitive and professional development in adulthood stress the importance of integrating subjective experiences and emotional responses in the learning. In addition, helping students become aware of their own thinking and learning styles and needs helps support their cognitive development.

■ *Be patient with the learning process.* The process of learning, like all significant human development, does not always proceed smoothly. Help students understand that frustration and discomfort are inevitable and are signs of growth. In addition, do not become impatient when learning takes longer than you had planned. Students who seem anxious about being right or wrong or who seem preoccupied with their own reactions and experiences may be reacting to the stress of learning a new professional role and may need help reaching the next level of development.

■ *At the same time, have high expectations of everyone.* Some forms of thinking and learning are more readily understood and validated in the academic context. Some learners relate more easily and readily to a particular teacher's style than others do. Fairness requires that as teachers, we provide a variety of learning experiences so that as many students as possible can benefit from them.

The next chapter covers different modes of teaching, along with tips to using them. A wide array of teaching techniques is the best way to ensure that each student has a chance to learn in the most effective way possible.

3

TEACHING COURSES:

METHODS AND MODALITIES

Teaching is above all an interactive process: learners interacting with teachers, learners interacting with other learners, learners interacting with the material being investigated or produced, and both learners and teachers in continuing interaction with the social and psychological forces around them.

M. TENNANT AND P. POGSON, *LEARNING AND CHANGE IN THE ADULT YEARS*

When education is oriented to the person who is to learn plus the situation to be mastered, there is something more to teaching than proving to the learner that one knows the subject.

B. C. REYNOLDS

OUR OWN EXPERIENCES AS STUDENTS may not have prepared us well to be effective teachers of adult learners. Most of us probably were taught using some version of what has been called the "empty vessel" or "banking" model of teaching and learning, in which students sit and listen while the professor "pours" his or her knowledge into them. In this method, learning is assessed by how much the students can retain and repeat what they have heard and read. While remembering and reproducing information is recognized as a basic form of learning (Bloom 1956), teaching today tries to engage the learner in more active, varied forms of learning. Teaching has moved from emphasizing the "sage on the stage" to the "guide on the side."

While teaching is indeed an interactive process, it is the teacher who is responsible for shaping the student–teacher relationship in a way that will enable the student to learn. This chapter is an overview of the major methods of teaching: lecturing and explaining, reflecting on experience, inquiry and discovery, training and coaching, and using groups and teams (Davis 1993). Each of these methods has strengths and best uses as well as drawbacks. Knowing these will help teachers choose and use the teaching technique(s) best suited to their goals. In addition, the use of several teaching techniques

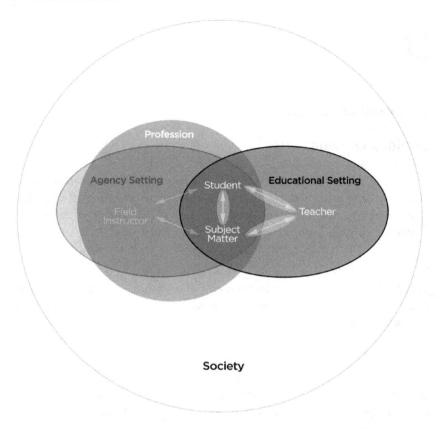

FIGURE 3.1 Model of teaching and learning that highlights teaching.

engages a wider range of learners. Finally, the chapter discusses the design of courses, planning course content and selecting the learning activities that best support the learning goals. Figure 3.1 shows the lines connecting student, teacher, and subject matter.

Although the teaching methods discussed in this chapter include those used in the field as well as the classroom, the emphasis is on classroom teaching. Field instructors and field advisers should consult the section in this chapter on coaching and training as well as chapter 5 on field learning.

INTELLECTUAL EXCITEMENT AND PERSONAL RAPPORT

Effective teaching must create intellectual excitement and establish interpersonal rapport (Lowman 1995). Teachers must know and care about course content and also about how they relate to their students. Being committed to both aspects of the teaching process is part of teachers' ethics and professionalism.

The tips in this chapter on using different teaching modalities are designed to help teachers maximize both intellectual excitement and interpersonal rapport with students. One of these often is easier than the other, and teachers need not be equally good at both in order to succeed in the classroom. With practice, however, it is possible to create intellectual excitement and interpersonal rapport.

Conveying knowledge to others requires developing a new level of command of that content. The ability to keep current with knowledge and ideas in the content area, to select the most salient content to emphasize, to organize the content in order to convey it clearly to others, to put that content into words in a variety of ways, to design activities through which students can gradually comprehend and demonstrate complex knowledge and skills, and to engage diverse learners with the material in many ways all are demanding tasks. For these reasons, Boyer (1990) spoke about the scholarship of teaching, urging colleges and universities to understand and value the intellectual work that goes into effective teaching.

MODES OF TEACHING, MODES OF LEARNING

Different modes of teaching tend to be best for learning different things and for different parts of the learning process (Friedman 2008). As table 3.1 shows, the knowledge, values, and skills forming the content of social work education call for different learning and teaching modes. The teacher's role differs according to the content being addressed. For knowledge, the teacher's primary role may be that of expert. For values, it may be that of a mentor and/or a role model. For skills, it may be that of a coach.

The other teaching technique discussed in this chapter—using groups and teams—can be used with various modes of teaching. Groups and teams are

TABLE 3.1 Content Areas Related to Teaching Modes and Learning Tasks

Nature of content	Teaching mode	Learning task (Bloom 1956)
Knowledge	Lecturing and explaining	Recall, comprehend, apply
	Inquiry and discovery	Analyze, synthesize, evaluate
Values	Reflection on experience	Apply, analyze, evaluate
Skills	Coaching and training	Apply, analyze, evaluate

most often used for inquiry and discovery and reflection on experience, depending on the activities or tasks.

DEVELOPING A TEACHING PHILOSOPHY

Part of what Royce (2001) calls "the mental groundwork of teaching" (1) is developing and articulating a teaching philosophy. In fact, in many settings, faculty members may be asked about their teaching philosophy when interviewed for a job or a performance review, including reviews for tenure and/or promotion. A teaching philosophy reflects the teacher's views of how students learn best, the most important goals for student learning, the most desirable or important classroom climate for learning, ethical principles in teaching, and teachers' roles and behaviors. For many teachers, this philosophy may be implicit.

As with all value systems, making this philosophy an explicit and considered one is essential to one's continuing development as an educator. Brookfield (2000) wrote about identifying one's implicit working assumptions as part of reflective teaching practice. These assumptions can be *paradigmatic*, addressing the basic categories and beliefs we use to understand the world; *prescriptive*, defining what should be happening in specific situations (e.g., teachers' and students' behavior); and *causal*, defining what actions can be taken to produce certain results (528). Although this kind of self-examination can be challenging, it can help identify opportunities for growth and change in our approach to teaching. These assumptions and our general philosophy of teaching strongly influence our teaching modes and methods.

Whatever the method of teaching employed, effective teaching requires *authority* (Banner and Cannon 1997). Authority flows from expertise in the subject matter as well as from the teacher's conduct in mentoring and advising roles. As Banner and Cannon (1997) stated,

> Teachers gain authority in the classroom through practice and experience, by thinking hard about authority's nature and use, by experimentation, and above all by their advancing self-knowledge. Although this process of learning extends over a long period, teachers . . . must strive to establish [authority] immediately, from the first moment of a class, and to evince those qualities of character that make students look to them for understanding and guidance. (26)

How we view and exercise authority as a teacher and how one addresses other ethical dimensions of teaching are critical parts of a teaching philosophy.

Part of this self-reflection in teaching is knowing when and how different modes and methods of teaching can best be used. Using a variety of teaching methods helps engage students with different styles or levels of thinking and learning. In addition, research and experience show that there are proven techniques for using each teaching mode most effectively. These hints for their use are designed to support active learning whatever the mode of teaching used.

CONTEXTUAL INFLUENCES

As figure 3.1 illustrates, teaching modes and methods are the arrows that join subject matter, teacher, and learner. However, the teaching context influences these connections in at least two ways, in the nature of the organization's teaching culture and in disciplinary influences. Because different teaching methods have come to dominate in different disciplines, fields, and professions, social work educators have an advantage in this respect. For example, the benefits of experiential learning and what is now called *service learning* have long been part of social work education in the field internship (Royce 2001:138). Field internship learning is considered the "signature pedagogy" of social work (CSWE 2008). In addition, by defining its scope in terms of knowledge, values, and skills, social work uses a greater diversity of teaching methods, such as using role-playing and keeping a journal, than some other fields do.

Another major influence on teaching is the organizational context. Colleges and universities diverge in their missions and the importance that they place on research, teaching, and service. Whatever the institutional mission is, organizational cultures or subcultures affect teaching and the value placed on it (Feldman and Paulsen 1998). Feldman and Paulsen (1998) talked about the need for an organizational culture "in which teaching and learning are the subject of serious, sustained discussion and debate; where people talk about teaching, inquire into its effects, and work together for improvement" (687). A supportive teaching culture contains the following:

- The upper administration's unambiguous support for teaching improvement activities.
- Faculty ownership of and commitment to the improvement of teaching.
- A broad definition of scholarship, following Boyer (1990), that includes the scholarship of teaching.
- Demonstration of teaching skills as part of the faculty hiring process.

- Interaction and collaboration among faculty members about teaching.
- Availability of a faculty development program for teaching, often in the form of a campus teaching center.
- Support at the level of the department chair.
- Rigorous evaluation of teaching as part of retention, tenure, and promotion decisions. (Feldman and Paulsen 1998)

Some experts argue that traditional research and scholarship support excellence in teaching, whereas others argue that too much emphasis on research and scholarship detracts from teachers' effort to improve their teaching skills. Whatever your point of view on that debate, the preceding organizational resources and practices both sustain and require teachers' efforts to make their teaching as effective as possible. They also indicate where an institution stands in its support of excellence in teaching.

LECTURING AND EXPLAINING

Lecturing is still the most common teaching method employed in higher education today (Bligh 2000). Even the architecture and equipment of many college classrooms (chairs in rows, projection equipment, lecterns, and the like) reflect the ubiquitous use of this teaching technique. "Smart classrooms" permit and encourage the use of instructor-generated visual aids, such as computer-generated slides or Web-based materials. By virtue of history and tradition, most settings seem to favor this form of teaching and the student–teacher relationship over others.

Bligh (2000) defines lecturing as "more or less continuous expositions by a speaker who wants the audience to learn something" (4). Even though lectures are not particularly effective at changing attitudes, teaching the values associated with a subject, or teaching behavioral skills, they are at least as good as other methods, such as independent reading and discussion, for conveying information.

Those who have studied and written about lecturing and explaining as a teaching technique typically turn to cognitive psychology to learn how to improve their lectures (Bligh 2000; Davis 1993). This research suggests that how material is organized and delivered can make a big difference in the information that listeners retain and in how they rate their satisfaction with the teaching. Most of all, a lecture's effectiveness seems to depend on the overall *framework* that the lecturer provides for its content. This framework should help listeners organize and hence retain the information being conveyed or that they may have read, so that it can be better retained in and retrieved from memory. Therefore, it is often recommended that the framework or outline for a lecture be provided to students on the chalkboard or in a handout so they can more easily follow the logic as the lecture progresses. This factor is so important to the success of lecturing that how well a teacher organizes information, often is part of course and teacher evaluations.

Lecturing can also be improved in other ways (Bligh 2000; McKeachie and Svinicki 1999; Nilson 1998). Nothing reaches long-term memory until it is noticed, enters short-term memory, and then is mentally filtered further, an active process. All the suggestions for lecturing presented here are designed to enhance these cognitive processes. In addition to making the framework for the class or lecture clear at the outset, these include

- *Varying your delivery.* Because an audience's attention always declines over time, you should review the points covered and still to come. Break up the point-by-point flow of content with illustrations and relevant personal experiences. Visual aids not only reinforce main points; they also break up the flow of spoken words. In addition, consider a break or some other occasion for a postural change especially if the lecture lasts more than an hour. Moving around the room and gesturing also help listeners maintain the audience's attention. If the size of the group permits it (and it usually does), inviting questions or comments periodically (checking in with the audience) may help.

- *Encouraging students to take notes.* Writing down the main points helps students process and organize the information as they are listening, and write and see while they are hearing (use multiple sensory pathways). Handouts with important topics listed along with space for writing may encourage students to take notes. But handing out detailed lecture notes can be counterproductive because they can distract from the lecture and do not help listeners organize the information in the best way for their own purposes.

- *Not writing out the lecture.* In most cases, it is better to lecture from an outline than to read from a prepared text. It is much easier to be animated and to maintain eye contact with the audience when you speak with some spontaneity. Sometimes reading the exact words that define a term or a direct quotation from someone else's work is necessary or desirable. But most teachers find, with experience, that their notes become less and less detailed and that this helps rather than detracts from making a successful presentation. If the teacher finds that a specific point has been missed, the omission can be rectified in the next class session. Whether brief or detailed, though, lecture notes should clearly convey the logical framework for the lecture, which is what will make it usable for the listener.

    ■   *Using visual aids.* The most common tools for making a point visually used to be the blackboard, whiteboard, or overhead transparency. These have the disadvantage of requiring the instructor to turn away from the audience in order to write (and it can be challenging to speak and write at the same time), although this change of instructor activity can actually help hold the audience's attention. PowerPoint and other computer-generated projection techniques are now commonly used, as well as audio and animated material. But when something that relies on electricity and/or technical equipment fails, the consequences are generally more disconcerting and distracting than when a piece of chalk breaks or a marker runs dry. Becoming familiar with any electronic devices and their use *before* a lecture or class session is always a good idea, and it also is good to have a backup plan in place (perhaps one that includes chalk and/or markers or printed copies of what was to have been projected).

    ■   *Stimulating thinking rather than emphasizing facts and conclusions.* For conveying facts and information, assigned reading can be just as effective as lecturing is (McKeachie and Svinicki 1999). A lecture is best for stimulating interest in the topic, synthesizing existing ideas in new ways, outlining the controversies surrounding a topic and why they are important, illustrating the implications and applications of ideas, and supplementing readings with new ideas and information not yet in texts and other publications.

Some simple techniques can help students better process lectures. One is the "buzz group," in which the lecturer pauses and asks students to talk to one another from their seats in groups of two or three for two minutes. The assignment may be to summarize the lecture's main points so far or to think of questions to ask the lecturer. The main points or questions can then be shared with the class or given to the instructor in writing before proceeding with the next portion of the lecture. While these mid-lecture interactions do take time away from the lecture, forcing students to process lecture content actively leads to greater recall and deeper understanding of the material.

    ■   *Asking questions instead of making statements.* One way to begin a lecture is to ask questions or outline a debate on which the lecture will elaborate or comment. Then, returning to these points or questions at the end can be a useful way of summing up. During the lecture, taking questions from the audience can be a good way of varying the flow of content and checking the audience's understanding. Often, the teacher's interest and enthusiasm conveyed is more important than the information or answers provided.

■ *Not trying to cover too much.* When preparing a lecture or teaching a course, the pressure is always to try to cover more content than is possible in given period of time. Trying to do a lot can actually overload students so that they actually retain less. Other common mistakes are overestimating what students know or assuming that their knowing as much as you know at the end of the lecture or course is a reasonable goal for students. We really are teaching students how to think and learn so that they can remain current in the field. In fact, over time, our students may end up knowing more than we do, and indeed, we hope they will. The challenge in each lecture or class session is to be selective about what you cover in order to stimulate interest in the content, to emphasize its importance, and to help students decide how to apply the content to their work.

Think back to the teachers you had whose classes you most enjoyed. What did you like and not like about the lectures, workshops, and professional presentations? Although a listener's intense interest in a topic can sometimes overcome a poor presentation, an analysis of a good lecture generally reinforces these suggestions. In the hands of a skilled lecturer, form and content appear to work together seamlessly. Experience helps, but even beginners can learn these techniques and skills and make lecturing more enjoyable for the teacher and more rewarding for the students.

Developing a framework for the content, knowing what points to emphasize, deciding which content is not as important, being able to talk about the content without a prepared text, being able to answer questions clearly and succinctly, being able to identify and articulate the current questions and dilemmas in a content area all require a high degree of interest in and knowledge about the subject matter. Moreover, the teacher's own learning process in preparing to teach is part of what helps make teaching a rewarding occupation.

REFLECTING ON EXPERIENCE

Many models of adult learning emphasize reflecting on experience as a way of making new meaning from it. The most common teaching mode that engages learners in this way is the classroom discussion. Lecturing and discussion are often combined, but in seminars, discussion may be the only or the dominant mode of teaching and learning. Discussion and the other methods of encouraging reflection on experience are, by definition, driven by what students themselves contribute. Teaching using discussion and other methods that encourage reflection on experience requires skill in shaping the conversation in ways that will lead students toward the learning goals for the course and will do so based on the students' expressed needs and concerns.

Reflecting on experience is a more active method of learning than simply listening to a lecture. The experience in question may be previous life or work experience, current experience in the classroom (when lectures and discussions are used together), and other class-related activities such as assigned readings, experiences in field, and internships.

Reflection on experience is one of the main teaching techniques for helping students learn how to think and for supporting and encouraging their cognitive development. In particular, it is related to encouraging critical thinking: "Critical thinking involves the careful examination and evaluation of beliefs and actions. It requires paying attention to the process of reasoning, not just the product. . . . Well-reasoned thinking is a form of creation and construction" (Gibbs and Gambrill 1996:3).

In the liberal arts, teaching students to think critically is seen as "a liberating force, freeing the individual from the ignorance that characterizes chauvinism and ethnocentrism, from narrow self-interest and 'small-mindedness'" (Davis 1993:174). Thus, teaching methods that involve reflecting on experience are closely related to the goals of professional education that involve increasing self-awareness, incorporating professional ethics and values, identifying underlying principles, considering the source and basis for knowledge and beliefs, transferring and applying knowledge and information from one situation to the next, and equipping oneself for lifelong learning and effective practice.

LEADING A DISCUSSION

When leading a discussion, teachers should draw out the participants and move toward the main learning goals for that class. Just as students' critical thinking requires creativity—making and remaking ideas and perspectives—so does leading a discussion. A skilled discussion leader answers students' questions and responds to what they say in ways that guide the conversation productively.

The following principles help make classroom discussion productive and effective (Davis 1993; Friedman 2008; Lowman 1995; McKeachie and Svinicki 1999):

■ *Set some ground rules for classroom interactions at the beginning of the course.* Doing so at the beginning means that rules will not be made in response to a specific comment or classroom interaction. These rules can then be invoked later if needed when points of tension arise. They should acknowledge that the group may have different points of view and that discussing them openly is good when done with mutual respect and civility. It also is important to encourage students to ask questions not only to the individual but also to the group. Most of all, you should let students know at the outset that you know that they will be able to contribute to the class. In a course that uses group discussion extensively, you may even have the students draw up the ground rules themselves (Brookfield and Preskill 1999).

Most of the ground rules for students' participation in a discussion pertain to civility. In social work, you might talk about social workers treating one another with respect. This means listening to each speaker, taking turns in speaking, speaking courteously even in disagreement, and speaking to and about the content of what is said, not the speaker. The process of discussion itself can be used to help students learn to give reasons for their opinions and how to express a difference of opinion clearly without attacking person who holds an opinion different from one's own. Reminding students that in practice, professionals often have to negotiate differences of opinion and perspective constructively can show that these skills will be useful in the future.

■ *Pose specific questions or problems to shape the discussion.* Posing a problem or asking a question can be a good way to open a discussion in the classroom. The problem can be a brief scenario or a description of differences of perspective or opinion for students to comment on. The problems to be used to stimulate discussion are generally best thought about while preparing for the class, although they sometimes emerge spontaneously from students' questions or comments during discussion. Being able to build a discussion on a student's issues and experiences tells the whole class that their ideas are important.

Asking productive questions is an art, which can be learned. Studies show that most of the questions that college teachers use ask for cognitive recall (facts, definitions, or review) (Barnes 1992). Such questions are useful for checking students' comprehension of the lecture's material, but they are not the best kinds of questions for stimulating a discussion. Questions that invite or elicit convergent, divergent, or evaluative thinking are more likely to enhance students' critical thinking than questions that have a right or wrong answer (Barnes 1992). Questions about applying the concepts being discussed, the limits of an idea, the assumptions or evidence underlying an idea, alternative views or theories all invite critical thinking. Just as beginning students learn not to ask clients "yes or no" questions, beginning teachers can practice asking questions that go beyond just checking students' comprehension and elicit diverse comments and perspectives.

One common question is whether to rely on volunteers to answer questions, perhaps by a show of hands, or to call on students at random. Because some students are uncomfortable being called on, the classroom ground rules should allow students to "pass" on commenting or answering a question. Embarrassment interferes with, rather than enhances learning. Nonetheless, although some students may have difficulty volunteering to speak in class, they may find that they become more comfortable once they have done so, perhaps by being called on or in small group discussion. Once the "ice is broken," these students may subsequently participate more comfortably and more often.

Calling on volunteers who offer to answer questions, ask questions, or comment on the discussion may be easier, but it can lead to some students—the more frequent volunteers—dominating the discourse. To avoid this, try calling first on those volunteers who are doing so for the first time or who do so less often, for example.

There is no one "right answer" to whether or not to call on individual students or to rely on volunteers, particularly in view of the overall culture and common practices in the department or school. The point is for each teacher to choose a strategy with some awareness of its risks and benefits.

■ *Show respect for all students and their contributions, even if they need to be reinterpreted.* Part of the art of leading a productive classroom discussion is to shape the participants' contributions to the class's learning goals. This may mean asking for an elaboration, clarification, or explanation of the question or comment to elicit a clearer articulation or to reframe the underlying idea. You might also ask the other students what they think about what has been said. Humor and other responses designed to defuse tensions should be used sparingly, however, as students may see them as dismissive.

Studies of teachers' behavior in the classroom have repeatedly shown that despite what teachers themselves believe, some students' contributions are more regularly noticed and acknowledged than others. Male students more often make comments, which are more often recognized, and more often answered positively than female students' comments are. Where a student sits in the room can also affect the teacher's attention and response. A classroom observer can give the teacher useful feedback on these issues.

■ *Consider how active you should be as the discussion leader.* All studies of teachers show that they talk for much more of the class session than they think they do. Even studies of teachers' questions show that interactions between teacher and student take up much less time in the classroom than does the teacher's lecture (Barnes 1992). As I walk through the halls of my own school while classes are being conducted (where smaller classes designed to permit students' participation are favored), I most often hear the voices of teachers, not of students.

A discussion leader must decide how much to allow the conversation to flow on its own and how much to intervene to shape it. You might consider letting students respond to one another rather than answering every question or comment yourself. Although most of us, myself included, tend to be too active, if students do not feel that the interaction is being managed by the teacher to keep it relatively productive and "safe," they will not feel free to talk openly or even at all.

■ *Consider using small groups for discussion.* A useful technique for getting more students to participate in the classroom is to form small groups for discussion of a specific question, problem, or scenario. When using this technique, the teacher may circulate among the groups to get a sense of the issues that are emerging but must not dominate these interactions. The first time a quiet student speaks in class can be important, and a small-group discussion may provide that opportunity.

Asking each small group to select a spokesperson to report to the class on what was discussed and the issues or questions that emerged can help the group stay on task and ensure that the whole class profits from the discussion. Students have a great deal they can contribute to the others' learning, and this kind of peer interaction may be easier in a small group than in a large group.

■ *Anticipate the kinds of problems that can occur in classroom discussion and plan strategies for handling them.* Many kinds of problems can arise during a discussion because students (and teachers) may not understand or possess the skills required for constructive participation. These skills include overcoming the habit of being passive in the classroom and the fear of being judged negatively for one's ideas and opinions; the ability to express oneself clearly and to give reasons for one's ideas and opinions; careful and open-minded listening; the ability to respond to ideas that are different from one's own without hostility; tolerance of silence; awareness of and tolerance for complexity and ambiguity; and the ability to explore alternative ideas without rushing to a conclusion or simply searching for what the professor wants to hear (Brookfield and Preskill 1999; McKeachie and Svinicki 1999). Developing these skills will be useful in many professional contexts, such as staff meetings and case conferences.

Specific strategies can be used to deal with some of the most common problems. One is the student who tends to *dominate or monopolize* the discussion. If the classroom ground rules include signaling a willingness to speak (e.g., raising a hand and waiting for recognition), the instructor can exercise some control over the situation by calling on those volunteers who have not yet spoken or who speak less often. Emphasizing the importance of listening as well as speaking may help. But if the student does not respond to these and other techniques, it may be necessary to arrange to meet with him or her outside class. Often students equate achievement with giving right answers to the teacher, and they may need to be helped to see how all group members can learn from the process of discussion as a whole. You could even then suggest that a learning goal for this student is to learn to listen and to trust in the group process, that learning can and often does take place best in this way.

Techniques for dealing with dominating voices also help draw out the quiet students. Whether or not to call on students who do not volunteer has already been discussed. During a classroom discussion, a "fishbowl" technique can be used in which a small circle discusses a topic with the requirement that every member participate; only after a certain period of time is the rest of the class, who are observing their discussion outside the circle, invited to comment and join in. Other group techniques are to require every member of a small discussion group to speak in turn without interruption or response (for several of these, see Brookfield and Preskill 1999). Many of these group techniques help get quiet students to speak, even once, which makes the next time much easier.

Some students may not participate regularly in discussions, no matter what techniques are used. If you are concerned about how well such a student is learning, you might arrange a meeting to discuss his or her experiences in the classroom. Students are usually able to tell whether this is their general learning style or whether they have a particular problem in this class.

An often unspoken fear about leading discussions is that strong opinions, feelings, or conflicts will emerge. Social work educators can use their practice experience to help them with this challenge, and often the instructor's simply showing comfort with the group's feelings has a calming effect. Teachers also must be prepared to help students who may say too much to maintain more appropriate boundaries and to invoke the class's ground rules about *how* feelings and opinions should be expressed in the classroom. Students will be able to share their feelings and opinions more readily if they have the sense that the teacher can bear them and believe that the teacher will help them maintain control and boundaries. However, in some classroom discussions, a student may be clearly having some emotional difficulty, and the teacher should then talk to that student after class to see whether he or she needs help.

Another fear about discussion is that it will deviate from the planned content for the class session. Here, too, the teacher must be prepared to redirect the discussion when needed, perhaps by posing a new question or remarking that new topics have emerged and then considering with the group when and how they may be discussed in the future. Even if some students resist this refocusing, others will be relieved to return to the planned topic of the day. A discussion that goes off on a tangent may, however, be revealing content that should have been included in the course or that can be addressed in another course or at another time. A teacher can learn a lot about students' concerns and learning needs by observing where classroom discussions are leading.

KEEPING A JOURNAL

In addition to discussion, some forms of writing can encourage learning through reflection on experience. Writing itself is currently regarded as an important tool for enhancing students' thinking in general. The process of committing one's ideas to paper usually forces the writer to clarify his or her thoughts. McKeachie and Svinicki (1999) talk about the usefulness of "low stakes writing" (133), that is, writing assignments that are not graded. For example, keeping a journal can be a course requirement for which credit is given for completing the assignment but the content itself is not graded or evaluated. Journals can be based on experiences, past or present, required or independent reading, or both. It has the advantage of forcing the student to think about a course's content outside the classroom. The assignment usually invites students to connect their experiences with concepts or content covered in class or in the required reading. Because a journal reveals how students think and write about their experiences and ideas, it can motivate them to learn about what the course offers (McKeachie and Svinicki 1999). Courses on diversity often require keeping a journals or even making a tape (Millstein 1999) because they reveal not only thoughts and ideas but also attitudes and values and their change over time.

INQUIRY AND DISCOVERY

Another teaching technique that encourages critical thinking and the development of problem-solving skills is encouraging independent inquiry and discovery. Many of the classroom-related assignments used in graduate education, like research papers, use these methods. Classroom activities also can encourage inquiry and discovery.

STUDENT PRESENTATIONS

The most common way to bring inquiry and discovery into the classroom is through student projects and presentations, individual or group. Because I talk about using groups and teams later, my comments here relate to class presentations by individuals. The assignment to prepare a presentation to the class can vary from reporting on information already identified, such as a critical analysis of an assigned reading, to reporting on a project or professional activity outside class, such as a case presentation or an analysis of a policy or an organization, and to generating information independently and then sharing it with the group. In any case, the student, rather than the teacher, must identify and decide on the important points to talk about. Critical thinking and an analysis and synthesis of information are needed. The student is also taking the role of the expert, and class members learn to learn from one another. These skills are essential to practice and can be reinforced in the classroom in this way.

RESEARCH

The most common form of learning through inquiry and discovery in social work education is research. It can be scholarly, as in a review of the literature, or empirical, as in a research project. Often students are required to write a literature-based research paper as a means of assessing their performance at the end of the course: the "term paper." These methods of encouraging inquiry and discovery are discussed in chapter 7, on assessing students' learning.

Other ways of reinforcing the importance of inquiry and discovery in a course involve using assigned readings are based on others' research, and using research findings and current scholarship in the lecture content. Class activities also can model and encourage the habits of mind—curiosity and critical thinking—are needed for research.

Students need many skills to learn through inquiry and discovery, from accepted research methods to a constructive use of existing information and information technologies. When an assignment in a course requires research, teachers should ensure that their students have the relevant skills to do research and to help them with any questions about how to do the work as it proceeds. Using the beginning or end of class to ask students about their progress with the assignment can help students do their best work and clarify the kinds of thinking and learning needed to succeed.

TRAINING AND COACHING

Training and coaching are teaching techniques primarily used with individual students (Davis 1993). This kind of teaching can take place in individual academic advising as well as in field instruction and field advisement. Social work has a vast literature on supervision, including supervising students in both practice and educational situations. It is not the purpose of this section to try to summarize that literature, although it is discussed to some extent in the chapter on field education. Next I define coaching, mentoring, and role-modeling as they are discussed in the literature on higher education and show how they can be used in contexts other than student supervision in the field.

MENTORING

Mentoring is the intense, long-term relationship that sometimes develops between someone more senior in a field and an advanced student, a partnership designed to help the student's career advance. As Kennedy (1997) pointed out, "It is through those relationships that the academy reproduces itself" (97). These relationships are mutually chosen, usually based on shared scholarly interests. They can be formative and gratifying both for the mentor and the mentored, but they can also be problematic. However, there are elements of the mentoring process in many less intense or long-term one-on-one relationships between students and teachers.

A classroom teacher who spends time with individual students, coaching them on course content and helping them develop the skills to succeed in the course, is mentoring. Being a student adviser, formally or informally, also is mentoring. Mentoring in this more limited sense means forming a relationship with an individual student to advance the student's learning and professional development, even when the development ultimately chosen may not serve the teacher's immediate interests. For example, a student may serve as a research assistant to a teacher, who teaches research skills and provides opportunities for increasingly independent work. The teacher may hope that he or she is investing in someone who will continue in this role and thus help with the teacher's scholarly productivity. But the student may decide to use these new skills for another area of interest. It is the mentor's responsibility to put the students' learning and professional development needs first and help them succeed in the new endeavor. In fact, sometimes a coach or a mentor's greatest contribution to a student's development is pointing out that a different area of activity or career may be a better choice.

The term *coaching* implies teaching skills, through instruction and perhaps other techniques, such as demonstration, as when the student can observe the coach performing the task or function that the student is trying to learn. Advising, especially in the field, and practice teaching, especially in the laboratory, through role-playing or demonstration of a specific technique, often include activities that would be termed *coaching* in other contexts. Mentoring may include coaching, but the term is used in a more general way to encompass a range of teaching activities and aspects of a relationship. Like a mentor, however, a coach can be a role model and provide more general orientation to a profession or field, including its attitudes and values, as well as specific skills.

ROLE-MODELING

Whether teachers want or expect it, some students will see them as a *role model*. In the professions in particular, there is an unwritten curriculum that has to do with being socialized into the profession in question. Students are learning how to behave like a professional social worker, explicitly and implicitly, and social work educators have long been aware of this part of social work education.

An unspoken aspect of teaching is that the teacher is always being observed very carefully. Students learn from what teachers do at least as much as from what they say, whereas teachers may be concentrating more on the latter than the former. Students study teachers in order to decide what to do or how to be as well as what not to do and how not to be. Their images of the profession and of what may (or may not) be possible for them as professionals (and people) are formed at least in part from their teachers. Teachers observe students as well, of course, in part to evaluate whether or not their students are being socialized to the profession. Although teachers cannot entirely control the messages or lessons, intended or unintended, that students may infer from observation, they can try to embody the norms of respectful, inclusive, and professional behavior that they want them to learn.

USING GROUPS AND TEAMS

While working in teams is now a common feature of social work practice in many settings, social work education does not yet emphasize working in teams (Opie 2000). Especially in this age of interdisciplinary practice and service delivery, we must prepare students to work well in groups and teams. Every class is itself a group, of course, with a shared purpose, interaction among themselves, and a tendency to act or react together (Davis 1993:243). Using groups and teams, however, applies to teaching techniques that create subgroups within a class—pairs, triads, and larger groups—specifically for completing structured learning tasks.

Using groups and teams is related to educational philosophies and movements that emphasize cooperative and collaborative learning (Steiner et al. 1999). Royce (2001) defined the difference between cooperative and collaborative learning as one of degree of structure and control provided by the instructor. Cooperative learning is designed to reduce competition among students and to enhance their skills for working in groups or teams by having them work together and support one another's learning in the conduct of a specific task or project designed by the teacher. In collaborative learning, the teacher cedes more of the responsibility for the design and even the evaluation of the work to the group members. These approaches call for designing tasks or projects that allow different solutions or approaches to the work, in order to stimulate collective creativity. They often also require applying, synthesizing, or conveying complex information to others. Peer evaluation (among small group members or among groups) is often part of the task (Steiner et al. 1999). Whether or not the task includes work done outside the classroom, some time must be allowed in class sessions for the groups to organize and to ask questions about the assignment.

For example, in a doctoral seminar on teaching, I divide a class into small groups, assigning each to prepare and "teach" the material on handling different diversity issues (race and ethnicity, gender, sexual orientation and gender expression, disability, age, and the like) in the classroom. Although I list some readings for each topic, the groups typically identify additional resources of their own. Each group or team must decide on the role of each member when he or she makes the presentation to the class (e.g., they either designate one or two speakers for their presentation or have everyone present some part of the material), and they decide on the content and the best ways of getting it across to other class members. They may use skits and videos as well as handouts and other more conventional teaching methods (see, e.g., Christensen 1995; Winston 1997). In addition, after the presentation in class, each group is asked to discuss the challenges they faced in preparing to teach, in other words, to reflect on both process and content issues. Steiner and colleagues (1999) give many more structured examples of using cooperative learning in a range of social work courses, such as jigsaw, structured controversy, and write-pair-share exercises.

Many teachers are reluctant to use groups, worrying about how much they should monitor and/or help the groups in the assigned task, whether all the group members contribute equally to the work, whether and how to evaluate the individual members' performance and contributions, the noisiness and lack of control of the process, and, most of all, whether the content can be as effectively conveyed as in a lecture (Royce 2001). Steiner and colleagues (1999) point out that cooperative learning emphasizes such skills as effective communication, interpersonal skills, and critical thinking, as well as the benefits of empowerment, interdependence, and diversity that come from working in heterogeneous student-led groups.

PREPARING A COURSE

Beginning teachers often assume that their first job will be designing the courses that they teach. But beginning teachers are often hired, full time or part time, to teach sections of required courses that have already been developed. Even though this reduces stress and work at the beginning of the course, it also means that the teacher must learn how to deliver course content that may not be what the teacher would have designed on his or her own. Next I review common elements in preparing and designing courses. McKeachie and Svinicki (1999) even suggest a time line for course preparation, which always must begin well before a class first meets.

The major elements of a course design that must be taken into account are the course title, the course description, the course's learning objectives, assigned readings, and assessments of the students' learning (required assignments and rules for grading). The course syllabus can be considered a kind of contract between the student and the department or school about what will be taught, how it will be taught, and what will be expected of the student in order to succeed in the course. Together, this profile of content to be taught and these performance requirements add up to the learning outcomes for the course of study as a whole.

PUTTING THE COURSE IN CONTEXT

Before designing a course, teachers must know where it fits in the students' curriculum. What can they assume that students will know from previous courses? What content will be covered in other courses to be taken along with or after this one? *Horizontal integration* of curriculum refers to how the content of courses and other learning experiences coordinate with each other at any one time in the students' program of study. *Vertical integration* of curriculum refers to how content is staged over time, what will be taught and learned first and what later. No course can be planned and taught effectively without knowing where it fits in the overall curriculum design. Course prerequisites cover only the basics, especially when students can choose different ways of completing their degree, such as through part-time study.

Unfortunately, beginning teachers are not always given as much information as they need about where their course fits into the whole. They therefore should ask for it when it is not offered, although much of the information is usually available on Web sites or other publications for students. Students will be frustrated if they feel a course is repeating what they already know or is not connecting well to the rest of their learning.

DEFINING LEARNING GOALS AND OUTCOMES

Every course, required or elective, has a few key learning goals. The teacher's and the students' activities are designed to help students meet specific objectives for the course or for segments (units) of the course (Grunert 1997; McKeachie and Svinicki 1999). Defining learning goals and objectives for each course helps *students* select courses, understand what is expected of them in a course and hence to meet expectations; and it helps *teachers* prioritize course content, select appropriate methods of teaching and learning activities; and it helps *departments and programs* monitor and develop curricula to ensure that students obtain the needed education.

Different educational settings have different requirements for course syllabi, but a well-designed syllabus always states the course's learning goals (Grunert 1997; McKeachie and Svinicki 1999). Such objectives should be stated as what students should know and/or be able to do at the end of the course. These goals should encompass the range of content to be covered but not be so many that it would be difficult to determine whether every student has achieved all the goals. For every goal on the list, there should be a corresponding activity or activities in either the classroom or assignments completed outside class, so that all students can show what they have learned. The wording of the goals is important. For a practice class, this might be demonstrating knowledge of specific principles of practice and perhaps application of this knowledge to written case materials, whereas demonstrating specific skills in actual practice with clients might be a goal in a field practicum.

In addition to a list of learning goals (and often preceding it), a syllabus describes the course and its content, stating any prerequisites. It may also say a little about the educational philosophy underlying the course to help students understand what will be expected of them. It is difficult to reduce complex ideas to a brief (usually one or two paragraphs) statement, and it generally requires several drafts and revisions to develop such a description.

For required courses in social work programs, a curriculum committee and/or the program faculty often write the course descriptions and learning goals. Each instructor then draws up a plan of teaching that will help students achieve those goals.

SELECTING COURSE CONTENT

In designing a course, as in lecturing, the most common frustration is trying to cover too much content. One way to avoid this is to map out the number of class sessions in advance, first sketching the beginning (getting oriented to the course) and ending (course wrap-up) sessions. By referring to the learning goals for the course, the rest of the course calendar can be filled in topically according to the amount of emphasis on each subtopic and the time needed in class for specific teaching and learning activities. This procedure may quickly show that the list of goals and objectives for the course may need to be more realistic. Or it may suggest that some class activities may have to be dropped in favor of others that better meet the students' learning needs.

In addition, one class session should be left unscheduled (McKeachie and Svinicki 1999), because even with the best planning, though, no two groups (or classes) are the same and hence getting "off schedule" at some point is usually unavoidable. This "unscheduled" session is a comfort to both faculty and students, enabling the teacher to follow the class schedule without worrying that some essential content may be dropped.

Always plan for a midcourse check-in with students for feedback. In fact, some instructors like to do this more often, after the first three or four sessions, for example. Planning for feedback also means that students do not have to initiate the conversation about how the course is going. Students appreciate their instructor's interest in their views of the course. It also is helpful to ask for feedback before any big problem or crisis has developed, since problems are usually more easily solved early.

This course planning—setting up goals and objectives and a general course calendar—is best done about three months before the class is scheduled to begin. Some colleges may have even more stringent requirements for advance planning. In part, early planning is needed because of the next step—getting course materials together—whose timing is often beyond the instructor's control.

COURSE GOALS AND LEARNING OUTCOMES

What takes place in the classroom each time a teacher meets with students in large part determines what they will learn. The other main element of planning a course is assessing what the students have learned. Again, some major parameters of this part of course planning is determined by the institution, such as the grading system, the academic requirements for the program as a whole, and the number and timing of formal assessment points. How the students' learning will be assessed—the course requirements—are important to grading, and they also should be designed to engage students in specific activities that in themselves can be significant opportunities to learn. This aspect of teaching—student assessment—is so important that it has a chapter of its own (chapter 7). The short discussion here is meant to underscore that when planning a course, students' learning goals are met through assessment and other course activities. In fact, some syllabi may explain how assignments can help students achieve specific learning goals (Grunert 1997).

The principal method of assessing students should not be an examination (in-class or take-home) or a paper simply because of custom or tradition. If self-reflection on certain issues is an important learning goal in the course, then a required assignment should be self-reflection. Skill in the applying of theory to practice situations, skill in oral communication, writing skills, critical thinking skills, the ability to collaborate, and the ability to gather, analyze, and synthesize existing information each requires different kinds of assessment. Required and graded assignments would likely be quite different in each case.

Finally, the course syllabus should clearly spell out the course requirements. Students need to know what the assessment of their performance will be based on, for both performance feedback and evaluative (grading) purposes. Some schools even require that for fairness, the percentages of a grade be allocated to each assignment and numerical standards for grading be calculated and used. This, however, can create tension between offering students feedback for continuing growth and development and fulfilling the demands of grading systems. The national problem of grade inflation suggests that colleges and universities have not addressed this problem well. Making performance expectations and standards for a course explicit does not resolve this problem, but it protects both students and instructors and can reduce students' anxiety so that more effective learning can take place.

MECHANICS AND MATERIALS

One reason for making a course's learning goals as explicit as possible is that you then can plan the use of specific teaching modalities, as illustrated in table 3.1. In addition, because students' learning styles differ, it generally is a good idea to vary the way specific classes are run. Even watching videos can get boring if they are shown every week.

Planning course sessions also requires arranging for the materials needed by the instructor and/or students each week. Required texts must be selected with enough time to arrange for books to be delivered. Copyright permission must be obtained for materials to be duplicated for students. Reading materials must be made available to students in the library and/or electronically. If videotapes, PowerPoint presentations, or other electronic media are used in class or in laboratory sessions, arrangements must be made for the needed equipment. All these requirements need some planning if the classes are to go smoothly.

Finally, every university and department has its own methods of assigning space to courses. In the week or two before a class meets for the first time, it is a good idea to visit the space and get a sense of its assets and limitations. How the furniture is arranged—chairs in rows ("theater style") or in circle, whether a lectern is present—indicates how the class will be conducted and what will be expected of the participants. If additional resources are needed (chalk, whiteboard, overhead projector, etc.), they can be identified before the first class.

BEING PRESENT TO ONE ANOTHER

One element of a course syllabus is information about the instructor's availability, which might be during office hours and by telephone and/or e-mail. In addition, a syllabus may outline the teacher's basic expectations in regard to attendance, timeliness, permissible absences, participation in class discussion, and the ground rules for class discussion and debate. Whether or not these matters, like attendance or class participation, are assessed (graded) depends on the course's learning goals. In any case, they can establish a working contract between the teacher and the students by making explicit the mutual obligations that all class members are undertaking to one another.

Finally, experienced teachers always suggest that the instructor arrive in the classroom a little early and perhaps also linger a short time afterward. Greeting students as they arrive for class may encourage them to participate in class discussions. Because it generally is easier for students to talk with teachers informally rather than formally, the before- and after-class contact can get questions answered and pave the way toward a more extended conversation at another time.

THE TEACHING PORTFOLIO

Teaching well requires a lot of work. Especially before hiring, tenure, and/or promotion decisions, teachers should document this work. The best way of doing this is with a *teaching portfolio,* a collection of documents and/or other materials illustrating the nature and quality of one's teaching activities.

Effort spent in research and writing is documented in publications, and effort spent working on the effectiveness of one's teaching can be documented as well. A teaching portfolio may contain the following:

- A *statement of teaching philosophy.* Some institutions request or require such a statement when teachers are hired or as part of the tenure review. Even if it is not required, this statement shows that you consider teaching to be a deliberate, professional, and self-reflective activity.
- *Student feedback.* Some kinds of evidence of effective teaching are obvious, like the *students' satisfaction ratings* of courses that are collected by the institution. However, student feedback may come in other forms as well and should be included.
- *Course syllabi and other materials.* Anyone who has taught knows that designing courses requires not just knowledge of how to teach but also current and substantive knowledge of the course content. Assignments, reading lists, and any other documents, like slides or other visual aids, can also be included.
- *Materials in other media.* Sometimes courses use other materials, like Web pages or resources or video- or audiotapes, or even experiences outside the classroom.

▣   *Outside assessments of teaching.* Outside evaluations or observations of teaching may be required for a tenure review or may be requested by the teacher. The results of any such evaluations should be included along with an explanation of how the feedback has been used to further develop one's skills. Sometimes model course syllabi or other materials are anthologized or requested by colleagues elsewhere, which should of course be mentioned.

Putting together a teaching portfolio, like other forms of professional assessment and self-assessment, can be a useful learning experience in itself that can suggest new ideas and new initiatives to make one's teaching as effective and enjoyable as possible.

CONCLUSIONS

Effective classroom teaching requires consideration of not only "what" but also "how." Planning a course therefore also includes considering the various teaching modes that might be used to address students' learning goals. These modes of teaching, especially inquiry and discovery and reflection on experience, are also related to the kinds of assignments and student assessment devices that you use. Not every teacher finds every teaching mode equally appealing or effective, and personal style and preference, of course, help determine how each person teaches. However, efforts to expand your repertoire of teaching methods and skills will pay off in keeping your time in the classroom lively and interesting as well as in engaging a greater variety of students in significant learning.

▣   *Incorporate opportunities for active learning.* Although it is more difficult in large classes, always try to find ways to encourage students' active participation in learning. Sometimes this can be as simple as pausing for students to write down thoughts, comments, or questions. Students' discussion of course content or reactions to it among themselves should also be encouraged. Even simply "checking in" with a class about unanswered questions or the pacing of the material indicates that you are interested in your students and are asking them to reflect on and be responsible for what they are and are not learning.

▣   *Vary the teaching modalities and learning activities within a course whenever possible.* While there is comfort in having a classroom routine, varying learning activities (e.g., instructor presentation versus student small group discussion) and modes of communication (e.g., visual and aural, talking and listening) over time both keeps up interest and reaches students with differing learning styles. It is generally better to plan for this kind of variation before a course starts—when constructing a syllabus—to ensure that the modes of teaching employed are best suited to the course's learning goals. And don't forget that the kinds of activities required for course assignments count as well.

   ▪ *Encourage higher-order thinking and learning.* Some situations require the recall of facts, but most professional education is *synthesizing* knowledge and *applying* it to complex and unique situations. Case-based learning has therefore been important to social work education since its inception. *Critical thinking* and questioning are skills that students should regularly practice if we expect them to graduate with these abilities. Some teachers, myself included, think that more *inquiry and discovery* would improve the rigor of social work education and enhance the field as a whole.

   ▪ *Mentoring and coaching also are teaching.* Various advising assignments, even working with student assistants, are not just administrative tasks but also teaching activities. Such interactions produce many "teachable moments," which can make them more interesting and rewarding.

   ▪ *Effective teaching includes continual self-reflection and self-evaluation.* Some gifted teachers may be able to rely wholly on improvisation, but most good teachers spend a lot of effort planning and organizing their materials, from readings to videos to Internet resources, as well as the methods they use in their teaching. Knowing where each course fits into the curriculum as a whole and where each student is in his or her studies helps. Every class is different, requiring the ability to adapt one's original plans. For most of us, having a plan for both content and process provides a structure within which we can spontaneously do our best work. Student evaluations of teaching regularly show that organizing course content and coming to the classroom well prepared are much appreciated.

   ▪ *Choose and prepare to teach in content areas that you care about.* This may be the most important suggestion, since being knowledgeable and enthusiastic about what you are teaching generally leads to the best learning outcomes. This does not mean, however, that you always teach just the courses in your area of specialty. It does mean that you should choose among the core required courses and adapt the required syllabi to incorporate your strengths. Renewing the curriculum with your colleagues can help keep alive your passion for the content.

Teaching can be a great joy and a source of deep satisfaction. These pleasures do not just come from the authority, status, and positive regard of others that can go with the role. The greatest pleasures are in observing students' excitement and growth when they learn the material and their insights and abilities grow. Learning "teaching tips" and using a variety of teaching modes and methods increase the odds that significant and gratifying student learning will take place.

Further Reading

Friedman, B. D. (2008). *How to teach effectively*. Chicago: Lyceum Books. [Available in traditional and electronic form from the publisher, this volume provides an easy-to-use handbook of successful training techniques]

McKeachie, W. J., and Sviniki, M. (2006). *McKeachie's teaching tips: Strategies, research, and theory for college and university teachers*. 12th ed. Boston: Houghton Mifflin. [The classic in higher education, accessible via brief chapters and full of useful tips, all based on current research on effective teaching at the college level]

Videos

Christensen, C. (1995). *The art of discussion leading: A class with Chris Christensen*. Cambridge, Mass.: Derek Bok Center for Teaching and Learning, Harvard University.

Winston, P. H. (1997). *How to speak*. Cambridge, Mass.: Derek Bok Center for Teaching and Learning, Harvard University.

4

AFFIRMING DIVERSITY IN THE CLASSROOM

THE DIVERSITY OF THE U.S. POPULATION is broadening, requiring that social work professionals be prepared to work with a wide variety of clients and communities. Diversity in higher education is broadening as well, although more slowly. In their social work courses, teachers encounter diversity among their students in ethnicity, culture, national origin, religion, age, life experience, class background, sexual and gender identity, and disability status.

The current statement on curriculum and accreditation from the Council on Social Work Education (CSWE 2008) requires that programs provide "a learning context in which respect for all persons and understanding of diversity (including age, class, color, disability, ethnicity, family structure, gender, marital status, national origin, race, religion, sex, and sexual orientation) are practiced," a context that is "nondiscriminatory" (16). This context encompasses "faculty, staff and student composition; selection of agencies and their clientele as field education settings; composition of program advisory or field committees; resource allocation; program leadership; speakers series, seminars and special programs; research and other initiatives" as well as curriculum (16–17). All these aspects of a social work program are enjoined to "model understanding of and respect for diversity" (17).

In addition to diversity in society, it affects all the elements in figure 4.1:

- Who the students are.
- Who the teachers are.
- What the subject matter is.
- Who the field practicum agencies serve, who staffs them, and how students experience them.
- What the makeup and organizational culture of the educational institution is.
- What the needs and requirements of the profession are.

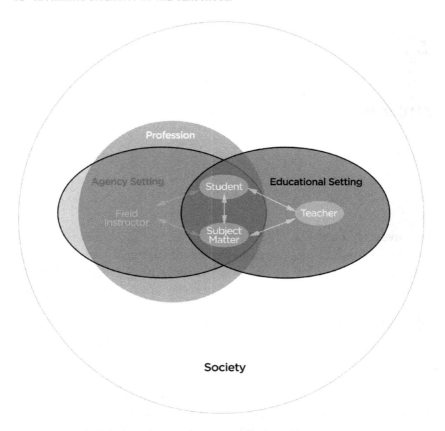

FIGURE 4.1 Model of teaching and learning that highlights the areas of diversity discussed.

Each of these, of course, affects all the others, and when one element changes, the others change, too. In addition, all are affected by the changes and unresolved tensions in society and by the clients, communities, and organizational cultures of the social agencies in which field learning takes place. Some social workers believe that there is an "illusion of inclusion" in social work programs, especially in predominantly white institutions "in which the curriculum, the personnel, and students reflect some level of diversity, but the organization itself is not transformed" (Roberts and Smith 2002:196).

Some approaches to multicultural teaching and practice incorporate the idea of making structural changes in organizations and society—the larger contextual rings and the background in the model—while others do not, focusing instead on students, teachers, subject matter, and perhaps educational settings. The "cultural competence" model adopted by CSWE in its accreditation standards largely represents what Ali and Ancis (2005) described as strategies to "facilitate success of diverse students in the mainstream," as opposed to "restructuring education and society" (71; see, e.g., Gutiérrez, Zuñiga, and Lum 2004). Others, such as Van Soest and Garcia (2005), devised a model for addressing diversity issues that "assumes change" (vii). Uehara and colleagues (2005) advocate a "transformative multicultural curriculum" in which "students . . . participate, with faculty, in the critical deconstruction and transformation of the curriculum itself" (117–118). While efforts at all levels are probably useful, you should decide for yourself where you stand on this continuum.

Many dimensions of human identity fit under the term *diversity*, but as Roberts and Smith (2002) noted, "a definition which includes everything is in danger of meaning nothing at all" (197). This chapter examines those that (1) are associated with oppression and discrimination and (2) have appeared in the literature on social work education. These dimensions are race, ethnicity, culture, gender, sexual orientation and identity, disability status, and aging. Although the issue of age also could apply to children and youth, we concentrate on "age discrimination" with respect to older people, since this is the aspect of age that civil rights and nondiscrimination statutes and policies address. Obviously, we cannot look at every relevant dimension of human diversity in one chapter. For example, immigration status, language differences, and the educational needs of international students are complex issues that the social work education literature has not yet dealt with extensively (for exceptions, see Abram, Slosar, and Walls 2005; Askeland and Payne 2006; Rai 2002; Zhou, Knoke, and Sakamoto 2005). While the place of religion in social work education and how to deal with students' differing religious beliefs have been discussed, I do not cover them here. Finally, sociologists of education regard socioeconomic status, sometimes called social class, as central to the social sorting functions of educational systems, especially higher education (see, e.g., Bourdieu 1990, 1996; Costello 2001, 2005). Even though the social work profession has been a gateway to professional status for many, class issues have not yet been addressed in depth, although what has been published (Costello 2005; Gasker 1999; Harding, Ferguson, and Radey 2005) suggests that this is an area ripe for further study.

As social work education begins to look at diversity issues, it has become clear that the interactions among students, teachers, and others—the teaching/learning process—must incorporate and foster self-awareness if they are to be effective. Continuous self-examination is required of students, teachers, and other actors in the educational situation. The systems of domination and subordination attached to diversity may cause discomfort (Garcia and Van Soest 1997), such as acknowledging unearned privileges that have come at the expense of others; losing a prior assumptive world; acknowledging multiple aspects of identity, some perhaps associated with privilege and some with oppression; and needing a safe space in the classroom which to explore these issues (Holley and Steiner 2005).

This chapter considers various diversity issues as they affect teaching and learning in social work. The question of what a curriculum should include often is specific to a program's location and the populations served by the agencies used for field instruction. Therefore, except for a brief section on general versus specific approaches to diversity content, this chapter looks at diversity issues as they can affect teaching and learning in the classroom (box 4.1).

So that readers will know the standpoint from which I write, my own understanding of dealing with diversity issues in social work education is affected by my identities as an older white woman, a feminist, and a lesbian. I was born in the United States and was raised in a white, middle-class, suburban environment. I am also the child of European immigrants, one of whom was a Jew who fled the Nazis. In striving to improve my own teaching, especially in the areas of race, culture, and ethnicity, I have been helped by (anti)racism and other diversity courses I have taken at various stages in my social work education, by formal faculty development experiences, by informal conversations with faculty colleagues, and, most of all, by the generosity of countless students who have shared their personal experiences with me and who have offered candid and thoughtful discussion and feedback in the classroom and elsewhere. Feminist consciousness raising, scholarly work on feminism and

---

BOX 4.1

EDUCATIONAL POLICY 3.1—DIVERSITY

The program's commitment to diversity—including age, class, color, culture, disability, ethnicity, gender, gender identity and expression, immigration status, political ideology, race, religion, sex, and sexual orientation—is reflected in its learning environment (institutional setting; selection of field settings and their clientele; composition of program advisory or field committees; educational and social resources; resource allocation; program leadership; speaker series, seminars, and special programs; support groups; research and other initiatives; and the demographic makeup of its faculty, staff, and student body).

CSWE 2008:11.

LGBT issues, and my continuing involvement with feminist scholarship and feminist colleagues across North America have given me helpful intellectual and personal tools. Nonetheless, dealing with these issues in my teaching and scholarship requires continuous attention and effort in a social and educational context that tends to obscure (or, to a Marxist, "mystify") or to silence.

Addressing diversity issues requires self-reflection and growth and, perhaps, unanticipated projects of organizational and social change. Because every society and educational institution has issues of diversity with which it is still struggling, increased attention to diversity issues in teaching and learning will likely face some discomfort and conflict. The opportunity for professional and personal growth, however, can be rewarding.

GENERAL OR SPECIFIC COURSE CONTENT

Given the social justice mission of the social work profession, those aspects of diversity most important to it are the needs of groups oppressed by society. One recurrent debate in designing social work curricula is whether to require and teach courses on oppression generally or on specific dimensions of diversity, usually racism. One benefit of general courses is that a program or instructor can choose the issues to highlight based on the populations in the region or the students' learning needs. The "equality of oppressions" paradigm implicit in this approach has been questioned, however, most recently by Schiele (2007). One disadvantage is that some difficult issues, for teachers or students, may be given short shrift. In addition, trying to cover all the relevant issues in one course may mean only a brief discussion of any one of them: the "oppressed group of the week" approach. The advantage of the narrower focus is the opportunity to address certain topics in more depth, albeit at the cost of not addressing others at all. For example, if race and racism are emphasized, LGBTQ or disabled students may object to the lack of attention to "their" issues. Finally, some instructors who work with this material may emphasize "diversity" more than "oppression" as a way to make the material more palatable (Singleton 1994).

Introducing all aspects of diversity into all courses is a third approach. Most social work programs try to do both: infuse content generally and also offer or require general or specific courses on diversity. The challenge of the "infusion" method of curriculum development is making sure to include the planned content and to cover it adequately. In other words, the problem is the horizontal and vertical integration of diversity content in a wide range of courses, which can be hard to document and monitor. One solution is for course evaluations to ask the students about the integration of diversity content in the course, specific or general. Since instructors usually want high marks for annual and tenure review purposes, this technique can increase their attention to content.

RACE, ETHNICITY, AND CULTURE

REQUIREMENTS OF THE PROFESSION

The social work profession and social work education have been strongly committed to addressing race, ethnicity and culture, and racism, at least in their stated goals and aspirations. For example, in the next decade, the profession should "address the impact of racism, other forms of social injustice, and other human rights violations through social work education and practice" and "continuously acknowledge, recognize, confront and address pervasive racism within social work practice at the individual, agency, and institutional levels" (NASW 2005:1). In addition, the National Association of Social Workers (NASW 2001) has published practice standards regarding cultural competence. Finally, the social work profession has been called on to work against institutional or structural racism (NASW 2007).

As in many areas of social work practice, we have little empirical evidence for what does and does not work well in culturally competent and antiracist practice and education. In addition, white social work students' prior experiences and comfort level with clients and fellow students of color and with race-related issues vary greatly. Krentzman and Townsend (2008) analyzed several measures of cultural competence used in social work and related professions for their content and possible use in social work education, and they recommend developing a measure based on NASW's practice standards in this area.

STUDENTS

One persistent concern in social work education has been recruiting and retaining students from traditionally underrepresented groups in BSW and MSW programs. The 2004 data show that of minority enrolled junior and senior undergraduate social work students, 35.4 percent were full-time and 46.7 percent were part-time students. In 2004, about 21 percent of baccalaureate graduates were African American, 9.6 percent were from various Hispanic groups, 1.1 percent were Native American, and 2.3 percent were Asian American and Pacific Islander, for a total of 35.2 percent (CSWE 2007b:32). There are fewer such MSW students. In 2004, minority students constituted 29.1 percent of full-time and 32.3 percent of part-time MSW students. Among MSW graduates in 2004, 14.6 percent were African American, 7.6 percent were from various Hispanic groups, 3.3 percent were Asian American and Pacific Islander, and only about 1 percent were Native American or from other native groups (CSWE 2007:40). As an example of the challenges in this area, Ortiz Hendricks, Finch, and Franks (2005) documented the pervasiveness of the problem of recruiting Latinos in social work programs in New York, despite the agencies' acute need for social workers to serve the growing Hispanic population in New York City and its surrounding areas. (The terminology here is inconsistent but reflects the data sources from which the information is originally drawn.)

As in undergraduate education generally, the number of students of color in baccalaureate programs in social work depends at least partly on the overall number of high school graduates. In the United States, this is a special problem for Spanish-speaking students, as national high school graduation rates are lower for them than for other groups. In addition, at the college level, attrition rates are higher for minority students than for white students, for reasons both complex and poorly understood. CSWE statistics show that at both the BSW and MSW levels, there are more part-time than full-time African American and Hispanic students. In addition, students from traditionally underrepresented groups are more often found in some kinds of educational institutions than others, like Historically Black Colleges and Universities.

Evidence shows that the experiences of students of color in social work education programs can be difficult (box 4.2). For example, Native American students report a lack of attention to them and their issues in the curriculum, which they see as invalidating their interests (Weaver 2000). Although while all social work students share many interests, their motivations and career goals may differ from those of students from traditionally underrepresented groups, as in their desire to meet specific community needs (Limb and Organista 2003). Nonetheless, it is likely that more will enter social work programs over time as their numbers increase proportionally in the U.S. population. The concern is that the populations served by social work agencies are becoming more diverse more quickly than are the undergraduate and graduate social work students. Thus many social work programs are trying to recruit racially and ethnically diverse students, especially those who can speak languages

BOX 4.2

STEREOTYPES CAN BE SELF-FULFILLING IN ACADEMIA:
A PSYCHOLOGICAL PERSPECTIVE

As Bain (2004) points out, research in social psychology can "help us understand the extra burdens faced by anyone who has been the target of some pervasive negative stereotype, and the especially onerous burdens female students encounter in certain subjects and African Americans and some other minorities carry in all academic pursuits—burdens that white males in our society do not experience" (72). The concept of stereotype threat (Steele 1997) or stereotype vulnerability posits that when a stereotype is triggered, people who identify as members of stereotyped groups tend to perform in a way that fulfills the stereotype, such as on tests of mathematics for women and any form of academic aptitude test for blacks. This effect occurs only when the person actually cares about performing well, thus most affecting the most able and ambitious. The effect seems to operate on both conscious ("hot") and unconscious ("cool") levels (Wheeler and Petty 2001). While the exact cognitive and emotional mechanisms that produce this effect are still being debated, research has shown that it also affects women in mathematics and other "masculine-typed" activities, as well as older adults with respect to memory. The general climate also makes a difference; for example, exposure to gender stereotypes in television commercials or to sexist jokes can be disabling to women. Some ways that teachers can reduce the effects of stereotype threat in educational settings are conveying positive expectations of potential and achievement, providing an appropriate and progressive level of challenge, stressing the expandability of aptitudes, affirming that nontraditional students indeed belong in the setting and among the high achievers, valuing multiple perspectives on what is being taught, and providing positive role models (Steele 1997).

other than English, often those of the populations served by the social work agencies and/or in accordance with demographic trends in the communities where the schools are located.

TEACHERS

Just as there are fewer students from traditionally underrepresented racial/ ethnic groups enrolled in social work programs than is desirable, there also are fewer faculty members from these groups than is needed. In 2004, about 13 percent of faculties of graduate and joint degree programs were African American; 6.0 percent and 4.5 percent, respectively, were from various Hispanic groups; and about 3 percent were Asian American. Only 1 percent or fewer were identified as being of Native or Pacific Island descent. In 2004, 16 percent of faculties in undergraduate programs were identified as African

American, and 5.5 percent were from various Hispanic groups. About 1.5 percent were Asian American, and 1.4 percent were Native American (CSWE 2007b:8). Students often seek mentoring and role-modeling from faculty members with whom they can easily identify, but many may not find faculty of their own racial, ethnic, or language groups in their programs.

Doctoral education is the gateway to the professoriat, but fewer students of color are enrolled in doctoral than in BSW and MSW social work programs (CSWE 2007b). For the last few decades, the federal government has provided financial aid and funded the mentoring of some doctoral students in social work through CSWE's Minority Fellowship Program (http://www.cswe.org/CSWE/scholarships/). This and other national and institution-based initiatives to increase the numbers of doctoral students and graduates of color should be continued and even raised in order to increase the number of full-time faculty of color.

We should distinguish between who faculty members are and what they must know and be able to teach. The widespread demand for faculty familiar with cultural competence and diversity issues is reflected in job advertisements for social work faculty (Anastas 2006). Faculty development efforts also are needed to enhance skills and confidence.

"The power relationships that structure social life do not stop at the classroom door" (Brown, Cervero, and Johnson-Bailey 2000:273) and affect teachers as well as learners. Students often challenge the credibility, authority, and expertise of teachers of color, so they must use strategies to defuse the tension and exert control in a nonconfrontational manner. Roberts and Smith (2002:201–203) reported that African American faculty members worry about the labels used to identify them, are concerned about how they dress or wear their hair, and experience various forms of invisibility and discounting of their theories, opinions, and/or expertise. In addition, students of color often seek them out for mentoring and support, and African American teachers often are asked to do much committee and other service work. Hence they may face extra challenges on the job and heavier workloads than do their white colleagues.

TEACHING THE CONTENT

Students may enter graduate programs in social work believing that they are already culturally competent in dealing with diversity issues (Holden et al. 2002:121). In fact, learning about these issues often means revising what we think we know (Garcia and Van Soest 1997), and in retrospect, by graduation

MSW students recognize that they know less than they had initially thought (Holden, Anastas, and Meenaghan 2003, 2005). On average, MSW students can become better at dealing with these issues by the time they complete their degree (Holden et al. 2002:121).

Including content on race, ethnicity, and culture in courses often brings strong emotional reactions in white students and students of color, which may interfere with learning. Tatum (1992) recommends using racial identity development theory to understand and work with students' reactions to content on race and racism. Although the process typically unfolds differently for whites and nonwhites in the United States, racial identity development theory posits that people normatively cycle through different feeling states and behaviors. For African Americans, these stages are described as *preencounter*, in which the values of the dominant culture are accepted uncritically, and group identity is not emphasized; *encounter*, an often painful crisis point at which the personal salience or impact of racism is acknowledged; *immersion/emersion*, emersion in their own racial identity and rejection of white dominance; and *internalization* or *internalization-commitment*, the secure establishment of their group (or racial) identity and engagement with the affirming aspects of the dominant white culture, often with a commitment to address their group's concerns (Cross 1991; Helms 1990; Tatum 1992). For whites, the stages are described as *contact*, characterized by a lack of awareness of cultural and institutional racism and its impact; *disintegration*, often precipitated by increased contact with people of color and/or with new information about racism, during which feelings of guilt, shame, or anger may arise; *reintegration* into the majority point of view, in which the outgroup may be blamed for their discomfort; and sometimes progress to a stage of *autonomy*, in which they affirm their white racial identity and commit to antiracism (Helms 1990; Tatum 1992).

Racial identity theory is most useful as a description of the varied emotional and social reactions and processes by which people cope with issues of race and racism, not as a prescription for how the process should take place. For classroom teachers, this theory helps explain why students have such strong feelings, because the material often taps into and/or threatens a hard-won aspect of personal identity.

Ortiz Hendricks (2003) used Bertha Reynolds's (1942/1985) formulation of stages of learning and teaching social work (see chapter 2) to delineate stages in the learning of cultural competence. The "acute consciousness of self" stage is developing new areas of *cultural* self-awareness, often embarrassment or avoidance along with self-examination. The second stage, "sink or swim" adaptation, is parallel to "cultural sensitivity," when learners or workers risk entering new situations and improvising ways of proceeding, but with anxiety because they are not yet able to deal with cultural differences. "Beginning cultural competence" is the third stage in which people have more confidence in their ability to handle cross-cultural situations and diversity issues, but without being able to articulate exactly how, followed by a stage of "relative mastery of cultural competence" in which, in Reynolds's terms, social workers can both understand and control their own activities—in this case, their methods of cultural competence. The final stage is learning to teach effectively what they have learned. These stages also may be useful in understanding how classroom teachers and field supervisors become culturally competent as well where students are located on this continuum of learning.

We must find a balance between content and process in teaching about race, ethnicity, and culture and effective techniques for teaching them. Comerford (2004) had students write about their identities and their experiences of both privilege and discrimination, which they shared in small groups at off-campus retreats as a way to support the affective and self-reflective dimensions needed for effective classroom learning about diversity. Millstein (1997) and Garcia and Van Soest (1997) reported using a "taping" technique, drawn from Tatum's (1992) work, which both encourages students' self-reflection on curricular content on race and racism and documents their changes in knowledge and feelings about these issues. The students' responses differed based on their ethnic and racial identities and their previous experiences of racism and other kinds of discrimination and oppression (Garcia and Van Soest 1997). This makes teaching the material in mixed groups difficult and underscores the importance of "starting where each student is." From students' reactions, however, it is clear that both *content*—information about social and economic inequalities, for example—and process contributes to changing them.

One way to teach diversity and white privilege (McIntosh 1988) is to discuss specific cases (Gillespie 2003). Well-crafted cases illustrate situations and complexities that students may not realize on their own. In addition, they can be a starting point for a discussion safer and less threatening than biographical or personal experiences and will likely produce varying perspectives of the case.

A lot of attention is currently being paid to incorporating content on racial and ethnic diversity in social work curricula (see, e.g., Carter-Black 2007; de Haymes and Kitty 2007), in teaching methods (Van Soest and Garcia 2005), and in field education (Van Soest and Garcia 2003). For example, Rozas (2007) suggests using a specific intergroup dialogue (IGD) model to strengthen participants' commitment to social justice, using a voluntary, extracurricular activity. Schiele (2007) and Abrams and Gibson (2007) suggest that education in social work should focus more on white identity and privilege as well as on the more subtle forms of racism in the United States. Discussing a case can be a way of addressing white privilege (Gillespie 2003; McIntosh 1988).

ORGANIZATIONAL AND INSTITUTIONAL CONTEXT

For nearly one hundred years, and sometimes longer, in the United States, social work has been taught in universities. Like all complex organizations, colleges and universities have histories and cultures that affect their climates and current practices, through mission statements and organizational structures and also in unwritten organizational norms and cultures. A few specifically educate people from traditionally underrepresented groups, while most are historically and traditionally white, often with a history of segregation or marginalization.

Being the few among many, students of color will likely have different levels of comfort in these different settings. For example, a student may feel responsible for speaking for the group in the classroom or the agency. Organized student groups and/or assigned faculty mentors are common methods used to reduce any sense of isolation and to provide social and emotional support.

Accreditation standards in social work and federal, state, and local law require that a social work program not discriminate against any student or group of students based on race, culture, language, or national origin. In addition, many social work programs are housed in colleges and universities with affirmative action policies. Following some widely publicized court decisions, some states and institutions are reexamining their affirmative action policies. But most have not abandoned their goals of affirmative action, even if how such policies are implemented may have been changed to conform to current legal opinion.

GENDER

REQUIREMENTS OF THE PROFESSION

Most adults who use social work services are women. From a biopsychosocial perspective, a person's gender affects his or her health risks from birth to old age; identity and psychosocial development; schooling; family roles and formation; employment patterns and opportunities; and retirement and aging. Across all racial and ethnic groups, women still earn less than men in comparable jobs. Gender determines how people view and participate in group, organizational, and community life, including political activity, access to political positions and power, and engagement in social movements and social change. There are significant gender disparities in health, mental health, substance use/abuse, and longevity. Therefore knowledge about gender issues applies to all areas of the social work curriculum, including our understanding of human behavior, social policy and the social environment, and intervention (McPhail 2008).

Gender inequities also exist within the social work profession (see, e.g., Anastas 2007b; McPhail 2004; Whitaker, Weismuller, and Clark 2006). Women in social work practice and social work education earn less than their male colleagues, and they also are at a disadvantage on many of the factors that reduce earnings and the potential for advancement in their careers. Thus, even though more women are in the profession, they still are at a disadvantage, as men continue to occupy a disproportionate share of the leadership positions in both practice and academia. Social work programs generally do not address this problem. Although when they enter the program, MSW students think they know a great deal about issues of sex, gender, and marital status they acknowledge later that they did not (Holden, Anastas, and Meenaghan 2003, 2005).

STUDENTS

Most undergraduate students in the United States are female, and given the numbers of women in the social work profession as a whole, this is true for undergraduate social work students as well: In 2004, 88 percent of full-time and 84 percent of part-time juniors and seniors enrolled in CSWE-accredited baccalaureate programs were women (CSWE 2007b:31). In 2004, women accounted for 83 percent of all MSW students in 2004 and 85 percent of MSW graduates. In addition, as in many other fields, while the majority of doctoral students in social work used to be male, women now predominate but not by as much: in 2004, between 71 percent and 78 percent of enrolled doctoral students in various phases and types of enrollment were women, and 69 percent of those awarded a doctoral degree that year were women (CSWE 2007b).

Costello's (2005) comprehensive ethnographic study of race, class and gender and how they affect graduate social work students makes two important points. The first is that students have *multiple identities* involving race, class, gender, and ability that affect them in complex ways. She found that "class-privileged white men" have the easiest and most successful experiences in

BOX 4.3

A SOCIOLOGICAL VIEW OF INEQUITIES IN HIGHER EDUCATION: PIERRE BOURDIEU AND *HABITUS*

Costello (2005) uses the sociological theories of Pierre Bourdieu, who studied, among other things, social class differences in taste (1988), perpetuation of class differences in France's educational system (1996), and masculine domination in "exotic" and western European societies (1990, 2001). Bourdieu's (1990) concept of *habitus* points to how aspects of identity are enacted in ways that are unconscious to the actor and reproduce social structures: "The *habitus*, a product of history, produces individual and collective practices — more history" (54).

According to Bourdieu's theory, both individual practices (actions) and social structures and institutions (re)create and perpetuate what others theories would call norms, roles, and/or meanings. *Habitus* encompasses worldview, that is, assumptions about how the world works and tastes, both of which relate to what others would term *culture* and/or *subculture*. These aspects of *habitus* are relevant to the socialization functions of professional education and the observation that some students feel more "at home" in social work education or in higher education more generally. *Habitus* also is *embodied*, that is, expressed physically in ways that are hard to change, "internalized as second nature and so forgotten as history" (Bordieu 1990:56).

Bourdieu's attention is not only on how social systems of "distinction" and "discrimination" (in both the generic sense of discerning differences and the sense of oppressive acts and practices) are enacted by individuals. It is also on the myriad ways in which organizations and institutions "discriminate" (again, in both senses of the word), subtly but powerfully. Costello (2001, 2005), for example, reports powerful contrasts in the comfort, elegance, and decor of the two settings she studied at the same university — the law school and the social work school — and the differing amounts of abstract theory and practical training (practicum experiences) in the two schools' curricula (38–43), illustrating the social sorting of fields of study and of students.

In Bourdieu's view, economic, political, social, and cultural capital are vital to understanding the relative power of individuals and institutions, with cultural and symbolic capital being especially important in contemporary society. Having these forms of capital enhances a student's chances of admission and success in educational programs. Conversely, educational systems confer on their students social and, especially, cultural capital that may also give them access to political and economic capital (Bourdieu 1996).

graduate school. The second point is that the social and psychological reasons for these differences are pervasive and subtle. In her study, Costello used the theories of the French sociologist Pierre Bourdieu to understand these mechanisms (box 4.3). She uses the term *identity dissonance* to indicate situations in which educational or professional norms do not fit an aspect of identity. For example, success in graduate school and the exercise of professional power and authority often are difficult for women. Costello notes, however, that some students experience "identity dissonance" as positive and hence feel empowered as they embrace new professional and behavioral norms. Others see it as negative and hence as a source of stress that hampers their ability to perform, thus following Meyer's (2003) minority stress model. For female students in social work, minority stress applies not because of actual numbers but because of masculine domination (Bourdieu 2001) in the institutions of higher education and the professions more generally.

TEACHERS

In general, studies of women teaching social work show patterns similar to those in other areas of academia: On average, women faculty members are lower in rank, tenure status, and salary and publish fewer books and articles than men do (Holley and Young 2005; Lennon 2005; Petchers 1996; Sakamoto et al. 2008). This gender difference affects faculty of color as well (Schiele and Francis 1996). One explanation for the difference in rank and salary may be that women are more likely than men to make employment decisions based on geographic, marital, and/or child-rearing factors (Holley and Young 2005; Petchers 1996). Although white men may perceive a disadvantage in the current academic job market (Holley and Young 2005), the data suggest that proportionally more men are hired for entry-level tenure-track positions than women are (Petchers 1996). These differences persist despite similar educational preparation and career aspirations in men and women doctoral graduates (Holley and Young 2005; Petchers 1996). In sum, although overall gender differences in rank and salary are lessening over time, they still exist (Valian 1998, 2003).

Students may not regard men and women in the same way in the classroom and may challenge the authority and expertise of women teachers, especially young ones, more often. Women on faculties may also be expected more often to advise students and/or to serve on committees or do other uncompensated work. They may also encounter subtle and not-so-subtle male dominance, such as men who talk over them in meetings (Holley and Young 2005). Institutional barriers surely play a role in this outcome (Petchers 1996).

TEACHING THE CONTENT

The CSWE has long mandated curricula on women in its accreditation standards. How well such content is conveyed and how women are faring in the social work classroom are not often discussed, however. Based on broader studies of gender in higher education, DeLange (1995) invites us to ask: "Do faculty call on male students more than female students? Do male students talk more frequently and longer? Are female students reinforced for speaking? Do any of these patterns change based on the sex of the instructor?" (80). Using an analysis of more general gender differences in communication, DeLange also suggests that cross-gender communication problems are more likely between teachers and students as well as among faculty.

Discussions of gender discrimination and curricular content in social work are still largely framed around male/female differences. At the end of the twentieth century, gender theory and queer theory in the humanities and social sciences also considered transgender and intersex phenomena (McPhail 2004), both in this and other cultures and because these issues offer an important perspective on otherwise unexamined assumptions in our thinking about sex and gender. In fact, students today interpret the invitation to discuss "gender" as how content on transgender and other gender issues is or is not addressed, which with the exception of McPhail (2004, 2008), the social work education literature has generally not yet discussed.

Theory and knowledge of gender issues have changed substantially since "content on women" was introduced to the social work curriculum (McPhail 2004, 2008). This is also reflected on campuses in the change from centers and departments of "women's studies" to "gender studies" and the many feminist theories that now exist (Saulnier 1996). As McPhail (2008) explained, boys and men now are also understood as having a gender, leading to the study and analysis of masculinity; the binaries of gender are being questioned, especially in regard to intersex and transgender issues; the *intersectionality* of gender with race and class is being emphasized; and queer theory is changing how sexual orientations, desires, and gender expressions are understood (McPhail 2004). Presenting current theory and knowledge in this area is essential to the analysis and improvement of social policy, research, social change, and social work practice, and McPhail (2008) provides excellent resources and suggestions.

Because the traditional classroom is not always hospitable to women, some people in social work have talked about using feminist methods in their teaching. Chapter 2 describes the influential theory that women may think, learn, and develop cognitively in ways that differ from how men do (Belenky et al. 1986). Belenky and colleagues call for "connected teaching" (214), a kind of teaching that "supports the evolution of . . . students' thinking" (218) and focuses not on the display of the teacher's knowledge (218) but on its use in "put[ting] the students into conversation with other voices—past and present—in the culture" (219). In addition, "connected teachers welcome diversity of opinion in class discussion" (223). All students, male and female, are likely to find that this style of teaching enhances their learning and critical thinking, that is, their professional growth. Feminist teaching has been viewed as a tool for teaching key principles of social work practice, especially empowerment (Dore 1994; Lazzari 1991; Parnell and Andrews 1994; Raske 1999).

ORGANIZATIONAL AND INSTITUTIONAL CONTEXT

CSWE's accreditation standards require that schools and departments of social work operate without discrimination against women. This mandate is usually evaluated by examining gender differences with respect to admissions, financial aid, and/or graduation rates for students and promotion, rank, tenure status, and compensation for faculty. Issues for staff and "softer" employment data, like working conditions for faculty, are less frequently considered. Another indicator of sensitivity to gender is the presence and publication of sexual harassment policies to protect students and faculty on campus and in the field. There still is a problem with gender in higher education generally, that is, a continuing underrepresentation of women at the highest ranks and seniority and in the academic administration (Petchers 1996; Sakamoto et al. 2008). Except at the doctoral level, social work education is not aimed specifically at producing future academics. Although the specific effects of male dominance in academic leadership on the performance of women students (or faculty) have not been studied, women students and faculty (Holley and Young 2005) may derive meaning from the absence of women in leadership (see box 4.2) in ways that may prevent them from reaching their full potential.

SEXUAL ORIENTATION AND GENDER EXPRESSION

REQUIREMENTS OF THE PROFESSION

The general public in the United States has become somewhat more accepting of gays and lesbians over time, especially in regard to equal opportunity and/or nondiscrimination in employment and housing (Avery et al. 2007; Newman, Dannenfelser, and Benishek 2002). The NASW continues to advocate for full rights for and affirmative practice with gay and lesbian people in this heteronormative and heterosexist society (Crisp 2006; Hunter and Hickerson 2003). Because U.S. census data now includes information on same-gender households and as states grapple with the issue of same-sex marriage, information about at least some aspects of gay and lesbian lives is becoming more accessible, suggesting that scholarship in this area will grow (Gates and Ost 2004). The child-bearing and child-rearing of gays and lesbians have also become more common, with all the attendant debates about child welfare and family policy. Finally, as the proportion of elders in society increases, issues related to the aging of gays and lesbians are now being addressed as well. Thus it is likely that social work professionals must be knowledgeable about and engaged with issues of sexual orientation and gender expression for the foreseeable future.

Problems for the social work profession remain, however, as in the continuing practice of conversion or reorientation therapies (see, e.g., Spitzer 2003), despite evidence that they are ineffective and even harmful (Jenkins and Johnston 2004; King, Smith, and Bartlett 2004; Shidlo and Schroeder 2002). Although a review of the current debates about conversion or reorientation therapies is inappropriate here, the social work profession's position on these "treatments" is clear: these are "misleading therapies" (NASW 2001:1), which *cannot and will not change sexual orientation* (2, italics in original). The American Psychiatric Association (1999) and the American Psychological Association (1997) earlier reached the same conclusion and made similar statements. Even if we were to accept the evidence that a *few* people may benefit from such "treatments" (Spitzer 2003), the great majority are not helped, and many can even be harmed by these methods.

Although the profession's ethics and policy statements are unambiguous, a consensus on the importance of nondiscrimination policies with respect to sexual orientation may not be as clear (Van Soest 1996). A study of social work textbooks not only documented the lack of inclusion of material on gays and lesbians but also found that about one-fifth of the texts studied actually presented the content negatively (Morrow 1996). Thus, the challenges for social work education are both what to teach and what not to teach.

STUDENTS

Until very recently, no data on the sexual identity (self-identified sexual orientation) of social work applicants or students had been collected, which makes sense in a legal context where civil rights protections are not in place nationally and not always locally (CSWE data with this information included have not yet been published.) Although we therefore do not know precisely how many gay, lesbian, bisexual, transgendered, queer, or questioning students are enrolled in social work programs, we know anecdotally and through other kinds of studies that there are some. NASW's members may voluntarily report sexual orientation if they choose, but very few do. As a result, we have no good estimate of the percentage of LGBT-identified people in the profession. If the current conservative estimates of 3 percent and 1 percent of the population as gay and lesbian, respectively—and remembering that this percentage is likely higher among college-educated people—straight and LGBTQ social work students must be prepared to deal with LGBTQ colleagues and clients and/or who have family members who identify as such.

Many schools and departments of social work have voluntary organizations for lesbian, gay, bisexual, transgendered, and/or queer-identified students and their allies. In these groups, students can support one another as well voice any concerns about curricular content (or its absence), field practicum experiences (positive and negative), or other aspects of school or campus life. Such groups are generally viewed as quite helpful (Hylton 2005).

Social workers' and social work students' attitudes toward gay and lesbian people have been studied since the mid-1980s, and the results suggest that at least some social workers and some social work students report homophobic or heterosexist attitudes (a good review of earlier findings is presented in Brownlee et al. 2005). A large-scale study of first-year graduate students in social work and counseling showed that only a few students in the two disciplines (6.5%) expressed negative attitudes on the self-report scale (Newman, Dannenfelser, and Benishek 2002:278). Self-reported sexual orientation and religious identity were the two strongest predictors of variance in attitudes, with conservative Protestants expressing the most negative attitudes and gay, lesbian, or bisexual respondents having somewhat more positive attitudes than heterosexuals. Some of the items most often reporting homonegative attitudes were the adoption of children by gay men, male homosexuality as a "natural expression" of human sexuality that should not be condemned, and female homosexuality as a sin. Similarly, Cluse-Tolar and colleagues (2004) found that undergraduate social work students had more positive attitudes than other undergraduate students did but that some social work students did have negative attitudes, ranging from 2 percent ("willing to accept a job with gay or lesbian customers") to 27 percent ("I feel that homosexuality is wrong") and 33 percent ("I would be uncomfortable with a gay or lesbian roommate"). Gender, political party affiliation, and religiosity were correlated with views of gay and lesbian people, willingness to socialize with them, and support for rights for gays and lesbians. The challenge in working with students' attitudes toward sexual orientation and gender expression is therefore likely to be helping the minority of social work students with negative attitudes differentiate between their personal, often religiously based, beliefs and convictions and the professional position required of them for ethical professional practice. Brownlee and colleagues (2005) reported similar findings among Canadian students.

TEACHERS

Until recently there has been no information about the number of faculty members in social work who identify as gay, lesbian, bisexual, or transgender. Those faculty members who are "out" are often sought out by LGBTQ students for mentoring and support, especially when they have problems in the classroom, campus residences, or the field. Martin (1995) argues that gay and lesbian faculty should assume these responsibilities, since LGBT students may encounter discrimination and stress. Although many schools actively recruit faculty who are members of traditionally underrepresented ethnic, racial, cultural, or groups, schools and departments of social work do not generally intentionally recruit LGBT faculty (Mackelprang, Ray, and Hernandez-Peck 1996). In fact, some academic jobs in social work require faculty to teach in accordance with the institution's religious mission, which may mean not "promoting" a "gay lifestyle" and which would likely not be comfortable for a LGBTQ faculty member (Anastas 2006).

TEACHING THE CONTENT

Mackelprang, Ray, and Hernandez-Peck (1996:23) found that deans and directors of social work programs reported much less emphasis on sexual orientation content in their curricula than on race, ethnicity, and gender content. Social work texts are only rarely "fully inclusive" of content on gays and lesbians (Morrow 1996). In addition, the mainstream social work journals have published relatively little in this area except in regard to AIDS and HIV (Van Voorhis and Wagner 2001). However important care- and prevention-focused studies related to the worldwide HIV epidemic may be, prevention studies now focus on sexual behaviors, not identities, and those affected with the virus are predominantly heterosexual, so it is correct to exclude HIV and AIDS content from such analyses. Those teachers who address LGBT content in their classrooms, then, cannot assume that students may have learned much elsewhere in their studies.

One of the issues faced by LGBT faculty members in teaching such content is identity management, that is, whether and/or how to disclose their gay, lesbian, bisexual, or "trans" identity in the classroom (Cain 1996; Lovaas, Baroudi, and Collins 2002; Martin 1995). Students' reaction to such disclosures varies, with some finding that it adds to their comfort and thus enhances their learning, and others becoming uncomfortable. In particular, gay or lesbian students who choose not to disclose their sexual orientation may feel pressured to do so when an instructor "comes out."

ORGANIZATIONAL AND INSTITUTIONAL CONTEXT

Because social work education takes place in both the field placement setting and the classroom, many self-identified gay and lesbian students have sexual orientation or identity issues in their field placement experiences (Hylton 2005; Messinger 2004; Newman, Bogo, and Daley 2009). They report individual issues, such as wanting more advice and support in managing the disclosure of their sexual orientation (to colleagues and/or clients) or in dealing with the pressures of hiding it. They also report encountering heterosexism and/or homophobia from staff and even in agency policy. Whereas they characterized some agencies as "gay friendly," they described others as "gay tolerant" or even "gay ignorant." Problems can be especially bad in some religiously affiliated agencies. Gay- or lesbian-identified field faculty may also have special demands when working with LGBTQI students, such as modeling identity management in the practice setting. Whether based on students' or field faculty's accounts (Newman, Bogo, and Daley 2009), these problems may be best described as "pervasive heteronormativity" unless the agency specializes in serving LGBTQI people. Every department or school of social work must look at sexual orientation in regard to its field placement settings to ensure not only that LGBT students are not placed in intolerable situations but that all students are given a gay-affirming education in the practice setting.

The challenges for gay, lesbian, bisexual, and transgender students go far beyond social work (Cramer 2002). Those who live in college or university residences may have concerns about comfort and safety. Because of the prevalence of violence against gay, lesbian, bisexual, and "trans" individuals, many campuses have established "safe zones" and ways to identify "allies" (Draughn, Elkins, and Roy 2002). Residence advisers and participants in campuswide safety and support programs should receive training and support. Both campuswide educational events and the inclusion of curricular content on LGBTQ issues (in queer studies, gender studies programs, and elsewhere) convey the message that the people and their concerns are important to the college community as a whole. How gay, lesbian, bisexual, and transgender social work students feel in the social work classroom depends a lot on how their concerns are addressed on the campus as a whole.

In a controversial decision regarding in its accreditation activities, the CSWE decided that social work departments and schools in religious colleges or universities can opt out of the requirement to support nondiscrimination with respect to sexual orientation when doing so would conflict with their religious norms and beliefs. To date, no programs have asked for such a waiver (D. Pierce, personal communication, 2005). Despite the existence of professional ethics and norms, such a policy recognizes how the educational institution as a whole affects social work. It certainly highlights the great variation among social work programs in how content on sexual orientation and gender expression is and is not being addressed.

Finally, colleges and universities vary greatly in how affirming they are of gay, lesbian, bisexual, and transgender people in all roles on campus (Sears 2002). In addition, basic civil rights protections for LGBT people are available in only a relatively few states and localities (National Gay and Lesbian Task Force 2007). The recent legal recognition in some states of same-sex partnerships through civil marriage and domestic partnership rights has triggered the passage of state-based and federal legislation (Defense of Marriage Act, or DOMA), enacted specifically to limit such rights. It has not yet been possible to enact federal legislation narrowly focused on ending workplace discrimination based on sexual orientation (ENDA), although equal rights for gays and lesbians in the workplace has widespread support in the U.S. population. Civil rights and other legal protections are only the beginning of ensuring social equity for oppressed groups. We must remember that students, faculty, and all social work professionals are dealing with diversity in sexual orientation and gender expression in a legal context that does not provide the same supportive legal framework that exists for other aspects of diversity.

DISABILITIES

REQUIREMENTS OF THE PROFESSION

Since its inception, helping people with disabilities and their families has been a core concern of social work. This commitment includes working in schools with students with identified special needs, which, however, can create some dilemmas for educators when between helping a student with an identified disability reach his or her full potential and determining whether or not the student can indeed perform the core responsibilities of the social work job well enough to be useful to clients.

For social work educators, the roles of social work rehabilitation and professional gatekeeping may conflict (GlenMaye and Bolin 2007). Legal regulation may also conflict with preferred professional practice, as when the program cannot tell placement agencies about a student's disability (only the student has the right to share this confidential information). Moreover, having a disability cannot be interpreted to mean that the person cannot perform adequately, especially when reasonable accommodations are made, but the service to clients and the student's interactions with clients and colleagues are legitimate areas of evaluation for all students, including those with disabilities. The courts do support the right and responsibility of programs and faculty to judge *all* students' performance, but they also require that programs make those needed accommodations that would not constitute an undue burden, in order to give a student with an identified disability a chance to prove themselves—to succeed or fail.

STUDENTS

Applicants with disabilities must, by law, be evaluated for admission to a social work program on the same basis as other applicants if the student is believed able to meet its requirements and if providing the accommodations needed for this to happen will not impose an "undue hardship" on the program, although no social work programs seem to actively recruit such applicants, and the number of such students enrolled seems to be low (Pardeck 2003). Pardeck's small-scale study found that although a variety of accommodations were offered to students, notice of disabled students' rights to these were not always well publicized.

A faculty survey of students with psychiatric disabilities found that most social work programs do deal with students with psychiatric disabilities, although their strategies for doing so varied (GlenMaye and Bolin 2007). Concerns about students with psychiatric disabilities were reported for both academic and performance in the field practicum: interactions with clients (and supervisors) in the practicum and behavior in the classroom (and with teachers). Faculty who had had such problems reported that the most common methods of addressing them were talking with the student or with the student and an advocate (perhaps someone from the campus disability service). This survey looked at issues with students who disclosed such a disability and sought accommodation from the social work program to support their learning. But because students are often reluctant to disclose a psychiatric or learning disability (Cole and Cain 1996), a program that provides accommodation may not always be a solution.

Library staff often know of assistive technologies that students with limited vision can use to read printed materials or of adaptations that can help deaf people use computers and the Internet. Technological and other mechanisms, like the use of readers, note takers, signers, or personal attendants, may be provided to disabled students in the classroom and field setting.

I vividly remember the first time I had a deaf student in class who, in addition to being fluent in sign language, could read lips, so it was hard to remember not to speak to the class while my back was turned to write on the blackboard. Making this adjustment actually benefited all students, though, for I wrote on the board less often and even before class (a recommended teaching method), and I was probably more understandable to everyone when I spoke facing the class. This illustrates why many people have embraced the concept of *universal design* because the adaptations to environments that help those with disabilities generally benefit all (Lightfoot and Gibson 2005). For example, I personally appreciate the ramps and curb cuts for wheelchairs when I use a briefcase on wheels to carry a heavy load of books and papers to and from my office.

In order to make sure that students know that help is available, we recommend that teachers and programs repeatedly make known students' rights to reasonable accommodation, as well as the procedures needed to document a disability and obtain help (Cole and Cain 1996). Individual teachers are generally encouraged to work with campus experts in disability services, who have the expertise and experience needed to determine which accommodations would work best and who also can support an instructor or a program in adhering to those requirements that must be met by all students, whether or not they have a documented disability, because they are essential to the program and the qualifications needed as a social worker.

TEACHERS

Besides students, apparently few social work programs actively seek disabled faculty either (Mackelprang, Ray, and Hernandez-Peck 1996). Indeed, the social work profession as a whole does not welcome professionals with a known history of mental illness (Stromwall 2002), and the same is likely true in academia. Faculty with disabilities that may require costly accommodations (e.g., deafness may require signers and/or technical equipment) thus worry about finding a job. But because most people are only "temporarily able bodied," teachers already in place may become disabled and need accommodation. We know essentially nothing about how teachers with identified disabilities are faring in social work education, how they negotiate their disabilities in the classroom and in other settings, and how students view having a teacher with a known disability, visible or not.

TEACHING THE CONTENT

Curricular content on disabilities has apparently been lacking in many social work programs (Mackelprang, Ray, and Hernandez-Peck 1996; Pardeck 1999; Quinn 1995), even though many social workers practice with people with chronic and disabling conditions, both physical and mental, and with their families. Quinn's (1995) review of program catalogs and survey responses found that the self-reported inclusion of disability content was far higher than that shown in catalog's content. Disability content was most often found in micropractice courses and least often in the research curriculum, but was not universal in any area. Response rates to the survey were low; the nature of the disabilities covered and not addressed was not specified; and the programs' field learning component was not studied. Nor was content on habilitation/rehabilitation or recovery models included, despite their importance to social work practice (see, e.g., Stromwall and Hurdle 2003). Finally, there is not yet widespread discussion in social work of the attitudes that nondisabled students must overcome or of teaching techniques that have been especially helpful.

ORGANIZATIONAL AND INSTITUTIONAL CONTEXT

Passage of the Americans with Disabilities Act in 1990 has had a far-reaching effect on higher education. The law mandates the reasonable accommodation of students with disabilities in all educational programs in order to give them a meaningful opportunity to "perform the essential functions and/or requirements of the program" in which they are enrolled (Cole and Cain 1996:343). Such requirements may not simply be traditional; they must be essential to the curriculum and the education needed for professional practice.

Since the act was passed, the number of students with identified disabilities enrolled in higher education has been increasing nationwide. The greatest increase among those seeking accommodation has been students with so-called invisible disabilities, including learning and psychiatric disabilities (GlenMaye and Bolin 2007). Other conditions requiring accommodation are vision and hearing impairments, speech and communication problems, mobility limitations and other orthopedic difficulties, and chronic health problems that might require periodic or continual monitoring, medication, or limitation of some activities or of exposures to certain environments.

These requirements are well understood in some areas but not in others (GlenMaye and Bolin 2007; Gordon et al. 2002; Simon et al. 2003; Thomas 2000). They also are subject to continuing interpretation through case law (Thomas 2000). Consequently, it is unrealistic to expect that every faculty member will be knowledgeable about all disabilities, all available assistive technologies and possible accommodations, and evolving law. Therefore it is best to rely on college- or university-based experts, usually based in a center for students with identified disabilities, for advice on implementing nondiscriminatory procedures, determining an individual's disability status, and recommending reasonable accommodations. This practice also helps safeguard students' privacy with respect to details about their disability. The most important organizational factor is likely to be the existence and effectiveness of campus-based centers for disabled students. Student (and employee) health and mental health services, accessibility arrangements on campus and in the community, and state and local benefits also should be available for people with disabilities.

AGING

REQUIREMENTS OF THE PROFESSION

The proportion of older people in the population is steadily rising in both the United States and around the world, but the number of professional social workers with expertise in working with older people is far too low to meet current and future needs (Whitaker, Weismiller, and Clark 2006). Over the past several years, the John A. Hartford Foundation has funded faculty education, doctoral student education, and curricula on aging, all of which have been very successful, although have not solved the problem. In fact, one study showed that the number of graduate programs offering aging content as a specialization or concentration or for a postgraduate certificate has actually declined. Thus, when identifying key issues for social work education for the twenty-first century, the emphasis is on increasing the expertise of all social worker students and social workers on aging as well as increasing the number of social workers working with older people in health, behavioral health, long-term care, and community settings (Cummings and DeCoster 2003; Scharlach et al. 2000). These efforts must also reflect the broadening diversity of the U.S. population of people aged 65 and older, with respect to race/ethnicity, language and culture, and national origin (Crewe 2004), family structure(s), sexual orientation and gender expression, and even age itself. In fact, the "oldest old," 85 and older, is the fastest-growing segment of this population (Rosen and Zlotnik 2001). Despite the need, social work practice in the field of aging remains the poorest-paying area of professional social work (Whitaker, Weismiller, and Clark 2006).

STUDENTS

OLDER STUDENTS The issue of aging affects the kinds of students who enter social work and, whatever their age, whether they are interested in working with older people. The greatest growth in enrollments in higher education nationally is in what are termed *nontraditional* students, that is, those who do not enter college immediately after high school graduation and/or who do not begin their graduate education right after college. Nontraditional students are often regarded as "older" students. Age also affects life stage and developmental tasks, family situations, and employment, factors that affect whether students can study full time and also what they will need in field instruction (Fox 2004). Some nontraditional social work students may also be "second-career" students, those who are changing their professions or careers. Despite all their previous experience and successes, older students and those reentering school after some years often worry about whether their age will be a barrier to admission or to their success in the program. Finally, Fox (2004) pointed out that collaborative relationships between teacher and learner, self-reflection and self-assessment, active learning, and ways to help students use their experience as part of their current learning are likely to be the most helpful for mature students (see chapter 2).

PRACTICE WITH ELDERS Regardless of their age, relatively few social work students enter programs with an interest in working with old people (see, e.g., Rosen and Zlotnik 2001). This reluctance is assumed to reflect our culture's ageism and "gerontophobia" and the stigma attached to aging and practice in aging. In addition to ageism, Kane (2004) cites "therapeutic nihilism" (23) as another attitudinal barrier, referring to the belief that cognitive impairment or other forms of ill health make interventions with elders futile, an attitude reflecting an unrealistic "cure" versus "care" orientation to helping in many areas of social work practice.

Scharlach and colleagues (2000), Rosen and Zlotnik (2001), and Rosen, Zlotnik, and Singer (2002) offer suggestions to enrich curricula and help overcome the stigma attached to the field, such as exposing all students to gerontological social workers, holding colloqia and inviting guest lecturers to speak on the topic, and introducing students to field placement settings early in their education. Anecdotal and other evidence suggests that many students' interest in aging develops out of exposure to older clients in their own lives and to the rewards of working with them in school-sponsored volunteer and/ or field placement settings (Kane 2004; Mason and Sanders 2004).

TEACHERS

When developing and evaluating social work programs for their ability to pre-pare students to work with old people and their families, it is important to have one or more faculty members whose area of expertise is aging, which is also still a problem in some settings (Rosen and Zlotnik 2001; Scharlach et al. 2000). Stipends and training opportunities are being used to recruit more stu-dents (and faculty, as in the Hartford Geriatric Scholars Program) into the field of aging. The Council on Social Work Education (CSWE Gero-Ed Center 2007) has received funding from the John A. Hartford Foundation to develop and disseminate curricular information and materials to improve gerontologi-cal content in social work programs. But since most faculty members were educated at a time when content on aging was not emphasized and because only relatively few will become aging specialists, faculty development efforts for the whole group are needed (Rosen et al. 2000; Scharlach et al. 2000).

TEACHING THE CONTENT

Relatively few social work programs offer concentrations or specializations in aging, so although they may offer elective courses on the topic, most insert the content into more general courses. The consequence is that curricula are still lacking in this area (Cummings and DeCoster 2003; Rosen and Zlotnik 2001; Rosen, Zlotnik, and Singer 2002; Scharlach et al. 2000), despite efforts to develop teaching materials and attractive field placements in aging. In addition, few social work educators have any specialized training in aging (Rosen et al. 2000).

Core competencies in aging are those that all social workers should have and also those that specialists in aging practice should have (CSWE Gero-Ed Center 2007; Rosen et al. 2000). Foundation-level competencies cover values, ethics, and theories, including self-examining myths and stereotypes about aging; promoting older adults' self-determination and decision making; respecting the diversity and cultural and spiritual beliefs of older adults and families; and being familiar with knowledge and theory of the biology, history (cohort effects), and sociology of aging, as well as information about grief, loss, and end-of-life issues. Competencies in assessment are knowledge of health and psychosocial factors affecting well-being; assessment of functioning, including activities of daily living, cognitive, and mental health concerns; and caregivers' needs and stresses. Intervention competencies are the use of psychoeducational techniques, and groups, case management skills, and advocacy, and knowledge of legal issues like competency, guardianship, and detection of elder abuse. The area of "services, programs, and policies" covers not only knowledge about entitlements and other services and how to access them but also attention to elderly who are disadvantaged and often underserved. It would be an interesting exercise to apply this list of foundation competencies for practice with older people and their families to each of the other groups discussed in this chapter. A checklist for assessing students' competencies in these areas has been drawn up. The original survey that formed the basis for this list of competencies found little difference among respondents between items that all social workers should know and those that specialists in aging should know (Rosen et al. 2000).

Practice in the field of aging requires interdisciplinary work, which in any case is becoming more common in all fields of practice (Damon-Rodriguez and Corley 2002). We have very little information about how best to prepare students for interdisciplinary practice, an area that needs research and curriculum innovation.

ORGANIZATIONAL AND INSTITUTIONAL CONTEXT

Institutions of higher education are, of course, affected by the aging of the U.S. population in many ways. When mandatory retirement was abolished in the United States, it at first did not apply to tenured faculty, but it has now been eliminated for this group as well. The result has been a "graying of the professoriat" both in general and in social work. As it will in many other fields, the next decade is expected to bring many faculty retirements (Anastas 2007c), and schools and departments will face both the challenge and the opportunity of replacing these experienced teachers and scholars. Therefore, the retirement policies (both incentives and disincentives) of colleges and universities will play an important role in shaping the social work professoriat of the future. Creative and/or transitional arrangements will likely use the expertise of older faculty members while making space for the next generation.

Many fields and professions besides social work are trying to fulfill the need for more knowledge about and better preparation for practice with older people. The journals *Educational Gerontology* and *Gerontology and Geriatrics Education* describe these efforts in many relevant disciplines, including social work. Some campuses offer opportunities to work with centers or institutes on aging or with faculty from other departments and schools, in research and teaching. Such collaborations support faculty interests and can be used to enrich curricula.

CONCLUSION

One theme common to our discussion of teaching and learning regarding all these dimensions of diversity is the need for a classroom climate conducive to both critical thinking and self-reflection. Interactions between teaching and learning interactions are most constructive when supported by the institution. For effective teaching and learning in all areas of diversity, all the elements outlined here must be considered. Fulfilling the profession's requirements—including the ethical mandate of professional social work that, uniquely among the helping professions (Payne 2006), mandates that oppression and social exclusion be addressed—supports curricular development and the inclusion of diversity content. The institutional and organizational context, in the classroom and in field education, can provide resources for and/or obstacles to this work, and eliminating any contextual barriers to change is necessary to avoid "the illusion of inclusion." Diversity in our students and teachers is one sign of a commitment to diversity but it is not sufficient. What *all* students know and are able to do in their practice with diverse clients and communities is the most important outcome.

Teachers addressing diversity issues in the classroom might remember the following:

- For various reasons, moments of *tension and conflict* are likely when discussing diversity issues. Do not assume that you can find a way to avoid this all the time; instead, prepare for it. View these events as "critical incidents" or "teachable moments" that can move the group and its members forward. Having classroom ground rules for interaction negotiated with and accepted by the group from the outset gives everyone something to fall back on. Theory reminds us that people of goodwill commonly have different perspectives on issues of diversity, identity, privilege, and oppression, which must be respected as phases of a journey even if they must sometimes be challenged.

• *Intersectionality* is the way that diversity and identity issues are currently understood. All our diversity statuses—privileged and oppressed ones alike—are multiple, not unitary. These identities are "visible and invisible, imposed and chosen, stable and changeable" (Enns and Sinacore 2005:179). Social work education has not yet even taken on all the dimensions of difference that we should teach in our curricula and in interacting with our students, such as religious and spiritual beliefs, socioeconomic status and poverty, and international aspects of teaching and learning, such as the embrace of both indigenous and dominant systems of knowledge. Just as no one can be fully "competent" in knowing everything about all ethnicities and cultures, it is impossible to understand all the intersectionalities that we, our students, and our clients inhabit and enact. Remembering these complexities is an important reason to make *curiosity* and *openness to alternative worldviews* central to approaching diversity and oppression issues, for teachers and for learners alike.

• Dealing with diversity in professional practice and in teaching and learning requires ongoing *self-reflection, self-examination, and support*. This includes being willing to consider, define, and share our position or standpoint (Swigonski 1993), that is, our understanding of our own social and locations and identities and how this understanding has developed over time. As we encourage our students to reflect on and articulate their own experiences and understandings of oppression and privilege, we can model this kind of self-reflection for our students.

I include "support" in this list because staying in contact with the historical record and the continuing instances of oppression, colonization, and social exclusion is painful. Challenging the status quo can be hard and sometimes lonely and risky. But as Enns and Sinacore (2005:194–196), the benefits also are many, such as discovering new ways of seeing the world, enriching one's appreciation of human and social differences, enabling professional and intellectual growth in students and colleagues, and facilitating change in the organizations and institutions in which we work. To this list I would add enhancing our understanding of history by including the experiences of those commonly written out of it and gaining better tools to work toward a more just society for all.

Further Reading

Costello, C. Y. (2005). *Professional identity crisis: Race, class, gender, and success at professional schools*. Nashville, Tenn.: Vanderbilt University Press.

Enns, C. Z., and Sinacore, A. L. (2005). *Teaching and social justice: Integrating multicultural and feminist theories in the classroom*. Washington, D.C.: American Psychological Association.

Gutiérrez, L., Zuñiga, M. E., and Lum, D., eds. (2004). *Education for multicultural social work practice: Critical viewpoints and future directions*. Alexandria, Va.: Council on Social Work Education.

Margolis, E., ed. (2001). *The hidden curriculum in higher education*. New York: Routledge.

Van Soest, D., and Garcia, B. (2003). *Diversity education for social justice: Mastering teaching skills*. Alexandria, Va.: Council on Social Work Education.

5

FIELD EDUCATION IN SOCIAL WORK:

TEACHING ROLES AMID OLD AND NEW CHALLENGES

K. Jean Peterson

All professional education suffers the Janus fate, with one head facing the aca-
demic world and the other head facing the workaday world of the profession.
The two faces of social work education appear in bold relief in field instruction,
in which learning and service to people go hand in hand.

K. A. KENDALL, *REFLECTIONS ON SOCIAL WORK EDUCATION, 1950–1978*

THROUGHOUT THE HISTORY OF SOCIAL WORK education, there has been tension between theoretical and experiential knowledge as the basis for professional learning. Social work education, however, both desires and requires that
supervised practice in the social agency setting—the field practicum—be an
integral part of its baccalaureate and master's programs. At a time when the value of "service learning" in higher education is now being recognized in many
fields, even in fields not substantively concerned with health care, education,
social provision, or social change, making the field practicum work well for
social work students is a more challenging and complex task than ever.

Despite new and ongoing challenges, social work education remains
committed to the field practicum. In its latest accreditation standards, the
Council on Social Work Education (CSWE 2008) called field education the
"signature pedagogy" in social work. Although the intensity and format of this
part of the curriculum may vary somewhat, the continued commitment to
field education flows from the idea that skills and behaviors are best learned
through experience and are best taught in an individual "coaching" or mentoring relationship with an individual field instructor or field "supervisor" (see
CSWE Council on Field Education).

A third person, the faculty–field liaison, is assigned to help integrate learning into the academic setting and the field setting (figure 5.1). For students, this
means relating simultaneously to two or three "teachers" (depending on the

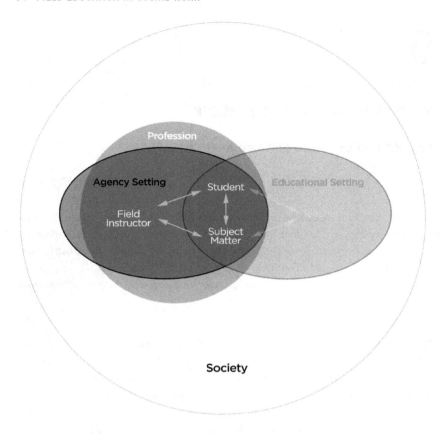

FIGURE 5.1 Model of teaching and learning that highlights field education.

program) who occupy three different places in the two settings for learning, the agency and the classroom. Although we have not yet mentioned the teaching role of the faculty–field liaison, it may be incorporated into the work of ten-ure-track, full-time faculty or may be undertaken by the field education office by part-time and/or full-time contract faculty. Even though social work faculty members with a BSW and/or MSW degree have been through field learning systems, the models and mechanisms supporting this part of social work educa-tion often remain ambiguous to them, even if they have been field instructors, until they join a faculty where they are discussed.

Graduates of social work programs often have had more hours of supervised training in practice with clients than their colleagues from similar disciplines have had, and graduates of social work programs generally remember their field experience as being the most important and most useful to them. This chapter is an overview of current teaching philosophies used in field education, the structures used, and current issues and debates about education in the field.

HISTORY OF FIELD EDUCATION

Tensions between the academy and the agency and debates about how best to integrate theoretical knowledge and practice experience started with the beginning of professional education. The first school of social work in the United States, the New York School of Philanthropy, grew from apprenticeship training in the new field of scientific charity (George 1982). Before the first formal training program for volunteers in 1898, providing service "was the means of training, with group meetings and individual conferences used to discuss the cases, determine what could and should be done to improve the conditions of the needy, and influence behavior in socially desirable directions" (George 1982:38). Mary Richmond called for the establishment of a training school in applied philanthropy in her speech to the National Conference of Charities and Correction in 1898, suggesting a two-year program of study. In her presentation, Richmond, speaking about the responsibilities of the director of such a program, stated that

it may be that he would seek connection with some institution of learning, though it should never be forgotten that emphasis is to be put on practical work rather than academic requirements. . . . Theory and practice would go hand and hand, and our best specialists would be engaged to deliver courses of lectures during the less busy months of the year. (Richmond 1898/2000:10)

The first six-week summer training program was started that same year for volunteers of the New York Charity Organization Society, combining lectures and field visits. In 1903 this program was extended to a full year, and in 1910 it became a two-year program under the auspices of the New York School of Philanthropy.

Similar events were taking place throughout the country, with other agency training programs evolving into schools of social work. This training was deemed necessary in order to impart the specialized knowledge and skills required by friendly visitors in charity organizations (Leighninger 2000). As George (1982) observed,

She [Mary Richmond] pointed out that while many learned from doing, learning by doing alone is not efficient and must be supplemented by theory. As in medicine, a long apprenticeship must still be served for skill, and training schools would allow volunteers and staff to profit from the experience of the more skilled. (39)

But unlike medicine, "many universities place schools of social work in a twilight zone between the traditional professional schools . . . and the graduate departments of the various social sciences" (Kendall 1978:70). As Kendall suggests, although the question that university administrators should be asking is why it costs so little to educate social work students compared to medical students, the question more frequently asked is why social work students cost so much more to educate than students in traditional social science disciplines. The answer, of course, is that the professional social work community—the agencies and organizations that furnish the sites and the instructors for field learning—shares a significant part of the expense by providing the staff time and agency resources that are not reimbursed.

According to Goldstein (2001), the distinctions between and responsibilities of classroom and field education became solidified with the establishment of formal training programs: "The former became responsible for the transmission of a body of knowledge to students, the latter for providing the experience with which students begin to master practice skills" (xi). Although many factors have influenced the growing divide between the academic and practice social work communities, according to Goldstein, the continuity he experienced in his own social work education "was that my education occurred in the pre-PhD era. Both my classroom and field teachers were themselves seasoned practitioners, rich in experience, comfortable with the theoretical as well as the imaginative and intuitive talents that allow for the emergence of individual styles" (x). And although the CSWE continues to require that university faculty teaching practice and performing liaison duties have a MSW degree and two years of post–master's degree experience, this minimum is far from Goldstein's description. It also means that students may see other parts of the curriculum, for which faculty are not required to have social work degrees, as having little or no obvious connection to their field learning. The result is a greater demand of field education programs to ensure the integration of the theoretical and the experiential, something that occurred more naturally in the past.

APPROACHES TO FIELD LEARNING

According to Jenkins and Sheafor (1982), the three different idealized approaches to field education are the *apprenticeship approach*, the *academic approach*, and the *articulated approach*, although "most schools operate with combinations or modifications of these approaches, or, too often, without specifying the approach used" (14). Given the reality of the "political econo-my" described by Grossman (1991), the particular approach used by a school may vary according to the available resources. Regardless of the approach to field learning chosen by a department or school of social work, two settings are always involved, the classroom and the field learning site, which student must learn to negotiate. The purpose of the faculty–field liaison is to facili-tate the connection between these two settings in order to support students' learning, with the expectations of the faculty–field liaison varying depending on the approach or model used. Each of these approaches places emphasis at a different point in the *knowing-understanding-doing* learning paradigm described by Gordon and Gordon (1982). This paradigm also is connected to the adult model of learning described by Kolb (1984), which is frequently used in social work education.

APPRENTICESHIP APPROACH

The apprenticeship approach, or experiential learning (Goldstein 2001), puts the field practicum at the center of social work education. This was the first approach used in social work education, requiring that students work from a solid experiential base. "If a school were to fully accept the apprenticeship approach, the curriculum would begin with a substantial practicum expe-rience. Students would be given a block field placement to allow time to develop a solid experiential base to which they could then relate the under-pinning knowledge" (Jenkins and Sheafor 1983:15). In other words, "doing" is the starting point in the knowing-understanding-doing learning paradigm (Gordon and Gordon 1982). Programs that expect students to be in their prac-tice/practicum setting at the same time they are taking practice courses at least partially reflect this model, as do those insisting on having experience before being admitted to the social work program.

For Jenkins and Sheafor (1982), "the primary responsibility for integration of class and field learning rests with the student and field instructor" (15), and the role of the faculty–field liaison is limited to periodic monitoring. Gold-stein (2001) might argue that integration is part of the seamless whole that characterized social work education "in the pre-PhD era," when classroom faculty were also experienced practitioners. Neither Goldstein nor Mesbur and Glassman (1991) say anything about the role of the faculty–field liaison in the apprenticeship approach to field education. Mesbur and Glassman do, however, discuss the role of the "faculty–field consultant" who helps translate the curriculum to the field instructor by describing specific behaviors and expectations that are then used as the basis for the mutual and continual evaluation of the student's field performance. Thus, the role of the faculty–field liaison is not only to establish and maintain mutual understanding and cooperation but also to serve as a consultant who also provides professional advice to the field instructors and/or students.

ACADEMIC APPROACH

In contrast, the academic approach is built on the premise that knowledge must be cognitively acquired before practice. This approach places the acquisition of knowledge at the center of the learning process and emphasizes cognitive ability as a priority in the student selection process. Field education may be delayed, reduced, or even eliminated in this approach until the student has a predetermined level of knowledge. At the extreme, social work could even abandon fieldwork all together and implement a practicum model after the course work has been completed (Blonstein 1988). Once the requisite knowledge has been learned, the student is given the opportunity to apply this knowledge in an agency setting. As Jenkins and Sheafor (1982) noted, "the paid faculty has assumed virtually the entire responsibility for the student's learning, and the field instructor essentially facilitates an experience where the students test out their knowledge" (16). The field instructor and agency provide practice experiences for the students, and the students are responsible primarily for the integration of field and classroom learning. The role of the faculty–field liaison becomes one of ensuring that the requisite experiential opportunities are made available to the student, who "is expected to deduce a practice approach from classroom learning" (Jenkins and Sheafor 1982:15). In this model, the faculty–field liaison rather than the field instructor is the primary resource for the students, given their presumed knowledge of the academic curriculum.

ARTICULATED APPROACH

In the apprenticeship approach, experiential knowledge (doing) is privileged, and students' understanding of practices comes through inductive reasoning, whereas in the academic approach, theoretical knowledge (knowing) is privileged, and students' understanding is achieved through deductive reasoning. In the articulated approach, all three components of the Gordon–Gordon paradigm are given equal weight, the objective being "for the student to be fully aware of what is involved in a practice act, know why that intervention is selected, and be prepared to determine how the necessary helping techniques should be performed" (Jenkins and Sheafor 1982:17). This approach requires collaboration between classroom and field faculty that is rarely achieved. Curricular development is continuous and must reflect the changing practice environment, and changes in the practice environment must change as the knowledge base of the profession evolves. The faculty–field liaison becomes the conduit between the field and classroom faculty, translating the changes in each arena to the other. Frequent and regular contact is required to ensure that students' learning is protected and achieved through the interaction of knowledge acquisition and practice experience.

STRUCTURE OF FIELD EDUCATION

The approach to field learning—apprenticeship, academic, or articulated—is affected by the structure of field education and whether field and classroom education are offered concurrently or sequentially. The two primary models of field education are concurrent and block placements. The most commonly used is the concurrent field education model, in which the field and classroom learning occur simultaneously. The student is enrolled in both academic and field hours, and academic and experiential knowledge are combined through one of the preceding approaches to field learning. Part-time students are required to take the academic practice course(s) and field practicum at the same time, even if they have previously completed other academic courses such as policy or research. In the block placement model of field education, students complete all academic courses before entering the field and then immerse themselves in experiential learning. This model requires students to apply the knowledge they have previously acquired to practice, with different approaches used to help them apply theory to practice. Perhaps the most common approach is the field seminar, in which students regularly meet with the faculty–field liaison to discuss their field experiences. Students may also be required to submit to the faculty–field liaison written material demonstrating this integration. In some instances, the students return to the classroom following the block placement for further instruction.

Proponents of the concurrent model of field education cite two major advantages: The first is the greater potential for integrating classroom and field learning as the students move back and forth between these settings. The second is the fact that students who are in the agency less often are more likely to maintain their student identity, and the focus of their activity will remain on their learning. Fortune (1994) reviewed studies of students' learning in different models of field education, which indicated that those in block placements were less conceptually oriented and more agency oriented than students who completed concurrent practicum placements. She concluded that "the important aspects of field placement are not the length of time or precise articulation with the classroom but having field work concurrent with academic coursework and having meaningful learning experiences in the field placements" (163).

Proponents of the block model of field education believe that the disadvantages of the concurrent model outweigh the ease of integration, limiting placement opportunities geographically and interrupting the provision of services (Hamilton and Else 1983). Other advantages of the block model are the opportunity for students to become more fully integrated into the agency culture through both formal and informal meetings, professional socialization, and greater access to learning opportunities targeted to specific areas of learning.

Regardless of the two models' educational advantages and disadvantages, the availability of placements may be the deciding factor for a particular social work program. Programs located in urban areas have the advantage of numerous and varied field education sites and thus may select the concurrent model of field education. Programs in rural areas may find few field education sites available, which either limits the number of students they can admit or forces them to adopt a block model of field education. Finally, the greater interest in international field placement opportunities may influence a program's model of field education, since a concurrent model is improbable in transnational work (Panos et al. 2002). Ideally a program might offer both options, but the resources needed to implement this ideal would be greater than most programs could afford.

The changing types of students being admitted to social work programs has resulted in the need to think creatively about field education (Wayne, Bogo, and Raskin 2006). Arguing "that radical approaches must be explored in order to overcome the roadblocks to high-quality field experiences" (161), Wayne, Bogo, and Raskin outlined some of the recent modifications in field education to meet the needs of employed students in the traditional structures of field education. Included are placements in agencies in which the students are currently employed, evening and weekend field placements, and individual planning. For example, a program with a concurrent model of field instruction may allow students working in a social service agency that provides practice opportunities to take the academic practice courses and complete the field education requirements at a later date by completing a block practicum or some other individual arrangement. Wayne, Bogo, and Raskin (2006) raise important questions about the erosion of quality field education experiences with these modifications, however, referring to their earlier report (Bogo, Raskin, and Wayne 2002), which indicated that "many students regret having availed themselves of employer placements and report that their agency was not successful in placing their learning needs above the agency's need for their employee-related services" (Wayne, Bogo, and Raskin 2006:165).

LIAISON BETWEEN FACULTY AND FIELD

"The faculty–field liaison provides the single most important linkage between class and field" (Jenkins and Sheafor 1982:112), and yet this role has received little attention in the literature on field education (Bennett and Coe 1998). As noted earlier, the role of the faculty–field liaison varies depending on the approach to field learning adopted by the school and the model of field education used. In the apprenticeship approach, the field liaison is a professional consultant, translating the curriculum and school expectations to the field instructor. In the academic approach, the faculty–field liaison is responsible for monitoring the field instructor's experiential learning opportunities for the students and for being a primary resource to the students for integrating academic knowledge. In the integrated approach, the responsibility for integration is shared equally, with the faculty–field liaison being the intermediary between the field and classroom faculty. Regardless of the approach to field learning and in both the concurrent and block models of field education, the faculty–field liaison is expected to be the voice of the school in the field. The academic and integrative approaches, however, require the faculty–field liaison to be more active in helping students integrate classroom and field education than does the apprenticeship model.

Brownstein, Smith, and Faria (1991) conducted the most comprehensive study, to date, of the role of the faculty–field liaison. In their three-phase study, they first asked field directors to describe the credentials, assignment, and evaluation of field liaisons, in addition to listing the field liaison's roles. Second, the field instructors were asked to describe their perception of the liaison role (Faria, Brownstein, and Smith 1988), and third, the faculty–field liaisons were surveyed to determine the congruence between their perception of their roles and responsibilities compared with those of the field directors and field instructors. Phase 1 defined ten roles and responsibilities through a content analysis of the field directors' responses:

1. *Linkage:* Acts as a bridge between the school, the agency, and the community; interprets school policies, procedures, and expectations to agencies; and assesses the fit between school curriculum and educational experiences provided by the agency.
2. *Mediator:* Helps resolve problems between students and the field instructor and/or other agency personnel; may involve reassigning students and/or termination of agency as placement.
3. *Monitor:* Continually assesses agency, field instructor, and students' assignments to ensure the quality of the educational experience.
4. *Evaluation:* Evaluates students, field instructor, and agency; assigns students' grades; makes recommendations for continued use of agency and field instructors.
5. *Consultant:* Helps field instructor develop teaching and supervisory skills in making the transition from practitioner to teacher.
6. *Teacher:* Helps students integrate course work and practicum.
7. *Adviser:* Helps students plan for practicum, including identifying learning needs and possible practicum sites.
8. *Advocate:* Provides relevant information for students under academic review.
9. *Practicum Placement:* Selects agencies and field instructors and matches them to students' learning needs.
10. *Administration:* Ensures completion of placement forms, letters to agencies, evaluations of agency; writes final summary of students. (Brownstein, Smith, and Faria 1991:240)

Field instructors from selected schools were then asked to describe the responsibilities of the faculty–field liaison as well as their perception of actual performance. Of these ten roles and responsibilities, providing a link between the school and the field was consistently rated as the most important and most frequently performed. In addition, more than 70 percent of the field instructors regarded the roles of mediator and monitor as an actual part of the field liaison role. Of particular note is that no field instructor described the role of teacher as a responsibility, and it was the least frequently cited role that field instructors perceived faculty–field liaisons as performing.

Faculty–field liaisons ranked the same three functions — linkage, mediator, and monitor — as being the roles/functions they most frequently performed (Brownstein, Smith, and Faria 1991), along with evaluation, being an advocate, and being an adviser. The faculty–field liaisons ranked the following roles in order of importance: monitor, linkage, adviser, consultant, and mediator as the top five, with teacher coming in seventh and advocate as eighth.

Using the same categories as Brownstein, Smith, and Faria (1991) did, Fortune and colleagues (1995) found somewhat different results. They examined the differences in field instructors' perception of the importance of liaison activities in two different faculty–field liaison models. The first model, the *intensive model*, was the more common, in which "the liaison is an active participant in the educational experience in the field and is central in the management of the field practicum" (277). This is the model used in schools adopting either the academic or the integrated approach to field education. In contrast, the *trouble-shooting model* "assumes that carefully selected and well-trained agency practitioners can carry out the field instructor role with minimal routine oversight by the university. However, when difficulties occur, intensive supports are mobilized to resolve the problem rapidly" (277). This model fit with the apprenticeship approach to field education. In the intensive model, field instructors ranked teaching functions as the most important roles for the faculty–field liaison to assume in supporting them as field instructors. The roles rated as most important were being a role model for students, evaluating students' progress and reading students' written materials, helping students integrate course work and practicum, as well as monitoring agency, field instructor, and learning opportunities for quality. Under the trouble-shooting model, field instructors placed much more importance on functions related to practicum placements and linkages, including interpreting school policies to the agency and field instructor.

In her doctoral dissertation, Coe "found that the satisfaction of field instructors with the academic program was correlated to their enjoyment of interactions with the faculty–field liaison and their perception of liaison support" (Bennett and Coe 1998:1). Using the same data, Bennett and Coe (1998) investigated factors associated with field instructors' satisfaction with the faculty–field liaison, hypothesizing that rewards and support for being a field instructor would be highly correlated with satisfaction. The results indicated that of all the variables studied,

those aligned with the field instructor's perception of support from the social work education program were most likely to explain variance in the field instructor's satisfaction with the faculty–field liaison. . . . These variables, along with a package of field instructor privileges, were among the strongest predictors of liaison satisfaction. All may be viewed as means of valuing and empower field faculty. (3)

An interesting question is raised when comparing the results of these three studies, which looked at three different aspects of the relationship between field instructors and field liaisons. Brownstein, Smith, and Faria (1991) focused on the roles and responsibilities most frequently performed, while Fortune and colleagues (1995) looked at what functions were most important from the perspective of the field instructors. Bennett and Coe (1998) concentrated on the field instructors' satisfaction. Although the liaison model used by schools in Brownstein, Smith, and Faria's series of studies was not defined, we may assume, because it is the most common, that the majority of these schools used the intensive model as defined by Fortune and colleagues. But when asked to rank the functions they most frequently performed, these liaisons seemed to perform more like the liaisons in the trouble-shooting model. The field instructors' satisfaction with the academic program was related to the quality of interactions with the field liaison and the perception of support, with the liaison's availability and the total number of contacts being the best predictors. The value of the faculty–field liaison became critical when viewed in this light, with the success of any BSW or MSW program depending on the availability and satisfaction of field instructors in agencies throughout the community.

Students' satisfaction with field placements also is relevant. Studying a number of factors related to students' satisfaction with their field placements, Fortune and colleagues (1985) found that items related to the field liaison received the lowest ratings. The quality of supervision offered by the field instructor and the relevance of learning were the most important factors. In a subsequent study, Fortune and Abramson (1993) found that the three most significant factors were quality of field instruction, agency desirability and inclusion, and explanations provided by the field instructor.

In summary, the limited research conducted on the roles and responsibilities of the faculty–field liaison has shown a disjuncture between what field instructors state would be most helpful, and the roles and responsibilities most frequently performed by the faculty–field liaison according to both field instructors and faculty–field liaisons themselves. Although the field instructors indicated that they would like faculty–field liaisons to teach more, the administrative and managerial responsibilities took priority. The field instructors were most satisfied when they spent time with and received support from faculty–field liaisons, whereas the students were most satisfied when they had high-quality field instruction. Students did not perceive the faculty–field liaison as critical to their learning, yet there is evidence that this role is critical to the overall quality of their field education. Raskin (1994) found little consensus among her panel of experts on the role of the faculty–field liaison, but these experts also stated that "the problem lies not in the definition of the role of field liaison but in the implementation of that role" (87). She also states that "an outcome study [should] be undertaken to show which (if any) of the faculty–field liaison roles and functions make a difference in student learning, in student field and job performance, and in student's ability to integrate theory and practice" (87). At this point, the research indicates only that the support of faculty–field liaison is related to the field instructors' satisfaction. Of equal importance would be a study to evaluate if any of the faculty–field liaison roles and functions makes a difference in the students' performance in their practice or in the performance of the field instructors, particularly in their ability to help students integrate theory and practice. But it is important, given the current state of knowledge, that faculty–field liaisons be available to field instructors, initiate contact, and provide overall support for these professional "volunteers."

CURRENT ISSUES

"There is general consensus that field instruction is the most significant, most memorable component of social work education. Within the general consensus this conclusion is most vehemently and most enthusiastically supported by social work students—present and former" (Kadushin 1991:11). Although critical to success of social work programs when compared with the importance of teaching and scholarship, being a faculty–field liaison comes in last (Brownstein, Faria, and Smith 1991).

Rhodes and colleagues (1999) listed seven threats to field education in schools of social work: academization, loss of autonomy, devaluation of field directors, growth of programs, gatekeeping, changes in student population, and a lack of faculty commitment. Critical to our current discussion are the changing demands on faculty in the current university environment and the conflicting expectations of faculty in professional schools such as social work. In Raskin's (1994) Delphi study of field education experts, the strong consensus was that "the lack of institutional support for field instruction in the

university creates the view that field work is administrative and non educa-
tion/academic" (82). According to Hartman (1990), professional schools were
able to maintain their unique identity within the university until the 1970s,
successfully arguing that the "primary objective of a professional school must
be to graduate knowledgeable and skilled practitioners" (46). Qualifications
for faculty positions, and subsequently standards for promotion and tenure,
reflected these differences, with faculty being supported and valued for their
practice competence. Increasingly the autonomy of professional schools has
been challenged by academization. One of the outcomes for schools of social
work has been the devaluation of field education by faculty who are having
"to make difficult choices about the use of their time, and in many cases, it
is time with students in the field that suffers the loss" (Rhodes et al. 1999:17).
More accurately, it may be time for the field instructors in "the field that suf-
fer the loss," hampering students' learning.

The reduced autonomy of professional schools within the university and
the reduced commitment by faculty to field education are two other threats
that Rhodes and colleagues (1999) mentioned, which are clearly related
to a fourth concern: the devaluation of field directors. In the university,
academic rank and tenure are two important criteria denoting status and
offering a legitimate voice to those who have achieved this status. But because the conflicting demands resulting from academization, "the role of
the field director [has been moved] into a non-tenured position" (Rhodes et
al. 1999:18). "This lack of faculty commitment to field work has resulted in
some schools electing not to use faculty in the role of field liaison and hiring
retired or part-time individuals for field support activities," with the result
that "faculty may have limited understanding of the function, structure, and
actual work of the field practicum and have little ownership of the field program" (Rhodes et al. 1999:22). But if field liaisons are not faculty, they may
have "limited understanding of the function, structure, and actual work" of
the curriculum. Either of these place enormous responsibility on the field
education office to ensure that classroom and field learning is combined
systematically and coherently, regardless of the school's approach or model
of field education.

With the trend toward the role of field liaison being assumed by adjunct
faculty, all faculty members must take responsibility for integrating classroom
and field learning, by working closely with field instructors and field liaisons.
The onus of this responsibility will most likely fall on the faculty who are
involved in the practice curriculum and on the director of field education.
Some points for faculty to consider are the following:

- Attending "field forums" and other events to meet field instructors.
- Asking the field education office to structure a meeting at which you can meet and talk with the field instructors of the students in your practice course.
- Conducting workshops for field instructors who are interested in your area of expertise.
- Giving field instructors access to the syllabi of the courses their students are taking (concurrent model) or have taken (block model) and urging students to discuss with them the course content and its application to their field learning.
- Asking students to share the parts of their field learning contract with course instructors when they are pertinent to a specific course.
- Inviting field liaisons to attend curriculum committee meetings to educate the practice faculty about pertinent issues in the field practicum, enabling practice faculty to educate them about the practice courses.

Essentially, any activity by faculty that demonstrates their interest in field education and acknowledges the importance of field instructors and field liaisons in giving students a quality education is important. Although conflicting somewhat with the self-image of many faculty, field instructors often put faculty in an exalted position and do not feel comfortable contacting them. Faculty need to let field instructors and liaisons know that they all have the same professional mission: educating the next generation of social work practitioners.

FUTURE DIRECTIONS

The tension between the two faces of social work education described by Kendall (1978:70) is not new. The earliest formal social work education programs were of two types. One type expanded from the agencies' training programs and included freestanding or agency-affiliated programs such as the New York Charity Organization Society. The other type was university-affiliated programs started by social reformers and sponsored by Harvard University and Simmons College. A third type was soon added: undergraduate, state schools, usually in the Midwest. These varying origins brought different traditions of education and fieldwork into social work education, creating issues that still have not been resolved (Fortune 1994:152).

During the twentieth century, social work educators tried to define and clarify some of these issues. The tension has heightened as research and scholarship demands placed on faculty by universities have increased (Wayne, Bogo, and Raskin 2006), with the result often being inattention to field education as new faculty concentrate on meeting tenure requirements. Both the academic and integrated models of field education depend on the active involvement of faculty to integrate experiential and theoretical knowledge, whereas the experiential model leaves the onus of responsibility on the field instructor and agency. Nevertheless, our limited research indicates that students remain generally satisfied with the quality of their field education experience. But as Fortune (1994) points out, this measure of satisfaction has not been shown to be associated with professional competence.

Although most schools of social work strive for an integrated approach to field education, with students in concurrent practicum placements and faculty–field liaisons operating under an intensive model, the reality appears to fall short of this ideal. Current writings in the area of field education center on the role of the field instructor and the need for training them (i.e., Bogo and Vayda 1998), which becomes the responsibility of the field education office. Raskin (1994) stated in her 1991 Delphi study of field education that one of the priority research agendas developed by the experts "includes the need for empirical analysis of outcomes related to field education; models to ensure quality of field instruction; and *processes to help field instructors assist students, especially in integrating classroom and field instruction*" (75, italics added). Although these studies mention the role of the faculty/faculty–field liaison, little attention is given to defining and improving this role. However, in discussing the faculty–field liaison role, one of Raskin's (1994) Delphi study experts stated,

> Reading the comments and reflecting on my experiences, I think there is a historical "ideal" model as reflected in the literature and guidelines which obviously does not work in today's environment. The panelists continue to identify why it doesn't work. Therefore, is it not time to start discussing and developing new models that meet educational goals and that faculty feel committed to enacting? (87)

Globerman and Bogo (2000) pointed out the paradox of developing ways to enhance the integration of theory and practice by enticing faculty back into field education at the same time that field education has been devalued by faculty in the university. These authors proposed a new model for faculty–field liaisons that they call an *integrated academic partnership*, which could bring the faculty's research interests into the field education setting. Faculty would be assigned to agencies in their area(s) of interest and work collaboratively with field instructors to conduct community-based research, thereby bringing together the academic and agency settings. In this model, faculty– field liaisons would assume more of the teaching responsibilities, combined with the trouble-shooting model discussed by Fortune and Abramson (1993). Globerman and Bogo (2000) supplied examples of how this model has been implemented in a school of social work and the benefits for students as well as academic and field faculty. The place of the field education office would be raised as they worked closely with faculty to facilitate this connection, placing the field office more fully within the university.

Building on the traditional model of field education in social work, Hartman (1990) proposed that the divergent expectations of the university and the profession may be resolved by faculty's joining community practitioners to challenge the criteria used by universities in awarding tenure. Challenging the notion "that the gap between education and practice is inevitable," she observed:

> I would like to suggest another course, wherein we stop accepting the alienation between practice and education as inevitable and recognize that it cannot be good for our profession for such alienation to exist. . . . Systemic change is required. Primarily, the profession's power to influence the direction of education must be enhanced and the power of the university must be challenged . . . we must join with other professional schools . . . to define professional education and bring this definition and the norms it embodies to the attention of the University hierarchies. (49)

In addition, coalitions must be built with the practice community and between CSWE and NASW. Our largest organization of practitioners (NASW) deals primarily with postgraduate and continuing education, and while CSWE's current governance structure and past accreditation procedures have tried to offer ways for practitioners' involvement, this representation has often been seen as minimal.

In contrast to this integrated model, Blonstein (1988) made one of the most radical suggestions about the role of field education in graduate programs in social work, recommending that graduate schools of social work "move away from the field instruction model into an internship model" (91). Providing a historical perspective and drawing on the earlier work of Schutz and Gordon (1977), Blonstein concluded that "a field instruction model is no longer functional" (95). This suggestion mirrors the approach currently used in other professional schools such as clinical psychology, in which students complete their practicums *after* finishing their academic work. Blonstein acknowledged the breadth of change that would be needed across the spectrum of social work practice and education but argued that a radical change was needed, since the problems, which were identified long ago, were no closer to being solved now than they were a century ago.

Wayne, Bogo, and Raskin (2006) reported the results of a meeting of thirty-three directors of field education who met to discuss enduring and reoccurring problems in integrating field education and academic programs. Although the meeting included directors from both baccalaureate and master of social work programs, they did not discuss how these different levels of professional education might respond to these problems. Given that social work is the only profession among those with which we are usually compared (e.g., psychology, law, and medicine) that grants professional status at the baccalaureate level, this oversight seems questionable, with many of the suggestions clearly more applicable to graduate education. "Thinking outside the box," the participants in this meeting suggested the following "radical changes to field education" (Wayne, Bogo, and Raskin 2006:166): new partnerships with agencies, field learning separate from the school, a hybrid model, and an individualized approach.

- *New partnerships with agencies.* In this model, based on the health science professionals, "institutionalized, formal, and continuing partnership between the university and its affiliated hospitals ensure the availability of learning opportunities in practice settings . . . faculty members are fully engaged in teaching practice in the setting, and there is greater integration between the academy and the practice site" (Wayne, Bogo, and Raskin 2006:167). Along with ensuring the qualifications of the field instructors, this also eliminates the need for the faculty–field liaison, since the field instructor is a member of the faculty.
- *Field learning separate from the school.* Perhaps the most radical model, reminiscent of Blonstein's (1988) suggestion, removes field education from the university and leaves the profession to provide practicum experiences for those who have completed the academic preparation. After completing the practicum, students would then be required to pass a professional competency/licensing exam for admission into the profession.
- *Hybrid model.* Combining the first two approaches, this model would focus on academic preparation during the first year of study and then form partnership agreements with "accredited" agencies for the second year of the program. Rather than having faculty supply field instruction, as in the partner-

ship model, these sites would have full responsibility for field learning, similar to an apprenticeship. Because of the permanent partnership agreement and the professional "accreditation" of these sites, the faculty–field liaison would no longer be needed.

■ *Individualized approach.* In this approach, each student would be assessed on "reliable and valid measures of practice competence" (Wayne, Bogo, and Raskin 2006:167) in order to determine whether he or she could be exempted from all or part of field learning. This approach would allow students with previous experience to focus on theoretical knowledge, with theory and practice being combined in the classroom.

Despite the challenges, researchers have not suggested that experiential learning is not a critical component of educating students for professional social work practice. Instead, the differences are where and how this experiential learning takes place. As long as professional programs are lodged in the academic setting, one of the main functions of the field education program is to make sure that the "two faces of Janus" come together into an integrated whole. There are differences between service learning and field education models, with the emphasis in the former on service and, in the latter, on learning specific practice skills. Even so, the current direction toward service learning in universities is in our favor, with "the movement towards producing graduates who are better prepared to apply knowledge and skills in 'real-world' settings and thus contribute to societal production and overall welfare" (Shera and Bogo 2001:199). The suggestion made by Globerman and Bogo (2000) to have faculty work collaboratively with field instructors to conduct research would integrate the current models of field practicum with the goals of service learning. Working closely with faculty involved in practice research and the agencies providing these services, a department or school's field education office would be at the nexus of developing these collaborative relationships.

Two other realities for professional social work education are the economic conditions requiring many students to continue working full time and the globalization of society requiring new and innovative approaches to field education. The economic conditions requiring students to work full time to support themselves and their families have increased the number of students requesting to complete their practicum at their place of employment. As noted earlier (Wayne, Bogo, and Raskin 2006), however, many students reported that their agency did not support their learning needs and regretted having completed their practicum in their work agency. The current reality is that the economic pressures on students is not apt to decrease in the near future, and so the field education office needs to take the initiative to build strong partnerships with agencies to ensure the academic integrity of the placement and to develop protocols for approving such arrangements. A review of selected schools in 2006 (J. Solomon, private communication 2006) found that some schools have developed innovative responses for these students. Among these schools are Hunter College and Case Western Reserve University, both of which have a specific application and admissions process of students who are currently working in social service agencies. Hunter College offers a one-year residence (OYR) program for those who have successfully completed at least two years of employment in a social welfare institution and whose employer agrees to provide a school-approved practicum in the second year of the program (M.S.W. Degree Pathways). This allows students to complete their course work on a part-time basis with a prearranged agreement that the last year of study will be full time. In this program, the entire nine hundred required field hours is completed during this full-time year of study. The Mandel School of Applied Social Sciences at Case Western University offers an "intensive weekend program" "to provide professional graduate level education to employed social workers and individuals working in a related capacity to pursue a M.S.S.A degree while maintaining full-time employment" (M.S.S.A. Overview: Intensive Weekend Program). Students in this program may use their place of employment for the field practicum if the agency can give them appropriate learning opportunities. No doubt, other schools are experimenting with innovative plans for working students and others, and published evaluations of their effectiveness would be a welcome contribution.

Field education directors must also take an active role in informing students about loan-forgiveness programs for social workers, as well as supporting the Dorothy I. Height and Whitney M. Young Jr. social work reinvestment act and other such initiatives. This support may allow more students to pursue their education without the burden of worrying about paying back student loans.

The globalization of society, increasing interest from students for international experiences, and the rising number of international students studying in the United States are current issues in social work education with particular implications for field learning. Johnson (2004) discusses the process by which one school internationalized its curriculum, including the development of international field placements and international exchanges. In their study of U.S. and Canadian schools of social work, Caragata and Sanchez (2002) found that "27 percent of US schools and 45 percent of Canadian schools place students in international practicum settings. These range from an occasional placement (primarily pursued at the initiative of the student) to more formal placements that include individuals as well as groups of students doing their practicum abroad" (230). They then discussed the advantages of developing institutional agreements between domestic and foreign universities, in which field placements and instruction are handled by the hosting social work program. As the demand for international placements by students increases, the field education office will be at the forefront of initiating these agreements.

A parallel issue is meeting the needs of international students studying in the United States (Rai 2002) and the acceptance or active recruitment of international students by U.S. institutions (Johnson 2004). International student enrollment in U.S. universities will likely occur in the same way that Caragata and Sanchez (2002) describe the development of international placements: on a continuum from "occasional" to "formal." Programs accepting the "occasional" student may find a disjuncture between the content taught in the classroom and its transferability to the student's home country. As Rai (2002) pointed out, "Some educators believe that, due to the lack of desired courses, finding appropriate field placements is the only alternative to meet the needs of international students" (29). These field placements must help international students transfer their knowledge and experiences back to their own societal context in order for them to be of value. Programs that actively recruit international students may be considered more "formal," with formal exchange programs part of the university-to-university agreements or by working closely with international programs within their university. These more formal arrangements may offer a closer connection between the academic content of the classroom and the practice experiences in the field, including both specialized course work and seminars. The field education program has the multifaceted responsibility of meeting the needs of the students, the agency, and the clients served by the agency. Language proficiency and comprehension are major issues in placing international students in field, but knowledge of social service "systems" and cross-cultural competencies are important as well. Field programs need to pay special attention to the interests and abilities of field instructors to work with international students as they develop these abilities and to design special seminars for the field instructors to learn these skills. These more formal programs may also contain structural supports for international students, working with them while they are still in their home country and offering field programs as part of these efforts.

CONCLUSIONS

Tenure-eligible faculty members in a school or department of social work who are not working primarily in field education can take steps to enhance their students' learning whatever courses they may teach. For example,

- Always remember that your students are (concurrent models), will be, or have been learning in the field, grappling with client and community problems, and trying to resolve them. In addition, since social work students commonly rank these experiences as the most meaningful to them, any efforts you make to bring field experiences into the classroom will likely enhance students' interest in and appreciation of your course and your teaching. But because social work programs often offer multiple "pathways" to the degree, make sure that assignments or class exercises involving students' field-learning sites or experiences offer alternative versions for those lacking that experience.

- Learn about the field education model used in your department or school. It also is helpful to learn about the settings being used for field learning or at least about those in which your students are working. This information alone can help you tailor your course content to show its relevance to field learning and, ultimately, to practice.

- Field education is the bridge between the university and practice communities, perhaps a professional school's most important role. Knowledge and the translation of skills into professional social work practice are integrated with the field practicum. Although confronted by many issues with the changing environment, field education programs remain strong and continue to provide leadership by initiating faculty/agency research collaboration, helping recruit and retain students who are struggling economically, and helping internationalize social work programs.

Further Reading

Bogo, M., and Vayda, E. (1998). *The practice of field instruction in social work: Theory and process.* 2nd ed. New York: Columbia University Press.

CSWE Council on Field Education: A Council of the Commission on Curriculum and Educational Innovation. Available at http://www.cswe.org/CSWE/about/governance/councils/Council+on+Field+Education.htm?PF=1.

Hendricks, C. O., Finch, J. B., and Franks, C. L. (2005). *Learning to teach, teaching to learn: A guide for social work field education.* Alexandria, Va.: CSWE Press.

6

TECHNOLOGY IN SOCIAL WORK EDUCATION

James W. Drisko

OVER THE PAST TWO DECADES, technological innovations have enabled several new approaches to teaching and learning. In teaching, the traditional "sage on the stage" lecture model, supplemented with one-to-one contact during limited office hours, still remains prevalent in social work, as it is generally an effective way to convey new material to many students. This model may not be an optimal fit for all adult learners, however. New forms of interactions between teacher and students as well as among students are possible with computer- and Internet-based technologies. These include increasing access to educational programs, courses, and materials for students in areas far from main program locations, allowing time-shifted or time-delayed communication between a teacher and one or more students and expanding both student-directed learning and collaborative learning among students. In this model, the teacher serves as both the new content "sage" and, equally important, the "guide on the side," facilitating, shaping, and encouraging students' work (Young 1997).

This chapter opens with a perspective on the ways that technology has influenced social work education, locating these new technologies within their larger societal, educational, and professional contexts. It also alerts readers to the many new opportunities and teaching–learning challenges accompanying the new technologies, such as differential access to technology coinciding with racial differences and class disparities in American society at large; high start-up costs; new classroom management, training, and workload challenges for faculty; and the very limited, mostly single site–specific, outcome studies of the efficacy of these innovations.

Second, this chapter examines several key technological innovations affecting social work education, including each technology's optimal uses, strengths, and challenges, as well as some perspectives on these technologies and some "how-to" information.

TECHNOLOGY AND TEACHING:
AN INTRODUCTORY PERSPECTIVE

Every new form of communication technology has affected teaching. The printing press made books more widely available to learners. Inexpensive, good-quality paper helped expand literacy. The metal quill pen reduced the cost of writing for both individuals and institutions. A reliable, low-cost postal service enabled correspondence courses, enhanced by the even faster delivery provided by televised educational programming. Current communication, data storage, data mining, and data delivery technologies also have created opportunities and challenges for teachers and learners alike. New technologies have altered the nature of "on-site" education as well as making "distance education" more comparable to "in-person" education, affecting not only the locations for learning but also the times and availability of lectures and events. Internet-based courses and e-mail communication allow the "time-shifting" of many educational contacts from set times to "24/7" flexible access. In addition, e-mail, instant messaging, and video conferencing allow faster, more frequent, and more individualized contact between teacher and learner. Despite concerns about cheating via cell phone text messaging (Associated Press 2003; Hulette 2009) and the potentially detrimental and disruptive roles of wireless communication in classrooms (Guernsey 2004; Hulette 2009), collaborative communication among students also is faster and more feasible. Time and distance have become less formidable barriers to learning (Drisko 1997).

Distance education "is the delivery of educational programs to off-site students through the use of technologies such as Internet, cable or satellite television, videotapes and audiotapes, fax, computer conferencing, video conferencing, and other means of electronic delivery" (*Peterson's Guide* 2000:3). Several social work programs have begun using distance education programs to better fulfill their institutional and program missions. For example, the University of South Carolina offers many graduate social work courses to students at remote sites using interactive television. This model is consistent with the university's mission of preparing skilled child welfare professionals across the state. Without distance education, travel time would be a major impediment to statewide access to social work education. With distance education, travel time is greatly reduced, and a wider range of candidates can obtain higher education.

Technology also affects on-campus teaching and learning. E-mail contact and instant messaging (IM) between the class instructor and the students allow information to be shared, resources to be exchanged, and assignments to be completed. Web-based courses may completely or partially move course content and materials onto the Internet, allowing students access whenever they choose. Many campuses have also established systems to use IM and cell phone contact to provide speedy information about campus emergencies to students, faculty, and staff.

Access to these new technologies requires an extensive infrastructure. Kreuger and Stretch (2000) note that this infrastructure is both a culture and an economy. Coupled with technology are enormous hidden ecological, health, and safety challenges linked to the many new marvels. Instant-on devices continuously use electricity even when in "sleep" mode. The rapid obsolescence of computers generates a steady stream of toxic materials that may prove hazardous to local water supplies (computer monitors are shielded with large amounts of lead; circuit boards contain many toxic metals). Despite the challenges and costs of technology, they have not slowed the expansion of technology-mediated teaching. Still, from the end-use consumer's point of view, cost and easy access are concerns.

NEW COSTS AND DIFFERENTIAL ACCESS

At the beginning of the twenty-first century, communication technologies hold the promise of enormously expanding access to people on a direct, worldwide basis. They have begun to offer access to vast information resources created by many different sources, each with their own interests and purposes. A key challenge is cost: computer and communications equipment, software, training, and maintenance all are expensive. In 2004, the U.S. Commerce Department reported that 62 percent of American households had a computer (Pew Internet Survey 2004) and that by 2007, 78 percent of households would have a computer. Somewhat fewer households—roughly 64 percent—are "online" (i.e., have Internet access) (Pew Internet Survey 2008a). On the other hand, only 55 percent of people with incomes under $30,000 per year had computer access, as did only 61 percent of persons living in rural areas (Pew Internet Survey 2004).

Social workers should note that white and Asian families in the United States are the most likely to own a computer. Although surveys have found that the most rapid growth in computer ownership is among lower-income and African American households, these groups still remain the least likely to own a computer. The surveys did not include Native American households. A "digital divide" separates those families with higher incomes from the less advantaged (Exploring 2001; Mehra, Merkel, and Bishop 2004; Servon 2002; Who's online? 2001). The surveys indicate that 75 percent of Hispanic American families and 72 percent of white families have computers but that only 62 percent of African American families do. Furthermore, while 67 percent of high school–educated and 84 percent of college-educated persons own computers, only 39 percent of persons with less than a high school education own computers. Findings of the Pew Internet Survey (2008a) reflect a deeper divide on broadband access: only 43 percent of African American families and just 25 percent of low-income families have fast Internet connections. Truly easy, equal access to technology currently does not exist. Social workers who seek to expand socially equal access to resources must be aware of the risk for further isolation and limited opportunity among low-income groups who have historically suffered social oppression.

The cost of owning a personal computer is the initial purchase (now ranging from about $400 to several thousand dollars), additional software (ranging from $50 to several hundred dollars), learning time, upgrades, and repairs. An additional hidden expense of great consequence to educators is that Internet connections are separate, monthly expenses for computer owners. In 2007, 74 percent of households had faster broadband Internet connections, and 26 percent had "slow" dial-up connections (eMarketer 2006). Internet connections range in cost from about $10 to more than $100 per month. Faster Internet connections may be available only in certain geographic locations. Whether broadband or dial-up, this monthly Internet access cost joins the initial purchase to widen the digital divide. In education, this means that social work educators may not be able to count on all students having easy, "24/7" access to the Internet. Thus students may have a very different view of the benefits of technology.

THE IMPACT OF TECHNOLOGY ON EDUCATIONAL INSTITUTIONS

The high cost of technology also affects educational institutions (Kreuger and Stretch 2000; Stretch and Kreuger 2002). The costs for educational institutions include not only computer and software purchase but also infrastructure (space, heating and cooling, wiring and furniture, waste disposal), Internet server setup and support, security measures, support staff salaries, as well as training time for technical staff and administrative, faculty, and student users. Some estimates put the total cost of institutional computer ownership at more than $5,000 each year per computer (Federal Electronics Challenge 2007), not including the wider environmental impacts (Kreuger and Stretch 2000; Stretch and Kreuger 2002). Recent "open source" software (including the Linux operating system and the Moodle course management software) can help reduce some costs but have not yet substantially lowered the total cost of computer ownership. Thus educational institutions must either find new funds for technology or reallocate existing funds to technology and away from other priorities. Technology support may be reduced in an economic downturn.

The costs of technology can be a significant percentage of a total institutional budget, so educators and administrators in social work and other fields must consider how technology costs will alter other institutional priorities. That is, if distance education reduces financial aid for students of color, social workers may choose to advocate for a change in priorities or alternative technology strategies.

The digital divide may also be evident at the institutional level. Larger, well-endowed institutions may be better able to implement new technologies more rapidly. In turn, they may appear more attractive to prospective applicants (if this "asset" is important to their educational needs and goals). Conversely, the relative impact of technology costs can be greater for the total program of smaller schools and programs. These schools run the risk of appearing as second-class citizens in the technology race, even though their programs may fit the needs of their intended applicants. Social work educators must bear in mind that finding the optimal educational uses for new technologies and developing institutional strategies for funding and implementing them are complex issues. Focusing on the educational mission and priorities must always shape discussion of the role of technology (Quam 1999).

THE IMPACT OF TECHNOLOGY ON FACULTY ROLES

Teaching and scholarship are key faculty roles. Traditionally, teaching has centered on giving lectures or leading seminars; providing advising and guidance; offering support and counseling; and encouraging or cajoling students to help them identify and overcome barriers to learning; providing career guidance; and serving as professional role models or mentors. These interactions take place on campus in class during office hours and through written or oral feedback on assignments. Classes or seminars are usually held at specified scheduled times in specific locations and may be coupled with scheduled discussion groups or labs and weekly office hours. Teacher–student contacts are generally planned, often structured, and "in person." An advantage of in-person teacher–student contact is the ability to develop personal relationships. Such relationships help motivate students to face difficult content, take risks, work harder, and persevere. Such personal relationships also model a key social work value (NASW 1999).

Technology can radically alter the nature of teacher–student interactions (Young 1998). Technologically mediated content can be provided without direct contact between teacher and student, which may make learning opportunities available to students located away from the main campus site. Little or no in-person contact may also allow students to access courses at times that better fit their schedules, again expanding opportunities for learners to use educational programs. "Asynchronous" communication (in which only one party is active at one time), such as e-mail or the use of Web-based resources, is another way for teachers and students to exchange information. From an institutional perspective, fewer direct contacts between teachers and learners may increase efficiency and reduce costs (Young 1998). Indeed, considerable in-service training in business settings is now provided online, without in-person contact (E learning 2001; Karrer 2006). Research on online training indicates that it is effective and efficient for content learning but less well suited to process learning. According to business researcher Chen, "It's often perceived as cold, sometimes less than stimulating, and not very responsive to an individual's questions and learning needs" (E learning 2001). Indeed, Karrer (2006) reported that dissatisfaction with CMS software is on the rise as its administrative tracking functions (i.e., reporting and compliance monitoring) are increasingly emphasized while its end-learner functions are deemphasized. Still, technology-mediated learning is easy to deploy, is accessible to many students without regard to location, may reduce costs for instructional personnel, and yields measurable results (though not always positive outcomes).

Many of the skills needed for traditional classroom teaching overlap with the conceptual and organizational skills needed in a faculty member's own courses, research, and scholarly writing. That is, lecturing and leading discussions in areas of the faculty member's expertise mimic how the faculty member was educated, although the skill and effectiveness of instructors trained as apprentices vary widely. The advent of computer technologies requires faculty to learn many new technical and teaching skills. Furthermore, new standards for several kinds of online discussions, known broadly as *netiquette*, are still evolving and not widely known (Hambridge 1995). Thus faculty must help create standards for professional behavior online, serve as technology consultants, and teach traditional content, which can be intimidating to those not technology minded or motivated. This also means that faculty must learn to use the new equipment, software, and communication conventions and convert previously successful teaching approaches to this new setting. As a result, faculty frequently depend on skilled technicians to make equipment work and to fix it when it does not.

Besides these new efforts, most institutions are maintaining their previous methods (Glassick, Huber, and Maeroff 1997). The workload and promotion "credit" for undertaking new technology-mediated teaching approaches have not been determined or even widely discussed. At the first social work Technology in Teaching Conference, many faculty participants complained that their efforts to create Web sites and materials for distance learning were not valued and were not considered as teaching or scholarship for promotion and tenure. Indeed, no standards exist for evaluating Web-based materials for tenure and promotion, whether for course materials, specialized information, or publications in many online journals. Encouraging educational innovation must be coupled with support for and acknowledgment of undertaking new efforts.

PRESENTATION SOFTWARE

One of the most widely used software packages in social work education is presentation software. Indeed, PowerPoint presentations at conferences and training sessions have become common here and in classrooms. Students, too, often use PowerPoint for their class presentations.

Although presentation software is widely used, the quality of its use varies widely, as presenters are rarely trained in its optimal preparation and use. Well-designed visual images can convey the complexity of events and information much more fully and quickly than words can and may add to the presenter's descriptions and credibility. Images also can shift some of the educational burden from the instructor to the content itself.

Visually enhanced presentations appear to work best with large groups of learners and groups meeting for a single session (such as in conference presentations). They also can be used to outline or highlight key points in the classroom. Slide shows fit well with the learning styles of "visual learners" and may also be viewed as an outline of the information that students "need to know," though they may inhibit further learning and exploration by some less motivated students.

Creating computer-based presentations requires mastery of specific software, which is roughly as difficult for most users as learning how to use a new word-processing program. Combining the visual and oral elements of a presentation is more difficult.

OPTIMAL USE OF PRESENTATION SOFTWARE

Computer-based presentations are created on readily available office software packages, like Microsoft Office's PowerPoint software, Corel Office's Presentation software, and the free Impress! software of newcomer Sun System's StarOffice (see "Resources" at the end of this chapter). Each package includes "themes" or "styles," which are professionally selected color schemes and backgrounds. Using such software is similar to using word processing, and rules and "tips" for the optimal use of presentation software are widely available.

When creating a presentation, remember that *content is key*. A slick slide "show" with no new content will always be disappointing (Applied Presentations Technologies 2000). But with good content, the following guidelines are useful as starting points:

- Be clear about the points you wish to make.
- Consider your audience. Some audiences respond well to clip art and animations, but others do not. Likewise, some audiences find detailed outlines useful, but others do not. Combine content and style for the learners in your audience.
- Every presentation should have an opening "title slide" to describe the presentation.
- Keep the slides simple. One common rule is to use no more than twenty-four words per slide. Another is to use no more than three fonts per slide and to limit the use of boldface, italics, and underlining.
- Use a single color scheme in each slide.
- Make sure the text is visible, usually by clearly differentiating between background and text. For example, yellow text on a white background may not show up well. Font sizes of twenty-eight points or larger are suggested.
- Use graphics, animations, and transitions between slides only to support the presentation, as too often they simply distract from it.
- Use between two and five bullets per slide and not more than two levels of bullets per slide.
- Clearly label all graphs and charts: The presenter loses an audience struggling to understand an unlabeled chart. The presenter also should explain

how to read graphs and charts within the first ten seconds in which the slide is visible.

- Keep graphs and charts simple. Pie charts with three or four "slices" or bar charts with three or four columns are the most effective.
- Use no more than five colors on a graph or chart.
- The closing slide or slides should offer recommendations or a clear summary.
- Handouts or outlines may help the audience follow the presentation, particularly when it is dense and mainly text.
- All scholarly presentations should be accompanied by printed bibliographies for learners to take home and explore (as with any scholarly presentation). Merely listing the references in a presentation is not sufficient.

A bulleted style "telegraphs" content, stating and elaborating ideas and needing no orientation. When using presentation software, the instructor should first explain orally what he or she will do, offering perspective, context, cautions, and examples.

Even though content is critical, the connection between presenter and audience is not generated by the presentation software, but by how the instructor engages the learners and uses the material to inform the audience.

The oral presentation or narration accompanying presentation software "shows" should not simply repeat the text on the slides. Instead, the presenter should word the oral narrative differently to retain the audience's attention and avoid the boredom induced by reading a paper to a live audience. The presentation software format is compatible with the open-question format in which learners can ask questions about each slide. Varying the oral delivery from the slide text invites clarification and challenges and maximizes the audience's involvement.

Presentation software is a flexible tool for in-person presentations and may also be saved in the Internet-friendly .html or .xml file formats, allowing the presentation to be made available on the Internet or e-mailed to others. This feature is as simple as using the "Save As" option in major presentation software.

INTERACTIVE MULTIMEDIA AND PROGRAMMED INSTRUCTION

USING CDS, DVDS, AND PODCASTS IN TEACHING

Another teaching technology that allows learners to work at their own convenience is programmed instruction or interactive multimedia on compact disk.

Some courses or content modules are now also available on disk as "podcasts": audio or video files that can be downloaded from the Internet to a personal computer or portable media player (i.e., iPod or similar device). Electronic books, with content identical to those in print versions, also are increasingly available (i.e., Ivey and Ivey's [2003] intentional interviewing textbook). Multimedia disks, such as Gibbs's (2002) multimedia add-ons for teaching evidence-based practice, are often attached to textbooks. Podcasts tend to be audio oriented, occasionally with video content, and allow students to learn when convenient, although this may mean that the podcasts are frequently interrupted. One advantage of podcasts is that they are easy to produce, allowing teachers, students, and a wide range of producers to create and share useful materials. An excellent example of a practice-oriented podcast site is Dr. Jonathan Singer's Social Work Podcast, with more than fifty files for educational download (see "Resources").

CDs and DVDs provide either enhanced lectures or interactive instructional programs. Because of these programs' multiple-media formats and the large file sizes, many are produced in CD or DVD format. The disk is "played" on the student's computer or portable device in the same way as is a video game or movie. That is, texts, sound, and sometimes video files are joined to guide the student through the content. Disks may include section-by-section quizzes, final tests, and reference materials.

The structure of an instructional CD or DVD is typically like that for a computer game: an executable file starts a series of programs including text, sound, graphics, and/or video. Each learner then moves through the content at pace that best fits the materials and his or her learning style. The content is often organized as programmed instruction.

Programmed instruction is a network of statements, related materials, and assessments based on behavioral learning theories (Krippendorf 1986). After an initial assessment (assuming the learners know little about the topic), students are presented with new material at their own pace. They move through the material based on the pattern of correct and incorrect answers. That is, when the student answers correctly, different new material is presented. When the answer is incorrect, the student is given additional repetitions of the material or related material. Thus the student moves through the material at a self-selected pace and is given additional "help" if needed (Maddux, Johnson, and Willis 1997).

The main advantage of programmed instruction in CD or DVD format is that students can use and review it at any time when a computer is available, usually eliminating scheduling issues and permitting self-pacing (Maddux,

Johnson, and Willis 1997). The materials must be clearly presented, and the networks guiding the students through the material must be responsive to differences in learning style. The materials also must be interesting or placed in relevant contexts to retain the learner's interest and offer encouragement o keep the learner going when mastery is slow. Programmed instruction via CD or DVD is used at many levels of education, from preschool to graduate school, although social workers have created a few CDs using programmed instruction. Programmed learning via CD or DVD requires careful design and, once completed, is difficult to revise and update.

Programmed instruction can also be delivered through the Web rather than on disk. The only limitation is the possible lack of broadband connections, which makes the downloading of large video and graphics files slow and time-consuming. Programmed instruction is generally a carefully designed set of static content, because the content on a disk is, of course, permanently fixed. Online, however, content is easier to change and update as necessary.

OTHER CD- AND DVD-BASED TEACHING MATERIALS

Some CD- or DVD-based courses do not use the programmed instruction model. Brooks/Cole Publishing and The Teaching Company offer a wide range of courses on CD, though only a few specific to social work. Continuing education courses in social work also are increasingly available, with full courses ranging from six to thirty hours in length and the purchase price generally increasing with the length of the video content. Courses consist of a series of thirty- to forty-five-minute audio or video lectures, with printed course guides providing additional information. This format allows students to work at their own pace and to move ahead or review at any time. Lectures may be "taken" at any time of the day or night, at the student's convenience.

Such courses allow outstanding lectures to be shared widely, avoiding distance and time constraints. Videos offer access to illustrations or vignettes of actions or processes. For example, Rittner and Struman (2002) used videos of mock cases to illustrate differential diagnoses, combining video CDs with lectures using presentation software, and Murphy and Dillon (1998) joined video to a traditional textbook. CDs can accommodate the very large file sizes of video material, produced separately and linked to the lecture.

Resnick's (1999) Paraphrase II is a CD-based interactive multimedia training program used to teach and refine listening and intervention skills with graphics, text, video images, and audio. Students see video presentations of mock cases, followed by multiple-choice questions about what happened and what the best response might be. Another example of an interactive CD instructional program is Chute and Bliss's (1996) Exploring Psychological Disorders, an introduction to the *Diagnostic and Statistical Manual of Mental Disorders-IV*. Content is read and case examples are viewed at the learner's own pace. The software ends each module with a computer-graded self-test, which either confirms new learning or directs the student to additional material and review. Ballantyne and Knowles (2007) found that multimedia case scenarios improved students' learning.

Because CD- or DVD-based lectures may be "taken" while students are exercising or doing something else, their concentration may waver, just as it does in classroom settings. Another drawback is not having a teacher to clarify or answer questions. Thus CD- or DVD-based learning is best for motivated learners who can manage their time wisely.

CD- or DVD-based modules and courses do not require that the end users be connected to the Internet, which may be an advantage for students in remote locations or while traveling. Furthermore, the number of such courses and modules is likely to increase as the cost of CD- and DVD-burning equipment decreases. Conversely, the growth in Internet access and availability may limit the growth in disk-based instructional materials except for those using very large video files. Seaberg (2001) found that only 5 percent of social work educators responding to a national survey (*n* = 102) used off-line video tools for teaching.

Research on the effectiveness of CD and DVD courses is extremely limited, and the research designs and samples used to examine its outcomes do not allow wide generalization of results. Cauble and Thurston (2000) found interactive multimedia to be an effective way to teach family and child welfare content. Nonetheless, the growth of "online teaching" has been rapid and widespread.

TEACHING ONLINE:
A CONTINUUM OF TEACHING APPROACHES

Some courses are now fully and solely available via the Internet, while other, more traditional courses are supplemented with online materials and resources. The terminology used to describe the continuum of online teaching options is still fluid and inconsistent. The two poles of the continuum between traditional face-to-face courses using no online resources and the solely electronic course with no face-to-face meeting—are clear. Less clear are the intermediate teaching options. Adkins and colleagues (2002) offered the following models and nomenclature, which form a rough continuum:

- *Web courses* that are fully online and require no in-person meetings.
- *Web-centric courses* in which communication and materials are predominantly available online but have some in-person meetings.
- *Web-enhanced courses* (also called *Web-assisted courses*) using a mix of in-person and online teaching approaches.
- Courses with a *Web presence*, such as online course descriptions or syllabi but with traditional class meetings and very few online resources.
- *Traditional courses* with no use of online resources.

Although we have no statistics on the use of online resources in social work teaching, it is likely that most courses are still traditional courses or those with a supporting Web presence. But the number of Web-enhanced courses is growing as many institutions offer course management software such as BlackBoard or Moodle to all faculty.

Courses may also be described by their use of time. Traditional courses are synchronous, meaning that sessions take place at the same scheduled time for all participants and lack scheduling flexibility. Online courses and many Web enhancements allow students and faculty to communicate "asynchronously" in an unscheduled, turn-taking fashion at the learner's convenience. For example, e-mail bulletin boards allow students to participate in discussion of a topic (called a *thread*) asynchronously at a convenient time to each participant. Web-enhanced courses make available materials and methods of communication asynchronously and include synchronous class meetings. Some Web-enhanced courses use synchronous live "chats," but such features presume that learners are not spread across different time zones or continents, which may be the case in online learning.

USING EXISTING INTERNET RESOURCES IN TEACHING

The infrastructure and start-up time for faculty are expensive when using technology in teaching. Faculty also must learn how to structure online teaching to maximize its advantages. Conventions for online courses are still being developed and are not widely shared. The three key issues in the use of Web-based content in education are using search engines and online resources in scholarship, using online journals and tools to search them effectively, and citing and saving Web-based materials.

OPTIMAL USE OF SEARCH ENGINES

Learners and faculty must be trained in the optimal use of Internet search engines. While human-vetted directories like Yahoo! are useful for some topics, and automated search "spiders" like Google and Bing can find many resources, both the quantity and quality of information can be daunting. Learners may be overwhelmed by the volume of data yielded by a simple search. Training in using "advanced" search techniques enables users to find more relevant results and can save time.

"Wikis" (user-generated encyclopedias) provide more specific information on a single topic. Wikis range in quality. They may be vetted by experts or be written persons with specific points of view or values. Although Wikis may offer specific information, their credibility, currency and thoroughness are not always apparent.

Evaluating Internet-based information is challenging. Accuracy and sources of online material may be unclear, and biases may be difficult to discern. Training in evaluating Internet information therefore is important to good education. Many good online resources explain how to use search engines (see "Resources") but must be supported and reinforced by faculty and staff. Who has primary responsibility for developing and implementing training in the evaluation of Internet resources is a matter of concern in a full social work curriculum, busy student schedules, and heavy faculty workloads. Some institutions have library or information technology specialists who offer such training. In other institutions, faculty who use Internet resources must offer courses on the use of search engine uses and critical evaluation of Web sources. Outlines of key issues in evaluating Web resources also are available online (see "Resources") but must be supported and supplemented by faculty, library staff, and class assignments.

OPTIMAL USE OF ONLINE JOURNALS

Students must learn how to access online journals using the software options purchased by their institutions and to use copyrighted materials appropriately. Both faculty and library staff can help identify those journals or databases likely to be relevant to specific search topics. In addition, products like J-Stor, CARL UnCover, and OVID each offer different search interfaces and different advanced search options. Students will likely need training and support to use these, and again, responsibility for such training is a matter of workload and cost. The cost is high owing to the relatively few institutions paying for these journals compared with medical and law journals. Search and citation skills, as well as consultation with or training from reference librarians, will help students make the most of available resources.

CITING AND SAVING ONLINE RESOURCES Software tools like RefWorks and ProCite make organizing citations of electronic publications easier, but Internet resources are not always stable. Weiner (2002) pointed out that Internet resources may move or disappear. In contrast to journals, some Web pages simply vanish when individuals or institutions remodel their Web materials. Thus learners and teachers need to be sure to print important Web pages, to save them using "cut and paste techniques" or to save the entire Web page in electronic form. Utility software like SnagIt or Scrapbook "downloads" a Web page or an entire site for later off-line use. For example, Scrapbook and Video DownloadHelper (both add-ons for the Firefox Web browser) save Web pages (see "Resources"). This process, however, can take a long time for complex Web sites and may be expensive. Once again, training in the use of these may be provided by faculty, library staff, information technologists, or a mix of each.

Using existing online resources can enhance many traditional courses. Dr. Gary Holden's long-running Information for Practice site offers a wide range of information and articles (see "Resources"). Making the transition to online communication between teacher and learner and among learners requires a revision of traditional standards, and faculty and academic administrators must help students interact online effectively and ethically.

ADVANTAGES OF ONLINE TEACHING

Online teaching has many advantages for businesses pursuing profits in higher education: limited physical plant costs, no need to house students (and often faculty), reduced (or no) library costs, and the possibility of exchanging faculty salaries for piecework payments to adjunct "consultant" teachers.

For more established institutions of higher education, the cost-benefit ratio is less positive but still impressive. Courses may be offered to a wider range of students in a wider range of locations (across a state, a nation, or even internationally). When an educational institution's mission emphasizes service to a state, online and distance education can help fulfill the mission equitably to everyone (Quam 1999).

Academic institutions, in turn, must support faculty with adequate equipment, technical support, and workload credit. Many online teachers find they spend more start-up time and effort on online courses than on traditional courses (Rittner and Struman 2002; Weiner 2002). Faculty need sustained support from institutional administration when teaching online.

Successful online courses must contain clear and well-structured content, enable learners to do more than read from the screen, and provide human resources to help and support when learner get stuck (E learning 2001). Using online resources in a professionally appropriate manner also is vital to effective teaching in social work. Faculty must help students learn the "ground rules" of online communication.

GROUND RULES AND "NETIQUETTE"

Faculty traditionally provide professional socialization to students, either explicitly or implicitly. Using online communication requires some socialization into the appropriate, courteous, and effective use of electronic communications (Hambridge 1995), generally known as *netiquette*. Netiquette has legal dimensions as well as ground rules for online communication. Indeed, the misuse of institutional resources and the violation of copyrights may be illegal as well as unethical. Many of these rules are contained in contracts required by the institution of all student and faculty users of institutional resources. Furthermore, as in all good academic work, dishonesty, plagiarism, and/or misrepresentation of other people's work are unacceptable. Although such policies are typically spelled out in student handbooks, they may omit issues raised by new technologies. For example, even though the misrepresentation of identity is possible online, it is unacceptable in all settings.

Faculty using online communications need to set standards for online communication and decide what forms of communication are professional and acceptable. Some institutions have their own netiquette guides, but many do not. In online communication and e-mail, netiquette means being respectful of others and their points of view, remaining open to divergent viewpoints, and building on and encouraging others' ideas. Other standards may be less obvious. E-mail users avoid using all capital characters, which some see as equivalent to screaming. "Flaming," or responding negatively and uncivilly to others' ideas, also is frowned on. Some groups find the use of emoticons — images meant to convey emotions, like ;) or): — acceptable, but others find them silly and inappropriate.

Instant messaging has generated new abbreviations that may not be suitable for formal academic work. Some, such as "u" for "you" are obvious, but others, like "lol" for "lots of luck" may be regarded as inappropriate. Faculty should establish the circumstances in which they are acceptable for academic work. Some general netiquette resources are available online (see "Resources"), but these should be tailored to course content, learning objectives, and professional standards.

Online communication may be either public or private. Weiner (2002) observed that public communications are like what someone might say out loud in class. Private online conversations are equivalent to office-based conversation between faculty and students and should include similar content. Students also use the private conversation standards for content communicated among their peers. They should ask, Would this content be appropriate for the whole class to know, or would it be better sent as a personal communication to just one other student? Confidentiality cannot be guaranteed. Similarly, students must be careful to use the "Reply to all" e-mail response only when the content is appropriate to, and meant for, all class members. Faculty also must decide whether messages should be sent to all students or only to specific students. For example, it may be useful to publicly affirm a student's helpful participation in an online conversation. Such communication also models helpful online communication skills. But affirmation or critical feedback should be offered privately when based on specific concerns or a student's particular interests.

Faculty should establish a clear policy regarding time lines for feedback to online assignments. Weiner (2002) found that students often want to know right away that their papers were received. In addition, faculty should set clear expectations regarding time lines for feedback on e-mail communication and for the return of assignments. Will feedback and grades take forty-eight hours or ten days? Being specific reassures students and models the correct behavior for online communication. Students, in turn, must be responsible for regularly checking institutional e-mail accounts or for ensuring that all institutional e-mail is correctly forwarded to their e-mail address of choice. Although e-mail is quick and generally reliable, not all computers may read file attachments correctly on all occasions. Students must be responsible for examining attachments and making sure that they come through accurately.

Faculty must make sure at the beginning of a course or online teaching module that students understand the ground rules for online communication. They must then continue to monitor the students' communication, reinforce communication that advances learning, and limit inappropriate or unhelpful communication. Once the ground rules are understood and faculty support is available in clearly specified times and modalities, maximizing the potential use of online teaching resources is the next challenge. Many commercial course management software packages can organize and expedite the use of online resources.

INTERNET-BASED COURSE MANAGEMENT SOFTWARE

More than one hundred different course management software (CMS) products are available to faculty and institutions (Centre for Curriculum Transfer and Technology 2000). Widely used CMS products include WebCT, Black-Board, and Moodle. The purpose of course management software is captured in the name of one product: Web Course in a Box. These products can be used to supplement traditional face-to-face courses or to make courses available on the Internet.

HOW DOES CMS WORK? WHAT DOES IT OFFER?

Either the instructor or the institution's registrar "enrolls" students by creating a list of legitimate students who may access the course. From campus, home, or elsewhere, students log on to the Internet to the course for which they are registered using a personal password. Thus only authorized users can access the materials for that course.

Once logged on, students find information about the course, which may include (1) recent class-specific or institutionwide announcements and an archive of past announcements for review; (2) the course syllabus; (3) the instructor's course assignments and materials (text documents, images, Internet links, sound files, and video files; (4) links to library resources, often including access to electronic copies of reserve readings; (5) links to contact the instructor by e-mail, such as options for electronic submitting papers or projects; (6) e-mail and/or real-time "chat" features for student-to-student and teacher-to-student(s) discussion, which is archived for review at any time; and (7) a search engine that can find desired content from either the course materials or a full Internet search.

The enrollees might not always be students but might be part-time field faculty or an international group working on a shared project. Authorized users of any kind can gain restricted access to materials on the Internet using CMS products. Faculty users can obtain in-service training or have access to grading options not available to students.

By using CMS, students (or other authorized users) have access to course materials at any time of day from both campus- and home-based computers. In addition, the burden of travel time (and/or campus parking) is reduced. Student-to-student discussion via the Internet is expedited, an advantage to many adult learners. Personal contact and in-person office hours may be maintained, as in traditional classes. Lectures and class attendance may be required as well. The most obvious loss is the opportunity for serendipitous learning when the book next to the one you seek in the library proves to be more interesting than the one assigned.

Reactions from student users of CMS products have been positive. Stocks and Freddolino (2000) found that students in research courses liked Web-based learning. Students found that it increased interaction, although they did wish for more face-to-face, live interaction. Wernet, Olliges, and Delicath (2000) found that students viewed Web-based courses materials as a helpful adjunct to learning, and nontraditional students had even more favorable responses to CMS options. Neither study, however, examined students' learning outcomes.

STUDENT-ORIENTED CMS FEATURES Some specific CMS features make them easy for students to use. *Student guides* explain how to use both the basic and advanced features of the CMS program and how to maximize electronic and online learning. In addition, student guides show how to get the most from communication options and materials available outside the classroom. Some "overview" aspects of student guides may be available from the software vendor, but many others must be developed by the institution and instructor. *Access to exemplars* of course-specific student and faculty work also can help students learn how to use online opportunities. These examples offer both content and usage information.

A *course index feature* and/or *course search engine* enables students to locate specific material quickly. Some CMS products allow searching either institutional course materials or more extensive library and Internet resources. CMS packages allow easy *bookmarking* of materials so that the student may leave and return to any location they choose. Bookmarking allows student-directed, nonlinear exploration of material and offers opportunities for serendipitous learning. Opportunities for students to *create their own Web pages* enable others to learn from them, consolidate learning, and can generate useful feedback and support. For example, I discovered a student's wonderful time line of key events on play therapy on her course Web page, which was available worldwide via a major search engine. (The page and its useful content vanished a year later, after the student graduated.)

CMS products *allow easy e-mail access* to work on group assignments and online discussions. Such software typically includes options to facilitate asynchronous (bulletin board or list-serv) communication, and some allow real-time (synchronous) chatting. None of these tools yet allows real-time oral or video conversation (the equivalent of an electronic conference call), although such features may appear quite soon. (These options now are available using software such as Skype.) Preliminary data suggest that many students who are unlikely to speak in class will participate in e-mail "discussions." Preliminary evidence from social work and other disciplines similarly shows that female students are more likely both to participate and to challenge the views of others in online discussions (Gohagan 2000).

Online *self-assessment exercises* enable students check their learning progress and identify areas of strength and weakness. Such tools may be *self-scored or electronically graded*. Machine-scored tests can also be used as part of the student's grade assessment. CMS packages can *document the frequency and/or content of all students' class participation*, which may be tabulated for grading purposes.

INSTRUCTOR-ORIENTED CMS FEATURES Most CMS packages start by directing the faculty user to a list of all available tools and options. These include personal options (changing your password or address) and course options such as course materials, contact information for instructors, and communication choices. *Templates* offer a common look for all courses offered by the host institution and help orient repeat users. Templates also organize course materials, but the instructor must supply the content and detail. Ideally, templates should be available automatically but be fully instructor customizable. Initial-course templates contain include course and/or institutionwide announcements, the course outline and assignments, contact information for instructors and enrolled students, and information links.

Course management software does not create course content; instructors must create it using different software, such as a word processor or photo editor. Other content may be found on the Internet or may be preexisting graphics and/or audio and video files in electronic formats. The resulting computer files must then be transferred or "uploaded" from the instructor's computer to an institutional computer "server," which allows Internet access. Easy-to-use *file management tools* are therefore important to using CMS. They make it easy to upload files one at a time or several at a time (known as batch processing) and to delete files from the server. You should learn *which file formats a given CMS package will upload* in "what-you-see-is-what-you-get" (WYSIWYG) form. Internet file formats may not preserve tabs and indenting or the locations of images or tables. Some CMS packages upload files in word processor formats and retain text formatting, whereas others require reformatting into Internet .html format before uploading.

Instructor guides are commonly available and very helpful. Some guides are available in printed format; others are online and must be printed. Such guides offer both examples and instructions. Online access to sound *exemplar courses* created by other instructors is another source of guidance and inspiration. Seeing how others use CMS features can point the way to useful innovations.

Automated glossary creation features are very helpful to students. Similarly, *automated table of contents creation* make indexing the material in the course site easy. Once generated, a table of contents can also be used to index *course-specific search tools* using common Internet search engines. The instructor must review and edit the automated results for each of these features to ensure complete coverage. Users may find detecting omitted items is more difficult than removing unwanted items.

Most CMS packages have *multimedia capabilities* to enliven and vary text-based materials, as well as provide useful illustrations and examples. The ways in which such files are displayed may vary widely. Some include built-in multimedia players through which audio or video files are displayed. Others use "plug-in" features that must be installed on the user's computer. Internet plug-ins like Apple's' "Quick Time" viewer and Adobe's "Flash" player are available as free downloads. Some students already have installed multimedia players on their computers. But end users must download these files, which often are large, from the Internet and install them in order to access multimedia files used for teaching purposes. This process may be time-consuming for students with dial-up Internet access. Plug-in features within CMS packages require user-friendly support pages as part of the course materials. (Such support pages may be used throughout the institution and may best be developed by technical support staff with expertise in this area.)

Despite the great range of features, most faculty find using CMS software about as difficult as learning to create presentations. There is a learning curve, and a good, hands-on training session is advisable. But once they have created a course site, reviewing and altering materials are easy.

COLLABORATION FEATURES The communication and collaboration features center on e-mail discussions, conferencing, and file sharing. Using e-mail for discussion is universal among CMS packages, which is not surprising, as most are intended to allow entire courses to be offered via the Internet. CMS discussion features may be equally useful as adjuncts to traditional classes in a single site. For example, Falk (1999) found that Web-based conferencing enhanced communication between teacher and students and among students. Asynchronous or time-shifted communication via e-mail is familiar to all e-mail users. CMS products allow *one-to-one e-mail* between enrolled students or between student and instructor. They also allow *one-to-many bulletin board communication* in which a message is posted and to which all participants may respond at times of their own choosing. The resulting files on a given topic, called a *thread*, remain available for later reflection, review, and study. Similarly, *many-to-many discussions*, known as *list-servs or text-based conferencing*, examine an issue from different perspectives. Experience has shown that many-to-many discussions quickly digress from the initial topic into new threads of conversation. Thus the instructor must establish the structure of the discussion to achieve specific learning goals. All such discussions take place at times selected by the student, maximizing flexibility and, one hopes, participation. The habits of students or instructors who routinely log on at 2 A.M. also become public knowledge. Many CMS packages enable synchronous, real-time chats. Faculty must schedule blocks of times for live chatting sessions, and participating students may reply to posting by other students immediately, allowing greater interaction than does asynchronous e-mail or bulletin board posting.

Some students find that participating in group discussions is easier on the Internet. Faculty may appreciate being to count the number of students' contributions to online class discussions. Thus CMS products may help set grading criteria for class participation. Faculty may also find e-mail communications allow them to give individual feedback to students beyond that in formal graded papers. Conversely, the burden of answering numerous e-mail messages may just be additional work.

WHICH CMS PRODUCT IS BEST?

Faculty opinions about which CMS product is "best" are highly subjective and varied (Future U 1999). Thus schools or universities should base their selection on ease of use for both students and faculty; the core features available for writing, organizing, and revising course materials; and administrative factors such as cost and ease of use and support for technical staff (Future U 1999).

IS ONLINE TEACHING EFFECTIVE?

Seaberg (1999) pointed out that determining the effectiveness of online questions is not simple. Online teaching falls along a continuum of course types based on the frequency of use of online components. Determining the effectiveness of online teaching therefore requires the careful matching of course types using appropriate research designs and methods. Unfortunately, the current research does not allow more than a tentative answer to this issue, as studies of specific course types and content are few and use mainly single-group or quasi-experimental research designs. Dependent variables are defined differently, often using grades on unspecified assignments. Outcomes are determined by the course instructor, which may be biased. The majority of the research addresses research or practice courses. Sections sizes are small, and traditional and online sections are rarely comparable. The validity of current research is limited, so conclusions must be viewed as preliminary.

Bearing this in mind, the literature generally shows that the yield of online and computer-based instruction in social work is equal to or better than traditional courses (Cauble and Thurston 2000; Freddolino and Sutherland 2000; Kulkin 2002; McFall and Freddolino 2000b; Schoech and Helton 2002; Seaberg 1999; Weiner 1999). Some contradictory studies, however, found that computer-based instruction may pose special challenges to particular groups of students, especially those not familiar with technology (Faux and Black-Hughes 2000). Beyond social work, Kulik and Kulik (1991) reviewed nearly three hundred "computer-based" courses offered across several disciplines and institutions and discovered that computer-based courses were more effective than traditional instruction, with an effect size of o.30. This means that on average, students in computer-based classes "would outperform 62% of the students from the conventional classes" (80). Outcomes measures were typically course grades, and the "state of the art" in 1991 did not include Internet access, e-mail, or course management software. But a survey of California State University students found that fewer than 30 percent of respondents believed that CMS software enhanced instruction but widely varied in their views of whether the software aided students' interaction (Munoz and Van Duzer 2005). Karrer (2006) reported that dissatisfaction with CMS software was rising in education and business, so the initial enthusiasm of early adopters may not linger for later student cohorts.

Additional research is needed on more varied course content using standardized measures and stronger research designs. Studies of businesses' use of online teaching suggest that it is good for teaching new content but not as good for teaching new skills and processes (E learning 2001). Even though the initial indicators are positive (Chambers 2002; Gohagan 2000; Wernet, Olliges, and Delicath 2000), refinement of optimal online teaching approaches for adult learners warrants further investigation. Overall, online teaching may be good for many but perhaps not all social work students.

E-MAIL AND INSTANT MESSAGING

E-mail is an important tool for personal and professional communication. E-mail software is included with all computer operating systems and is offered free by most Internet service providers. In most educational institutions students are automatically assigned an institutional e-mail address when they register.

Seaberg (2001) found that 93 percent of social work educators ($n = 102$) used e-mail. The median number of e-mails was twenty-three per day (sent and received). Seaberg (1999) also reported forty-seven e-mail messages per student per semester in his own online course. E-mail may indeed enhance contact and communication but can pose an additional out-of-class burden for faculty, which may be considerably more time-consuming than are traditional in-person office hours.

Weiner (2002) noted that students often want rapid confirmation that assignments sent by e-mail were received. Such communication may be quick but require that faculty continually read their e-mail messages. Weiner also proposed that faculty contract with students regarding time lines for responses and periods of availability. That is, if a forty-eight-hour response time is the established norm, some form of response should be made within that time. Similarly, if the teacher will be unavailable for a specified period (conference, vacation, etc.), he or she should send these dates to all students. Teachers are responsible for informing students of their expectations and schedules.

Academic institutions and course instructors must draw up rules for e-mail usage. If faculty expect students to use their institutional e-mail account, they must send messages to only these addresses. In most cases, students can set their academic e-mail account to "forward" e-mail to their most commonly used e-mail account. Students and faculty should check their e-mail on some defined periodic basis (such as every other day). Faculty should also send a message to all students early in the course, attaching the file formats that will be used in the course. Specifically, if Adobe Acrobat (.pdf) document files, Microsoft PowerPoint (.ppt) slides, or SPSS data files (.sav) are to be exchanged by e-mail, students must verify that the files have been delivered and can be used on their own computers. Such expectations and policies help limit technical challenges to e-mail communication. Crook and Brady (1998) found that most e-mail problems were due to technical problems with local Internet service providers or end-user equipment rather than with institutional service. Students must take responsibility for ensuring that their e-mail software will successfully send and receive the necessary file types.

Despite the little research on student-to-student peer interaction in online learning, there is anecdotal evidence that students may prefer scheduled times for synchronous online chats over asynchronous list-serv communication (Weiner 2002). Chat sessions allow student to use "online messaging" services such as ICQ or America Online's Instant Messenger, which show who is currently online and available to chat and send messages to a defined, limited group. Such online messaging services are widely used, but not all students may have access to them, and the different software types are not always compatible. Thus all students must use the same software to chat. Most CMS packages allow for such synchronous chatting among students enrolled in a course.

In all forms of text-based communication, the teacher must be responsible for setting the ground rules and monitoring the communications. Faculty must establish a netiquette to help students understand appropriate versus inappropriate content and to distinguish between public and private communications (sent directly to teacher or a single student, but not to the group as a whole). Teachers should support useful content and note when potentially productive ideas receive no responses from peers. The teacher must also affirm good content and good peer process. For instance, the teacher might send a private message to a student who has reinforced a peer's message. Alternatively, the message could be sent to everyone to ensure that all students understand the need for affirmation in group e-mail communications. Faculty should also encourage novel and productive threads to encourage such work.

One of e-mail's limitations is its text-only format. Nonverbal cues like facial expressions, posture, and proximity are not communicated easily in text. Participants must also be able typists and good spellers. But several studies indicate that students find e-mail increases class communication and creates new learning opportunities (Ouellette 1999; Stocks and Freddolino 2000), although e-mail must be carefully structured and continuously supervised to be productive. E-mail may add to faculty workloads and may require continuous rather than periodic interaction with students. But e-mail also can be structured to create new, cooperative learning assignments and could be a resource for collecting data across great distances.

INTERACTIVE TELEVISION AND VIDEO CONFERENCING

Interactive television (IT) is another technology used in distance education. Interactive television adds to the one-way televised courses of the 1970s the possibility of immediate two-way communication. IT courses may be offered to groups of students in a classroom setting or, using video conferencing, to small groups of students working from multiple locations in different settings. Recent software and expansions in Internet bandwidth also permit video conferencing using software like Skype.

In some educational settings, several forms of interactive television are already widely used. Although its use began before the development of Internet tools, IT has matured and begun to merge with online learning. IT began with an instructor in a central location whose lecture and discussion were "fed" live to remote sites via closed circuit cable or satellite connections. Questions from the remote sites were asked using simple telephone connections. The result was a lecture-based format with opportunities for questions and exchange, and both home and remote sites had access to the same content. But this was offset by a lack of spontaneity in discussion. The instructor could speak with only one person or site at a time. The instructor viewed each remote location via a separate television monitor, requiring him or her to handle notes and materials and monitor the live section and each remote location by video all at once. In many cases, local teaching assistants oversaw the discussion and were available to answer questions from students in the remote sites. This made the program available at distant sites and made students feel more connected to the program as a whole. Recent increases in Internet bandwidth (the ability to handle ever-larger volumes of data at one time) have enabled the Web to handle video communication. In addition, "compressed video," which sends smaller files from place to place while maintaining the video's quality, has improved to nearly lifelike quality, with little "lag time" between sending and reception. Many current IT classes are handled by video-conferencing technology.

In Internet compressed video courses, the instructor's presentation is sent live to remote sites via Internet connections and displayed on one or more computer monitors. Discussion takes place via microphones placed in a central location, usually the center of a conference table. Multiple microphones may also be used. Because video-conferencing microphones are voice activated, any question asked by a class member turns on the microphone and sends the comment to all sites simultaneously. Multiple microphones enhance interactive discussion, but students and the instructor must "queue up" to speak, one at a time. The video's quality varies from excellent, with fast, broadband Internet connections, to choppy and pixilated (composed of square blocks), with slower connections.

Interactive television allows some universities to better meet their mission and goals, especially in providing access to an entire state or region and increasing access to high-quality educational programs and courses. Students from different locations (urban and rural, diverse and monolithic) are able to share their varied perspectives on the course content. Students' questions may open new avenues for discussion. In addition, students may feel more connected to their program and course of study and may develop new peer networks and learning alliances. For some students, the ability to see the faces and reactions of others makes the sense of connection more vivid than does text-based communication.

Video conferencing may support both traditional and IT classes. Most video conferencing using personal computers is limited to relatively small group interactions, limiting its usefulness as a class or even a seminar replacement. It may, however, be a valuable tool for faculty advising and as an adjunct to in-person supervision. It proved effective at the Smith College School for Social Work, where students often work on master's thesis projects at far away from their thesis advisers (LaTerz 2008). Here, students and their advisers have already established a personal relationships before using video-conference advising. Internet video "feeds" to large classrooms or multiple recipients, in which content is delivered to a large group, functions much like IT. The limitation of this medium is that feedback from participants is limited, lacks spontaneity, and is often difficult to arrange.

IS IT EFFECTIVE?

Like online teaching, IT is not a single entity but a range of approaches coupled with varying technology. Evaluators must be careful not to compare apples and oranges, such as courses using telephones for communication versus teleconferencing formats. As is true of the research on online teaching, dependent variables lacked standardization and often were based on the instructor's own evaluations of student performance. While comparative methods are often used across sections, the equivalence of students across sections cannot be established through pretest; the number of students in each section is usually very small (ten or fewer); and the course content is variable.

Haga and Heitkamp (2000) reported equivalent outcomes for students in IT and traditional sections of their social work program as a whole. Petracchi and Patchner (2000, 2001) found no differences in performance or attitudes between students in traditional and IT sections of foundation practice or in students' experiences and attitudes in three different sections of research. Hollister and McGee (2000) found no differences in performance or quality of communication in substance abuse and child welfare courses. Huff (2000) found no differences in critical thinking skills between IT and traditional sections of a policy course. But Thyer, Polk, and Gaudin (1997) and Hylton (2006) found that live instruction was rated significantly higher than was IT or online course sections. Besides evaluating students' performance, studies have examined attitudes and some specific skills. Outside social work, Lim, Morris, and Yoon (2006) found that differences in students' motivation and investment significantly correlated with success in online courses.

Quam (1999) noted that evaluations of IT and other forms of distance education must begin with the student learners' needs. Tesone and Ricci (2008) argued that Web-based learning requires extensive efforts by instructors to develop and maintain student–teacher and student–student relationships. Macy (1999) examined the experiences of fourteen students who completed an IT-based MSW program. These students believed that IT enhanced their learning and could be a useful method for graduate education in social work. Notably, Macy's sample believed that IT increased the diversity of students, which contributed to learning. The sample also pointed to the importance of support from the on-site coordinators and from within the on-site cohort. Similarly, Harris and Parrish (2006) found that students often felt isolated when learning by computer. Attention should be given to the overall structure of an IT program, the selection of on-site personnel, and the forms of IT instruction. Ways of using IT in social work have not yet been developed, as both more experience and research are needed to determine its efficacy. As in online education, IT's strengths appear to be in delivering technical content. Indeed, new information, delivered lecture style, is the core IT content. The use of IT in courses that emphasize process and skill building has not been fully studied and warrants additional attention.

Many new teaching technologies are available for use in social work education. These technologies may fit well with institutional missions and help equip students for the technologies they are likely to use in their education and service. Research on the optimal use of these new technologies is limited, and well-designed studies using standardized outcome measures are needed.

At the same time, the new innovations suggest ways to expand access to social work education. Current and new faculty should be trained in using the new technologies. Criteria for workload, tenure, and promotion credit are lacking to guide institutions and faculty who use these new technologies. For peer support, the Council on Social Work Education's Distance Education and Technology Symposia have been active in the past several years, providing new ideas, potential collaborators, and encouragement for faculty who "take the plunge."

CLASSROOM CONSIDERATIONS REGARDING WIRELESS DEVICES

Both the planned uses of technology in teaching and the simultaneous explosion in use of wireless communication devices by students have significantly altered the educational environment (Stewart 2008). As stated earlier, technology offers wonderful resources for teaching and learning. At the same time, faculty must keep pace with the social changes that electronic devices have made in the broader social context of education. Because 62 percent of all Americans have mobile data connections (Pew Internet Survey 2008b), all educational institutions need policies regarding the in-class use of cell phones and text messaging, as they may be either distractions or educational assets (Hulette 2009). Finding their optimal use will require thoughtful engagement with students to develop reasonable standards and policies to reduce distraction and benefit learning.

Similarly, the use of personal computers in class may replace the active learning involved in writing pencil-and-paper notes and may help students with specific learning challenges to use classroom time more effectively. Alternatively, computers may lead to distractions in personal e-mailing and Internet surfing. Faculty members may find it difficult to distinguish between appropriate and inappropriate computer usage by students in class. Social work educators should develop "appropriate usage policies" that both ensure suitable and legal use of institutional resources and teach students how to use the new technologies. Teachers should talk with students about the educational use of electronic devices and services, so as not to leave discussions of netiquette solely to institutional technology and library personnel. Social workers should promote the ethical and considerate use of resources consistent with their professional values and ethics.

AREAS NEEDING FURTHER ATTENTION
BY EDUCATORS

The technology is rapidly changing, but several areas of concern to social workers and social work education still need attention: access and ease of use, specific content areas, and changes in both student and faculty roles.

Advances in technology in teaching raise important issues of social justice regarding access and accessibility. As previously noted, an economic and racial "digital divide" limits access to technology for many people of color. Likewise, resources regarding human diversity and cultural competence have been slow to develop online. Since social work students who have completed interactive television and online courses know that diversity is a key strength of these technologies, social workers should create and promote such resources. Dumbrill and Green (2007) found that little native knowledge is found in Web-based learning.

Many useful resources are available online for the "differently abled" and disabled. The Internet has been a valuable source of connection among people with similar abilities and life needs, but using technology in teaching requires considerable attention to the abilities of student learners. "Improvements" in graphical computer interfaces have come at the price of requiring good vision to use computers easily (Stretch and Kreuger 2002). Blind, visually impaired, and dexterity-challenged students may find using many technological resources very demanding and challenging, so faculty and institutions need to be sensitive to and respond to their needs.

Advances in Internet technology have added to the visual demands of using the Internet. Many Web sites do not offer fully equivalent text-based content in tandem with their graphical interfaces. This is important because the screen reader software used by blind and visually impaired individuals can speak only text-based content, and graphics often contain no text-based (alternative) content.

Text-to-speech or "screen reader" software, such as Freedom Scientific's JAWS program, is fairly well developed. Many products are now available with a range of both male and female "voices" and a wide range of tools to adjust the cadence and rate of speech output. Less well developed are speech-to-text or "voice recognition" software products, which feed electronic text documents from speech into a computer microphone. Products such as ScanSoft's Naturally Speaking and IBM's ViaVoice operate, with training, with 90 to 98 percent accuracy (see "Resources"). These programs are an asset to visually impaired and blind computer users, but the written results still require substantial editing. There is a very real "ability divide," especially regarding vision, like the race- and class-defined "digital divide" in technology access.

Social work education in the United States is taught predominantly in English, and most of its literature is written in English. Although the majority of Internet resources appear in English, many are in other languages, and access to Internet resources and communications may be significantly limited by the language barrier. Several search sites, including Google, offer computerized translation services (see "Resources"). Separate computerized translation programs also exist, but all contain significant translation errors. But as these products mature, they may improve cross-language communication and become a valuable aid to multilingual and international social work education.

Using technology fully and easily may be a serious challenge to the differently abled teachers and learners. Technology may ultimately become a resource to overcome certain limitations, but it currently poses some significant obstacles for certain groups of users. Reasonable accommodations for these challenges are not always clear or easily available (see "Resources").

LEARNING STYLES

Technology can make a learner more active and more self-directed (Chambers 2002; Ouellette 2002), attributes that characterize most adult learners and their learning approaches. Many technologies fit cognitively oriented learners well (Chambers 2002), although the use of technology by learners who need movement or who learn best through intuition and affect has not been evaluated. Others may need more face-to-face, in-person interaction. Macy's (1999) students observed that certain course content seemed better suited to interactive television. They also noted that the careful selection of on-site personnel was necessary to build and maintain a sense of connection to the host institution and the program. Further attention to defining the learning styles that do, and do not, mesh well with technology-mediated learning is needed.

APPROPRIATE MARKETING FOR ONLINE EDUCATION

Kulkin (2002) reported high dropout rates (more than 60%) from her online course sections. While bearing in mind that many students "try out" introductory social work courses, dropout rates of more than 50 percent raise concern. Gustafson (2002) stated that dropout rates from online BSW courses appear to be higher than those for in-person courses. One reason may be that students misinterpret the marketing of online courses. The "convenience" of online courses may be misinterpreted as meaning the courses are easy, or easier, than in-person counterparts. In fact, online courses are convenient in regard to scheduling but require time-management skills, persistence, and a high degree of self-direction. Without scheduled classes and in-person contacts, it may be easy to fall behind in readings and assignments. Further research regarding the marketing of online teaching is warranted to make sure that students fully understand the requirements of online learning.

FACULTY WORKLOAD AND REWARDS

Anecdotal and preliminary survey evidence suggests that more effort is required to prepare an online or IT course than traditional courses (Seaberg 2001). It is unclear whether this includes the time spent on becoming familiar with new technologies or only the time preparing the course content and materials. Faculty should understand both their institution's plans for educational technology and the effort needed to develop technology-mediated courses and modules (Monaghan 1998). Anecdotal evidence also suggests that institutional support for developing technology-mediated courses is widely available (Seaberg 2001) but that its extent and quality vary considerably. Still unclear is whether or not additional workload credit is offered to faculty to develop new technology-mediated courses and the extent of such additional credit. No standards are publicly available at this time.

While many educational institutions and the culture at large are promoting the use of technology in teaching, it often is not clear how the creation of online materials will be evaluated, especially for tenure, promotion, and merit raises. Currently, online journals, whether or not they are peer reviewed, may not always be viewed as "legitimate" publications, although as the open-source movement begins in social work, this problem is likely to diminish. Nevertheless, standards for the assessment of online work, used in both teaching and scholarship, need clarification.

Seaberg (2001) found that disproportionate numbers of senior faculty were involved in online teaching. He speculated that this may be because senior professors are more established, teach fewer courses, and may desire a change in approach to repetitious content. He also suggested that "assistant professors may not be able to take the risk of spending time on an activity that may not be recognized in the university's promotion and tenure criteria." Clarifying the weighting of online teaching and materials preparation appears crucial to encouraging junior faculty to become involved in online efforts.

PRIVACY

Many computer users fear virus contamination by malicious computer "hackers," but they may fail to recognize the many larger but more subtle threats to their privacy and comfort inherent in computer and Internet use. Stretch and Kreuger (2002) pointed out that technology allows network administrators "to peek at employee screens in real time, scan data and e-mail at will, tabulate keystroke speed and accuracy, overwrite passwords and even seize control of a remote workstation if they deem it necessary" (7). Karrer (2006) observed that administrative compliance monitoring is a key use of course management software, especially in business settings but also on many campuses. Similarly, "spyware," installed without the user's knowledge by many commercial software packages, allows the monitoring of Internet usage and specific sites that the user visits. User privacy cannot be ensured by either current technology or legislation, as privacy laws have not kept pace with technological innovation, leaving computer and Internet use only minimally regulated.

While some teaching content may not raise privacy concerns among users, other content is protected by copyright and/or other laws addressing privacy and confidentiality. The use of case materials, student papers, and copyrighted materials all are restricted by federal and state laws. Protections of privacy and confidentiality may be further protected by social work ethics and values (NASW 1999). Academic institutions, faculty, and students all must be careful to use materials accessed or distributed online appropriately.

CONCLUSION

■ *Teaching technologies can be extremely valuable resources in social work education.* They offer ways to include a wide range of students in professional education programs. They can help make higher education feasible for learners with many learning styles and in varied circumstances. Assuring access to technology aids and empowers all learners.

■ *Technology is an increasingly prominent part of our daily lives* and will be an increasingly vital part of teaching. Learners will increasingly expect technology to be an important part of their learning environments. As new technologies emerge, aging teachers will need to explore and use them to stay current with student expectations.

- *Each teaching technology should be put to best use.* Simply using technology without a clear purpose will likely yield confusion, not enhanced learning. Joining technology with learning processes and learning goals produces the best outcomes and best serves students' needs. More research on the best uses of teaching technologies, as well as their optimal target student populations, is needed.

- *Technological changes are continuous and ongoing.* The speed of technological change imposes a significant demand on educators and educational institutions. Understanding teaching technologies and how best to use them requires considerable time and effort. More outcome research on the *impact of teaching technologies* is needed.

- *Learning to use teaching technologies effectively takes resources, time, and effort.* Instructors need to make this effort, and institutions need to support them.

Technology can enhance teaching in many ways, but each innovation will bring new challenges and barriers as well. Social workers need to "try out" these new teaching technologies and simultaneously determine their strengths, limitations, and omissions. Teaching innovations, research on teaching processes and outcomes, and the development of ground rules and policies for using technology all need further development and professional discussion.

Resources

Presentation Software

- Corel Presentations is part of Word Perfect Office. Information on Corel Presentations is available at www.corel.com.
- Star Office is available for download from Sun Microsystems at atwww.sun .com/software/staroffice/www.sun.com/staroffice/get.html.

Using Presentation Software

- Formatting individual slides in PowerPoint is available at www.iasted.org/ conferences/formatting/Presentations-Tips.ppt.

- Using Corel Presentations (from start to finish) is available at www.uaex.edu/pres8/default.htm.

Using Existing Internet Resources in Teaching

- Gary Holden's Information for Practice Web site offers a wide range of information and full-length articles useful for social workers. It is available at www.nyu.edu/socialwork/ip/.

Effective Web Search Strategies

- The Department of Educational Technology at San Diego State University offers a four-step strategy to effective Web searches at http://webquest.sdsu.edu/searching/fournets.htm.
- The Georgetown University libraries offer a very thorough outline for Web searches at www.library.georgetown.edu/Internet/effectiv.htm.

Site Rippers (Web site Copiers for Offline Use and Saves)

- HTTrack Site Copier allows downloading of entire Web site contents for off-line viewing and saving for later review. It is available free at www.httrack.com/.
- Scrapbook is an "add-on" for the Firefox Web browser that allows screen capture and site downloading. In Firefox, click on Tools and then Add-ons, and search for Scrapbook.
- SnagIt screen capture software captures and edits Web sites and pages and is available for purchase at www.techsmith.com.
- Video DownloadHelper is another Firefox add-on that allows the capture of flash videos and YouTube videos for later review. In Firefox, click on Tools, then Add-ons, and search for Video DownloadHelper.

Netiquette

- Hambridge's full netiquette guidelines for users and administrators (Intel RFC 1855) are available at http://www.dtcc.edu/cs/rfc1855.html.
- Virginia Shea's rules of Internet etiquette are available at www.albion.com/netiquette/corerules.html.

Different Abilities/Disabilities

- CAST, the Center for Applied Special Technology, offers resources on "using technology to improve opportunities for all people, including those with disabilities." Information and links are available at www.cast.org.
- Bobby is CAST's software for evaluating the accessibility of Internet sites. You may evaluate a site at www.cast.org/bobby.

Screen Readers

- The JAWS for Windows screen reader is available for purchase at www.freedomscientific.com/fs_products/software_jaws.asp.
- ZoomText is a windows magnification program with an optional screen reader. A USB device version of Zoomtext allows portability to any Windows-based computer. It is available for purchase from www.aisquared.com/.

Voice Recognition Software

- Dragon Naturally Speaking speech-to-text software is available for purchase at www.nuance.com/viavoice/.
- IBM ViaVoice software speech-to-text software is available for purchase at www.nuance.com/viavoice/.

Translation Programs

- Babylon offers multiple language translation with good accuracy as well as encyclopedia information. It is available for purchase at www.babylon.com.
- Free online translation sites for short text passages include SDL's Free Translation at www.freetranslation.com/; Google's Language Tools at www.google.com/language_tools; and Yahoo's Babelfish at http://babelfish.yahoo.com/.
- @promt is a multiple-language online translation and dictionary site and is available for purchase at http://translation2.paralink.com/.

7

ASSESSING LEARNING AND TEACHING

ACCOUNTABILITY AND CALLS FOR MEASURABLE OUTCOMES have recently become nearly universal watchwords at all levels of education in the United States, affecting models of accreditation and professional education (Palomba and Banta 2001) in social work (Baskind, Shank, and Ferraro 2001) and other fields. In the past, the accreditation and evaluation of social work programs were based on the setting (program and college/university resources, curriculum, qualifications of the faculty, screening of students for admission) and the assumption that traditional mechanisms for evaluating student performance, like grading, were enough to ensure that social work programs graduated students competent to serve clients capably.

Although we generally assume that completion of a degree program will improve practice skills and abilities, we should examine this assumption empirically. For psychotherapy, Dawes (1996) reviewed the evidence and found that educational qualifications and postgraduate experience did not convincingly translate into improved outcomes for the people served. In social work, Wodarski, Feit, and Green (1995) found evidence that aspects of MSW social work students' "interpersonal helping skills" might actually decline from baseline or, when improved, have not been shown to generalize to real clients in the agency setting. The research they reviewed on outcomes in other areas, like teaching policy practice skills, was quite promising, but in areas like the human behavior and social environment curriculum, there are almost no studies. While the research they reviewed is now quite dated, it is clear that more and better research on the effectiveness of our educational methods in a range of areas is needed.

Colleges, universities, and schools and departments of social work compete with one another for the best applicants, the best faculty, and the best resources on their own campuses. This competition is increasingly driven by various kinds of rankings, even though their validity has been questioned (Be-less 1994; Green et al. 2006; Kirk and Corcoran 1995). This chapter discusses the rankings of schools of social work because they now are so influential in driving many of faculty's activities. In social work as in higher education more generally, however, these rankings may not always say much about the quality of students' education. But because this book is meant primarily for teachers, I emphasize assessment not *of* but *within* programs and schools: in courses, in the field and of the educational experience overall.

Assessments of teaching and learning have different purposes: to borrow language from the field of program evaluation, their uses may be *formative*, to provide feedback on learning or teaching in order to improve performance. These uses have no implications for recorded judgments of learning or teaching but are meant for use in self-improvement. Other uses of assessment are *summative*, serving a gatekeeping function with respect to students; as part of faculty evaluation for employment, tenure, promotion, or merit; or in accreditation processes. Summative evaluations, however, are best connected to learning and professional growth. Here we examine both uses of assessment.

The assessment of *learning* is sometimes assumed to be an assessment of *teaching* or some combination of teaching and curriculum ("subject matter" in figure 7.1). The best teachers try to reach a variety of students with a range of learning styles and needs. Teaching also can be defined as creating the conditions in which learning can take place and in which students are inspired to succeed. The curriculum's design must take into account differences among students as well, although not all individual students are motivated or able to take advantage of the learning opportunities that teachers and curricula provide. Even if we assume that the quality of teaching is related to students' learning, it still can be useful to assess the teaching *input* directly or in addition to student *outcomes*. Therefore, I look at the assessment of learning and the assessment of teaching separately, despite the obvious relationship between the two.

Learning and teaching can be assessed at various levels in addition to the institution (college or university), such as the school or department or a specific program within it (e.g., BSW, MSW, or doctorate); a component of a school or program, such as resources, students, or faculty; and a course, a segment of a course, or a series of courses, including an internship or a segment of it; or a specific assignment or activity. (This chapter does not address the assessment of doctoral education in social work, a special topic in its own right. See, e.g., Maki and Borowski 2006.) Meaningful assessments can be elicited from a variety of sources: students; classroom teachers, field instructors, and

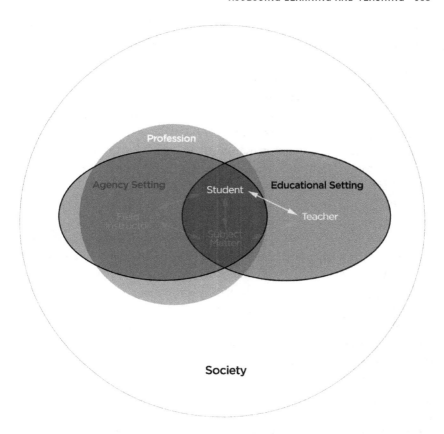

FIGURE 7.1 Model of teaching and learning that highlights areas of assessment.

faculty–field liaisons; trained observers; and clients and/or employers. Many methods of assessment can be used , which should ideally relate well to what is being assessed, although feasibility and costs often limit the options. Grading is not always a good method of assessing students' performance and is a source of anxiety to many beginning teachers, so we discuss grading specifically as well.

Assessing students for admission to degree-granting programs in social work is an important issue that will not be covered here, because admissions processes in social work programs are often greatly constrained by practices in the college or university as a whole. Admissions issues have not been extensively studied in recent years, with some notable exceptions (Fortune 2003; GlenMaye and Oakes 2002; Miller and Koerin 1998; Pardeck 2003). Comparative data on selectivity in graduate admissions have only recently been published (Kirk, Kil, and Corcoran 2009), although many complex factors may influence these figures in ways that are hard to assess. Any admissions screening system can only imperfectly predict students' success, meaning that gatekeeping via unbiased student evaluation *within* social work degree programs remains an important issue to consider.

This recent emphasis on this assessment of educational outcomes has both progressive and regressive possibilities. The well-known debate about using standardized tests of student achievement to evaluate teachers and public schools at the elementary and secondary levels illustrates both progressive and regressive possibilities. "Blaming the victims" in overcrowded and/or underfunded classrooms and "teaching to the exam" are negative consequences. Inspiring teachers and schools to find ways to bring out the best in their students and publicizing and disseminating educational practices that improve academic performance are positive possibilities. Most important, however, is that some philosophies and definitions of professional practice and professional competence are better reflected in the dominant models of educational assessment. Yelloly and Henkel (1995), for example, offer critiques and alternatives based in Schön's concept of reflective practice. It is important to choose practices in the assessment of teaching and learning congruent with the educational philosophies being used.

ACCREDITATION AND LICENSING: ENSURING MINIMUM PROFESSIONAL STANDARDS

ACCREDITATION

Institutions of higher education are accredited on the college or university level. In addition, social work has a profession-based system of accreditation (Palomba and Banta 2001) that covers baccalaureate, graduate (MSW), and joint (BSW and MSW) programs, although not doctoral programs. Social work is accredited by the Council on Social Work Education's Commission on Accreditation (http://www.cswe.org/CSWE/accreditation/). This system is designed to ensure that basic indicators of quality social work education are present, including curriculum content that defines the core of the profession. Just as students do, programs may "perform to the test," meaning that the published standards for program assessment, including curriculum guidelines, which are periodically revised, often drive curriculum changes and program practices.

One example of how accreditation standards can be used directly in out-comes assessment is apparent in Holden, Anastas, and Meenaghan's (2003) study of MSW students' pre- and postratings of self-efficacy with respect to specified foundation-level competencies. Although the authors recommend-ed also including program-specific learning objectives in any outcome as-sessment (Holden et al. 2002), changes in self-efficacy could be shown in students' scores in areas defined in the accreditation standards as basic to beginning-level social work practice, although causal attribution is not pos-sible, of course, without a control group.

The accreditation system is based on a peer review of a self-report that each program submits to CSWE's Commission on Accreditation, generally accompanied by a campus visit for further assessment. The self-study preced-ing a program's self-report to the commission is an occasion for an internal re-examination of educational goals, educational methods, curriculum content, and the assessment of students and graduates. Because accreditation by the profession is linked to the program's reputation and graduates' ability to qual-ify for public credentialing (state licensing or certification) and hence to the recruitment of applicants, programs and schools invest a great deal of energy in preparing for their periodic reviews. Recent changes in social work accredi-tation policies and practices have been designed to give educational programs greater latitude in defining their own missions and program emphases, with their "inputs" and outcomes evaluated with respect to the missions and goals they define for themselves, as long as their missions and activities fall within the recognized scope of social work. Social work programs, however, become frustrated with the accreditation standards for program assessment (Garcia and Floyd 2002). Current accreditation standards and other information on accreditation in social work are available at the CSWE Web site.

Only the overall outcomes of program reviews (successful candidacy for accreditation of a BSW or MSW program, initial accreditation, reaffirmation of accreditation for a specific time period, or some less successful outcome, like probationary status) are published. The more detailed comments about areas of strength or concern are confidential and are submitted only to the program and its university administration. Hence this information cannot be used to rate programs comparatively or to learn about best practices.

LICENSING

Over the past twenty-five years, state-based methods of licensing or credential-ing social workers, at least at the MSW level, have become universal throughout the United States. All licensing systems have at their core the mission of protecting the public by setting minimum standards for professional practice. Hence, "pass rates" on state licensing examinations have become another standard measure of outcome for master's and baccalaureate programs in jurisdictions that require licensing at that level. The Association of Social Work Boards (ASWB, http://www.aswb.org/) represents all states' regulatory bodies and is a good source of information about the examinations and other requirements for licensing.

While the topic of the range of credentials that exist and/or should exist for social work professionals is beyond the scope of this chapter, before discussing assessments of teaching and learning within social work education, I should note that through state legislation, society now exercises some control over who can practice professional social work, has defined the nature and scope of social work practice, and can discipline social workers found to have violated ethical or other standards of practice in order to protect those they serve and the general public interest. As in higher education, the licensing bodies themselves cannot assume that having certain structures or processes in place, like carefully crafted examinations or licensing boards adequately financed and staffed, automatically ensures that the goals of the licensing—requiring minimum standards of competence in social work practice—are being achieved.

There are some inevitable tensions between the licensing system and educational programs. Because MSW programs use graduates' pass rates on licensing examinations as an outcome measure, they assume that the adequate preparation of students for licensing examinations is a legitimate service to students and graduates. Academic institutions also, however, have the sole legal and moral authority to determine curriculum content and degree requirements in all disciplines and professions and hence do not allow licensing examinations to determine the curriculum. To ignore them entirely, however, risks ignoring what others in society believe is relevant to professional practice. The relationships between the legal regulation of practice and the assessment of social work educational programs and how both are (or are not) relevant to what defines social work practice require more study.

PROGRAM RANKINGS:
RELEVANT TO LEARNING AND TEACHING?

National rankings of undergraduate and graduate programs, primarily those of *U.S. News & World Report* (*U.S. News*), have taken on ever-increasing importance as colleges and universities compete for tangibles, like well-qualified students and faculty, and intangibles, like renown, that can support fund-raising. The findings of the U.S. News survey, that is, the published ranking of an academic unit in its field, can also influence the allocation of resources and prestige among units within a college or university.

The U.S. News survey findings are based on reputation, as reported by deans and directors as well as a sample of senior faculty in the field. Because the U.S. News ratings are subjective and limited in what they measure, some undergraduate liberal arts colleges have recently opted out of this system, but for the time being, most colleges and universities participate in the poll. The methodology used in the U.S. News rankings of graduate programs varies. Green and colleagues (2006) found that the rankings of schools of social work were based on responses to a single item rather than on several items, as for some other professions. Survey respondents are instructed to rate each program *of which they have knowledge* as "distinguished" (5), "good" (4), "average" (3), "marginal" (2), or "poor" (1). The top ten social work programs in 2004 were rated 3.9 or higher (to 4.6), and the top fifty-one schools were rated 3.0 or higher. The average scores for many schools, therefore, differ only slightly (perhaps by a fraction of a decimal point) from those of others. Nonetheless, these very small score differences are magnified by the rank differences. Departments and schools of social work naturally seek to enhance their national rankings, despite questions about what the rankings may actually mean for the quality of student or faculty life or the quality of teaching and learning.

Not surprisingly, social work educators have been discussing the meaning and usefulness of the U.S. News rankings (Green et al. 2006; Kirk and Corcoran 1995). Kirk and Corcoran (1995) and Green, Baskind, and Conklin (1995) found that the U.S. News rankings correlated highly with faculty publication rates and, in particular, that the top ten schools also were rated at the top in earlier studies of faculty publication rates. To examine further the validity of the U.S. News ranking for the top fifty social work programs, Green and colleagues (2006) surveyed samples of deans and directors, CSWE members, graduate student members of NASW, and practitioner members of NASW. They found the 2004 U.S. News rankings to be correlated with selectivity in graduate admissions, the age of the MSW and doctoral programs, and, again, most strongly with faculty publication rates. The program ratings by deans, directors, and senior faculty were more closely correlated with the U.S. News rankings than those of the students and practitioners were, although there were some striking differences for individual schools: Programs *not* in the

U.S. News top ten that students ranked in the top ten included Smith College and the University of Pennsylvania, and programs *not* in the top ten that practitioners ranked in the top ten (including ties) included Smith College, Case Western Reserve, the University of Illinois at Urbana-Champaign, CUNY / Hunter College, the University of Kansas, and New York University. Whether focusing on the overall correlations or on the discrepancies between students' and practitioners' rankings and academics' rankings, this analysis can be read as either support for the validity of the *U.S. News* ranking system or a reason for skepticism.

ASSESSING STUDENTS

Whatever a school's accreditation status and the overall ranking, assessing students' learning and graduates' accomplishments is considered central to accountability (Crisp and Lister 2002). Student performance based on grade point average has always been part of gatekeeping in educational programs, but the usefulness of grades is quite limited, and grade inflation is a widespread problem. Palomba and Banta (2001) define assessment as "the systematic collection, review, and use of information about educational programs undertaken for the purpose of improving student learning and development" (13). According to this perspective, grades might figure in a course's or program's "pass rate," but they would count as educational assessment only if grading outcomes as a whole were analyzed and used as feedback to improve program or teaching practices.

Brown (1997) observed that assessing students has both developmental and judgmental aspects affecting their right to continue their course of study, and students tend to focus on the latter. Therefore,

> assessment defines what students regard as important, how they spend their time and how they come to see themselves as students and as graduates. Students take their cues from what is assessed rather than from what [teachers] assert is important. Put rather starkly, *if you want to change student learning then change the methods of assessment*. (Brown 1997:7, italics in original)

Assessment is a powerful but underutilized tool for both enhancing professional development and shaping a whole educational program, but assessment is usually carried out by traditional methods (e.g., individually produced written papers and/or pencil-and-paper examinations in courses), rather than through the hard work of thinking about what to assess and how best to do it.

Methods of assessing student classroom work, in particular, need more attention (Crisp and Lister 2002).

AUDIENCES FOR ASSESSMENT

The calls for accountability in higher education suggest larger audiences for assessment: legislators who fund public higher education; donors who help support public and private colleges and universities; prospective students and their families seeking and faced with paying for quality undergraduate and graduate education; alumni invested in the prestige of the institutions from which they obtained their credentials; and, in the end, the general public. College and university administrators seek reasons to invest (or not) in specific programs and units on their campuses. Accrediting bodies, charged with maintaining minimum standards on behalf of this public interest, stress accountability for outcomes.

Perhaps the most important audiences for educational assessment are the most immediate ones—teachers and students—whereas the audiences just listed are generally more concerned with outcome or summative assessments. Teachers and students can and should use assessments not just to ensure that educational goals are being met but also to inform their own efforts to learn and to teach well, that is, for formative as well as summative and for developmental as well as judgmental purposes. Assessing education does require work, and making assessments meaningful and useful is the only way to ensure that this work is actually carried out and used.

STANDARDIZED MEASURES

Some people in higher education advocate using standardized instruments to assess educational experiences and outcomes. They suggest standardized instruments in part to take advantage of the work of people experienced in and knowledgeable about measurement and instrument construction (see, e.g., the SAT used in college admissions or the GRE used by graduate programs) and in part because they provide a common metric for comparing institutions and programs as well as for giving programs information about areas of strength and weakness in comparison with others. When discipline-specific accreditation requires outcome assessment, as it does in social work (Baskind, Shank, and Ferraro 2001), it encourages the development of assessment methods and tools, both those specific to a program and the standardized ones that many programs might employ.

Some social work educators have actually developed and begun using a standardized approach to assess baccalaureate social work education programs: the Baccalaureate Educational Assessment Package (BEAP, http://beap.socwk.utah.edu/; and see Buchan et al. 2004, 2007). The system has six elements or instruments: an entrance survey and a pretest of knowledge of social work values, both of which should be administered when a student declares a social work major; an exit survey and a social work values posttest given to students at graduation; and an alumni/alumnae survey and an employer survey that alumni/ae administer to their employers. The survey instruments are administered to students and graduates by each participating BSW program, and the surveys are scored and findings by program (along with overall data for comparison) are reported by a national center. In 2001, about 30 percent of BSW programs in the United States were using one or more parts of this system (Buchan et al. 2004:246).

Buchan and colleagues (2004) reported on the development and first years of use of the BEAP measurement package. The content of survey items covers most areas of accreditation-mandated program objectives at the baccalaureate level except for critical thinking (247). While the system contains many of the characteristics considered desirable for educational assessment, including acceptable psychometric properties (249–250), it lacks others, such as the ability to tailor the instruments to the specific program mission and the ability to capture directly (rather than by self-report) the practice skills of students or client outcomes, the latter two being the outcomes most difficult to capture in any system. While the BEAP has the capacity to assess changes in students' knowledge in one curriculum area—social work ethics and values—there have been problems with locating graduates at the planned two-year-post-graduation data collection point, and contact with employers at this point is necessarily indirect, thus compromising response rates for this part of the system. Despite these acknowledged shortcomings, which the BEAP developers are working with programs to remedy, the BEAP system is a commendable effort by the profession to develop and implement a standardized system of educational program assessment that can be used *formatively* to monitor and improve programs and *summatively* to report on program outcomes, such as graduates' employment rates and employers' satisfaction with them.

Another standardized measure of knowledge in undergraduate social work is the Area Concentration Achievement Test (ACAT) (Project for Area Concentration Achievement Testing 1997, for social work majors, http://www.collegeoutcomes.com/ACATS/socwork.htm). This examination has three versions and is available online and in a paper-and-pencil format. The ACAT system allows for the addition of individualized (program-specific) items along with standardized ones. As of 2007, the fields in which this system was used most often are psychology, social work, political science (under revision), biology, and criminal justice. Noble and Stretch (2002), who used this examination in their study of student self-evaluation as affected by GPA, reported that the ACAT system for social work has been used in more than 250 colleges and universities in the United States.

Although there are two standardized examination systems for baccalaureate education in social work, none has been developed for the MSW level. Outcomes on state licensing examinations may be thought to be equivalent, but as Noble and Stretch—who advocate a standardized examination at the graduate level—pointed out, social work has the highest pass rate and the lowest required passing score on licensing examinations among the helping professions (2002:229).

CULTURAL COMPETENCE

Given the ever-increasing diversity of U.S. society, social work programs want their students and graduates to have knowledge and skills in cultural competence, or antioppressive practice. Krentzman and Townsend (2008) comprehensively reviewed nineteen instruments measuring cultural competence in disciplines close to social work, evaluating the content of the scales and their psychometric properties (e.g., reliability and validity) and their suitability for social work. This article is an excellent resource for faculty and programs who may wish to assess this aspect of student learning.

WHAT TO ASSESS   The first step in assessing students and graduates is developing "statements of what graduates should know, be able to do, and value . . . often called 'expected learning outcomes' or 'expected competencies'" (Palomba and Banta 2001:13). These often are listed for graduates of the program as a whole and then broken down for program components, such as specific courses or the field internship. Social work has long touted knowledge, skills, and values, which include professional ethical standards, as what students must learn.

Current accreditation processes in social work, as in higher education as a whole, are moving to mission-driven models of assessing learning outcomes, including student learning, and in 1992, the standards included such a model for evaluating programs that emphasized this. For the individual teacher thinking about assessing students, this means locating the course or

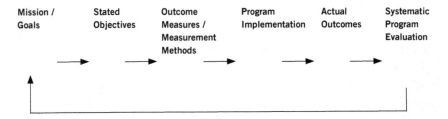

FIGURE 7.2 The Council on Social Work Education's model of program assessment (Holloway, n.d.).

other learning experience (e.g., field internship) as an element of the total program being implemented and specifying the program objectives being met through that specific course (figure 7.2). Based on the course or field-learning objectives, outcome and other assessment measures should be chosen because they give feedback to the student and the instructor about what the student has achieved.

Perhaps the most important elements in figure 7.2 are "Systematic program evaluation," or monitoring, and the arrow that connects this evaluation to the program's mission, goals, assessment methods, and implementation (curriculum). This process means that assessment outcomes must be shared with relevant audiences, and in turn, deliberations on this information must be used to affirm or alter a program's stated mission and objectives, refine the measurement methods if needed, and, especially, to consider whether the program needs to be implemented differently, in either the classroom (courses or teaching methods) or the internship. Of course, other changes are also possible, such as in admissions or graduation standards, requirements or prerequisites, the structures of study, gatekeeping practices, or student advising. While this part of the process may be the most important, it is not always documented and not even always carried out. Without it, however, the real goal of assessment—improvement in learning and teaching—will not be achieved.

Professional education in social work has long been conceptualized as learning the knowledge, skills, and values, ethics, and norms of professional behavior. Assessing student *knowledge* often relies on traditional methods like examinations and oral or written papers and reports. Changes in levels of knowledge usually are measured only for a specific study of a new course or of a teaching method, often with the eventual publication of findings in mind, meaning that the areas of knowledge assessed are generally specific to the educational innovation being studied. Some of my own research with colleagues suggests that pre- and post-assessments of student learning can be valuable and that tools to assess broad areas of student knowledge about practice should be developed (Holden et al. 2002; Holden, Anastas, and Meenaghan 2003).

Values and ethics can be assessed, as the BEAP and licensing examinations do, in terms of knowledge about them. How well students and graduates have absorbed them and especially how well they can deal with ethical dilemmas in actual practice situations have not been assessed except through field instructors' and faculty–field liaisons' assessments of students based on their work in the internship. Some research has looked at social workers' professional ethics and problematic behaviors based on complaints to the NASW (see, e.g., Strom-Gottfried 1999a, 1999b, 2000a, 2000b). There also has been a little research on social work educators' self-reported ethical beliefs and practices in the area of dual relationships (Congress 2001) and authorship (Apgar and Congress 2005). But there are no published studies of outcomes for teaching ethics in social work.

Skills, or practice *behaviors*—the application of knowledge and ethics to complex and diverse cases—are the most difficult to assess. Using Bloom's taxonomy of knowledge, taking classroom knowledge and understanding into the field internship or practice setting and *analyzing* clients' problems and needs, *applying* that knowledge to practice with real clients, and *evaluating* and perhaps reanalyzing the work with each case or in each session call for higher-order thinking skills (Anderson and Krathwohl 2001). Traditional ways of assessing practice knowledge, including knowledge about ethics, often rely simply on recall and similar lower-order thinking. For this reason, case study methods—whether based on students' own cases or cases supplied by the instructor—are widely used in teaching about practice. Field instructors and others, like supervisors, routinely render subjective and nonstandardized judgments of students' skills and offer feedback, often very useful, on areas for students and graduates to improve. The systematic assessment of practice skills remains the area of greatest challenge for social work education and the profession as a whole.

WHO ASSESSES

TEACHERS Traditional models of educational assessment assume that the assessment that matters is what the teachers (the experts) think of a student's performance. After all, professors are responsible for designing the instructional program (the curriculum) to ensure that all students have the opportunity to learn everything essential to professional social work practice at the

BSW or MSW level. Each student must fulfill all curricular requirements (pass all courses and complete all required internship activities satisfactorily) as specified by the faculty as a whole and as evaluated on an individual basis by their instructors. These aspects of assessment—further guided by external requirements, primarily the discipline's accreditation standards—are part of any professional program's gatekeeping responsibilities, which later are confirmed by state licensing and regulation. Assessing students by grading alone or by reporting a program's pass, graduation, or attrition rates is now considered necessary but not sufficient.

STUDENTS Theories of adult learning stress the importance of self-direction and the capacity for self-reflection (see chapter 2). CSWE's accreditation standards (CSWE 2008) require being able to be self-critical and to evaluate one's own practice, meaning both practice processes and outcomes. For these reasons, students and graduates should assess their own learning, as well as the teaching and other aspects of the education they have received.

Although the familiar course questionnaires are used primarily to assess teaching, they usually contain items requiring students to reflect on themselves, such as how much they learned, how much effort they put into the course, and how much they initially wanted to enroll in the course. These items are most often used to place in context students' collective evaluations of their courses and teachers, but they do offer an opportunity for self-reflection. More meaningful are the surveys administered upon the program's completion, which sometimes have versions given at program's beginning, in order to determine change before and after. Some surveys intended for undergraduate social work majors are standardized (e.g., ACAT, BEAP) whereas others are tailored to the specific content of a program's curriculum. While these "home-grown" measures have high face validity with respect to the curricular content of the particular program in which they are used, their psychometric properties are generally unknown (see, e.g., Noble and Stretch 2002).

Some in social work education, myself included, have used a self-efficacy framework to develop students' self-assessment questionnaires to measure before-and-after changes in self-perceptions of knowledge and skill (Holden, Anastas, and Meenaghan 2003, 2005; Holden et al. 2002). While self-efficacy measures are self-reports, a long research tradition based on Bandura's work in cognitive psychology documented a moderate correlation between self-efficacy measures and actual performances independently assessed. Holden and colleagues (1999, 2007, 2008) also used this technique to assess research learning specifically. One benefit of self-efficacy measurement techniques is that they can be anchored to universal criteria, such as the CSWE statements of foundation social work practice competencies (Holden, Anastas, and Meenaghan 2003, 2005), and to "local" or program-specific learning objectives. Holloway (n.d.) specifically mentions the use of self-efficacy measurement techniques as promising and feasible for measuring educational outcome.

A common criticism of students' self-assessments is that they can result in an overappraisal of achievements and capacities. In a complex small-scale study, Noble and Stretch (2002) examined the effects of GPA on undergraduate students' appraisals of their knowledge of generalist practice. The study found that an assigned GPA had a moderate relationship to students' self-appraisals, which, they argued, was evidence of one harmful effect of grade inflation. Noble and Stretch were also able to draw interesting conclusions by comparing areas of self-assessment and finding, for example, that self-assessments of practice skill were less strongly affected by GPA than those in policy and research, which are more traditionally "academic." My studies with colleagues using self-efficacy–based self-assessment measures have been similarly useful for examining pretest, then-test, and posttest changes and for determining the areas of students' greatest confidence and change as well as their areas of least confidence (e.g., evaluating their own practice) or in which they had changed the least from program entry to graduation.

PEERS   Having students take on the hard work of evaluating one another's work, based on cooperative learning models, is often suggested as a way for students to develop self-assessment skills, to learn and internalize the standards by which their own work is being evaluated, and to prepare for working in teams and supervising (Lemieux 2002). Making this activity reciprocal is necessary to prevent students from becoming too critical of one another. Accordingly, they might assess each other in pairs, one reading and commenting on the other's paper. Peer assessment can be used as a form of feedback that does not actually count in the grade for the course but is designed to show work in progress. It also is possible to offer the instructor's feedback in addition to peers' critiques, and sometimes students can even be evaluated by the instructor on their evaluation of a peer's work. How peer assessment techniques are used also depends on the course's learning goals. For example, if one activity in a practice class is to present a case to develop skills in assessment, treatment planning, and the use of consultation, students could apply the same skills to others' cases and learn from this how to give useful feedback to colleagues.

In trying to use peer assessment in social work courses, I have encountered resistance from students, which I have interpreted in part as wanting to "get one's money's worth" for a course by getting the feedback of the "true" expert, the instructor. Some of this resistance may also stem from the realization that it is hard work to develop insight into the quality of someone else's work and to communicate that insight constructively, especially when it is not positive. It may also reflect that students can depend on teachers' ethical commitment to fairness and the like (see chapter 9) and may not believe that they and their peers have the same commitment. A common problem is that students are reluctant to mention any fault in a colleague's work, perhaps to protect their supportive social relationships.

GRADUATES A commonly used technique in program evaluation is asking social work graduates to evaluate their experiences as students and to share their perceptions of the usefulness of their education based on their subsequent work experiences. While response rates to surveys of graduates are sometimes low, even the self-reported employment rate of recent graduates and the nature of the professional (or other) work they are doing are useful information. As noted earlier, reports from state licensing boards on the percentage of a school's graduates passing licensing examinations are another source of information on graduates' performance in the field. Some programs and schools have used focus groups of recent graduates and/or employers of graduates as sources of detailed information on the strengths and weaknesses of program graduates and the areas of satisfaction and discontent expressed by graduates themselves.

OTHERS Finally, the stakeholders in educational assessment go beyond teachers and learners to include college and university administrators; funders of and donors to programs, colleges, and universities; the general public; internship sites and employers of graduates; the profession as a whole; and, especially, the people served by students and graduates (Gambrill 2002; Noble and Stretch 2002). While methods to include clients' outcomes in what social work educators can realistically assess have not yet been fully developed, feedback on students, qualitative or quantitative, individual or collective, from such key informants as internship agency personnel and employers of graduates can be incorporated into program assessment systems, as the BEAP system does with employers. In another example, Green and colleagues' (2006) study of the rankings of top graduate schools in social work incorporated ratings of program reputation from the perspectives of a sample of social work practitioners ("the profession") and students, finding that academics and practitioners often, but not always, evaluated programs similarly.

HOW TO ASSESS How best to assess students' learning and practice skill depends entirely, of course, on what you are measuring and what may be feasible to do. Both quantitative and qualitative data can be useful in educational assessment.

Paper-and-pencil measures, such as survey instruments, are the most commonly used techniques in educational assessment because they are the easiest way to gather data from the largest number of people. The multiple-choice questions used in quizzes and examinations also are well known and widely used examples of paper-and-pencil assessment techniques. Especially in the classroom, short, open-ended written statements from students about their learning can be a useful source of information about a class session or course. Statements can be collected in class on index cards, posted electronically on an electronic course "site," or e-mailed directly to the instructor. Students should be allowed to refuse to comment and also should understand that their comments will not used outside the immediate teaching context except in a formal, research-based evaluation of the course and if they have given formal permission to participate in such research.

Written papers are one of the most common ways to evaluate and grade students' learning. These can be research-based papers or essays on personal or professional experiences, case summaries, analyses of social policies or organizational practices, or even journals. Sometimes a group of students working together on a project can write a report together, although group papers raise some special issues in student evaluation when they are used to grade individuals.

Graded written assignments should reflect the course's learning objectives. For example, if developing the habit of and capacity for self-reflection is a goal, keeping a journal or another form of personal essay might be a useful assignment. Similarly, since writing case summaries or progress notes is often a part of professional practice, a practice course or field internship might require them. It even can be useful to write memoranda and other forms of interprofessional communication, with feedback on how to make such documents more effective.

Social workers are concerned, as are those in other fields, about students' writing skills (Rompf 1995). Campus-based centers often are available where students (and faculty) can go for help in improving their writing skills, although the services of these centers sometimes are overwhelmed. Some social work programs have therefore developed in-house mechanisms for students to obtain writing help. Problems in writing, however, are often hard to separate from problems of knowledge or thinking, making the boundary between the teacher's and the writing teacher's job sometimes difficult to determine.

Oral performance, although not called by this name, is another method used in student assessment. Examples are class presentations and oral presentations of cases in either the classroom or the agency (field learning). Usually, this kind of work is judged on its content, but if the goal is to help students make effective presentations, it also is useful to evaluate oral presentations on clarity of speech, the use of visual or other aids for the audience, and other "performance" factors. As with written work, all the criteria on which students' oral presentations will be evaluated should be made known to them in advance.

Observation. Since practice is a set of skills and behaviors, *direct observation* of students' interactions with the people they are serving would seem the most logical way to evaluate their practice. Family therapy has long incorporated team observational methods into its training and practice, and social work students may therefore encounter *formative* evaluation through observation in some of their field education, that is, situations in which they are given feedback from observers based on one-way mirror or videotaped work. Role-playing in the practice classroom is another way in which instructors and peers can offer students feedback. Schools and departments of social work may (or may not) have "labs" in which students can be observed in role-playing or other practice encounters. The immediacy of the feedback here is particularly helpful.

Despite the logical and intuitive appeal of these assessment methods, no published report that I know of examines what has been learned in this way regarding students' strengths and weaknesses *in general* or how that information might affect social work's educational standards or curriculum. Unlike grading and examination scores, which have been studied for their (limited) predictive validity for the workplace, we do not know whether or not such student evaluations can predict on-the-job performance.

Since the inception of social work education, a "proxy" method of observation—the *process recording*—has been widely used in the field internship (Neuman and Friedman 1997; Ortiz Hendricks, Finch, and Franks 2005; Urdang 1979; Walsh 2002). As Ortiz Hendricks, Finch, and Franks (2005) noted, the traditional verbatim record, written based on recall after the fact, lies on a continuum of session recording methods from a verbal summary given to a supervisor through audio or video recordings and even one-way mirror observation. Formats for process recording generally describe the interaction and provide a space in which to record students' comments on the interaction after the fact and a space for the instructor's feedback. While Mumm's (2006) study suggests that process recordings are not so widely used in field education and are not viewed as very helpful by students, Knight (2000) found that it was how, rather than how often, process recordings were used that mattered.

Some argue that process recordings are still used in social work education because they are inexpensive (although time-consuming), whereas others argue that they teach important skills of recall, writing, and self-reflection, despite their possible inaccuracies. It is also an unobtrusive measure, unlike audio and video recording, and better protects clients' confidentiality. Some people recommend structuring the recording in various ways, to draw students' attention to specific issues, like affective versus cognitive responses to the interview content, to specific phases of the work, or to specific issues like clients' strengths (Neuman and Friedman 1997; Walsh 2002).

What students learn from process recordings depends greatly on the feedback they receive, which entails the field instructor's analyzing the recording and considering when various issues should be raised with each student (Ortiz Hendricks, Finch, and Franks 2005). Students make their best recordings and most productive reflection when they trust the student–teacher relationship and when the burden of doing them does not discourage their careful preparation. Perhaps for this reason, process recordings are generally used in formative rather than summative student evaluations, even though what students' process evaluation show about the quality of their work with clients is part of what field instructors take into account when rating or grading their field performance overall. Finally, unlike case interactions or role-playing used in the classroom, written process recordings are more permanent documents that can be revisited over time and/or compared with later recordings, when advances in skill are expected. However process recordings are used in student evaluation, the *process* is meant to instill in students the commitment to self-reflection in their practice.

STANDARDIZED CASES Evaluating students' performance in actual cases has disadvantages. One is that the cases students encounter in the internship vary greatly in complexity and other characteristics. One solution has been to standardize the cases that students are presented when assessing their skills. In the past this effort has been aimed at developing written case studies that students are asked to analyze, but the exercise then becomes one of paper-and-pencil. As we know, a written case study is not likely to elicit the personal reactions in a professional that a videotape (or even a photographic image) does, and managing these reactions is an important part of professional practice in both assessment and intervention. All kinds of useful information, like "body language" and other aspects of appearance, also are lost in written evaluations.

The literature on the use of standardized cases in social work practice classes, as both a teaching tool (formative) and a possible outcome measure of students' practice skills, is growing (Badger and MacNeil 2002; Mooradian 2007, 2008; Petracchi 1999; Petrachi and Collins 2006). While this method builds on traditional in-class role-playing, the use of standardized cases is complicated. First, realistic scenarios (case situations) must be devised that include content on the assessment and treatment issues that students must show that they can address but that are ambiguous enough to be challenging. When assessing advanced graduate students' family practice skills, Mooradian (2008) prepared scenarios involving marital conflict over sexual intimacy and conflict between adolescents and parents. The performers (often theater or acting students) also had to be able to improvise as they interacted with the student interviewers. The students' interactions with these "clients" must be then be judged. After the event, talking with those taking the role of the therapist and/or with those simply observing these interactions is essential to maximizing students' learning, to point out both what went well and where improvement is needed. Because of the expenses in time, labor, and dollars of assessing students in this way, the social work studies of using standardized cases have been of students observing and commenting on tapes of these interactions. Students reportedly find the experience—both being a simulated "treater" and observing simulated case interactions—realistic, "better than role-plays," and an effective method of learning practice skills. Obviously, this method of assessment prevents the threats to privacy in taping interactions with real service users.

Videotapes of interviews with clients can be shown in the classroom or on the Web, and students can be asked for written assessments of them or written "treatment plans." The student's interaction—the ability to ask the right question to get the information needed in assessment or skills in connecting affectively—cannot be assessed as reliably in this way as it can if a student takes the part of the practitioner in a simulated case scenario. The student's "body language" and other ways of reacting to the client are lost as well. But the ability to analyze the practice behavior of others and to formulate approaches to assessment and intervention based on real cases can be examined in this way, as when students observe and comment on simulated case interactions that they view in the classroom. The opportunity to observe different students or clinicians interacting with the same (or similar) clients, real or simulated, can also suggest new or improved approaches to the students who view them. The most common obstacle to using real clients, however, is the legal and ethical need to ensure that consent is obtained and the client's privacy is safeguarded in ways conforming to current HIPPA regulations.

Because of these problems and the promise of using simulated cases, medicine and related fields such as nursing have raised the assessment of students' skills in "patient" interactions to a very sophisticated level through the OSCE (Observed Structured Case Evaluation) methodology (Baez 2005). Two dimensions of the students' interactions with the simulated client are assessed: the *content* of what was done (Was all the relevant information elicited? Was any assessment or treatment recommendation made correct/ defensible?) and the *manner* in which the interaction was conducted — body language, service user's comfort level, and the like. One feature of the OSCE procedure that was apparently not included in the social work studies of using simulated cases published so far was the absence of feedback from both the simulated service recipient and the faculty observer/rater to the student being assessed, that is, comments on how it *felt* to have been interviewed. This assessment of clinical skill is being used in formative (as a teaching tool) and summative (for passing a clinical course, being relicensed) student evaluation in these other fields, and there has been an extensive literature on its use since the 1970s.

Baez (2005) reported on a federally funded interdisciplinary project (medicine, nursing, and social work) in which the OSCE was used both to evaluate students' skills in screening for substance abuse problems in a range of client situations and to give students individual feedback on how they could improve their work in this area. Whatever the practice skill to be assessed, a valid OSCE procedure requires enough cases/scenarios/"stations" to adequately sample the variety of client situations and problem areas that the prospective practitioners are likely to encounter. The amount of time interacting with each simulated patient can also vary, depending on the actual practice (e.g., shorter client encounters in emergency medicine, longer encounters in psychiatry). Social work students who participated in Baez's project found the experience to be excellent for learning, despite the performance anxiety generated. Even though student actors (rather than professionals) were used as standardized clients in this project, the expense of developing scenarios and implementing the student assessments was such that it was possible to do only with grant support. Having observed this OSCE project in action, I was impressed with it for student assessments, and the extensive literature on the

OSCE methodology has established its reliability and validity. Whether targeted at generic skills in assessment and intervention or at specialty practice areas, as in the substance abuse area described by Baez (2005), the profession must decide whether it can or should invest in developing this kind of technology in response to the need for greater accountability for its educational outcomes (Gambrill 2001; Holden et al. 2002).

PORTFOLIOS Although not wholly based on cases, an innovative method to assess learning is *portfolios,* collections of works that also are analyzed (self-reflection) for what they reveal about learning (Moran 1997:chap. 6). Students might select assignments completed for various courses or in their field internship, perhaps from the beginning of their educational program through those completed later on, and then analyze and reflect on their content and the changes in their skill level or complexity of understanding of an issue. Reports of portfolios used in last-term, "integrative" courses or as required capstone projects (Schatz 2004; Spicuzza 2000) and in field education (Risler 1999; Schatz and Simon 1999) have been published. Fitch and colleagues (2008) discussed the use of e-portfolios, meaning the use of available software for developing and recording students' portfolio materials.

Whether or not the medium used is electronic, several elements of the process are necessary for its usefulness as a teaching and evaluative tool. One is that the portfolio requirement should be introduced to students early in the educational process being assessed, for two reasons. The first is that students' "products" from the beginning of the program are often compared with those produced later. The second is that thinking about learning outcomes at the outset often helps students clarify their learning goals and select or develop the best "end products" for inclusion in their portfolio. Any parameters for what is required to be included should be clear as well.

The advantages of using portfolios for grading purposes are that students can choose which pieces of work to include and that the assessment does not depend on any single product. Sometimes a portfolio evaluation can contain more than one person's assessment (e.g., by a committee), which, although a time-consuming process, can also reduce the hazards of having only one grader/evaluator. Most of all, portfolios ask students to reflect on their performance, determine their progress, and identify areas to work on in future (McKeachie and Svinicki 2006).

When a portfolio is compiled to evaluate teaching, Sidell (2003) observed that students' learning is a major focus. For example, Sidell's teaching portfolio included students' weekly comments on what they had learned in each class and her reflections on them. Portfolios might even be substituted for major (comprehensive) examinations in doctoral programs in social work (Thyer 1993).

Portfolios are apparently not yet widely used in social work education, perhaps because there require considerable work to evaluate and provide feedback. This kind of assessment tool has advantages over and above the usual assessment work, like grading students' work for each course, as integration of areas of study often is emphasized. The practice shows great promise, however, especially because it encourages students to self-reflect and incorporates the idea that whatever has been achieved, learning should continue.

GRADING Whatever the logic and methods guiding the assessment of students' learning, the traditional method of grading remains central to virtually all social work education, even if that grading system for some or all courses is a version of the pass/fail system. Grading is such a universal experience for students and teachers that even "pass–fail" systems are operationally defined using grades (e.g., a "marginal pass" is equivalent to a grade of "C," and a "P" at the graduate level is equivalent to A or B). Grading separates the helping function of teaching, which is fairly comfortable and familiar to social workers who become academics, from the authority and power aspects of the teaching role. The responsibility of assigning grades is a common source of anxiety for beginning teachers, in part because they are more used to being graded and in part because they may have an intuitive or realistic sense of the broad social ramifications and hence the perils of making academic judgments (for a complex and convincing analysis of the social sorting functions of educational institutions and practices, see Bourdieu 1990, 1996; Costello 2005).

Finally, as Hu (2005) demonstrated, problems in the grading system in U.S. colleges and universities are grade inflation and disparities in grading across different fields. Grades are designed to evaluate, communicate, and motivate honestly, but when the system is distorted, they are compromised. The research on grades, student characteristics, and grading practices over time is complicated. Sadly, however, there may now be an unspoken "disengagement contract" between teachers, who need to put more time and effort into scholarship than into student evaluations, and students, who need good grades to qualify for scholarship aid and graduate school but who are working and facing other pressures, making maximal academic effort difficult. Changes in the grading policies and practices of academic institutions are likely necessary to restore more integrity to the grading system.

Most of the advice to individual teachers about assigning grades does not pertain to the grading system itself but is designed to make the "rules of the game" as transparent as possible to both students and teachers (see, e.g., Gibelman and Gelman 2001a; McKeachie and Svinicki 2006:chap. 11). This practice is sometimes referred to as developing a *rubric* for assessment so that students know what they will be evaluated on when they begin their work. Aviles (2001) argued for "criterion-referenced" grading rather than grading on a curve, that is, for performance standards determined by the instructor that most students can achieve. Student handbooks should contain the program's and/or college's or university's definitions of each grade level (e.g., "A" indicating excellence and/or outstanding work), and these definitions should also be made available to all the evaluators (instructors) who will be assigning grades to students.

While grading contains some unavoidably subjective elements, part of the academic freedom of college and university teachers is their right to evaluate (grade) students as they see fit as long as they follow due process and are not biased. Although students are free to complain to an instructor about a grade or to ask that a grade be changed, teachers are free not to honor such requests. Departments, schools, and colleges or universities, however, always have some way for students to make a formal complaint if they are alleging bias or some other problem in how a grade was given. Simply wishing for another opinion or outcome, however, is not sufficient cause for such a complaint to be heard.

ASSESSING FIELD LEARNING

It has long been recognized that the simple assignment of a grade does not provide sufficiently detailed and meaningful information about a student's performance in the field. Much of the early literature on student assessment and evaluation in social work concerned field learning (see, e.g., Gitterman and Gitterman 1979; Pease 1988), and social work programs have methods to provide feedback to students on multiple aspects of their performance in the field, in part to model professional educational processes that should continue after graduation as well. When professional development and performance in real-world settings are at issue, evaluation should be "longitudinal, contextualized, and collaborative" (Scanlon and Ford 1998:104).

Assessment of student learning in the field needs further development (Raskin, Wayne, and Bogo 2008), especially as social work accreditation standards now add students' *behaviors* to the usual description of knowledge, values, and skills as goals or outcomes of social work education that should be assessed (CSWE 2008). Efforts to improve the assessment of students' practice skills, as through the use of standardized cases, would seem relevant to the internship as well (Risler 1999; Schatz and Simon 1999).

GATEKEEPING

Social work programs have a responsibility to promote students' learning and also to confer professional degrees on only those who can meet the academic and personal performance standards necessary for informed and ethical practice. While postdegree licensing procedures are designed to protect the public, graduation from a CSWE-accredited social work program is a precondition for obtaining a license in the United States. Gatekeeping therefore remains a core responsibility for programs, and programs usually have procedures for dismissing a student, providing a "second opinion" process that goes beyond any single instructor's judgment (Cowburn, Nelson, and Williams 2000). For example, if an instructor were concerned about a student's poor performance in the classroom or the field internship, he or she might not give the student a failing grade if it could lead to dismissal from a program. In actual practice, however, when a student is marginal or failing, usually no one instructor's grade alone can result in dismissal from a program without a deliberative group process.

Legally and in educational practice, professional programs have the right and the responsibility to judge students' performance in areas including but not limited to traditional academics (Urwin, Van Soest, and Kretzschmar 2006). Lack of selectivity in admissions, other demands placed on faculty that make spending time on student performance issues undesirable, and pressures on programs to maintain enrollments have been some of the factors bringing gatekeeping issues to the fore in recent years (Urwin, Van Soest, and Kretzschmar 2006). Even so, social work programs have the right to "determine the suitability" of those seeking a professional degree, especially because clients' rights and safety are implicated.

To avoid unnecessary problems, effective gatekeeping procedures must have a number of characteristics: explicitly stated criteria for students' performance in the classroom and the field; a system for communicating information to students about deficiencies in their performance with a chance for improving them (including re-review); students' grievance procedures to correct for any prejudicial evaluation; and, at all steps in the process, due notice, written documentation of concerns and decisions, clear and direct communication with affected students, and safeguards for students' privacy (Cole and Lewis 1993; Urwin, Van Soest, and Kretzschmar 2006). These procedures are designed to balance the promotion of student learning with professional safeguards, faculty autonomy in evaluative judgment of students' rights, and individual faculty perceptions of students and situations with those of peers and others. A final key issue is administrative support for those faculty members and faculty groups who make the hard decisions about some students. This must be balanced, of course, with safeguarding students' rights to due process. Admissions decisions and faculty judgments about students' performance are imperfect, but there is no right to program admission or program completion; these are privileges that must be earned.

ASSESSING TEACHING

The focus of accreditation efforts has turned to "outputs" (student learning) rather than "inputs," such as the quality of the teaching and other educational resources that support students' learning. Nevertheless, the assessment of teaching remains an important factor in faculty tenure and promotion decisions as well as in more routine evaluation of the quality of their work, as in annual performance and merit reviews. The most common measure of faculty teaching is the essentially universal use of *students' course satisfaction questionnaires*, whose results are also usually used in tenure and promotion decisions. *Teaching portfolios* and *peer observation in the classroom* are two other measures used in tenure and promotion decisions. Whether or not a formal teaching portfolio is prepared, course and/or curriculum development work, efforts to refresh teaching, and how scholarship informs teaching also constitute information about teaching quality beyond students' opinions.

FORMATIVE FEEDBACK IN THE CLASSROOM

A universally recognized "best practice" in teaching is checking in with students early and often when teaching a course. Feedback can be sought through class discussion ("Let's take a few minutes to hear any comments you may have on how the course is going so far"). Asking for both what students like and what they don't like or might like to see changed is useful. Students can also hand in written comments or be invited to post them to a course

Web site. If comments are elicited and submitted outside the class session, the teacher should bring his or her comments to class so that students will know they were "heard." If the requested changes cannot be made, they should know why. This formative feedback can permit useful "midcourse corrections" and can remedy a specific course section that has become unproductive. While the time taken for this process can be seen as reducing the time needed to cover course content, the teacher's willingness to consider the students' point of view and suggestions for changes in how the course is being taught ensures that more will actually be learned.

STUDENT SATISFACTION QUESTIONNAIRES

Having students complete questionnaires describing their (dis)satisfaction with their courses and classroom instructors, in class on paper or online, has become universal in higher education. Often these instruments are adopted across campus, with the option to customize or add items in different departments. Ratings from these instruments are widely used in social work for faculty and course development and also in tenure and promotion decisions (Jirovec, Ramanathan, and Alvarez 1998; Wolfer and Johnson 2003). Although instructors often regard the ratings from these instruments with suspicion, Pike's (1998) study of a specific social work questionnaire found that it reliably identified the most capable teachers but not always the least capable ones. In Wolfer and Johnson's study using the "overall" rating from the same social work instrument, however, there was so little variation in satisfaction (everyone was in the "A" range) that no correlates of students' satisfaction except the instructor gender (women were rated more highly) were found. Overall, these instruments were found to consistently identify important correlates of what students and professionals viewed as important elements of effective instruction, such as treating students with respect, and were not much influenced by confounding factors, like grades given, that often make low-rated instructors want to dismiss them.

As in other fields, Jirovec, Ramanathan, and Alvarez (1998) found in a social work study that instructors' abilities to organize course content effectively, provide prompt feedback and have clear grading policies, and develop rapport with students were strongly correlated with global ratings of teaching skills. Ratings differed by course content area but not in the direction expected, suggesting that skilled instructors can succeed when students are not initially so eager to take the course (policy versus practice in the particular setting studied). Conversely, instructors teaching elective courses did get higher ratings than on the required courses in this study, so the authors recommended that views of the ratings of tenure candidates who teach mainly required courses be tempered by this information. Giving individual instructors information about how their ratings compare with the averages for others teaching sections of the same course or courses in the same content area (e.g., research or practice, other electives) can help them place their ratings in context and may reduce the tendency to "explain away" low ratings. But Wolfer and Johnson (2003) rightly warned that "above or below average" scores may differ in decimal points only to a degree that does not reflect anything but measurement error. In addition, even the best and/or most experienced teachers occasionally encounter a course section in which things do not go very well from the students' point of view. What is important is not that one set of course ratings shows less than outstanding student satisfaction; it is how the instructor responds to them: defensively, by blaming students, courses, or colleagues (the others grade too leniently, the others pander to popularity, etc.) or constructively, by trying to learn from the experience. Finally, no one has yet found a good way to relate students' satisfaction ratings to how much students have actually *learned* in a course, since we have no way to measure complex learning outcomes validly and feasibly.

TEACHING PORTFOLIOS

Doctoral students beginning a teaching career and full-time teachers renewing their contracts or trying to obtain tenure and/or promotion are often urged to assemble a portfolio documenting their achievements in teaching. A teaching portfolio might contain a statement of teaching philosophy, with the rest of the materials supporting it. New or substantially revised course syllabi often are included; other useful documents are assignments or classroom exercises. Certainly, an innovative use of technologies—videos, Web links or resources, content summaries (e.g., PowerPoint slides and handouts)—belongs in the collection. Students' feedback in a variety of formats (students' satisfaction rating summaries are only one possibility) are important. Like students' portfolios, the effectiveness of a teaching portfolio for evaluating an instructor depends on how the portfolio is structured and will be assessed. Finally, a written statement about the contents developed and assembled is essential. Therefore, even if a portfolio is not a part of the formal evaluation system, it can be useful for a job search or career advancement and for the self-reflection process that is part of best practice in teaching.

TENURE, PROMOTION, AND ANNUAL EVALUATION

Although effective teaching is no longer as important as scholarly productivity to tenure and promotion decisions, it is generally the second most important factor considered. Sometimes "excellence in teaching" is described as a necessary but not a sufficient criterion for promotion and tenure. Therefore, your ability to document success in teaching is important to retaining and advancing in your job. For adjunct instructors, success in teaching is the only criterion affecting retention, with a limited opportunity to document work beyond the standard students' satisfaction questionnaire results.

The effectiveness of your teaching must be documented in the context of your teaching philosophy. When applying for renewal of a contract, at the one- or three-year point before tenure, or for promotion and tenure, you should describe your teaching philosophy, as well as your curriculum development and teaching achievements. As when assembling a teaching portfolio more generally, you should include such materials as classroom exercises developed, new courses designed and delivered and the syllabi describing them, and/or students' comments. Some standard measures, particularly students' satisfaction questionnaire data, are always required. You can use the narrative accompanying these data to address any seeming shortcomings or special successes (i.e., ratings higher than usual for a specific course). In framing the information presented on teaching, remember that readers of the material for tenure and promotion (as opposed to annual or other reviews) come both from within the discipline (department or school) and outside it, so they may not be familiar with social work concepts or jargon.

In most settings, direct observation of teaching is permitted or required only for a tenure decision. Candidates normally have some control over the situation, as when (on what date, during which class session) a classroom visit is permitted, in part so that students can be alerted that a visitor will be present, since they also are being observed. It usually is nerve-racking to be observed, but this is only rarely decisive.

CAMPUS-BASED CENTERS FOR TEACHING

Many campuses now have teaching resource centers for teaching assistants and other faculty members. Many offer one-time or ongoing seminars and workshops, and some have a library of publications and resources like videos. Others even offer individual coaching that may include classroom observation and feedback on it. For performance issues in teaching, the opportunity to improve by using these on-campus resources is generally welcomed.

Annual conferences for social work educators held by the CSWE and BPD provide preconference sessions on teaching techniques and teaching in specific curricular areas as well as sessions throughout the regular program on how and what to teach. These discipline-specific meeting resources can also be helpful as venues in which one's own teaching techniques and curriculum innovations can be disseminated to others. Transforming one's investments in teaching excellence into the scholarship of teaching can be a way to manage the tensions between teaching and scholarly performance.

ASSESSING FIELD INSTRUCTION

Assessing students and teachers in social work education is not confined to the classroom. The field practicum, now termed the *signature pedagogy* in social work (CSWE 2008), has students in practice interact with actual service users in real-world service delivery settings where they are instructed, or "coached," individually and perhaps also in groups, in ethical and effective practice. The language of "field instruction" itself reflects a transition from what used to be an apprenticeship model of "agency internships" to an explicitly educational framework for understanding both students' and field instructors' activities (Bogo 2005). As Bogo and McKnight (2005) noted, field instruction often is still called *supervision*, but what is known about effective supervision for graduate clinicians and students must be considered separately because the supervisor's responsibility to the agency and to effective and ethical service to clients must be balanced with an educational responsibility to students' learning (Bogo 2005). The effectiveness of and students' satisfaction with their field liaisons or academic advisers are areas needing new scholarship, since there is essentially no empirical literature in these areas and because the liaison role is increasingly being relegated to part-time faculty (Wayne, Bogo, and Raskin 2006). Finally, although agency context matters, how contextual factors influence students' learning and/or teaching activities has not yet been studied (Bogo 2005).

EVALUATING STUDENTS' PERFORMANCE Bogo and colleagues (2007) synthesized findings from several studies of their own addressing field instructors' experiences in evaluating students' performance in the field practicum. Giving feedback to students about their performance is a gratifying part of a field instructor's work when students are doing well or are open to learning and use critical feedback to improve their subsequent performance. Just as with grading for class room instructors, however, providing corrective feedback is less comfortable than supporting learners. Field instructors do not always feel supported by social work programs when making negative judgments about students' performance. In addition, working with students with performance problems has been described as very stressful and time-consuming, which again mirrors what classroom teachers say in similar situations. The close personal relationship that develops between student and supervisor is both a necessary medium for conveying corrective feedback constructively and an emotional context that can make the process difficult. Simply put, positive teacher–student relationships are essential to learning and professional growth, but even though strong students can tolerate and use this feedback, it can be challenging to introduce criticism into this relationship when the student is weak, which is when it is most often necessary.

Social work programs are increasingly using quantitative rating scales to guide field instructors' evaluations of students (Bogo 2005). One benefit of using such techniques is that students know ahead of time the specific dimensions of their performance that will be rated. Bogo described four such scales (Bogo et al. 2002; Koroloff and Rhyne 1989; O'Hare, Collins, and Walsh 1998). In addition, a scale based on self-efficacy has also been developed (Fortune et al. 2002; Fortune, Lee, and Cavazos 2005). These represent only those rating scales whose use has been described in published articles in peer-reviewed journals; many if not most social work programs likely have "home-grown" tools. These assessments are completed in the context of the student–instructor relationship, which can compromise their validity in action (Bogo et al. 2007). Regehr and colleagues (2002) reported on a method for students and field instructors to negotiate learning priorities. But as Bogo (2005) pointed out, students' learning outcomes have generally not been studied in relation to the models of field instruction being employed. Nor has there been cross-instrument study and description of the areas in which social work students tend to be more or less strong in their general performance. In sum, these tools have been studied for their validity and utility for making judgments about individual students' performance, but findings from their use have not been mined for information about the social work curriculum content or instructional design more generally.

STUDENTS' SATISFACTION WITH FIELD INSTRUCTION As with students' satisfaction with their course instructors, many departments and schools of social work have standardized forms and procedures for students to provide feedback on their agency internship and field instruction experiences. But since internship learning is not part of the curriculum across campus, these systems, unlike classroom evaluation forms, are usually "home grown" and can be somewhat specific to each setting. In addition, feedback from these evaluations is generally used only for making decisions about individual settings or field instructors, but in the aggregate they can also be useful for guiding programwide curricular and system change.

Bogo and colleagues (2002) subjected their program's student evaluation scale to factor analysis and found stable dimensions related to differential use of self, intervention planning and implementation, empathy and alliance, assessment, values and ethics, and presentation and writing skills. All programs likely assess similar dimensions of students' performance, but not cultural competence and diversity issues (or items). Although Ortiz Hendricks (2003) proposed a theoretical framework for understanding students' progress toward cultural competence in their practice, the assessment of this area of student knowledge and skill remains underdeveloped.

Fortune, Lee, and Cavazos (2005) also studied student ratings of satisfaction with their field education, looking primarily at students' characteristics rather than field instructors' activities. Higher satisfaction with the field experience was most strongly related to the value students placed on the tasks they were performing, their intrinsic motivation to do the work, and their sense of self-efficacy (confidence in their ability to succeed). Interestingly, as with students' course satisfaction ratings and instructors' grades, field instructors' ratings of students' performance were not significantly related to students' satisfaction with the field experience or to any student characteristics other than self-confidence.

Some studies examined the teaching methods used by field instructors and students' satisfaction with them. Mumm (2006) found that discussion of next steps or intervention options, observation of the field instructor to model skills, and the provision of readings were the most common teaching techniques used, with the first two viewed by students as the most helpful. Students also liked the use of "co-counseling" opportunities, although they were less often available. Strozier, Barnett-Queen, and Bennett (2000) found that students valued field instructors that they described as honest, likable, expert, reliable, sociable, prepared, sincere, warm, skillful, and trustworthy. More time spent in interaction with field instructors (frequency and length of meetings) also affected students' satisfaction, as did perceptions of how engaged or supportive the field instructors were (Knight 2000, 2001). Activities encouraging self-reflection and self-critique also were highly valued, especially by advanced concentration graduate students (Bogo 2005; Knight 2001). Knight (2001) found that at the end of the field internship, discussing openly, integrating theory with practice, encouraging self-criticism, requiring self-evaluation, assigning specific readings, and the field instructor's applying classroom learning all were strongly predictive of students' self-ratings of how well prepared for practice they were, suggesting that the articulation model of field instruction (see chapter 5) was useful to them. Time spent in supervision (both frequency and length of supervisory meetings), availability outside planned sessions, and quality of feedback on process recordings were, not surprisingly, related to students' satisfaction with their field instructors. Feedback from field instructors through "live" sessions (sitting in with the student) or audio or video recordings of students' sessions with clients was generally regarded as very useful by students, but these techniques did not appear to be widely used (see, e.g., Knight 2000, 2001). Finally, just as field instructors are encouraged to integrate classroom content into their teaching, there are ways to incorporate supervisory-style learning experiences into the practice classroom. Shibusawa, VanEsselstyn, and Oppenheim (2006) described a technique of using the Web to "simulate couples therapy supervision" into a family practice course, a teaching technique that students rated very positively.

CONCLUSION

The assessment of learning and teaching depends on one's beliefs about learning and philosophy of teaching (Anderson and Speck 1998). Is learning an active or a passive process? What is the relative importance of process and product in learning? Is assessment subjective or objective? Should learning and assessment processes be individual or collaborative? How multidimensional (knowledge, values, and/or skills) should assessments be? These are key questions to be asked in student assessments, but they are relevant to the assessment of teaching as well. But unlike in other areas of higher education in which knowledge of a content area may be different from teaching skills, most teachers of social work are educated as social workers and therefore bring skills in relating constructively to people of varying backgrounds, the ability to handle group dynamics in the classroom, and the motivation to be helpful to their students to their work. The quality of classroom instruction in social work education programs is therefore generally (but, of course, not universally) high. Even so, continuous reflection on and evaluation of teaching activities and student learning are still required. The following are specific suggestions for assessment:

- *Plan for student assessment as integral to course and curriculum development.* While assessment activities play a role in judging the adequacy of students' performance in specific areas, students' efforts should pay off in some intrinsic learning as well. Students are also less frustrated by these demands ("requirements") when the activities seem directly related to the course objectives and their professional experiences.

- *Fit student assessments to their learning outcomes.* Examinations can test for the recall and application of specific knowledge. Oral presentations and term papers can involve discovering, analyzing, and synthesizing new information. Journals and other methods can be used to encourage and evaluate the capacity for self-reflection. Role playing, case analyses, process recordings, and similar activities can be used to assess practice skills.

- *Offer variety and options in assessment activities.* Choices can maximize students' opportunities to learn in different ways. They also allow the instructor to experiment over time with what seems to work best. Because students' learning needs can differ dramatically (as when a student with an advanced degree in another field enrolls in a social work program), I include a one-line statement on my syllabi that anyone is free to propose another assignment, although I do not guarantee that I will accept the proposal. This strategy has reduced frustration for students enrolled in a required course who already have significant background in the area, which can in turn translate into an easier time in the classroom.

- *Don't rely solely on the institution's standard mechanisms for feedback on your teaching.* The information from ratings and comments on the standardized end-of-quarter or end-of-semester questionnaires should not be dismissed. But many such mechanisms also permit instructors to customize the questions asked, a feature rarely used. Most important, it is never a good idea to wait until the end of a course to ask your students for feedback. Fellow instructors often enjoy an invitation to discuss teaching and curriculum development issues, so it may be helpful to reach out to others, and not just when problems arise, to tap into or share "practice wisdom." Finally, there are often excellent resources on campus, as in centers to support excellence in teaching, which may offer general and even individual assistance to improve your teaching effectiveness.

Many of the problems identified by Wodarski, Feit, and Green (1995) in their review of empirical research on the outcomes of social work education remain. At both the BSW and MSW levels of social work education, students' self-reports of practice skill or their satisfaction with their learning and teaching experiences remain the norm. Unless specific findings are published as research reports, information captured by individual programs about their educational outcomes and described in their self-reports for accreditation will not be available to other educators, and findings have not been examined collectively to see what, if anything, might be learned from them. In addition, promising practices for assessing students' practice and other professional skills have been identified but are not yet in widespread use. As in most professions (Palomba and Banta 2001), better assessment of our learning outcomes will continue to be a challenge that we will have to strive to meet, individually and collectively.

Further Reading

Anderson, R. S., and Speck, B. W., eds. (1998). *Changing the way we grade student performance: Classroom assessment and the new learning paradigm.* San Francisco: Jossey-Bass.

Angelo, T. A., and Crossman, K. P. (1993). *Classroom assessment techniques: A handbook for college teachers.* 2nd ed. San Francisco: Jossey-Bass. [Published a while back but a classic work]

Area Concentration Achievement Test (ACAT) (Project for Area Concentration Achievement Testing, 1997) for social work majors. Available at http://www.collegeoutcomes.com/ACATS/socwork.htm.

Baccalaureate Educational Assessment Package (BEAP) homepage. Available at http://beap.socwk.utah.edu/

Bogo, M. (2005). Field instruction in social work: A review of the research literature. *Clinical Supervisor* 24 (1/2):163–193.

Hu, S., ed. (2005). *Beyond grade inflation: Grading problems in higher education.* ASHE Higher Education Report, vol. 30, no. 6. San Francisco: Jossey-Bass.

Palomba, C. A., and Banta, T. W., eds. (2001). *Assessing student competence in accredited disciplines.* Sterling, Va.: Stylus.

8

ACADEMIC JOBS AND FACULTY WORK

TEACHERS USUALLY FOCUS ON *what* they teach, not *where* they teach. One point that I have emphasized throughout this book is that all formal teaching and learning is greatly, although often implicitly, affected by their social and organizational contexts. This chapter puts the *educational context*—the department or school, the college, the university—in the foreground (figure 8.1). It also places classroom teaching in the context of the full range of faculty roles and responsibilities, including those job requirements that can enhance and/or detract from excellence in teaching.

The academic workplace is an industry like any other, with cultures, norms, and performance standards, both written and unwritten. As in many other employment sectors in the early twenty-first century, higher education is an industry undergoing rapid change. Major current trends in the academic workplace include the use of new technologies (see chapter 6), pressures on faculty members for increased productivity and accountability, changing demographics in students and faculty, and changes in faculty appointments (Finkelstein, Seal, and Schuster 1998; Schuster 1999). The academy also is a place where, because of its age and governance structures, both functional and dysfunctional traditions endure.

Social work is a profession, and being a professor is a profession as well (Melko 1998). Often the characteristics and functions of the two professions complement each other in their ideals of service to others, competence, ethical conduct, and commitment to the work. The missions of the two professions also differ, sometimes in ways that produce strains. For example, both professions enjoy a degree of power and autonomy in their work based on credentials, but full-time academic work and social work practice require different credentials, which is currently an area of debate (Zastrow and Bremner 2004).

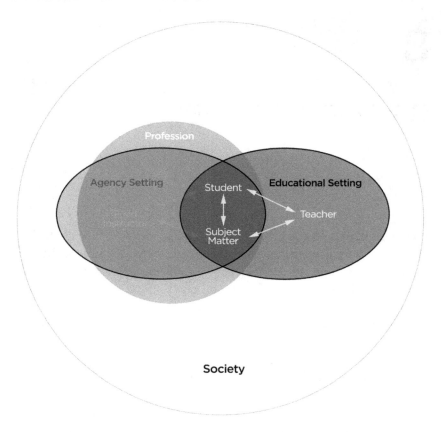

FIGURE 8.1 Model of teaching and learning that highlights job factors.

Besides looking at being a professor of the profession of social work, this chapter is meant to be a short survival guide for those seeking a full-time academic job in an accredited social work program in the United States and for those beginning work in these programs. Although the use of adjunct faculty is growing in social work, as it is in other fields (McMurtry and Mc-Clelland 1997), and although many doctoral graduates in social work teach part time (Whitaker, Weismiller, and Clark 2006) , this chapter focuses on full-time academic work. It examines what academic jobs are *meant to be* as well as what they currently are—their ideals—and it also is meant to (re)inspire and inform our choices for our careers. We begin with the second topic, because searching for a job is most likely to be successful with an informed sense of what academic work should be as well as what it currently is.

TYPES OF INSTITUTIONS OF HIGHER EDUCATION

The United States has more than 2,500 four-year colleges and universities (Eckel and King 2003), of which 397 have accredited graduate and undergraduate social work programs (CSWE 2007b). These colleges and universities have different missions and cultures and emphasize different kinds of scholarship, teaching, and research. For example, some are private, nonprofit organizations of higher education; some are affiliated with a religion; and some online degree programs are private, for-profit enterprises. But because only one CSWE-accredited social work program is offered wholly on line, this discussion is limited to "bricks and mortar" and nonprofit programs. Although the Carnegie Foundation's system formally recognizes only tribal institutions as a separate type, the mission of some institutions is to educate historically disadvantaged subgroups of the population, like undergraduate programs that serve only women and historically black colleges and universities (HBCUs).

The Carnegie Foundation devised a system of classification for colleges and universities based on the goals and standards appropriate for its type (a summary can be found in Levine 2007:10). I discuss only those Carnegie categories containing accredited social work programs. For example, I do not discuss two-year colleges, from which students often transfer into undergraduate social work programs, even though a doctoral graduate in social work might choose to teach in a two-year college.

One major classification is *doctorate-granting institutions*: (1) RU/VH, "research universities with very high research activity"; (2) RU/H, "research universities with high research activity"; and (3) DRU: doctoral research universities. All these institutions award more than twenty doctoral degrees each year. The level of research activity ("high" or "very high") is determined by the amount of external funding received. The earlier Carnegie category of "Research 1" remains in common usage and generally is the same as the RU/VH, the largest subtype in this category.

The next group is *master's colleges and universities*, with three subgroups based on enrollment. Then come *baccalaureate colleges*. Although a baccalaureate institution may award up to twenty doctoral degrees per year and also associate's degrees, the term *liberal arts college*, still in common use, has been dropped from the classification system. The report on the classification system adds that "baccalaureate" institutions now are granting more graduate degrees. Similarly, the trend in social work education has been toward "combined" programs, that is, accredited programs offering both the baccalaureate and MSW degrees. Although many BSW-only departments and programs remain, many BSW programs have added the MSW option.

For faculty jobs in social work, the most useful and clearest distinctions are between (D)RU institutions and all others. Most social work programs offering doctoral degrees are (D)RUs, and the vast majority of these are actually HRUs. Conversely, most social work programs offering only BSW degrees are in baccalaureate colleges, although there are many exceptions. Therefore, these Carnegie types describe the kinds of degrees typically awarded and the amount of externally funded research as well as the institutional priorities that affect faculty (and student) life. Even though all institutions insist that excellence in teaching is a priority, the greater emphasis on research productivity in (D)RUs drives faculty priorities and job requirements, even the kinds of faculty appointments offered, and they affect students' experiences as well.

FACULTY WORK

When faculty work is discussed, *research, teaching,* and *service* always come up, especially in regard to the relationship among them and the relative importance of each. In addition, much faculty work is not captured in the formal assignment of specific courses to be taught each term or semester. Teaching accounts for about 50 percent of professors' self-reported work, for senior and new faculty members alike, whereas research averages from 20 to 30 percent (recently hired faculty do more), and service averages about 5 percent for all (Finkelstein, Seal, and Schuster 1998:66).

The American Association of University Professors (AAUP) describes faculty work beyond classroom teaching and research as "student-centered," "disciplinary—or professional-centered," and "community-centered" (AAUP 2003:1–2). The first category applies to individual assistance to students in their research, learning, or career advancement; alumni relations; and curriculum and course development. The second is institution-based (i.e., faculty selection, promotion and tenure reviews, and other departmental and universitywide committee work) and "outside" activities, such as editing for scholarly journals and publishers, conference presentations, and involvement with professional associations. The third covers such activities as serving on boards and consulting for local, state, and national governments and community and business groups, often free of charge.

Another role, administration, is often not discussed or is defined as a form of institutional service or "discipline-centered work." National data on faculty work collected in the 1990s suggested that faculty spend about 12 percent of their time in administration, although they would prefer less (Finkelstein, Seal, and Schuster 1998:66). Academic administration, like enrollment management, is increasingly being defined a specialty of its own, a job for those who have never been in traditional academic positions or who have different skills. Even though academic administration can enhance or detract from teaching and learning, we talk about it here only to the extent that institutional service often involves participation in faculty governance and departmental administration.

The description of the Carnegie types of institutions of higher education shows that "research," "teaching," and "service" are emphasized differently in different settings. What counts, or should count, as research or scholarship differs as well.

SCHOLARSHIP

When discussing scholarship, the order of the items and the choice of words ("research," as in the previous paragraph, and "scholarship" here) are significant. Colleges and universities promise not just to teach but to teach the most up-to-date and trustworthy content. Indeed, the generation of new knowledge and new ideas is a goal of university life in itself, and the evaluation of faculty job performance is often most heavily weighted toward research and scholarship. Scholarship enriches and renews teaching and curriculum development, but the amount of time in a week, a semester, or a year is finite, and most faculty members believe that investing time in research, especially externally funded research, is more likely to pay off in promotion, tenure, and merit pay than is investing time in teaching. As a result, many people criticize U.S. universities for shortchanging teaching, especially undergraduate teaching (Boyer 1990; Boyer Commission 1998). The Boyer report on undergraduate teaching recommends not only preparing doctoral students as apprentice teachers but also engaging undergraduate students in more active and inquiry-based forms of learning in a strong community context (see chapter 2).

In the 1990s, the Carnegie Foundation for the Advancement of Teaching tried to resolve this tension by examining the nature of scholarship itself and arguing for a broader definition of it. The definition was designed to encompass more of the kinds of work that faculty in different disciplines and in different kinds of colleges and universities do. The result, the widely cited Boyer report of 1990, lists four kinds of scholarly work of value. This conceptualization has great promise for both maintaining the value of research as traditionally defined in scientific fields and recognizing accomplishments and intellectual work that might be more characteristic of faculty members in the arts or in the professions, for example. Because the report is often cited inaccurately, I quote from the original, which is well worth reading not just for this discussion but also for the national faculty survey findings on which it is based.

The *scholarship of discovery* is the term for what is normally called *research*, that is, the generation of new information and ideas through independent inquiry. It embodies a central ideal of the academy:

> the commitment to knowledge for its own sake, to freedom of inquiry and to following, in a disciplined fashion, an investigation wherever it may lead. . . . The intellectual excitement fueled by this quest enlivens faculty and invigorates higher learning institutions, . . . and in our complicated, vulnerable world, the discovery of new knowledge is critical. (Boyer 1990:17–18)

Doctoral programs in social work typically emphasize preparing their students for this form of scholarship (Golde and Walker 2006). As Richardson (2006) said about doctorates in education, a profession also needs a scholarship of the enterprise, that is, a study of its practice(s) and service delivery systems. Such work may be considered the *scholarship of application* and is accorded less prestige than "basic" research endeavors.

The *scholarship of integration* means giving meaning to isolated facts and developing knowledge that may cross disciplines and/or bring information from one field productively into the work of another. Much has been said about the interdisciplinary perspective needed to address many contemporary issues and problems, but traditional disciplinary structures and credentialing systems often remain firmly in place, making such appealing and limited ventures as joint appointments potentially hazardous to incumbents. By nature, social work is a profession that combines sociology, psychology, and many other fields, which has sometimes been viewed as a weakness rather than as a strength. Boyer (1990) describes this kind of scholarship as being directed to the possibility of "interpret[ing] what's been discovered in ways that provide a larger, more comprehensive understanding," which in turn requires synthesis and "critical analysis and interpretation" directed to questions of what these discoveries may mean (19).

The *scholarship of application* addresses "how knowledge can be responsibly applied to consequential problems" faced by individuals and institutions as well as how "social problems *themselves* define an agenda for scholarly investigation" (Boyer 1990:21, italics in original). This type of scholarship seems typical of much social work research and scholarship. Some forms of professional and community service might actually be this form of scholarship, as when best practices are disseminated and/or evaluated. Boyer also pointed out that such activities can lead to new knowledge and/or the identification of new problems needing scholarly attention. Such service activities not only are good citizenship, but they also are "tied directly to one's special field of knowledge" (Boyer 1990:22).

Finally, Boyer's (1990) report talks about a *scholarship of teaching*:

> Teaching both educates and entices future scholars. . . . Teaching begins with what the teacher knows. Those who teach must, above all, be well informed, and steeped in the knowledge of their fields . . . widely read and intellectually engaged . . . teaching, at its best, means not only transmitting knowledge, but *transforming* and *extending* it as well. (23–24, italics in original)

Teaching means leading others into scholarship; it also requires one's own scholarship to do it well. Finally, some people have used this formulation to advocate paying more attention and respect to scholarly work that examines and evaluates teaching practices and educational outcomes, but the legitimacy and importance of this form of work may be questioned when one's expertise is not education as a discipline.

The Boyer report considers all four forms of scholarship necessary for good teaching and for colleges' and universities' fulfillment of their missions. It is unclear, however, whether this widely read and well-regarded report has had much real impact, especially on research and doctoral institutions, since the scholarship of discovery has remained the most highly rewarded. Social work is a profession, meaning that its practice—the *application* of concepts to interventions in the real world—is a focus of its research, although much less is published in this area than is needed (Reid, Kenaley, and Colvin 2004). It is likely that reward systems are driving faculty efforts elsewhere, especially in research-oriented institutions. Nonetheless, this typology of scholarship can help faculty members choose scholarly projects based on how they may be viewed. It also helps convey the value of scholarly work, especially if it is not in the category of the scholarship of discovery using a framework familiar to those in higher education.

TEACHING

Teaching may seem the easiest part of a faculty member's job to define, and in some ways that is true. Each academic department usually requires a certain number of classes per quarter or semester that each faculty member must teach. But sometimes several sections of the same course are treated differently from sections of different courses; some departments provide teaching assistants and others do not. Constructing or teaching a new course may or may not receive "workload" credit. And sometimes different arrangements are made for new faculty and/or at points in the pretenure process. Accordingly, job applicants should ask about variations in the numbers of courses taught and how these are decided. Few schools or departments are enthusiastic about applicants who seem to want to teach the minimum.

Besides teaching a certain number of classes or course sections, teachers often must advise students. In professional programs like social work that include internship and/or service learning, someone must take responsibility for both field instruction (usually agency employees in social work) and liaison or field advising (see chapter 5). This responsibility may be shared by full-time faculty, delegated to specialized faculty in the field department, carried by adjunct (part-time) faculty, or some combination of these. Also, if the institution has a doctoral program, it is important to know how service on doctoral examinations or dissertation committees and the advising and mentoring of doctoral students are figured into faculty workloads, since practices seem to vary widely in this area. Mentoring and role-modeling may be at least as important to faculty work as classroom instruction but may be harder to "count" in faculty work.

Finally, the extent that one's teaching is *scholarly*, as Boyer (1990) suggests it should be, may be harder to evaluate. Assigning new and up-to-date readings in a course may be evidence of this, as may student evaluations suggesting that a teacher knows much about the subject matter and conveys intellectual excitement. Quantifying the effort to keep abreast of the field and make knowledge exciting and relevant to students is difficult, however.

SERVICE

Based on the kinds of work that students in their practicum training and faculty do, schools and departments of social work are often hailed by college and university administrators as symbolizing their overall service mission. This emphasis on service activities, however, is declining as standards for scholarly productivity for tenure and promotion are rising. *Service* may be defined as service to the department or school (e.g., committee work, curriculum development activities) or to the college or university, and some service is generally the norm for all. Junior faculty members may be informally encouraged to limit their service until they have earned tenure, in order to protect their time spent on scholarly work.

Service activities may be engagement with social service agencies or organizations, through, for example, pro bono consultation or board service or other kinds of noncompensated work. Service may be in local and national professional or scholarly organizations, such as reviewing articles for journals, which is regarded as recognition of one's areas of professional and scholarly expertise. But since service activities are often "counted" and valued differently, you should find out how they are defined and evaluated in your institution. For example, service may be valued only if it leads to related scholarship or is connected to students' service-learning activities.

ADMINISTRATION

Some academic positions are purely administrative. Some may be held by people who also have professorial appointments, tenured or contract based, but some are not. Since academic administration has become a specialty in itself, a full discussion of it is beyond the scope of this book, but you can find an excellent, brief overview of typical university governance structures in Eckel and King (2003).

Full-time faculty members may assume administrative responsibilities, sometimes on a rotating basis, like chairing a curriculum area or directing a program or subprogram (e.g., part-time study). Sometimes, if the work is like chairing a faculty committee, it is counted as service to the institution. Sometimes it is compensated, especially if work is required outside the normal academic calendar. At other times, especially if the number of faculty is small, it is expected of everyone and/or is rotated among the group. Again, how expectations and practices in these areas are handled is a topic that should be discussed when considering a job and in a faculty group.

PROFESSIONAL DEVELOPMENT

Professional growth and development refers to attending conferences and other meetings to keep abreast of developments in one's areas of teaching and research, attending specialized workshops on writing grant proposals and research methodologies, traveling for research (and obtaining funding for it), and arranging faculty development activities for all or part of the group on campus, including services from campus-based centers on teaching. In social work, national conferences often include preconference institutes for teaching, research methods, and/or research funding development. Those who receive external funding for their research often attend specialty conferences for grantees and others that provide similar opportunities to learn about new research findings and develop research skills. Except when these activities are linked to external grants, professional developmental activities may be more common for new faculty. Colleges, schools, and departments vary greatly in what is available on campus and in what they provide in financial and logistical support and in release time for these activities.

AN ALTERNATIVE PARADIGM?

Because of changes in academic work, including the increasing number of non-tenurable full-time appointments, Gappa, Austin, and Trice (2005) argue for a different, values-based framework for thinking about faculty work. They cite five "essential elements" important to all faculty: *employment equity*, including open and transparent employment policies; *academic freedom* in research and scholarship, in the classroom and as a citizen; *balance and flexibility* in work arrangements and career development over time; opportunities for *professional growth*; and opportunities for *involvement in the institution* (through governance) *and the community*. These faculty benefits and entitlements provide another tool for assessing specific academic employment opportunities.

RESEARCH ON FACULTY JOBS IN SOCIAL WORK

In the 1990s, several national studies examined faculty work in general and in social work. The findings of the social work studies were similar to what studies in other fields showed: an aging professoriat; increasing demands on faculty for scholarly productivity, especially in institutions offering doctoral degrees (Anastas 2006; Green 1998, 2008; Hull 1991; Sansone, Bedics, and Rappe 2000; Wergen 1994:17); and the increasing use of adjunct and nontenured, full-time faculty in departments and schools of social work (McMurtry and McClelland 1997).

QUALIFYING FOR A FACULTY JOB

Currently, there is a shortage of doctoral graduates available for full-time faculty jobs, especially those who hold both a doctoral and a professional, usually a MSW, degree (Anastas 2006, 2007c; Feldman 1999; Zastrow and Bremner 2004). Overall, social work programs reported an 8 percent faculty vacancy rate in 2006/2007, and 43 percent of programs had one or more vacancies in that year (Anastas 2007c). This problem is expected to continue because 74 percent of programs anticipated faculty retirements in the next five years and 89 percent expected them in the next ten years. Teaching part time, that is, on an adjunct basis, is quite different and is briefly discussed later.

My own study of job ads for one recent year (Anastas 2006) looked more specifically at what competencies and areas of expertise schools and departments of social work are seeking when hiring new full-time faculty for entry-level positions. My findings show that this information about faculty vacancies and the competencies sought in applicants needs should be considered in accordance with the types of institutions in which programs are located and the level of social work education, graduate or undergraduate, being offered. In fact, because types and level are correlated and earlier research on this topic used a method of comparison specific to social work (Feld 1988), my study's findings are based on the highest social work degree offered: baccalaureate, master's, or doctorate.

Only military and paramilitary (e.g., law enforcement) jobs emphasize rank more than academia does. The faculty "pecking order" and tenure-track and "contract" (not tenure-eligible) positions have their own language, which generally seems self-explanatory to those in the system but may be unintelligible to outsiders. The "tenure system" is explained in box 8.1 (AAUP 2001).

Because I designed my study of job openings in social work education to examine opportunities for doctoral program graduates, I focused on job ads for positions at the assistant professor level or for those whose the rank was "open," meaning that it could be filled by a beginner at the rank of assistant professor or higher (Anastas 2006). This and previous studies describe the kinds of expertise sought in new faculty in social work as well as the job responsibilities listed in the ads.

Most of the jobs advertised in the year studied were for institutions with both BSW (82%) and MSW programs (88%). Almost half the jobs (45%) were in "doctoral-level" programs (RU or DU in the current Carnegie system). Only about a third of the advertised jobs were in settings with a social work

---

BOX 8.1

DECODING FACULTY TITLES AND RANKS

The traditional system of faculty titles and rank is tied to the granting of tenure, although the proportion of tenured faculty seems to be declining. While the qualifications for faculty rank and the titles used vary institution by institution, you should know the general language of faculty rank in the tenure and nontenure systems. In the tradition of peer review and faculty self-governance, faculty rank is usually recommended and assigned, in accordance with the particular college's or university's policy, by a faculty committee, that is, by fellow faculty members in one's own department or school, with subsequent endorsement within the college or university. Salaries are generally tied to rank or title.

Assistant professor is the most common title given to beginning, full-time, tenure-eligible faculty. In tenure systems, this title is used for most or all faculty members who have not yet been granted tenure. In some institutions, especially if the candidate has not completed the doctoral degree, the lower rank and title of *instructor* is used, but often for only a limited time. Pretenure appointments are formally "probationary," that is, not permanent, as they are for tenured faculty.

Qualifications for promotion to the rank of *associate professor* are usually the same as those for tenure. Some institutions award this title before granting tenure, either for outstanding accomplishment but more often for someone who has joined a faculty after full-time faculty work elsewhere.

The highest rank granted is simply *professor*, or sometimes *full professor*. Not all associate professors attain the rank of professor. Although "temporary" and "visiting" are not permanent titles, a "temporary" appointment can sometimes be converted to a continuing one.

Many titles are used for those in full-time faculty positions without the possibility of tenure, that is, on contracts of varying lengths. These titles may also reflect different roles and work assignments, such as *clinical (rank) professor* or *research (rank) professor*. Note that "clinical" may or may not have anything to do with practice or "clinical practice"; it may simply indicate a contract (full time, nontenured) rather than a tenured position. The term *rank* means that someone may be a clinical assistant or a clinical associate professor, for example, reflecting length of service and/or promotion based on accomplishments. Sometimes the term *lecturer* is used. A generic term for these various kinds of positions is *contract faculty*, indicating finite terms of guaranteed employment and recurrent periodic reviews. Sometimes these appointments are made administratively (as by a dean), but sometimes they, too, fall under faculty governance systems to one degree or another.

---

doctoral programs; 23 percent were for institutions offering only the BSW, and 42 percent were in MSW programs not offering doctoral degrees in social work. Thus many of the schools/departments in which faculty jobs were available were unlike the institutions in which social work doctoral students were earning their degrees, although many were in research-active and/or doctoral-level *institutions*.

As Zastrow and Bremner (2005) predicted, almost all the job ads mentioned that the MSW degree was required or preferred (93% combined), and a majority of ads also wanted some amount of post-MSW practice experience (71%). The areas of expertise most often sought were practice and diversity and/or cultural competence. Experience in teaching (58%) and research or scholarship (50%) usually was necessary, although the latter was more likely to be mentioned in ads for schools with doctoral programs. The responsibilities most often listed were MSW teaching (50% of ads) and BSW teaching (53%), although scholarly productivity was commonly sought, too (44% of ads), again usually in ads for schools with doctoral programs in social work. These data suggest that preparation for and experience in teaching at both the MSW and BSW levels are likely to be necessary for obtaining a faculty job. Especially for those wanting to teach in a research institution, research and publication or presentation experience at the time of application also was likely to be advantageous. Most current doctoral students have a MSW degree and some post-MSW experience (Anastas 2007a). Candidates without these may have fewer opportunities, although they may be better compensated if they are hired (Sakamoto et al. 2008).

Most important, more full-time faculty jobs currently are available in social work each year than there are graduates from social work doctoral programs to fill them (Anastas 2006, 2007a; Zastrow and Bremner 2004). An unknown number of people with a MSW degree obtain their doctoral education in another, related field (e.g., sociology, public policy, developmental psychology), and they are eligible for these positions as well. Conversely, many social work doctoral graduates already are employed when they graduate or may not be seeking a job in the academic sector. In addition, this job market is national, and not all doctoral graduates are able to relocate for postdoctoral employment (Anastas 2007a). Therefore, some localities and types of institutions may very well have available few full-time academic jobs, and the programs may be in the enviable position of receiving many applications for each opening. Overall, however, this problem of a shortage of doctorates is expected to continue for some time, especially when the impending retirements of current faculty are taken into account.

FACULTY WORK IN SOCIAL WORK

Social work falls into the broader category of professional education (in contrast to the "traditional disciplines"), which affects faculty work in a variety of ways. Social work is both a discipline, that is, a field of knowledge with its own content and typical modes of study, and a profession, that is, a field whose core is service and action, what Richardson would call an "enterprise" (Anastas and Kuerbis 2009; Richardson 2006). As Shulman (2005) observed, "A professional is not someone for whom understanding is sufficient. Understanding is necessary, yes; but not sufficient. A professional has to be prepared to *act*, to *perform*, to *practice*, whether they have enough information or not . . . they [professionals] have to *be* certain kinds of human beings" (3, italics in original).

This affects curricula in a variety of ways, such as the inclusion of a field internship, which necessitates the selection of field-learning sites and the supervision and evaluation of students' practice. It also means the inclusion of professional values and ethics in what is taught and an obligation to evaluate students' general suitability for practice as well as their intellectual achievement. It means that knowledge and understanding generally emphasize their value and application to practice.

How does this affect faculty work? As we noted, job applicants with a professional practice degree and some practice experience are likely to be preferred because they are more likely to be able to convey the practice relevance of what they teach effectively, as in providing case examples to illustrate their points. In addition to deciding on the courses to be taught, every department or school of social work must decide how to handle students in field learning sites and who will instruct and evaluate students' learning in the field. Thus, advising students in social work may have both academic and field-oriented aspects, and many institutions expect full-time faculty members to be field liaisons or advisers in addition to their other responsibilities. Faculty members may want or be expected to maintain their social work practice or their ties with community agencies and organizations. Therefore they may spend more time advising or on service-related activities than do their colleagues in other disciplines. Because of these differences (and other factors), since its migration from agencies to universities social work education has been concerned about being "in" but not "of" the university (Austin 1997).

Seaberg's (1998) national survey of social work faculty provides the best data showing both how our work is like that in other parts of the university and how it differs. Studies suggest that all faculty work for about fifty-five hours per week, spending a little more than half their time teaching. The average number of hours worked reported in Seaberg's study was only fifty, which might be explained by the fact that some did professional but non-university-based work, such as social work practice. Tracking workload by the number of courses taught was the most common measurement, and this part of faculty work is the easiest to quantify. The typical teaching load in the Seaberg study was four courses per year. The respondents reported spending about eleven hours a week in the classroom, ten hours a week on class preparation, and additional time on grading students' work and meeting with students outside class. Very few had teaching assistants, and most carried a heavy advising load (more than seventeen students each). Lack of faculty workload credit for thesis and dissertation advising was a common complaint.

In regard to Seaberg's findings about faculty scholarship over a period of two years, a number of study respondents recorded no specific scholarly activities (a finding not likely to be replicated today), while others were quite productive, thereby underestimating the averages for the active scholars. Overall, the respondents averaged about six conference presentations, three published articles, and one to two grant applications in two years. A less common activity was writing books and monographs. In addition, active scholars reported having two articles or other manuscripts "in progress" or under review but not yet published. The respondents averaged about thirteen hours a week on scholarly activities, the area in which there was the most dissatisfaction with workload policies, because they did not allow enough time for scholarly work. Seaberg's study did not look at time (and funds) spent on such activities as professional development.

Other aspects of work studied were service, which took up more than one full workday per month, practice (six hours per week), and administration, which was another area of dissatisfaction with workload policies that did not give credit for this work or for travel time to teach at distant locations. In sum, respondents reported spending 42 percent of their time teaching, 29 percent in research and scholarship, 16 percent in service, and 13 percent in administration. The amount and kinds of work done by the sample varied considerably, but they were not linked simply to the size of the faculty. Other characteristics of the employing school, department, or university were not measured. In other words, local workload norms and practices may vary fairly widely.

Among faculty in the social work study, as in other fields, women tended to teach more courses, serve on more university committees, and publish fewer articles on average than did their male colleagues, and minority respondents had more students overall than did their white colleagues. Both in this study and others, junior faculty were found to be spending *more* time teaching than senior faculty did, despite their need to prepare for their tenure review (Seaberg 1998; Finkelstein, Seal, and Schuster 1998).

Compensation for social work faculty also is an issue. In the 1990s, Howe (2000) found that faculty salaries in social work were lower than for other fields at the same institutions at both private and public colleges and universities; social work salaries increased more slowly than did those for other disciplines during the decade; and fewer assistant professors were hired. Besides salary and benefits, it is important to consider the full range of workload issues outlined in this research when negotiating for a faculty position and, once hired, when negotiating annual workload and other assignments.

GETTING THE FACULTY JOB YOU WANT

Although many doctoral students in social work are limited to a particular location (Anastas 2007a), the job market for full-time teaching jobs in social work is national. In some areas of the country and for some types of schools, obtaining a full-time faculty job may be difficult. Because I cannot cover everything on this topic in this chapter, I recommend, for example, Sowers-Hoag and Harrison's *Finding an Academic Job* (1998) and Formo and Reed's *The Job Search in Acacdeme: Strategic Rhetorics for Faculty Job Candidates* (1999). The first book, although aimed at all disciplines, is written by social work educators and is an excellent and practical step-by-step guide, although it assumes that the hiring process is rational and that faculty committees and deans will behave well toward all candidates. The second book compares the process of getting a faculty job with landing a job on stage or screen, as both require a "script" and a "screen test," and it offers tips on handling those searching institutions that play it "tough." Both books use "cases" to illustrate both successful and problematic scenarios. In addition, the *Chronicle of Higher Education* (published weekly by the American Council on Education) often contains useful articles on searching for an academic job, many of them with helpful tips and reflections on the process.

The following might make it easier to obtain a full-time job:

- Having an MSW.
- Having post-MSW practice experience.
- Having *completed* the doctoral degree.
- Having *some* successful teaching experience, preferably in a school or department of social work.
- Having a record of scholarship.
- Having some expertise in diversity and/or cultural competence.

- Having a well-defined specific area of expertise that *fits well* with the hiring program's mission and needs.
- Having a well-articulated teaching philosophy.
- Having a five-year plan for future research and scholarship.

It is important to understand why these are considered desirable as well as how to develop and articulate these qualifications. Some of what I present here is based on earlier writings (including Formo and Reed 1999; Sowers-Hoag and Harrison 1998) and research, but much is based on many years of service on faculty search committees at different schools, on observing and advising doctoral students applying for faculty jobs, and on listening to doctoral program directors, deans, and others discuss how best to prepare students to search for a job.

DEGREES AND OTHER QUALIFICATIONS

Having a MSW degree is desirable because it is the terminal practice degree for the profession. Candidates with a MSW degree presumably know and are committed to the ethics, values and knowledge base of social work that will influence their teaching, whatever the specific curriculum content they teach. Moreover, in accordance with current accreditation standards, those who teach required practice courses and are involved with certain aspects of field instruction must have a MSW degree. Faculty members are increasingly expected to teach in a variety of traditional curricula—practice, HBSE, policy, and research—and faculty members with a MSW can cover practice courses as needed. A social work practice degree also is seen as desirable because it enables teachers to connect for students what they are teaching in other areas (e.g., research, policy, HBSE) to its relevance to practice.

What about applicants who do not have a MSW degree or post-MSW practice experience? Without a MSW, an applicant is likely to find a job only in programs that are large enough to accommodate faculty with relevant specialized knowledge because they already have many faculty members with a MSW degree. Even medium-size and large programs have different philosophical beliefs about the desirability of recruiting such faculty members. Job seekers should check out this attitude in advance (if there is no one else on the faculty without a MSW, this may be a dead end). Some programs whose universities are working toward greater interdisciplinary collaboration are actively seeking faculty members who might hold joint appointments (with or without the MSW) and/or demonstrate expertise in another discipline, a more promising scenario. It is, of course, possible to earn a MSW during or after doctoral study, and some faculty members have done so to advance their careers.

What about the BSW degree? While it turns out that quite a large proportion of doctoral students in social work have a BSW degree (25%: Anastas 2007a), no data are available on how the BSW degree is viewed in hiring. The qualifications in job ads did not mention it (Anastas 2006), and many states do not recognize the BSW degree for licensing purposes. Therefore, it is unlikely that the BSW degree is a sought-after qualification, especially because BSW education is considered roughly equivalent to the first year of a MSW program, and many institutions with a BSW program add a MSW program if they do not have one already, thus becoming a "joint" program, the fastest-growing group among CSWE-accredited social work programs.

Those who enter their doctoral studies without post-MSW practice experience (usually a minimum of two years of agency practice is sought) may want to gain this experience while they still are students. Of course, this experience can be gained after earning a doctorate, but the "opportunity cost" may be greater. Even though gaining this experience (often through part-time practice) during a doctoral program may delay obtaining the degree, doing so after being hired as a full-time faculty member will definitely take away time needed to develop a portfolio of teaching and scholarship for tenure and/or to carry out heavy job responsibilities.

The mention of a *completed* doctoral degree addresses *when* during one's doctoral studies to look for a job. (These comments apply primarily to doctoral students seeking their first full-time academic job after completing their doctorate. Those enrolled in part-time or other doctoral programs while already employed full time probably do not need to know how to get an academic job, since they probably already have one.) Some programs state that they will consider "ABD" (all but dissertation) applicants. *This generally means that the applicant has at least defended his or her dissertation proposal* and can offer a firm date to defend the dissertation itself. Some colleges and universities are restricted to offering appointments to such candidates only at a lower rank (i.e., instructor) and lower pay, or they have policies that do not permit hiring ABD candidates at all. But it is acceptable to begin looking for a job in the academic year in which the dissertation will be defended. Generally, a "completed degree" means that the degree requirements (dissertation defense and deposit) will have been fulfilled *by the time the appointment begins,* and sometimes letters of initial appointment actually state that the appointment will take effect only when this has been done.

While you may be tempted to think about a full-time job while completing your dissertation, the time needed to complete the dissertation on the job will conflict with doing what may be necessary to obtain tenure (to keep the job), and adjusting to a new job is time-consuming in itself. Sometimes this arrangement works, but it is not ideal. Unfortunately, doctoral students from historically underrepresented groups are sometimes recruited *very* aggressively and offered opportunities like this. In my opinion, they should be considered only when *both the school and the university/college* commit in writing that the tenure "clock" can be "stopped" until the degree has been completed. In contrast to taking a full-time faculty job ABD, if you can invest time in a postdoctoral fellowship, you will have a real advantage in getting that first faculty job because your research career will already have begun.

Another reason to be well along in your dissertation research when applying for a full-time job is that formally presenting your research is almost always part of the on-campus "job talk" required of finalists for faculty positions. Although it is possible to talk about literature, theory, and research methodology without presenting actual findings, this kind of presentation is generally less compelling.

TEACHING EXPERIENCE

Even though doctoral study is demanding, it is an excellent time for gaining experience in both teaching and research. Some doctoral students are funded through teaching assistantships, which can offer mentored experiences in teaching undergraduate or graduate social work students. With or without such experience, doctoral students may teach part time (as adjuncts). Some teaching may earn money and also looks good on your résumé.

Some doctoral programs offer courses in teaching (Dinerman, Feldman, and Ello 1999; Hesselbrock 2006; Valentine et al. 1998). Many campuses also have teaching centers that offer doctoral students, teaching assistants, and faculty at all levels individual and/or group-based instruction and coaching in how to teach. The national conferences held annually by the Council on Social Work Education (CSWE) and the Baccalaureate Program Directors (BPD) offer workshops on curriculum development and teaching. If full-time teaching is your goal, it is a good idea to take advantage of these opportunities. Some people recommend assembling a *teaching portfolio* containing documentation of your teaching development activities; teaching assignments, including syllabi and other course materials; and student evaluations (see chapter 7).

The two drawbacks to teaching part time while studying for your doctorate are that, first, many doctoral students fall in love with teaching, and feel that they have already obtained the reward they were looking for. Their motivation to complete the research requirements therefore may wane. Second, social work programs are relying increasingly on adjunct teachers and advisers (McMurtry and McClelland 1997). If you are still relying on teaching part time to get through your doctoral program, it may be hard to refuse. But carrying a heavy teaching load as an adjunct can delay obtaining your degree if it detracts from your dissertation. Although I have no data to support this conclusion, I think that having taught *many* rather than *some* courses successfully probably is not important in a job application. Having had some experience teaching means that the candidate has the basic skills to succeed in teaching (or field liaison work), making him or her a "safer bet" as a beginner.

RESEARCH EXPERIENCE

Doctoral studies offer many forms of research experience (beyond the dissertation), such as research internships, assistantships, and other part-time employment on research projects, as well as opportunities to present conference papers and publish, with other students and/or faculty, or on one's own. Doctoral students report that access to these opportunities varies across and within doctoral programs (Anastas 2007a). Although new social work faculty used to be hired based on the "promise" or "capacity" for productivity in research and scholarship, some institutions hiring now are looking for previous accomplishments (Anastas 2006), although the emphasis on this varies across settings.

Even attending scholarly conferences while studying for your doctorate can be a good way of learning about current research in your area of interest and learning how to write a conference abstract and present your research results. As in teaching, some national conferences and organizations, the Society for Social Work and Research (SSWR) and the meetings of the major social work education organizations, offer methodology and other workshops to doctoral students. Attending these also is evidence of serious preparation to become a productive scholar after graduation.

DIVERSITY, CULTURAL COMPETENCE, AND INTERNATIONAL ISSUES

Because of the changing demographics of the U.S. population and the current shortages of social work (and other) professionals to serve them, being able to serve diverse clients and communities, to teach content relevant to practice, and to shape both research methods and findings to oppressed and underserved groups is essential to social work education today. Even in very expensive and short job ads, knowledge of diversity and cultural competence emerges as an area often desired by social work schools (Anastas 2007a). Everyone, not just members of minority groups, who teaches at a school of social work is required to incorporate this content into his or her teaching. In addition, health disparities are emerging as central to much of NIH-funded research, and social workers are often interested or involved in studies in this area. The most recent revision of U.S. accreditation standards requires educating from a "global perspective," and increasing numbers of universities and colleges are developing or expanding claims to a "global reach." Although not yet commonly mentioned in faculty job ads (Anastas 2006), international interests and involvement are advantages when applying for a faculty job in social work. Hence it is not just who you are but what you know and know how to do that matters.

PART-TIME TEACHING

So far, we have talked about those seeking full-time academic jobs. As we noted, however, social work programs are increasingly relying on part-time (adjunct) faculty, and many doctoral graduates (and others in social work) are choosing to make teaching one of their *secondary* career activities. To illustrate, about 88 percent of licensed social workers with doctoral degrees were teaching (Whitaker, Weismiller, and Clark 2006), although only about a third of them listed an academic position as their primary employment. While overreliance on adjunct faculty may not be good for programs and students, classroom faculty actively engaged in practice, research, and administration in nonacademic, community-based settings bring valuable knowledge, skills, and perspectives to the classroom.

Hiring adjunct faculty is entirely different, as it is local and often informal. Even though the compensation is low, the satisfaction is often great, especially when the job is well connected to the full-time faculty and the larger program. Thus getting a job as an adjunct faculty member is a matter of networking: at geographically convenient schools and programs, at a program from which you got one of your degrees, at a program specializing in an area of interest, and through full-time faculty, especially those chairing curriculum areas (e.g., practice, social policy) or directing programs.

Do make clear what your practice experience, research, academic background, and interests best prepare you to teach. Find out about the specific curriculum at the school or department you are interested in and think about where you might best fit in. Do *not* assume that you can develop and deliver a specialized elective course in a very specific area of your expertise. Although this sometimes is possible, especially if a school wants to develop a course in an area that is not well represented by its full-time faculty, it usually is staffing for core curriculum content (basic and advanced courses in practice, policy, research, and human behavior theory) that is most needed. Finally, do not overlook the possibility of teaching in associate degree programs, human service programs, specialized programs in addictions or family services, or other relevant fields such as public health. While these may not be particularly oriented to social work, bringing social work expertise to other areas may help increase the field's general reputation.

SEARCHING FOR A JOB

The phases of searching for a full-time academic job are finding out what jobs are available and applying for them, preparing for the first interview, preparing to be interviewed as a finalist, and negotiating a job offer (Formo and Reed 1999; Sowers-Hoag and Harrison 1998). At all phases in the process, you should clearly explain what you have to offer to your audience, the hiring institution.

HOW FACULTY ARE HIRED

The details of the hiring process (and of all faculty governance rules) vary, but it is a long-accepted faculty right and responsibility to participate in deciding who is hired to join the group as a full-time colleague. The administration, in the department or school as well as at the college or university level, also is involved. Thus there are actually two "audiences" to address in your search, and while they often agree on what they are looking for in a new faculty member, they may emphasize different things and approach job candidates differently.

Most often a *search committee*, made up in whole or in part of faculty members, initially screens the applicants. This committee is the first audience that will see the applicants' materials. They compare the applicants' qualifications with the posted job requirements and desired characteristics in new faculty. The administration, however, is often the key actor at the final stages of the hiring process when salary, benefits, work assignments, and professional development resources are discussed.

FINDING A JOB

The two main sources of information about available faculty jobs are published advertisements and networking, especially at national professional conferences. The affirmative action policies of most institutions require that faculty job openings be advertised regionally or nationally. Annual conferences like those held by CSWE and SSWR offer specific information about available jobs to members and attendees, and the job openings listed there may not have been published yet. You also should consult the newspapers and professional publications, such as the NASW and CSWE newsletters, that are most widely used in the region in which you are seeking work. The *Chronicle of Higher Education* is the national publication in higher education in which the majority of jobs in all fields appear, but do not overlook other journals aimed at specific underrepresented groups.

FRAMING YOUR EXPERTISE AND PROFESSIONAL GOALS

Articulating what you have to offer as a faculty member requires both knowing yourself and understanding how others will see you and your résumé. Although their knowledge of your doctoral program may be dated, search committee members will know something about you based on where you have studied, at both the MSW and doctoral levels. Everything you do during the search process—the letters you write, telephone calls you make, e-mails you send, reference letters you request, and your behavior during interviews and social events surrounding an interview—is information about you that will be used to evaluate your job application. Each of these gives you an opportunity to shape the "message" you want to convey to a prospective employer. All colleges and universities are looking for teaching and the ability to shape and improve curriculum, scholarly productivity, and a willingness to engage constructively in academic life (Adams n.d.). The following is a brief overview of the steps in the job search process.

THE APPLICATION

The first information that a prospective employer has about you is your letter of application and the attached materials, usually a curriculum vitae, or CV. Most applicants know that they should carefully produce and update their CV and be truthful in all respects. Some applicants do not seem to realize that a perfunctory or generic cover letter may be viewed unfavorably and is certainly an opportunity lost. When applying to several places, you may use a similar cover letter, containing content that summarizes your experience and mentions things not in your CV, such as your approach to teaching and your goals for the future and how they build on your past experiences and achievements. However, at the least, the letter's first and last paragraphs should be shaped to each particular school or department you are applying to, showing how you meet its specific needs as outlined in its advertisement or job description and how you might be a "good fit" in that environment. You need to convey your interest in *that job*, not just any job. Addressing your suitability for *this* job may take some homework on your part, such as visiting the school's Web site and learning more about the school and its curriculum, for example, as well as finding out more through networking.

The first step for the search committee is to review all the applications and decide on those candidates they want to talk with further. Some candidates are rejected right away as not demonstrating the basic qualifications for the job or as having a poor fit with the school's requirements. Normally all members of a department's or school's faculty have some say in faculty hiring, so search committee members will also be thinking about whether or not an applicant will be supported by faculty members in an interview. Therefore, if you have the basic qualifications for the job and are rejected at this early stage, do *not* necessarily view it as a judgment of your value because it may be only an assessment of "fit" with that particular group at that particular time.

Academic job searches are generally very slow, and managing one's anxiety during the application process can be difficult. It is fine to show interest in a particular position by making *judicious* follow-up contacts, but collegial and committee processes take time. Being seen as too pushy or as a "pest" is not good, since your ability to be a colleague who will be easy to live with if hired is also being assessed.

A NOTE ON REFERENCES Sometimes applicants are asked to submit letters of reference with their initial application, but more often, this is merely a list of names and contact information for those people who will write a letter of reference for you. Of course, you will have obtained permission from these people to give their name to the committee. If your application advances beyond the preliminary stage, your references will be contacted by telephone so you can be discussed and specific questions can be asked and answered off the record. A written recommendation often is needed only if and when the application advances to the finalist stage or a job will be offered. As with your cover letter, letters of recommendation are most persuasive when they are specific to a particular job and are not entirely generic. Therefore, be sure to give each person who will serve as a reference for you enough information to support your application. This information should include copies of materials you are sending to each school (CV and cover letter) so the recommendation can emphasize some of the points you are trying to make about yourself. Also provide *information about each position you are seeking*, such as a copy of the job ad and position description. This information will enable those recommending you to talk about how you might fit in well and contribute, in each position.

THE FIRST INTERVIEW

When a search committee has identified the best applicants, the next step is usually a preliminary interview. This can take place in a variety of forms—on the telephone, on site (if the applicant is local), or at a professional conference. In social work education, the most common sites for these first-round interviews are the annual SSWR and CSWE meetings. For the search committee, the main purpose of the first interview is learning more about the candidate: his or her research interests, teaching experiences and ideas, community involvements, and the like. All job search handbooks and even university career centers have information about the kinds of questions that are likely to be asked.

The first question commonly is, Why are you interested in this job with us? Too often, job seekers are well prepared to talk about themselves but not as well prepared to talk about the hiring institution. Your answer to this question should be about both you and the institution interviewing you. While many questions can be anticipated, some cannot, and you must show that you know about and are interested in those you might be working with in the future. You will, of course, learn more about "them" as you go through the search process, which will ultimately help you decide whether or not a particular job will appeal to you. Even though these first interviews usually are short, you should be prepared with some questions of your own, for not having any may be taken as a sign of disinterest on your part. You want to demonstrate that you are taking this job possibility seriously, by asking about the job and the place. Finally, a preliminary interview may be an occasion to offer the search committee other materials to support your application, like a writing sample (if it has not already been requested), teaching evaluations, or teaching materials you may have developed (such as a syllabus or creative student assignment).

Based on the preliminary interviews, the two to three strongest candidates are typically invited to campus for a "final interview." But the preliminary interview process may be an occasion for *you* to decide that some job possibilities that you thought were promising will not actually work for you. Recognizing this early on can be a gift to yourself and to those searching, and the best outcome for all may be for you to withdraw your application at this stage.

THE ON-CAMPUS INTERVIEW

The on-campus interview process for finalists goes well beyond a simple interview. At best, it should be an occasion both for the hiring school to get to know you better and for you to get a better sense of the hiring department, school, and university, as well as the community in which it is located and where you will be living if hired.

THE "JOB TALK" The on-campus interview usually is made up of a formal presentation to faculty (and perhaps others, like students, alumni representatives, and community members). This presentation most often is about your research, typically your dissertation research. In addition to the content of the presentation, that is, the soundness of the research and the relevance of findings to the profession, two other things are being assessed: your command of the material and whether you convey it in a lively and interesting manner. The methods and content of the research are seen as bearing on your potential as a scholar, and your delivery is seen as relevant to your potential as a teacher. *You should therefore rehearse this presentation, time it carefully, and seek feedback on it from others* before the interview.

One important tip is to leave time for questions from the audience. Being able to speak about your work spontaneously is a good way to show your command of the content, and faculty members enjoy having a chance to speak and ask questions themselves. Everyone knows, however, that giving a "job talk" is stressful and may reduce your ability to recall everything relevant. So if there is a question that you cannot answer on the spot, just say so and promise to provide the answer later (an excellent technique for the classroom as well). Finally, you will learn something about your future colleagues from how they treat *you* in their questions, as a colleague whose work they are curious about or as a "quasi-student" whom they just want to "trip up."

The "job talk" is not the only important part of the campus visit, but it is hard work to overcome a boring or disorganized presentation, and some work ahead of time can ensure greater success. Finally, make sure that any needed equipment (as for a PowerPoint presentation or videotaped material) is available, although be prepared with backup material, since even well-prepared technology can fail.

Another variety of job talk that is less often used is preparing and presenting some material that you could use in actual classroom teaching. All the preceding points about how best to prepare for a presentation of one's research apply to this kind of "performance" as well. When invited to a campus for an interview, be sure to ask about what kind of presentation is expected and prepare accordingly.

MEETING THE FACULTY Another feature of the campus visit is meeting, usually both formally and informally, with the dean or director of the program and various members of the faculty. In fact, the campus visit usually includes a full day of appointments with individuals and groups, and candidates should be given this schedule in detail beforehand in order to be able to prepare.

Much of the conversation in these meetings, formal and informal, will be about your teaching and research interests, because both you and the faculty members taking part in the meetings are trying to determine whether or not there may be a good fit between you and the job. You should be prepared to answer several common questions: about your plans for *future* research and scholarship, the areas in which you would like to teach and/or develop curriculum, and your teaching philosophy and/or style, especially in relation to students. People will especially want to know why you want to come to *their* school in particular. There may be other questions specific to the setting or job, and in fact you will likely be repeating answers you have already given to the search committee. In preparing for a campus visit, it is legitimate to ask what questions the committee thinks you are likely to be asked.

Being invited to a campus visit means that you (and the others at this stage) are qualified for the job; the rest is "fit" and "chemistry" on both sides. Therefore these events usually include social interactions, over lunch and/or dinner, at receptions that may include students, and the like. Do not forget that these are "interviews" as well, and your interpersonal skills as well as what you are saying are being carefully observed.

To make the best impression during these conversations, it is important to have done some homework before the event, learning a bit about the work of the faculty members you will be meeting and, most important, knowing something about the curriculum and the school's mission and students. Not only will this show your motivation to be hired; it will also allow you to ask intelligent questions and to talk about your qualifications and future plans in ways that illustrate what you could contribute to that specific institution. Not only will people expect questions; they will expect you to lay out politely but candidly what *you* want in a faculty job. If relocation will be needed, they will also expect and be ready to answer questions about housing, the community, schooling for children (if relevant), and other factors that might affect your willingness to move and/or to live there. Overall, the general advice to "be yourself," meaning your best professional self, in any interview situation always is best: You need to know whether or not the school you are visiting will, in fact, be a congenial environment for you.

In most faculty governance systems, members of the faculty (not just the search committee) must vote to approve appointing a new faculty member. Faculty search committee members, who now are invested in those they have chosen to make a campus visit, often serve as hosts and even "coaches" during the visit. Since these are people you already have met, their familiar faces can be quite reassuring during the visit.

MEETING THE DEAN/DIRECTOR A key part of the visit is, of course, the meeting with the dean or director, with whom you will talk about your teaching and research interests, as you have done with the faculty. For most institutions, it usually is only here that such matters as rank, salary, expenses, and other terms and conditions (e.g., timing, benefits) of a possible appointment are discussed. While these often are negotiated *after* an appointment has been offered, the parameters of what may be possible are usually set forth at this stage. During this meeting, you will, of course, be aware that this person will be your "boss," at least for a time (successful faculty appointments generally outlast those of any dean/director), so both you and the dean/director will be considering whether you can work well together.

TOUGH TOPICS AND SITUATIONS

This brief overview has not addressed such topics as being asked inappropriate and illegal questions, including those about age, marital/partner status, children, and a range of other personal matters, including a partner's employment issues if relocation is required. When and how to disclose a LGBT identity and/or find out about the availability of domestic partner benefits also should be weighed carefully. You should also consider when and how to discuss a disability that will require accommodation on the job, especially if the disability is a visible or known, meaning that it will be on people's minds early in the process. Finally, although this does not happen often in social work, you may encounter "stress interview" techniques at any stage of the interview process, which can be unnerving. The handbooks on job searching cover ways to handle each of these as deftly as possible (Formo and Reed 1999; Sowers-Hoag and Harrison 1998).

THE OFFER

As Golde (1999) observed, "Searching for a job (and the waiting game that follows) is unlikely to leave you feeling empowered and confident. But once an offer has been made, the power balance shifts in your favor" (45). Decisions made at this crucial time can affect compensation and working conditions for years to come. Nonwhites and women have been found to be less likely to negotiate job offers, and you are unlikely to get everything you may hope for. But you can expect that some terms of the job offer can be altered, within the time limits, resource constraints, and norms of constructive professional relationships. Prestige, not money, may be regarded as the most important currency in academic job searching and hiring (Youn 2005), which can work in your favor if you have graduated from a highly ranked program, especially if you are thinking about accepting a job in an institution that has less national prestige. It also follows that a job offer from highly ranked programs may be less generous, since it is assumed that any job applicant would be eager to work there.

RANK AND TERMS OF APPOINTMENT The rank of appointment is usually listed in the job advertisement, but sometimes this is flexible. Rank is tied to both compensation and the terms of employment (length of initial contract and timing of performance reviews, tenure status, timing of review for tenure and/or promotion, etc.). In addition to talking about initial rank, therefore, you should be familiar with the school's or university's tenure and promotion systems, and it is fine to request and review the relevant written policies. Don't be afraid to ask about expectations for achieving tenure and about how recent applicants for tenure have fared; everyone will expect and be prepared to answer this question, although their answers are often guarded and complex. Finally, clarify the *length* of annual appointment. The norm for tenure-track positions is nine or ten months (although salaries are paid out on a twelve-month basis). Finally, you should make sure of the starting date.

SALARY AND BENEFITS Salary is tied to rank, and there usually are ranges within each rank, making the salary itself negotiable. Sometimes it is possible to supplement your base salary through such activities as intersession or summer teaching. Employment benefits (health insurance, retirement, etc.) in college and university settings are generally good, but these, like the levels of compensation for a specific rank, vary, including time until enrollment in and vestment in pension systems, how soon health insurance benefits will take effect, and the share of the costs that the faculty member contributes. Housing or help in locating it, help with moving costs, and other benefits may be available as well but may not be offered unless the applicant asks for them.

SUPPORT FOR SUCCESS Once on the job, managing time and competing demands is often the biggest problem for a new faculty member (Golde 1999), so you may want to consider specific work assignments and available resources to help with work. In addition to classroom teaching, will you be advising students? Where will you teach and/or advise students—on or off campus—and can you adjust your workload for activities that call for travel or online teaching? Will you be protected from undue committee work? Are teaching or research assistants available? What about teaching support, technological support, and/or research development resources in the school or on campus? What about office space and equipment? You should also try to assess the possibility of *keeping* the job over the long run, especially if the appointment offers the possibility of tenure.

Some institutions have specific protections to help new faculty get adjusted, such as a reduced teaching load in the first semester or year, release time at key points in the tenure-preparation process, and mentoring from senior faculty. Some institutions offer specific orientation for new faculty—at the school or university/college level—which can be helpful not just for performing the job but also for getting to know one's colleagues in the department and beyond.

This discussion obviously is suggestive but not exhaustive of the issues that may be discussed when negotiating a job offer. Mentors and search committee members may be helpful guides to what may be possible. Finally, if you are in the enviable position of having more than one job offer, you should compare them according to the suggestions here rather than decide on the basis of just one factor, like initial salary. As important as it is to be smart about the economics of a job offer, intangibles, especially a sense of "goodness of fit" with the institution and future colleagues—even with the community in which the school or department is located—matters as well. Whatever the prestige of the place, can you feel "at home," and can you do good work there? Since so much time and energy are invested in the job search—by the hiring institution as well as by the job applicant—everyone wants the process to succeed and the new faculty member to thrive.

KEEPING THE JOB

THE TENURE SYSTEM

In most social work education institutions, faculty jobs are tenure track, although in most places, *nontenure* appointments may be available as well. This chapter does not go into detail about tenure systems; the AAUP publishes guidelines that most colleges and universities use in developing their own governance systems and tenure standards (AAUP 2001). For example, the standards for obtaining tenure usually are exactly like those for being promoted to the rank of associate professor, although in some systems promotion may be possible *before* tenure is granted. The rigor of these systems, that is, the interpretation of the requirements for tenure and/or a promotion in rank, varies greatly.

One thing that makes negotiating a faculty job different from other kinds of jobs is that tenure is an "up or out" system. Therefore, even if your performance on the job is *satisfactory* in those first six years, the job is probationary with respect to permanent employment. That is, if you are not given tenure within a specific time period (usually six years), all that usually is possible is a final one-year appointment while seeking a job elsewhere. (While periodic posttenure reviews are becoming more common, they usually are meant to determine merit-based levels of compensation; a tenured appointment can be terminated only "for cause" or in cases of financial exigency.) Given the system's "up or out" nature, you may want to ask about flexibility in the time lines, or "tenure clock," such as the ability to take time "off the clock" for specific family needs. Those who have had previous full-time faculty service may want to ask about being able to be considered for tenure and/or promotion early, that is, before five or six years.

If a faculty job is offered, you will be expected to ask about the possibility of securing tenure before deciding about the offer. You should, of course, read the rules—for the department and the college or university—and ask how the rules are interpreted: How much weight is given to scholarship, teaching, and service? How is "excellence" in teaching and scholarship judged? What has happened in recent years to those from the department who were considered for tenure? These issues are often discussed throughout the search, but the questions often become more pointed once an offer has been made, and in addition, questions about any supports available— tangible and intangible—to help new faculty get tenure can be part of the negotiation of the appointment.

MENTORING

Those who enter the job market with a mentor already in place, from graduate school or elsewhere, have a valuable guide to seeking a job and negotiating job offers. But even those who do, as well as those who do not, may want
to ask about mentoring resources available to new faculty. Some schools and
departments of social work actually assign someone from the faculty to serve
as a mentor to each new faculty member (Wilson, Valentine, and Pereira
2002). Dixon-Reeves (2003:16) described the functions of a mentor as including being a peer counselor, adviser, role model, sponsor, and coach. Some
new faculty members report having several mentors (Dixon-Reeves 2003; Wilson, Valentine, and Pereira 2002), using different people for assistance with
different aspects of their career development.

The reported emphasis in mentoring relationships for new faculty in social
work is most often on research, publication, and getting tenure (Wilson, Valentine, and Pereira 2002:325), an emphasis that has existed for some time (Berger
1990). Much time also is spent becoming familiar with the institution and its
resources, teaching issues, and general support and encouragement. Not all
"formed" (or other) mentoring relationships succeed, for a variety of reasons,
and new faculty often seek out a variety of people, including peer groups of
other new faculty, for valuable support and advice. In particular, new faculty
members from traditionally underrepresented or oppressed groups may find it
helpful to connect with a mentor who has coped with similar issues (Dixon-
Reeves 2003; Wilson, Valentine, and Pereira 2002).

OTHER OPTIONS

The focus of this discussion of getting (and keeping) a faculty job has been
on tenure-track positions. As noted, social work is increasingly relying on
non-tenure-track, full-time faculty positions (Baldwin and Chronister 2001;
Gappa 1996; Gappa, Austin, and Trice 2005). These *contract* positions are
often research or teaching specific, with some administrative responsibilities or are completely administrative, that is, without an associated professorial title and teaching load. These kinds of positions may be excellent for
someone who loves the educational enterprise and has teaching, administrative, and/or managerial skill and experience but who is not interested
in research and scholarship at the level that a tenure-track faculty position
would require. Although the number of institutions that do not grant tenure
at all has *not* increased (Gappa, Austin, and Trice 2005:35), the number of

full-time, non-tenure-track positions has increased in those institutions in which many (although a declining proportion of) faculty members *do* have or are eligible for tenure, meaning that the groups may have status and role differences. The use of full-time, non-tenure-track positions has also been seen as a way to decrease the use of part-time or adjunct faculty, which is thought to benefit both the teachers in these positions and the students who study with them.

Based on a national study, Baldwin and Chronister (2001) divided full-time, non-tenure-track faculty positions into teaching, research, administrative, and "other." Some of these positions require a doctoral degree, though others do not (98). Roles and job satisfaction vary among these groups, but self-reported job satisfaction is comparable to that of tenured colleagues and higher than that of those on the tenure track. Women and minorities are overrepresented in all these groups compared with tenured and tenure-track faculty, which is very troubling because of the common "second-class status" of many of these faculty members in their institutions.

The employment practices affecting contract positions are extremely variable (Baldwin and Chronister 2001). For example, in some places they are always technically one-year appointments, while in others they may be for longer-term (e.g., three-year) contracts. Although saving money is often a reason for colleges and universities to employ contract faculty, the compensation may be comparable (50). In addition, how fully contract faculty members can participate in faculty governance regarding future appointments, curriculum, and other academic matters is variable. But these jobs can actually be quite stable and rewarding *if* you are prepared to be a "second-class" citizen, at least with respect to traditional faculty rank, and if they allow you to do most of what you like best (e.g., teaching, research, or administration). The benefit, of course, is sidestepping the sometimes extreme stress and anxiety of achieving tenure that new faculty in traditional roles often face. The danger is that the values that should underlie faculty employment for all may not be extended as fully to non-tenure-track faculty. Social work education urgently needs to examine the work and work lives of this growing segment of our academic workforce.

CONCLUSION

A few keys points to remember when thinking about the realities of faculty work, especially for those beginning their academic careers, are the following:

▪ *Faculty work is multifaceted,* which is both a great virtue and a big problem. The advantage comes, of course, from the variety, autonomy, and self-determination that this affords. The obvious disadvantage is that the work is essentially limitless, which means that setting priorities is a constant challenge. To the extent possible, choose a job that will allow you to do the kind of work you are best at and that you love the most. For some, this may even mean a "contract" or adjunct position or an administrative job (e.g., director of field education) rather than a tenure-track or tenured job. Once you have a job, you must balance your work commitments and demands, and your choices will vary in different settings and at different stages in your career.

▪ The colleges and universities in which a department, school, or college in which a social work program is located *have very different missions, which in turn drives hiring and promotion requirements for faculty.* Every program expects a faculty member to achieve in the areas of scholarship, teaching, and service, but the emphasis differs for each and in the amount of teaching, advising, and publishing that is normative. Conversely, resources and infrastructure to help obtain external funding for research vary greatly. Although higher rankings and prestige may be associated with research-intensive settings than with others, *think instead about what faculty activities are most possible and most rewarding for you* when deciding on where you want to work. A goodness of fit between what you want and what the hiring organization needs is what is most important for you both.

▪ It is easy to see teaching and scholarship as opposing demands, but they are "inextricably linked" (Boyer Commission 1998). Currency and renewal in your teaching requires keeping up with scholarship in the relevant fields. In addition, research and scholarship enrich all aspects of your teaching. Despite the tensions in balancing a workload, the ideal of scholarly teaching—of students learning from those at the "cutting edge" of knowledge development—remains precious and worthwhile. In sum, the *very* best teachers are accomplished scholars as well.

Faculty work can be incredibly satisfying and rewarding but also complex and multifaceted. In return for great autonomy and self-direction, the time demands are great, especially in the pretenure period but also for those who remain most productive as scholars and teachers. The settings for teaching also differ, and these differences affect getting a faculty job, keeping a faculty job, and other aspects of ongoing faculty work. As with all employment situations, the challenge is to find the best match between a teacher's skills, interests, and personal needs and a specific job. This match is unlikely to be perfect in all respects, but knowledge of the academic workplace coupled with self-knowledge and a thoughtful approach to choosing employment opportunities to explore will help ensure success in getting and keeping an academic job. Despite the demands of faculty work, it is a privilege to teach and, through teaching and scholarship and service, to shape the future of one's field.

Further Reading

Boyer, E. L. (1990). *Scholarship reconsidered: Priorities of the professoriate.* San Francisco: Jossey-Bass.

Chronicle of Higher Education. Published by the American Council on Education, a weekly newspaper of higher education.

Sowers-Hoag, K., and Harrison, D. F. (1998). *Finding an academic job.* Thousand Oaks, Calif.: Sage.

9

ETHICAL ISSUES IN TEACHING

HUMAN BEINGS MAKE MISTAKES. When, whether by error or design, human actions harm or can harm others, ethics are involved. "Others" must be defined broadly to include students, colleagues, employing institutions, and public trust in the academic enterprise itself. To write about ethical matters may seem bold, since it may imply some special knowledge or special ability in this area, which I emphatically do not have. But including this chapter represents a hope that all of us can advance in our ethical awareness and conduct by continuing our self-reflection, much as we do in regard to diversity.

Like social work itself, teaching can be considered a calling, meaning a commitment to serve and a set of standards of conduct. Social workers who are educators are familiar with and strive to adhere to the profession's ethical standards, which, for social work education programs in the United States is the National Association of Social Workers' (NASW) Code of Ethics (1999). With some notable exceptions, however (Cole and Lewis 1993; Collins and Amodeo 2005; Congress 1992, 1996; Strom-Gottfried 2000b; Strom-Gottfried and D'Aprix 2006), little of what has been written about ethical norms and their violation in the profession addresses teaching situations or academic issues. Indeed, ethical issues in research, rather than general academic ones, are more often discussed (Braxton and Bayer 1999; in social work, see, e.g., Anastas 2008; CSWE 2007a). Sometimes the ethical norms of the academy, such as upholding academic freedom, seem to conflict with professional norms, like honoring the profession's commitment to social justice and social change.

Students in social work programs are required to follow the professional code of ethics (NASW 1999) in addition to the ethical standards that guide scholarship and academic endeavors as defined by the college or university in which they are enrolled. Current accreditation standards explicitly state that they must follow the NASW's Code of Ethics (CSWE 2008:4), but these standards refer to professional, not academic, values and ethics. In their field internship and on campus, students must be able to function within the profession's norms and standards, and educational programs in social work have the right and duty to graduate only those who have demonstrated that they can do so (Cole and Lewis 1993). In addition, the accreditation standards state that the research curriculum must address "ethical approaches to building knowledge" (5) but does not specifically mention more general academic ethics and norms. Cheating and other forms of academic dishonesty are widespread on U.S. campuses (Whitley 1998), and the student manuals of departments and schools of social work typically state that students must adhere to the standards of conduct of the host college or university. Nonetheless, plagiarism and other forms of cheating, which are included in the NASW code but are understandably not its focus, are common problems.

When searching the term *academic dishonesty*, only books and articles addressing students' dishonesty come up, even though cases of faculty's fabricating or altering data and of plagiarism surface from time to time in the press. And though rarely reported, some faculty members engage in questionable practices toward students, ranging from having sexual relationships with them to publishing material based on their work without crediting it (Gibelman and Gelman 1999; Strom-Gottfried 2000b; Strom-Gottfried and D'Aprix 2006). Like students, faculty members are required to adhere to the norms of academic conduct of the colleges and universities that employ them. Federal law protecting student privacy and confidentiality (FERPA) also affects faculty's day-to-day work, although its provisions may not be well known. (Issues of disability law (ADA) are briefly discussed in chapter 4 and are not the focus here.) Adherence to general employment law and provisions for confidentiality in peer review processes (and for upholding other virtues, such fair-mindedness and the avoidance of personal biases) are necessary for safeguarding faculty colleagues and other employees. Little guidance, however, may be available to faculty members for ethical dilemmas regarding student, faculty, or administrative conduct.

This chapter is an overview of ethical issues that can arise in classroom teaching involving the conduct of both students and faculty. Its goals are to make teachers aware of these problems and to help them resolve them fairly, since teachers are role models and agents of socialization for their students. This chapter is not about teaching courses in ethics, about the responsible conduct of research (RCR), or about research ethics specifically, although some the ethical dilemmas discussed with respect to faculty and students pertain to the ethics of scholarship, as in authorship issues or plagiarism. Finally, I do not address issues related to employment decisions or employment law. Instead, I focus on how the norms of the profession, the academy, and the internship all must come together to shape the education and evaluation of our students.

For educators, ethical standards pertain to "thou shalt": regarding academic duty and serving the best interests of students while also serving the profession and the field. They also pertain to "thou shalt not": avoiding some of the ethical pitfalls and temptations common in scholarship and teaching. Teachers must both model and inculcate professional and academic norms and standards and respond to violations of academic and/or professional integrity (Simon et al. 2003). Teachers may face ethical issues when deciding on course content, evaluating and assessing students' performance, and managing the classroom (MacFarlane 2004). Ethical issues also may arise in what are characterized as dual relationships (Congress 1996), and both parties in these relationships (e.g., teachers and students) may encounter problems because of the power differential involved (figure 9.1). Because internship learning is the "signature pedagogy" of social work (CSWE 2008), additional complexities may arise regarding the safety and well-being of those being helped by students, in negotiating the boundaries between the academic and community service settings in which students learn, and when teachers are also professional practitioners accustomed to therapeutic rather than educational ways of relating to students (and others). By describing these problems in both the academy and the profession, this chapter is designed both to make readers aware of the issues and to suggest principles and practices that can improve students' education. Finally, schools and departments of social work are employment settings, and some issues of academic ethics involve administrative issues and fairness (or the lack thereof) in employment practices, such as equity in pay, retention, promotion, work assignments, and working conditions (for a discussion of gender equity issues for faculty in social work, see, e.g., Sakamoto et al. 2008). As important as these topics are, especially since contextual factors are crucial to promoting academic integrity among students and faculty members, this chapter looks at only those ethical issues involving students and faculty (not administrative) conduct.

STUDENTS AND ACADEMIC INTEGRITY

Studies consistently find high rates of self-reported cheating by college students in the United States, on exams, homework, and written assignments: 9 to 95 percent "ever," about 30 percent in any one semester, and 70 percent

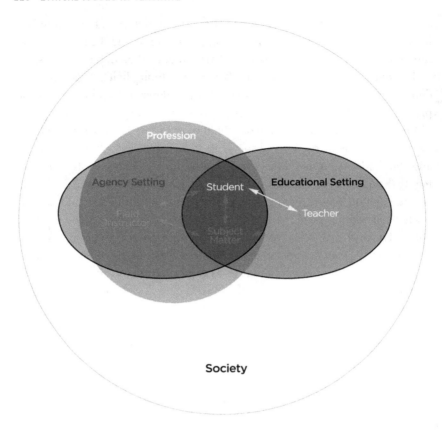

FIGURE 9.1 Model of teaching and learning that highlights the areas of ethics discussed.

on average (Vandehey, Diekoff, and LaBeff 2007; Vowell and Chen 2004; Whitley 1998). Although rates of cheating vary by discipline or major, we do not have any specific data on the rates of graduate or undergraduate social work students' cheating (Collins and Amodeo 2005; Marson and Finn 2006; Saunders 1993), although some studies have looked at undergraduate psychology and sociology students (Vandehey, Diekoff, and LaBeff 2007). The rate is also unacceptably high among graduate students (73% in one study when naming specific dishonest behaviors), especially when the students are enrolled in master's degree programs that are terminal for the field (90%) rather than a step to the doctoral degree (Wajda-Johnston et al. 2001). Students who admit to cheating do understand that the behaviors named in these surveys are dishonest and believe that their professors think so, too (Wajda-Johnston et al. 2001). Many studies, however, have found that students who are aware that their programs have policies addressing academic dishonesty, especially honor codes that are taken seriously on their campuses, cheat less often than others (Wajda-Johnston et al. 2001; Whitley 1998).

Even if we assume that rates of student academic dishonesty in social work may be lower than in some other, more highly competitive fields like business, it is hard to argue that social work students would be so different from others, such as psychology students, or that the problem is not fairly widespread, especially since many believe that Internet access has made some forms of cheating easier, such as the purchase of term papers and access to material to incorporate into written work without attribution (Groark, Oblinger, and Choa 2001).

Researchers studying student cheating more generally have explored both psychological and sociological explanations for this behavior. Undergraduate students who admit to cheating are typically younger, more immature, more involved in "partying," less able academically, more anxious about their ability to perform well, lacking in study skills, and lower in industriousness than noncheaters are (Whitley 1998). They also are more likely to have cheated previously (at a lower level of education). Students who cheat often rationalize this behavior by insisting that "everyone is doing it" (Kisamore, Stone, and Jawahar 2007; McCabe, Treviño, and Butterfield 2001; Vowell and Chen 2004) while distancing themselves from the behavior, stating that others are more likely to cheat than they themselves or their friends are (McCabe, Trevino, and Butterfield 2001). The more that his or her friends are known or thought to cheat, the more likely a student is to regard cheating favorably and to cheat himself or herself (Vowell and Chen 2004; Whitley 1998).

Situational factors are at least as powerful as personal ones in influencing the prevalence of student cheating. Working students may cheat more often than others (Vowell and Chen, 2004), a situation faced by more and more graduate and undergraduate social work students. The mere presence of a well-publicized academic honor code that is taken seriously on campus does lower the likelihood of cheating (Engler, Landau, and Epstein 2008). Examination conditions, such as spacing between seats, affect the amount of cheating on tests (Whitley 1998). High academic workloads also contribute to cheating, but so does the perception of the likelihood of detection and punishment, which brings our discussion back to how professors should handle standards of academic ethics.

REPORTING STUDENTS' ACADEMIC DISHONESTY

Despite its prevalence and the fact that academic dishonesty may well relate to the conduct of students and graduates in the workplace (Marson and Finn 2006; Whitley 1998), professors report cases of academic dishonesty by students *far* less often than they occur. This fact is especially disturbing because the most important deterrent to cheating from the student's point of view is the risk of being caught and its potential consequences, such as receiving a failing grade or being dismissed from the program (McCabe, Treviño, and Butterfield 2008). Understandably, however, teachers often state that dealing with unethical student behavior is the most onerous and unpleasant aspect of their work.

Researchers have explored why college teachers so rarely report instances of student academic misconduct, since "foster[ing] honest academic conduct" (AAUP 1996:171) is a core ethical commitment of college and university teachers. Teachers give four reasons for not "directly confronting" instances of student dishonesty (Keith-Spiegel et al. 1998). One is avoiding negative feelings, such as the stress and anxiety of confronting a student and/or guilt over the negative impact on the student's future. Students' protests can exacerbate these factors. As one student found to have plagiarized extensively in a term paper complained to me, "How can one paper ruin my chances to have the career I want so badly?" Another reason for teachers is fear of the consequences for themselves, such as a threatened or imagined lawsuit, bad student evaluations (a baseless worry, since students actually prefer to know that standards of academic integrity are being upheld), or other kinds of retaliation. Although I am not aware of data to support this idea, it would seem logical that untenured faculty may be more vulnerable to these concerns. Denying the need to report students' cheating reflects such beliefs as the worst cheaters do not get caught (so why punish the inept ones) or that cheating students are poor students and therefore will ultimately fail anyway. A few professors actually admitted not reporting students because they reminded them of their own cheating as students.

The last reasons—those related to the difficulties that are inherent in or will follow from confronting suspected cheating—may be the most important, since department, school, and college practices can help minimize them. Professors with less confidence in the administrative support they might receive when submitting a formal complaint about professors' (more women than men) academic ethics are less likely to address such problems either formally or informally (Simon et al. 2003). They also are less likely to be familiar with the procedures for doing so. All the structural aspects of teaching are becoming less salient to success in academic careers, which also affects the willingness of faculty members to confront students' academic dishonesty (MacFarlane 2004; Simon et al. 2003).

Insufficient evidence that cheating or plagiarism has in fact occurred (despite suspicions or partial evidence) is naturally the most common reason that cheating is not reported (Keith-Spiegel et al. 1998). Professors are well aware that the process of confronting a student's dishonesty is time-consuming, both the time spent compiling solid evidence of the infraction and in the hearing that follows a formal accusation of dishonesty. These processes usually must be carried out alone and silently, since confidentiality for the student means that the matter cannot be discussed with peers. An institution with a strong "honor code," from which faculty can expect administrative support for raising concerns and whose processes for pursuing complaints are fair but not unduly burdensome, can reduce these concerns. For example, proprietary software to detect plagiarism is available to make the detection of such problems easier (Groark, Oblinger, and Choa 2001).

NEW METHODS OF DETECTING PLAGIARISM

Just as access to the Internet may make some forms of cheating by students easier, proprietary Web-based plagiarism detection programs now are available, the best known—but not the only—being turnitin.com® and plagiarism. org®. The latter offers free access for students and teachers to information about plagiarism, and the former can be used to check documents for instances of plagiarism, although its use requires an individual or institutional subscription to the service. In order for teachers to use plagiarism detection software, students must submit their work in specific electronic formats, and these texts can then be uploaded and scanned for the inclusion of known works by others. A few social work programs now require that students submit all written work for screening in this way, usually based on college or university policy. Other programs make the use of such plagiarism detection software available on a case-by-case basis. Whether to purchase and use plagiarism detection technology is a program- or campus-specific decision.

"NONACADEMIC" OR PROFESSIONAL ETHICAL ISSUES

Much attention in social work's accreditation standards and in the social work education literature has been paid to "nonacademic" behavioral problems among social work students, referring to activities that violate professional ethics and norms in ways that are not directly related to examinations, homework, or written classroom assignments. These often, but not always, are activities that take place in the field internship or involve students' conduct with service users or colleagues. For example, Finn and Marson (1998) reported an incident in which a student requested (and was granted) a specific field internship placement that she later asked to have changed. It turned out that the reason she had asked for the placement was to obtain a copy of the mental health treatment records of a friend's husband for use in a divorce proceeding. Dual relationships with clients (or supervisors), other boundary violations, and assaultive or harassing behavior on campus and elsewhere also have been reported and discussed anecdotally. Unsatisfactory experiences in addressing these kinds of problems have led social work programs to try to improve their ways of resolving them (see, e.g., Urwin, Van Soest, and Kretzschmar 2006).

Educational programs that produce professional practitioners must teach the ethics of that profession. The content of courses on socials work ethics is not the topic here. Studies suggest that our educational programs may have little positive effect on our students' professed values, as least as traditionally measured, which is indeed a humbling finding (Baretti 2004). Students' ethical (or unethical) conduct commonly is found in social work education's gatekeeping issues, in the classroom, in on-campus behavior, and in the field.

Gatekeeping issues start with the admissions process, and one crude measure for ensuring that those who enter social work programs will be able to function ethically and within the law is to talk to applicants and perhaps exclude them if they have been convicted of certain felonies in the past (Urwin, Van Soest, Kretzschmar 2006). But with the increasing number of social work programs and, at best, a stable national applicant pool (Feldman 1999), there is concern that students who are academically or ethically "unsuitable" for the field may be gaining entry to social work programs. No admissions screening process is perfect, and social work programs often have to deal with decisions about whether or not to allow a student to continue in the program to which he or she has been admitted. In addition, at the baccalaureate level, students may choose, rather than be admitted to, the social work major, thus being covered by only the general undergraduate, and not the profession-specific, admissions process. This may explain why there may be a second, specific screening for "admission" to the field internship or the major and why more has been published about gatekeeping for BSW programs than for MSW programs, that is, about deciding to dismiss a student from a program.

Urwin, Van Soest, and Kretzschmar (2006) summarized the legal precedents that determined that because of the need to protect service users, admission to professional education is not a right and that it is legitimate to use more than grades to assess students' professional skills. They also believe that gatekeeping issues involving "unsuitable" behavior are found in BSW, MSW, and doctoral students. My own experience confirms this, so policies and due process procedures should apply at all levels. Faculty members are as reluctant to confront students' nonacademic as academic behavioral or ethical issues. Having well-articulated and well-accepted written policies and procedures in place is necessary to deter students' infractions, to clarify for students the performance standards against which they will be judged, and to support faculty in upholding these policies.

Because social work programs are preparing professional practitioners, students should be evaluated for their conduct in the classroom and the field internship. Most often, it is in the field that students' ethical behavior, especially involving service users, becomes a problem. Koerin and Miller (1995) found that few MSW programs had explicit policies about terminating students for nonacademic reasons, instead stating that informal "counseling out" procedures; university policies covering issues such as plagiarism, cheating, and sexual or racial harassment; and educational review procedures covered the problem, since nonacademic issues often were related to poor academic performance. When confronted with specific instances of questionable student behavior, social work educators are often torn between considering a student's "ability . . . to change and grow" and their responsibilities to current and future service users (Koerin and Miller 1995, 260). These tensions can be especially pronounced when a student's problems include substance use/abuse and/or mental illness (see, e.g., GlenMaye and Bolin 2007), especially when he or she has not disclosed a disability and has not requested reasonable accommodation for it (see chapter 4).

One approach to students' behavioral, ethical, or other nonacademic problems is to make the demonstration of an ability to practice and behave in accordance with professional ethical standards a criterion for awarding a grade, especially in the field internship, thereby transforming nonacademic or professional performance standards into academic (graded) ones. Nevertheless, very few social work students flunk out of their programs, raising questions about whether their problems in professional ethical performance are being adequately addressed.

If a student is terminated from a program, other students may become concerned and seek information about the situation. Obviously, as in employment-related terminations, specific information about what has happened cannot legally or morally be divulged to anyone not already directly involved in the situation. Even though this can be painful for faculty members who may be directly or indirectly accused of being unfair, in the end it is a comfort to students to know that their own situation would be safe in similar circumstances.

Finally, some of the most difficult problems of student professional performance that I have faced have been situations in which one or more (usually a small group) of students raises concerns about the behavior or well-being of a fellow student or a faculty colleague. A student may in fact know more about the behavior or suffering of a fellow student than an instructor does. Nevertheless, the information received in such situations is secondhand. In addition, any follow-up with the student or faculty member cannot be shared with those who raised the concern. Obviously, the first recommended step is to ask the concerned student(s) to speak directly with the fellow student or colleague about the problem, which he or she may or may not have done or be willing to do. When the concern is about a faculty member, the institution should have a procedure for making a formal complaint, which students should be told and urged to use if appropriate, although they often are, individually or collectively, too frightened of retaliation to do so. Sometimes honor boards or other mechanisms can take care of concerns about a fellow student, although these are less common. Remembering that the safety (of students and clients especially) must be the first concern, a faculty member's recourse is then to consult with the student's adviser in the program and/or with the appropriate administrator (e.g., the dean of students or program director) about what, if anything, should be done. Best practices in dealing with workplace issues can be useful guidelines in these situations.

OTHER INTERNSHIP-RELATED ETHICAL ISSUES

The confidentiality of student information is safeguarded legally under FERPA and the ADA, if it pertains to a disability or reasonable accommodation for one. These laws limit programs from discussing a student's academic or other performance issues with those in the field, especially if a disability or accommodation is involved. Only the student can choose to share this information. Sometimes the issue is other sensitive information, like matters of personal history that might affect a student's ability to practice effectively. This situation is often frustrating to both program-based faculty (especially field department personnel) and field instructors (Duncan-Daston and Culver 2005). The best option is to urge all students to talk openly with faculty and field instructors about their learning needs and limitations, beginning what should be a lifelong professional process of self-evaluation and growth. Those students who are least able to judge themselves accurately or are at least willing to talk openly about themselves are the most likely to have problems behaving professionally.

Students also need help from both program and agency staff in protecting the confidentiality of those whom they serve in the agency. When case materials are used in classroom assignments, protections like disguise may be needed. The NASW Code of Ethics's (1999) statement on confidentiality is very helpful, and the ability to practice in compliance with it is often stated by programs as a requirement for a passing grade in the field.

Dual relationships between students and service users is another area in which students may have difficulty with professional conduct in the field. A survey of MSW students about sexual contact with clients suggests that students' attitudes may be more permissive than we would like (Berkman et al. 2000), especially when former clients are involved. Findings also suggested that students would like more classroom discussion of sexual ethics and handling sexual feelings toward service users.

Dual relationships with field instructors, both sexual and nonsexual, may become a problem. The most common boundary issue is between providing supervision, in which personal and emotional issues are discussed in order to advance the student's practice skills, and providing counseling or psychotherapy per se, which is not considered ethical (Neufeldt and Nelson 1999). Sexual relationships may have a lasting impact (Barnett-Queen 1999).

A student unhappy with a field internship assignment may simply stop going to the site rather than waiting for the fieldwork department to agree to and find a new placement. Does this amount to abandoning the client? Students' completion of agency paperwork or other documentation for the field instructor, such as process recordings, may be a problem. Should the consequences be the same as those for an agency staff member or a student who does not turn in required written assignments, or should it be treated as a more minor infraction? These and other situations can be interpreted as ethical violations with serious consequences or as signs of immaturity and/or the need for professional growth. Faculty members regularly struggle with complex judgments about such situations, sometimes in the face of subtle or not-so-subtle administrative concerns about enrollments. Other factors that may affect such judgments are relationships with valued field education sites and long-standing professional relationships with agency-based and other colleagues, which students generally believe outweigh their needs in the eyes of faculty. Courage is needed to face the problems of taking professional ethics seriously.

IS THERE A CONFLICT BETWEEN
ACADEMIC AND PROFESSIONAL NORMS?

Social work education has been accused of being ideologically rather than intellectually driven. Some years ago, a child died while being given "rebirthing therapy" by a social worker in Colorado. Could more emphasis on the use of evidence-based practices in our educational programs prevent such rare but intolerable occurrences (Myers and Thyer 1997)? When educating our students about policy practice and advocacy, are we requiring that they adhere to specific political positions rather than educating them about the profession's values and teaching them how to practice when personal and professional beliefs conflict with each other? We as professors enjoy academic freedom, which the institution of tenure is designed to protect specifically so that governments, social norms, or our own academic administrations cannot constrain our thinking and scholarship. As citizens of the academy, our students enjoy the same freedoms, even though as graduate professionals, they must be able to practice in accordance the profession's values and ethics.

In an infamous example, a student at a school of social work successfully grieved an assignment in a course designed to teach advocacy skills, which was writing a letter to legislators in support of gay marriage. Because the student's religious and personal values conflicted with this, she did not complete the assignment and received a failing grade, an incident that received national attention. Even though the social work profession has certain ethical standards and policy positions (as all disciplines and professions do), students must be free to express their personal values and/or politics *in the academic setting,* as long as they do so civilly and also are taught what to do when professional and personal values conflict.

On a more concrete level, I recently consulted with colleagues about a student whose work on a final paper in one of my MSW social policy classes merited a failing grade (F). Despite passing work on previous smaller assignments, the weighting system of the assignments meant that she would fail the class (and the student was close to graduation). The question was whether to assign the course grade based on the paper submitted or to offer the student the opportunity to rewrite and resubmit it. As McKeachie and Svinicki (2006) observed, if a student were offering money to change a bad exam grade, the choice would be clear, but if the student is asking for the chance to retake the exam and thus demonstrate the competencies required, what is the ethics of granting such a request? If the student were allowed to rewrite and resubmit the paper, should all class members have the option to do so, if only to improve their grade? Would it make a difference to know that this was the second time the student was taking the course, having already failed it once? Would it make a difference if the class in question were a practice class rather than one in social policy? Would it make a difference if this were a student from a historically underrepresented group? During my consultations abut this situation, someone pointed out that the student had done well in her field internship, that is, with clients. How is this relevant to evaluating her in the social policy class? Although I remain conflicted about what I did, I allowed the student to rewrite and resubmit the final paper. It earned a C, which was just good enough via the announced point system to earn a B- (passing) grade for the course. Having chosen this option, was I able to evaluate the resubmitted paper fairly? If I am prepared to do this for one student who does not well on an assignment (without a policy to guide the program as a whole), am I obligated to make this opportunity available to everyone in the class in the future? Fundamentally, this dilemma is about how central "academic" performance is, or should be, to deciding who should graduate from social work programs.

TEACHERS' ACADEMIC INTEGRITY

One of a teacher's roles is to be a role model for students, and social work students become indignant when the conduct of a teacher or the practices of a program seem to contradict the professional values and ethics they are required to follow. Braxton and Bayer (1999) describe four types of "professorial impropriety": scholarly or research misconduct, such as plagiarism or the falsification of data; teaching misconduct, such as failing to meet classes or ridiculing students publicly; service misconduct, such as failing to meet committee and other professional obligations; and employee misconduct, such as the misuse of funds and other resources or unacceptable behavior toward staff or colleagues. In practice, social workers like to assume that fewer ethical violations are attributed to them than to those in other professions, at least as reflected in the number of formal complaints made to licensing boards and the like. Similarly, we assume that the kinds of ethical misconduct in which professors may indulge are not common in the social work professoriat

---

BOX 9.1

3.02 EDUCATION AND TRAINING

(a) Social workers who function as educators, field instructors for students, or trainers should provide instruction only within their areas of knowledge and competence and should provide instruction based on the most current information and knowledge available in the profession.

(b) Social workers who function as educators or field instructors for students should evaluate students' performance in a manner that is fair and respectful.

(c) Social workers who function as educators or field instructors for students should take reasonable steps to ensure that clients are routinely informed when services are being provided by students.

(d) Social workers who function as educators or field instructors for students should not engage in any dual or multiple relationships with students in which there is a risk of exploitation or potential harm to the student. Social work educators and field instructors are responsible for setting clear, appropriate, and culturally sensitive boundaries.

NASW 1999.

(Strom-Gottfried 2000b), although we have no hard data on this. Unfortunately, Braxton and Bayer (1999) found that professorial misconduct in other disciplines is "not as rare" as might be hoped or assumed, suggesting that a discussion of professorial ethics might be necessary.

The NASW's Code of Ethics for social work includes a section specifically addressed to educators and trainers (box 9.1). While these standards address some issues that arise in social work education, especially those pertaining to field instruction, they do not cover all the issues that are relevant and are addressed in discussions of academic ethics more broadly.

MacFarlane (2004) gives some excellent (although not social work–specific) ethical dilemmas that can arise in teaching itself, assessment, evaluation, and course management. Many of these are much more subtle than the kinds of problems that may result in formal charges of ethical misconduct, such as sexual harassment or other exploitation of students or colleagues. Norms of conduct in scholarship also must be considered. Currently, the national organizations of social work educators (e.g., CSWE, BPD, and GADE) have not published ethical standards to guide professorial conduct, but two other organizations have well-known codes (boxes 9.2 and 9.3). CSWE's National Statement on Research Integrity in Social Work (2007a) is available on its Web site (www.cswe.org) but does not address teaching roles per se.

BOX 9.2

STATEMENT OF PROFESSIONAL ETHICS:
AMERICAN ASSOCIATION OF UNIVERSITY PROFESSORS

1. Professors, guided by a deep conviction of the worth and dignity of the advancement of knowledge, recognize the special responsibilities placed upon them. Their primary responsibility to their subject is to seek and to state the truth as they see it. To this end professors devote their energies to developing and improving their scholarly competence. They accept the obligation to exercise critical self-discipline and judgment in using, extending, and transmitting knowledge. They practice intellectual honesty. Although professors may follow subsidiary interests, these interests must never seriously hamper or compromise their freedom of inquiry.

2. As teachers, professors encourage the free pursuit of learning in their students. They hold before them the best scholarly and ethical standards of their discipline. Professors demonstrate respect for students as individuals and adhere to their proper roles as intellectual guides and counselors. Professors make every reasonable effort to foster honest academic conduct and to ensure that their evaluations of students reflect each student's true merit. They respect the confidential nature of the relationship between professor and student. They avoid any exploitation, harassment, or discriminatory treatment of students. They acknowledge significant academic or scholarly assistance from them. They protect their academic freedom.

3. As colleagues, professors have obligations that derive from common membership in the community of scholars. Professors do not discriminate against or harass colleagues. They respect and defend the free inquiry of associates. In the exchange of criticism and ideas professors show due respect for the opinions of others. Professors acknowledge academic debt and strive to be objective in their professional judgment of colleagues. Professors accept their share of faculty responsibilities for the governance of their institution.

4. As members of an academic institution, professors seek above all to be effective teachers and scholars. Although professors observe the stated regulations of the institution, provided the regulations do not contravene academic freedom, they maintain their right to criticize and seek revision. Professors give due regard to their paramount responsibilities within their institution in determining the amount and character of work done outside it. When considering the interruption or termination of their service, professors recognize the effect of their decision upon the program of the institution and give due notice of their intentions.

5. As members of their community, professors have the rights and obligations of other citizens. Professors measure the urgency of these obligations in the light of their responsibilities to their subject, to their students, to their profession, and to their institution. When they speak or act as private persons, they avoid creating the impression of speaking or acting for their college or university. As citizens engaged in a profession that depends upon freedom for its health and integrity, professors have a particular obligation to promote conditions of free inquiry and to further public understanding of academic freedom.

AAUP 2006:171–172.

BOX 9.3

FROM ETHICAL PRINCIPLES IN UNIVERSITY TEACHING

The purpose of this document is to provide a set of basic ethical principles that define the professional responsibilities of university professors in their role as teacher. . . .

Principle 1: Content Competence

A university teacher maintains a high level of subject matter knowledge and ensures that course content is current, accurate, representative, and appropriate to the position of the course within the student's program of studies.

This principle means that a teacher is responsible for maintaining (or acquiring) subject matter competence not only in areas of personal interest but in all areas relevant to course goals or objectives. Appropriateness of course content implies that what is actually taught in the course is consistent with stated course prerequisites and prepares students adequately for subsequent courses for which the present course is a prerequisite. Representativeness of course content implies that for topics involving difference of opinion or interpretation, representative points of view are acknowledged and placed in perspective. Achievement of content competence requires that the teacher take active steps to be up-to-date in content relevant to his or her courses . . . and to provide adequate representation of important topic areas and points of view. . . .

Principle 2: Pedagogical Competence

A pedagogically competent teacher communicates the objectives of the course to students, is aware of alternative instructional methods or strategies, and selects methods of instruction that, according to research evidence (including personal or self-reflective research), are effective in helping students achieve the course objectives.

This principle implies that, in addition to knowing the subject matter, a teacher has adequate pedagogical knowledge and skills, including communication of objectives, selection of effective instructional methods, provision of practice and feedback opportunities, and accommodation of student diversity. . . . To maintain pedagogical competence, an instructor takes active steps to stay current regarding teaching strategies . . . and will provide equal educational opportunities for diverse groups.

Principle 3: Dealing with Sensitive Topics

Topics that students are likely to find sensitive or discomforting are dealt with in an open, honest, and positive way.

Among other things, this principle means that the teacher acknowledges from the outset that a particular topic is sensitive and explains why it is necessary to include it in the course syllabus. Also the teacher identifies his or her own perspective on the topic and compares it to alternative approaches or interpretations, thereby providing students with an understanding of the complexity of the issue and the difficulty of achieving an "objective" conclusion. Finally, in order to provide a safe and open environment for class discussion, the teacher . . . sets ground rules for discussion, is respectful of students even when there is need to disagree, and encourages students to be respectful of one another. . . .

Principle 4: Student Development

The overriding responsibility of the teacher is to contribute to the intellectual development of the student, at least in the context of the teacher's own area of expertise, and to avoid such actions as exploitation and discrimination that detract from student development.

According to this principle, the teacher's most basic responsibility is to design instruction that facilitates learning and encourages autonomy and independent thinking in students, to treat students with respect and dignity, and to avoid actions that detract unjustifiably from student development. Failure to take responsibility for student development occurs when the teacher comes to class under-prepared, fails to design effective instruction, coerces students to take a particular point of view, or fails to discuss alternative theoretical interpretations. . . .

In some cases, the teacher's responsibility to contribute to student development can come into conflict with responsibilities to other agencies, such as the university, the academic discipline, or society as a whole. . . . There are no hard and fast rules that govern situations such as these. The teacher must weigh all conflicting responsibilities, possibly consult with other individuals, and come to a reasoned decision.

Principle 5: Dual Relationships with Students

To avoid conflict of interest, a teacher does not enter into dual-role relationships with students that are likely to detract from student development or lead to actual or perceived favoritism on the part of the teacher. This principle means that it is the responsibility of the teacher to keep relationships with students focused on pedagogical goals and academic requirements. . . . Although there are definite pedagogical benefits to establishing good rapport with students and interacting with students both inside and outside the classroom, there are also serious risks of exploitation, compromise of academic standards, and harm to student development. . . .

Principle 6: Confidentiality

Student grades, attendance records, and private communications are treated as confidential materials, and are released only with student consent, or for legitimate academic purposes, or if there are reasonable grounds for believing that releasing such information will be beneficial to the student or will prevent harm to others. . . . Violation of confidentiality in the student–teacher relationship can cause students to distrust teachers and to show decreased academic motivation. Whatever [laws,] rules or policies are followed with respect to student records, these should be disclosed in full to students. . . .

Principle 7: Respect for Colleagues

A university teacher respects the dignity of her or his colleagues and works cooperatively with colleagues in the interest of fostering student development.

This principle means that in interactions among colleagues with respect to teaching, the overriding concern is the development of students. Disagreements between colleagues related to teaching are settled privately, if possible. . . . If a teacher suspects that a colleague has shown incompetence or ethical violations in teaching, the teacher takes responsibility for investigating the matter thoroughly and consulting privately with the colleague before taking further action. . . .

(continued on next page)

(continued from previous page)

Principle 8: Valid Assessment of Students

Given the importance of assessment of student performance in university teaching and in students' lives and careers, instructors are responsible for taking adequate steps to ensure that assessment of students is valid, open, fair, and congruent with course objectives.

This principle means that the teacher is aware of research (including personal or self-reflective research) on the advantages and disadvantages of alternative methods of assessment, and based on this knowledge, the teacher selects assessment techniques that are consistent with the objectives of the course and at the same time are as reliable and valid as possible. Furthermore, assessment procedures and grading standards are communicated clearly to students at the beginning of the course, and except in rare circumstances, there is no deviation from the announced procedures. . . .

Principle 9: Respect for Institution

In the interests of student development, a university teacher is aware of and respects the educational goals, policies, and standards of the institution in which he or she teaches.

This principle implies that a teacher shares a collective responsibility to work for the good of the [college or] university as a whole, to uphold the educational goals and standards of the university, and to abide by university policies and regulations pertaining to the education of students. . . .

STLHE 1996.

College and university professors enjoy much more autonomy in their work than others, including those in other forms of professional practice, so adhering to strong professional norms is even more important to their work (Braxton and Bayer 1999, 2004). Braxton and Bayer assert that since service is central to all professional work, professors must serve their academic discipline and its knowledge base, the cause of learning, students in groups, and students as individuals.

Expanding on this idea of service, Stefkovich (2006) proposed an ethical framework for educators based on an ethic of justice, an ethic of care, and an ethic of critique. Promoting social justice is, of course, a key value of the social work profession, and the various conceptualizations of social justice can be part of the content taught in social work programs. In educational decision making, following Rawls (1999), Stefkovich argued for an ethic of social justice that calls for equal access to tangible and intangible goods but offers greater access to those who are socially disadvantaged. An ethic of care and compassion places the best interests of the student and/or the educational community at the center of all ethical decision making. Finally, rooted in critical theory, an "ethic of critique seeks to challenge the status quo and give voice to marginalized sectors of society" (Stefkovich 2006:11). These ethics may sometimes conflict with professional, community, and/or personal norms and standards, so educators must continually self-examine in order to negotiate the dilemmas they encounter. Stefkovich contended that the best interests of students, individually and/or collectively, and the educational community (the department, school, or college) are best served when educational practice is guided by ethics of justice, care, and critique. She also implied that students' best interests are served when individual, collective, institutional, and professional needs are balanced.

Every college and university has faculty handbooks and policies concerning sexual harassment and discrimination that all members of that community—faculty, staff, and students—must follow. Faculty members also are responsible for informing students about the protections they enjoy under these policies as well as the procedures they may use to ensure that those who have been victimized have ways of seeking redress from discriminatory practices. As the statements from the American Association of University Professors (AAUP) and Canada's Society for Teaching and Learning in Higher Education (STLHE) make clear, the virtues and ethical guidelines for teachers in higher education go far beyond doing no harm in obvious ways. The AAUP statement embraces both scholarly and teaching issues, but the STLHE statement does not, although it covers ethics in teaching more completely. McKeachie and Svinicki (2006) summarized teachers' ethical responsibilities to their students (beyond avoiding exploitation, harassment, or discrimination) as encouraging the free pursuit of learning, demonstrating respect for students, respecting confidentiality, modeling scholarly and ethical standards, fostering honest academic conduct, and ensuring fair evaluation. None of the foregoing sources explicitly addresses ethical issues concerning students in internships or agencies, although the statement at the end of principle 4 of the STLHE talks about conflicts between the responsibility to support students' development and the responsibility to "other agencies." Such "agencies" would clearly include the internship and the best interests of service users, current and future, with whom students interact.

ETHICS OF SCHOLARSHIP

Teachers must incorporate the institutional, professional, and general norms of scholarship in all that they do. For example, they should appropriately cite others' work in course materials; present a complete and balanced point of view on the subject they teach, whatever their own interests and convictions are; respect differing points of view, including those expressed by students; and encourage students to discuss sensitive and controversial matters constructively

AUTHORSHIP Sometimes ethical problems arise when students produce materials, either for classroom assignments or as research assistants, that professors use in their own published work. Currently, social work has no specific guidelines for authorship issues, and the kinds of contributions to a written work that merit authorship credit is debated even among social work educators (Apgar and Congress 2005; Gibelman and Gelman 1999). In addition, many social work researchers, especially when they are students, seem to have had adverse experiences with authorship (Netting and Nichols-Casebolt 1997). Social workers' beliefs about the weight given to certain tasks when determining what merits authorship credit, such as data analysis, which is often assigned to student research assistants (Apgar and Congress 2005), differs from that in other fields. In sum, student–faculty collaborations in research and publication have both risks and benefits (Baretta-Herman and Garrett 2000).

Washburn (2008) drafted a "model policy" for determining authorship. Although it is aimed at enhancing university–agency collaborations, it has some helpful suggestions, such as differentiating "carrying out data analyses specified by the supervisor" (57) from the more general task of "selecting, preparing, directing, running, and interpreting statistical analyses" (nothing is said about qualitative data analyses), with the latter, but not the former, meriting authorship credit. This recommendation follows the general principle that "to be considered for authorship, a contribution must be creative and intellectual, be necessary for the project to be completed, and require a comprehensive understanding of the overall project" (56). In addition, "all authors must be involved in drafting the manuscript or revising it critically for important intellectual content. Authors must also have final approval of the version to be published" (56). Stated in reverse, should a problem be discovered in any part of a manuscript, all those listed as authors are considered responsible for the violation, whether or not they worked on the specific section in question. Thus the listed authors must be ready to take responsibility for the entire product.

For a teacher using a student's work in a publication, then, giving credit for work actually performed and offering an opportunity to help with the research and/or publication process must be balanced against assigning only appropriate responsibility. As is always noted when authorship is discussed, understanding authorship at the outset of a project is the best protection against later conflict. This issue may need to be revisited during the project, as when I worked with a student who agreed to help collect and analyze data for a project to an extent that I thought would merit coauthorship of the published study. But during our work together, I lost confidence in the student's conceptual understanding of the project, which limited the usefulness of her analyses and limited her ability to comment constructively on the text of the paper as a whole. Accordingly, I told her that I would acknowledge only her data collection and analysis, since she had ended up doing less than I had initially planned. Though disappointed, she accepted this decision, perhaps because I had regularly discussed my problems collaborating with her, trying to resolve them, which we were not able to do.

Many (student) respondents cited problems with issues in authorship on a survey I conducted in 2007 of social work doctoral students in the United States and Canada (Anastas 2008). Even though ethical issues were not the focus of my study, these comments were in response to a request for suggestions to improve doctoral education in social work or simply for comments about their experiences as students. As social workers engage more baccalaureate and master's students in inquiry-based learning and sometimes directly as collaborators in faculty research (Barretta-Herman and Garrett 2000), such problems are likely to become more rather than less common, especially owing to the increased pressure on faculty members to publish in order to obtain tenure and/or promotion. As MacFarlane (2004) said, virtue is indeed under pressure among academics today.

ETHICS IN THE CLASSROOM

Braxton and Bayer's (1999) national survey of faculty misconduct in undergraduate teaching covered course design and content, the first day of class, behavior in class, interactions with students in and out of class, examinations and grading, and relationships with colleagues. Most of these areas of potential problems directly involved the classroom. Their analysis divides ethical concerns into those of greater and lesser severity: (1) inviolable norms or proscribed behaviors, including moral turpitude, condescending negativism, inattentive planning and noncommunication of course details, particularistic grading, personal disregard of students' needs, and uncooperative cynicism; and (2) admonitory norms pertaining to negligence in advising, an authoritarian classroom, inadequate communication, inadequate course design, instructional narrowness, avoidance of inconvenience, insufficient syllabi, teaching secrecy, and disparagement of colleagues (Braxton and Bayer, 1999). While many of these seem to reflect teaching quality, in that they reflect a lack of responsibility in meeting students' learning needs, they also have an ethical dimension, as the case examples in Braxton and Bayer's book illustrate. Social work educators should also consider each of these dimensions in relation to field advising and other internship-related responsibilities.

COURSE CONTENT Ethical dimensions pertain to how teachers deal with the content of their courses, the first being intellectual honesty in representing up-to-date knowledge and varying points of view on the subject matter. Remaining up-to-date requires constant review and renewal of course materials. Having a point of view or theoretical position is fine, and stating it may help students detect any bias in what you are presenting. But students' *academic* freedom entitles them to know about and express differing perspectives, and learning to articulate these within the norms of intellectual discourse is important to their thinking and learning skills (see chapter 2).

Designing a course also has pragmatic considerations. Because the teacher's primary responsibility is to the students' overall educational success, the content of a course, especially if it is required, must build logically on any prerequisites and prepare students for subsequent courses. It must also relate sensibly (without excessive overlap of content) to concurrent courses. Social work educators should also consider course content with respect to its relevance to the field internship. A teacher's intellectual passions and interests must be balanced by students' learning needs and the structure of the curriculum as a whole.

TEACHING METHODS As noted in chapter 2, most teachers tend to teach in the ways that they were taught or that they most enjoyed as students. Nonetheless, teachers have a responsibility to learn about and use a variety of instructional methodologies to ensure that their teaching is as effective as possible and to accommodate the full range of students' learning styles. This also means that teachers may need to incorporate new technologies into their work in the classroom because of what students currently find most engaging and what they may have come to expect based on recent experience (see chapter 6). As when working on course content, the best interests of students require that teachers constantly consider *how* as well as *what* they teach.

CLASSROOM MANAGEMENT In an intellectually lively classroom, conflict among points of view is inevitable. In addition, social work degree programs involve "sensitive topics," such as policy and politics, diversity and the "isms," trauma and its treatment, child abuse, sexuality, and others too numerous to enumerate. As part of their professional development, students are encouraged to examine their opinions on these issues and often to reflect on and share personal and professional experiences. Students depend on their teachers to protect these discussions in the classroom. One of the best ways to do this is to set ground rules for students' conduct at the beginning of each course. Distractions from the classroom learning environment, such as habitual lateness; side conversations with friends; and texting, phoning, or electronic messaging during class sessions hamper everyone's learning (for managing the classroom, see chapter 3).

ASSESSMENT AND EVALUATION OF STUDENTS Ensuring that the "assessment of students is valid, open, fair, and congruent with course objectives" (Murray et al. 1996) is easier said than done. Grading is often one of the most burdensome and time-consuming aspects of classroom teaching. Chapter 8 discussed the importance of assessing educational outcomes for individual students and educational programs as a whole, as well as ways to assess teachers' performance. Besides substantive and technical aspects, these assessments also have ethical aspects.

Many of the ethical issues discussed in the organizational statements about teaching pertain to the need to be respectful of each student's dignity and worth, that is, to not be insulting or demeaning when providing feedback. But when teachers are more eager to please students than to do the hard work of evaluating their performance honestly when problems are evident can cause difficulty. For example, that it takes much more time and energy to read and comment on a weak than a strong term paper. Teachers who "go easy" on students, individually or collectively, are not helping students learn, and they are not fulfilling their responsibility to maintain the integrity of the course (and curriculum) content. Teaching is not a "popularity contest," and those instructors seen as encouraging positive student course evaluations are resented by their colleagues and undermine the efforts of the group as a whole to provide a consistently excellent education.

Dual relationships obviously interfere with student evaluations, at the extreme leading to "quid pro quo" situations. They also taint the *perception* of the evaluation. The harm of these situations extends beyond the parties directly involved. Students are motivated to do their best work when they perceive the academic system as fair. Thus, honesty in student evaluation, including constructive criticism designed to improve students' work, enhances the learning of everyone, not just the individual student involved.

MacFarlane (2004) devotes a chapter to dilemmas that can arise in student assessments, for example, evaluating the work of groups of students, perhaps students' complaints about the quality of work or lack of effort of fellow group members. Techniques that can be used to gather "artifacts" of the group's product or processes in order to identify each participant's work are keeping logs of the group's work or separating elements of a final report. Most teachers who use groups in learning find that it is common in the workplace, and therefore group members should also be expected to resolve these issues on their own, that is, to deal with them themselves. Other problems are a student offering an instructor a gift, which can involve cultural issues, or a student requesting an extension to a deadline. In both situations, instructors can be helped by referring to agreed-on rules, practices, or guidelines for a program or department.

ETHICS OUTSIDE THE CLASSROOM

Responsibilities to classroom students do not end at the classroom door, and most colleges and universities reflect this by requiring teachers to schedule office hours to meet with students, by telephone, e-mail, and electronic course software. When an instructor will and will not be available to students outside class should be made clear at the outset.

Dual relationships may be formed when engaging in nonteaching relationships with students. Accordingly, it may be best *not* to form a teaching relationship with a family member, close friend, client/patient, or business associate. Even when the teacher is working hard to maintain "objectivity" in dual relationships, they often appear to involve favoritism. The STLHE (1996) statement about dual relationships also recommends not "introducing a course requirement that students participate in a political movement advocated by the instructor."

In student advising, field instruction specifically and supervision more generally, a boundary must be maintained between the educational and professional development aims of these relationships and therapeutic aims and activities. A dual relationship in social work that is not addressed in higher education generally is becoming a service provider to a student or a student's family member or becoming the teacher (or field instructor) of someone (or a family member of someone) who is or has been a service user. Some people who receive services from a social worker are then inspired to become social workers themselves and may even ask their social worker to write a letter of recommendation for admission for them or for advice about obtaining a social work degree. Whatever the implications of this situation for the therapeutic (professional) relationship, firm boundaries must be maintained around the educational relationship, that is, no dual relationships. In large educational systems, a therapist and ex-patient may be able to avoid any educational contact with each other, but in small systems, this is unlikely to be possible.

In states that require postgraduate supervision for advanced levels of licensure and when MSW graduates themselves are paying for supervision to fulfill the needed hours, policies should be in place spelling out what is appropriate and ethical for teachers and students or former students who want to form such relationships.

RELATIONSHIPS WITH COLLEAGUES AND THE INSTITUTION

Students are often most indignant when they see the policies and practices of programs or professors as inconsistent with social work values and ethics that they are being taught and are required to follow. The NASW's Code of Ethics addresses ethical responsibilities to colleagues and employers as well as responsibilities to clients and society in general. A social work academic's "employer" is both the social work program or department and the college or university in which it is housed. Departments, schools, and colleges of social work have differing relationships to the larger systems they inhabit and are rarely described as the core or central units of these systems. In today's parlance, then, they are often challenged to demonstrate the "value added" that they provide beyond their enrollments. This relative marginalization can lead social work educators to take a defensive and/or critical position toward the colleges and universities that employ them. But colleges and universities are, by definition, multidisciplinary organizations, and no professor will find that his or her department, discipline, or profession is always the institution's top priority.

The NASW's Code of Ethics regarding social workers' ethical obligations to employers suggests that social work educators should try to help their departments, schools, and universities improve their educational services and advance their mission, which includes advancing knowledge and service to the community (box 9.4). The NASW's Code of Ethics also cites the commitment to support and improve the organization as a whole.

Being a social worker teaching in a program of higher education is just one of many examples of social workers in a "host setting." As the NASW's Code of Ethics suggests with respect to social work practice in the agency,

---

BOX 9.4

3.09 COMMITMENTS TO EMPLOYERS

(a) Social workers generally should adhere to commitments made to employers and employing organizations.

(b) Social workers should work to improve employing agencies' policies and procedures and the efficiency and effectiveness of their services.

(c) Social workers should take reasonable steps to ensure that employers are aware of social workers' ethical obligations as set forth in the NASW Code of Ethics and of the implications of those obligations for social work practice.

(d) Social workers should not allow an employing organization's policies, procedures, regulations, or administrative orders to interfere with their ethical practice of social work. Social workers should take reasonable steps to ensure that their employing organizations' practices are consistent with the NASW Code of Ethics.

(e) Social workers should act to prevent and eliminate discrimination in the employing organization's work assignments and in its employment policies and practices.

(f) Social workers should accept employment or arrange student field placements only in organizations that exercise fair personnel practices.

(g) Social workers should be diligent stewards of the resources of their employing organizations, wisely conserving funds where appropriate and never misappropriating funds or using them for unintended purposes.

NASW 1999.

---

sometimes the social work point of view may conflict with the university's priorities and practices. The NASW's code recommends that social work ethics and values prevail, but the AAUP statement on ethics states favors the defense of academic freedom and the unfettered pursuit of knowledge. As the AAUP statement notes, professors are obligated to balance "their responsibilities to their subject, to their students, to their profession, and to their institution." Perhaps social work education could benefit from more exploration and discussion of situations in which these commitments—to the goals and standards of the academy and those of the profession—conflict and how such conflicts are best resolved.

Finally, social work educators must be honest employees, honoring contracts and commitments, being good stewards of organizational resources, and generally being "good citizens." Since full-time academic employment generally has flexible hours, as the AAUP policy statement points out, professors must be judicious about their other commitments (e.g., outside employment) and should honor institutional policies on these matters.

ETHICAL RESPONSIBILITIES TO COLLEAGUES

The AAUP and STLHE ethical statements and NASW's Code of Ethics addressing conduct toward colleagues, such as being respectful of and cooperative with colleagues and settling differences and raising concerns privately (box 9.5). The box omits the sections on confidentiality, interdisciplinary teamwork, referral for services, and consultation, as they are related to client services and not relevant to the educational situation. The statements about sexual relationships and harassment in the NASW's code (which explicitly mentions "trainees") are likely to be more restrictive than college or university policies. As in the practice situation, measures for dealing with impairment, incompetence, or unethical behavior in a colleague are generally not well developed in academia.

EVALUATING COLLEAGUES Peer review is a well-established practice in academia, especially for the promotion and/or retention of full-time teachers, which usually means tenure. The NASW Code of Ethics states, "Social workers who have responsibility for evaluating the performance of others should fulfill such responsibility in a fair and considerate manner and on the basis of clearly stated criteria." Nonetheless, stories abound in both academia generally and social work education, about the political and interpersonal horrors that have occurred in peer evaluation. MacFarlane (2004) discusses common problems in evaluating teachers and teaching and managing a faculty group. Is a teacher's popularity among students equal to teaching excellence? How is a department's desire to standardize and improve the work of the group best balanced with a teacher's right and responsibility to innovate and bring his or her expertise to the teaching? These and many other subtle but important dilemmas have ethical as well as substantive dimensions that need to be addressed.

BACK TO STUDENTS

This chapter began with students in regard to potential ethical problems, but remembering what universities owe their students is a useful way to remind instructors of their responsibilities. The excerpt in box 9.6 does not include the statements' recommendations for students' obligations, which are useful to review. Complaints about the quality of students' writing are ubiquitous in social work education. How well are we helping students to do better in this area? Do we expose our students to "pursuers of knowledge at every level of accomplishment," from senior research scientists to fellow students at different

BOX 9.5

2. SOCIAL WORKERS' ETHICAL RESPONSIBILITIES TO COLLEAGUES

2.01 Respect

(a) Social workers should treat colleagues with respect and should represent accurately and fairly the qualifications, views, and obligations of colleagues.

(b) Social workers should avoid unwarranted negative criticism of colleagues in communications with [students] or with other professionals. Unwarranted negative criticism may include demeaning comments that refer to colleagues' level of competence or to individuals' attributes such as race, ethnicity, national origin, color, sex, sexual orientation, age, marital status, political belief, religion, and mental or physical disability.

(c) Social workers should cooperate with social work colleagues and with colleagues of other professions when such cooperation serves the well-being of clients. . . .

2.04 Disputes Involving Colleagues

(a) Social workers should not take advantage of a dispute between a colleague and an employer to obtain a position or otherwise advance the social workers' own interests.

(b) Social workers should not exploit clients in disputes with colleagues or engage clients in any inappropriate discussion of conflicts between social workers and their colleagues.

2.07 Sexual Relationships

(a) Social workers who function as supervisors or educators should not engage in sexual activities or contact with supervisees, students, trainees, or other colleagues over whom they exercise professional authority.

(b) Social workers should avoid engaging in sexual relationships with colleagues when there is potential for a conflict of interest. Social workers who become involved in, or anticipate becoming involved in, a sexual relationship with a colleague have a duty to transfer professional responsibilities, when necessary, to avoid a conflict of interest.

2.08 Sexual Harassment

Social workers should not sexually harass supervisees, students, trainees, or colleagues. Sexual harassment includes sexual advances, sexual solicitation, requests for sexual favors, and other verbal or physical conduct of a sexual nature.

2.09 Impairment of Colleagues

(a) Social workers who have direct knowledge of a social work colleague's impairment that is due to personal problems, psychosocial distress, substance abuse, or mental health difficulties and that interferes with practice effectiveness should consult with that colleague when feasible and assist the colleague in taking remedial action.

(b) Social workers who believe that a social work colleague's impairment interferes with practice effectiveness and that the colleague has not taken adequate steps to address the impairment should take action through appropriate channels established by employers, agencies, NASW, licensing and regulatory bodies, and other professional organizations.

2.10 Incompetence of Colleagues

(a) Social workers who have direct knowledge of a social work colleague's incompetence should consult with that colleague when feasible and assist the colleague in taking remedial action.

(b) Social workers who believe that a social work colleague is incompetent and has not taken adequate steps to address the incompetence should take action through appropriate channels established by employers, agencies, NASW, licensing and regulatory bodies, and other professional organizations.

2.11 Unethical Conduct of Colleagues

(a) Social workers should take adequate measures to discourage, prevent, expose, and correct the unethical conduct of colleagues.

(b) Social workers should be knowledgeable about established policies and procedures for handling concerns about colleagues' unethical behavior. Social workers should be familiar with national, state, and local procedures for handling ethics complaints. These include policies and procedures created by NASW, licensing and regulatory bodies, employers, agencies, and other professional organizations.

(c) Social workers who believe that a colleague has acted unethically should seek resolution by discussing their concerns with the colleague when feasible and when such discussion is likely to be productive.

(d) When necessary, social workers who believe that a colleague has acted unethically should take action through appropriate formal channels (such as contacting a state licensing board or regulatory body, an NASW committee on inquiry, or other professional ethics committees).

(e) Social workers should defend and assist colleagues who are unjustly charged with unethical conduct.

NASW 1999.

BOX 9.6

AN ACADEMIC BILL OF RIGHTS

By admitting a student, any college or university commits itself to provide maximal opportunities for intellectual and creative development. These should include:

1. Opportunities to learn through inquiry rather than simple transmission of knowledge.
2. Training in the skills necessary for oral and written communication.
3. Appreciation of arts, humanities, sciences, and social sciences. . . .
4. Careful and comprehensive preparation for whatever may lie beyond graduation. . . .
5. Opportunities to interact with people of various backgrounds, cultures, and experiences different from the students' own and with pursuers of knowledge at every level of accomplishment. . . .

BOYER COMMISSION 1998:12–13.

levels of professional development? Are we providing opportunities for all students to learn through inquiry and discovery? The "Academic Bill of Rights" was written for undergraduate education but is relevant to all of us.

CONCLUSION

MacFarlane (2004) lists the "virtues for university teaching," which apply equally to relationships with students and with colleagues, individually and collectively (the department and the institution). These are respectfulness; sensitivity to others (students or colleagues); pride in one's work; courage both to innovate and to confront difficult situations with students and colleagues; fairness; openness to peers' and students' feedback and to self-examination; restraint with respect to the primacy of one's own ideas and in one's emotional reactions on the job; and collegiality in managing courses (with one's students) and working with one's colleagues.

The following are suggestions for social work educators in regard to handling student and faculty ethics:

■ *Individual instructors* and *social work programs* and *the colleges and universities that house them all play a role in addressing students' academic ethics.* It is difficult for instructors to take action on ethical violations without the collaboration and support of their colleagues and administration. Conversely, institutional policies are effective only if instructors have the tools and the will to take action when a violation is suspected. Policies concerning academic ethics and the consequences of violating ethical standards (e.g., cheating, plagiarism) must be drawn up and promulgated. Students also must be educated about them in the classroom, just as they are about ethical issues in client services. When violations occur, the standards must be enforced through procedures that include due process for students, instructors, and any other party involved.

■ *Honor codes* have been shown to strengthen students' adherence to academic ethics, but we have no data on how many social work programs have them. These codes exemplify instructor-department-institution collaboration in addressing the problem. Most important, they have the additional advantage of enlisting students in safeguarding the program's ethical standards. If there is no such code in place, one should be developed and implemented.

■ *Faculty ethics are based on both institutional and discipline-specific standards.* In social work, the NASW's Code of Ethics (1999) is widely invoked, but its content on the ethics of teaching is minimal, especially in regard to the "*shoulds*," as opposed to the "*should nots*." Reviewing the AAUP's and STLHE's standards may be useful for bringing out the best in us as teachers.

▪ As our social work ethics reminds us, *some kinds of ethical violations are more likely when there are power differentials between people: teachers and students, senior and junior faculty, and administrative leaders with respect to all others*. Since we know that not all people are comfortable or fare well in our academic communities (Costello 2005; Sakamoto et al. 2008), *academic relationships that span ethnic, gender, class, and other social differences must be observed especially carefully*.

The table of contents of Kennedy's excellent book on the research university, *Academic Duty* (1997), reminds us of all the obligations that we in the academic community undertake in return for the academic freedoms we enjoy and for the many ways in which society supports the work of colleges and universities, materially and morally. These include the duty to prepare, to teach, to mentor, to serve the university, to discover, to publish, to tell the truth, to "reach beyond the walls," and to change. Each of these duties and many of these problems are addressed in the U.S. and Canadian statements on professorial ethics. In managing complex and multifaceted workloads, teachers may put more or less of their energies into performing different aspects of these duties at any one time and over time, but they all are important. In addition, we as social work educators may face dilemmas related to field learning and students' conduct with service users in settings in which we do not exercise as much control as in the classroom. Since academic norms for teaching conduct vary substantially across disciplines and problems in professorial conduct may be fairly widespread (Braxton and Bayer 1999), our educational practice would no doubt be helped by a more detailed exploration of these problems and better articulation of principles to guide our work, especially when academic and professional norms may seem to conflict. Working to support and enhance norms of ethical behavior for the professoriat may be one of the most powerful tools we have for improving student behavior as well.

Further Reading

American Association of University Professors (AAUP). Statement of professional ethics. Available at http://www.aaup.org/NR/rdonlyres/3B3F65BF-AA8F-4EC2-90C2-DA83380C8CB4/0/StatementonProfessionalEthics.pdf.

Murray, H., Gillese, E., Lennon, M., Mercer, P., and Robinson, M. (1996). *Ethical principles in university teaching.* Hamilton, Ont.: Society for Teaching and Learning in Higher Education. Available at www.mcmaster.ca/stlhe/documents/Ethical%20Principles%20in%20University%20Teaching.pd.

10

CONCLUSION

SOCIAL WORK IS, IN MANY WAYS, A CALLING, and social workers who become teachers bring both their interpersonal skills and their passion for their subject matter to their educational work. Overall, although the quality of teaching in social work programs is good, reflecting on practice is as useful a habit for educators as for practitioners. This book is intended to assist in that process, and it also has identified areas—old and new—that require our continuing attention now and in the years to come.

"BIG PICTURE" ISSUES

GOING GLOBAL

Among the many areas of teaching and learning that will continue to require our collective attention in the twenty-first century is one not addressed in this book: bringing a global and international focus to our work. Even after September 11, 2001, enrollments of international students at U.S. colleges and universities have risen, although more in some institutions than others. National economies are now more interdependent than ever, which affects both the resources available to fund health and social care and the health and social welfare systems in which social workers will practice. Rapid travel and electronic communication speed the dissemination of ideas. Migration, voluntary and involuntary, brings international issues into the United States, and policies affecting immigration and services to immigrants, documented and undocumented, remain a hotly contested and unresolved political issue.

How will social work education respond to these and other forms of globalization? One doctoral student in my 2006 study offered this observation:

"Much of the literature coming out of the United States is extremely limited in scope . . . with respect to a serious lack of acknowledging the work that goes on outside of the United States . . . a very narrow and parochial perspective [on] the world." To what extent might this observation apply to what we offer in BSW and MSW education in social work? Because we have more international students and overseas experiences (for students and teachers) are becoming more common either during or before enrollment in our programs, how might our curricula, student support, and/or teaching methods need to change?

THE COLLEGE/UNIVERSITY CONTEXT

Public and private U.S. colleges and universities are evolving, especially in their economic structures, which in turn affects faculty employment and work, not always in ways that enhance academic freedom or teaching quality. I finished writing this book at a time when the United States had entered a serious economic downturn, coupled with a change toward a more progressive ideology, at least in the national government. Economic hard times affect both private and public institutions of higher education, but in somewhat different ways. Some people are critical of the corporate model adopted by many university economics and governance systems (Aronowitz 2000) and hope that the recent failures in the corporate sector will make business a less desirable model for higher education to emulate. Instead, colleges and universities may continue to increase their use of lower-paid contingent workers or cut supportive services for students. As a society, just as in our financing of health care, we have not yet acknowledged that most other developed economies provide much greater access to (often tuition-free) higher education, although examination-based entrance requirements are often required.

The professoriat in general has been criticized for not resisting or at least not questioning these institutional arrangements. Will the social work professoriat, whose students are often from less wealthy and privileged sectors of society, deal with these issues? Is accommodation or resistance the better strategy? As an occupational group, do we have the organizational structures needed to consider and answer these questions?

Social work has accredited programs of social work education in a wide variety of institutions, from small liberal arts colleges with local or regional student bodies to top-ranked research-extensive universities with national and international student bodies. A social work department may be a "jewel in the crown" on a smaller campus or a small and relatively devalued part of a very large campus. A social work faculty may consist of only a few full-time employees who also teach courses in other departments or a much larger group that is either self-contained or interdisciplinary. The conditions of faculty work, including such basics as course load and faculty performance standards, differ in these different settings and circumstances. The rewards and frustrations of faculty life differ as well. Embracing and valuing this diversity remains a challenge.

LEGITIMATING THE SCHOLARSHIP OF TEACHING

Boyer (1990) made a brave and much-praised attempt to elevate the scholarship of teaching and learning to equality with the classic idea of scholarship of discovery. Traditional university reward systems, including promotion and tenure, nonetheless continue to give greatest value to the scholarship of discovery, and many social work programs do so as well in order to improve the standing of discipline or department on campus, especially in research universities. How can social work improve its scholarship of teaching? New developments in this area might benefit non-tenure-track faculty, whose numbers continue to increase. Our profession is not alone in having to grapple with this problem and should take note of developments in other practice-oriented academic fields. For example, medicine has an electronic gateway to peer-reviewed syllabi and other teaching tools, and dentistry is developing a similar gateway. Such a system is designed to legitimate the intellectual work of preparing for tenure and promotion. The Council on Social Work Education's (CSWE) practice of printing compendia of peer-reviewed syllabi is an effort along these lines but may need to be updated.

If social work education is to have a vibrant scholarship of teaching and learning, it will need funding. The CSWE currently supports such efforts through its Visiting Scholars Program, which helped me in 2006/2007 when working on doctoral education. The Silberman Fund also has supported this kind of scholarship in the United States. But in an era when obtaining funding for research has become important to tenure and promotion, these resources are not enough to support the amount of scholarship needed.

Finally, useful data probably are buried in various studies conducted by accredited departments, schools, and colleges of social work as part of their self-study (re)affirming disciplinary accreditation. The amount of information generated has likely grown as a by-product of the recent option for well-established programs (with prior approval) to conduct focused studies as an alternative to the traditional self-study. All self-study documents and self-evaluations are now treated as confidential data, however, so they cannot be used for information that might help the enterprise as a whole.

OTHER KNOWLEDGE NEEDS

In a period of evidence-based practice, how will our profession develop and disseminate knowledge? Much (but not all) social work research and scholarship takes place in the academy. Social workers often are involved in a *scholarship of application*, moving toward "engagement" and asking, in Boyer's (1990) words, "How can knowledge responsibly be applied to consequential problems? How can it be helpful to individuals as well as institutions? . . . Can social problems *themselves* define an agenda for scholarly investigation?" (21, italics in original). Reviews of the social work literature suggest that research on practice processes and outcomes is only a small fraction of what is published. Does this suggest a need for closer university–agency or university–community relationships?

The field will need knowledge brokers to disseminate knowledge (Hall 2008), since most practitioners must concentrate on assessing each client's situation, preferences, and choices rather than evaluating the research itself. Resources like the Cochran Collaboration (www.cochrane.org) and Campbell Collaboration (www.campbellcollaboration.org) must be made more widely known and affordable to students, educators, and practitioners. Information services, like Gary Holden's Information for Practice (IP) (www.nyu.edu/socialwork/ip/), need to be developed, supported, and made available to teachers, learners, and graduate practitioners.

EMPHASIS ON OUTCOMES

The widening use of electronic technologies to enhance curricular content and the learning environment is one example of how instruction affects what is possible in teaching and learning. An issue less obvious to outsiders and newcomers to academia is the current emphasis on accountability and assessment. Some of this emphasis no doubt reflects conservative suspicions about higher education in general and is similar to the emphasis on testing of such federal legislation as the "No Child Left Behind" efforts of the second Bush administration. Colleges' and universities' competition for resources, both public and private, their marketing, the competition among units and departments on campuses, and the shift in accreditation standards toward outcomes at all levels suggest that this emphasis is likely here to stay.

Classroom assessment techniques are designed to provide *formative* feedback to instructors that will help improve a specific course or class experience. Except for the effort to implement these processes, their usefulness is clear. But determining how well we achieve the educational outcome we want—an expert social work practitioner—is difficult. Many kinds of approximations are being tried, which is good. So far, though, the profession and its educational institutions have not been willing to undertake the conceptually demanding and costly development of better and more comprehensive methods for assessing practice skills in the way that the medical and other professions have done. This may hurt the field in the long run.

All these issues—higher education in the United States and its global aspirations, the changing nature of faculty work, the evolution of social work knowledge, the emphasis on educational outcomes, and the continuing change in social work practice sites, roles, and methods, coupled with the increasing racial, ethnic, cultural, and religious diversity of the U.S. population—draw attention to the "teacher-in-situation" framework. How we understand social agencies (internship or practice settings), educational institutions, and the social work profession affects how we teach, although these contextual influences have not yet been adequately analyzed and explored with respect to students and their learning or teachers and their teaching.

LESSONS IN LEARNING

The latter half of the twentieth century produced much knowledge about learning as a lifelong, developmental process, and standards for professional education, along with the liberal arts education in which it has long been the tradition, now recommend teaching our students thinking skills, specifically critical thinking, along with discipline-specific content. Social work education has always emphasized self-knowledge and self-reflection as necessary for practice. We also need to act on all the research showing that high expectations bring out the best in students, especially when coupled with support in an environment free of stereotype-related fears.

Social work educators have considered Kolb's learning theory with respect to field learning in particular, but many other frameworks for understanding adult learners' development could be used more systematically to inform teaching, analyze student–teacher interactions, or assess learning outcomes. Bertha Reynolds's (1942/1985) profession-specific framework describing a practitioner's stages of development still influences thinking in field education, and Bandura's (1997) construct of self-efficacy can also be used to examine students' self-assessed progress in learning. Schön's (1983, 1987) framework could help us examine the heuristics characteristic of practice expertise, that is, the ways we all simplify problems in order to make quick decisions (Gigerenzer 2007). Theories of adult learning help teachers go outside their own preferred styles and techniques of learning in order to engage a greater variety of students.

Using a variety of teaching techniques, at the group (classroom) and individual (advising, supervising) levels, is the best way to ensure both that learning is taking place and that students who learn in a variety of ways will engage with the material. The increasing use of electronic technologies in the classroom and the field makes this easier. Finally, learning extends to peer interaction as well as instructor–student interchange, which also is good preparation for the group and team interactions common in and important to health and human services.

The Social Work Congress of 2005 adopted the imperative that the social work profession "increase the value proposition of social work by raising standards and increasing the academic rigor of social work education programs" (NASW 2005:1). What evidence do we have that suggests we are addressing this call to action or making progress in achieving this goal? Social work education, with its "signature pedagogy" of field internship learning, has been a leader in higher education in learning through doing and in coaching by the field instructor and field liaison. Most social work programs work hard to help students integrate classroom and field learning, but tensions between them remain. Both curricular development and decisions about faculty qualifications and deployment will affect this balance in the future.

Graduate social work education in the United States does not use inquiry methods of teaching as much as, for example, social work programs in the European Union do, for which a thesis is generally required for the master's degree. How might the wider engagement of social work students in research and scholarship affect their development as professional experts and lifelong learners?

Because the experiential learning of the field internship and many practice classrooms has been driven by national accreditation standards, social work is ahead of many other fields and disciplines in dealing with diversity and oppression issues in its curriculum and, although not yet successfully enough, in recruiting diverse students and faculty. Nevertheless, these efforts still generally lag behind the changing demographics of U.S. society and the scholarship and new conceptual frameworks being developed in gender, cultural, and global studies. As Costello (2005) reminds us, our educational programs remain less hospitable to some people than to others, so this area requires continuing efforts.

Finally, social work has always stressed ethical standards for professional practice, but it has not as often discussed academic ethics in the field. Useful documents in both Canada and the United States discuss the ethics that must guide scholarship, including students' work and teaching. The CSWE proposed a set of ethical principles for research (CSWE 2007a), and the NASW Code of Ethics (1999) refers specifically to research and teaching, but no social work education organization has yet drawn up a profession-specific academic code or endorsed an existing one. Should we talk about whether or not social work education might benefit from such an effort?

LEARNING TO TEACH

Beginning a career as a social work educator, usually during doctoral studies, is intellectually, professionally, and personally challenging (McGranahan 2008; Sussman, Stoddart, and Gorman 2004). Doctoral students often are moving from a practice to a research role (Mendenhall 2007) as well. When offered a teaching assistant position, for either financial aid or professional development, it can be difficult to manage simultaneously the dual identities of teacher and student in addition to the dual relationships with the faculty the student is assisting. If doctoral students are employed as adjunct teachers, they become both employees and tuition-paying students. As both teachers and scholars, they are learning to be comfortable using authority. Doctoral programs currently incorporate various kinds of teaching experiences and so must address these potential conflicts in both the program and its policies for the educational programs in which doctoral students teach. These are some of the "new" problems arising from the profession's efforts to better prepare future faculty.

IN CLOSING

Despite the challenges to the field that I have just outlined, my career as a social work educator has been immensely rewarding. I have found social work students at all levels—baccalaureate, master's, and doctoral—to be dedicated to helping others in need, interested in social justice and social change, and ethical in all they do. But they sometimes lack confidence in their academic abilities. My students have appreciated my confidence in their ability to achieve while holding them to firm performance standards. Even though their statements may be motivated by a desire to please me (and they do), they motivate me to persist in these behaviors, even when I must fail a student in an assignment or a course.

I also have been rewarded by my intellectual engagement with my subject matter: How many jobs pay a person to learn continuously, which is necessary for keeping course and curriculum content current and fresh? Every time I read students' papers, I learn something from them. The first great pleasure of my academic career has been helping students grow professionally; the second is my engagement with ideas—old and new, others' and my own. Some people would no doubt reverse the order of these two activities, which probably does not matter if both are significant.

To use Bertha Reynolds's still useful terminology, becoming a social work educator, as in the rest of academia, used to be a matter of "sink or swim." Now much more is available now in the literature of social work and higher education, in campus-based teaching centers, and in social work doctoral programs, to help the new or renewing teacher. There is much to admire in the current state of teaching in social work, but there also is much we could improve on, individually and collectively. If this book helps others in this process, I will have achieved my goal.

REFERENCES

(AAUP) American Association of University Professors. (1996). *Policy documents and reports*. 9th ed. Washington, D.C.: American Association of University Professors.

(AAUP) American Association of University Professors. (2003). What do faculty do? Available at http://www.aaup.org/Issues/workplace/facdo.htm (accessed February 3, 2003).

(AAUP) American Association of University Professors. (2006). Statement of professional ethics. Available at http://www.aaup.org/NR/rdonlyres/ 3B3F65BF-AA8F-4EC2–90C2-DA83380C8CB4/0/ StatementonProfessionalEthics.pdf (accessed July 16, 2008).

Abram, F. Y., and Cruce, A. (2007). A re-conceptualization of "reverse mission" for international social work education and practice. *Social Work Education* 26 (1):3–19.

Abram, F. Y., Slosar, J. A., and Walls, R. (2005). Reverse mission: A model for international social work education and transformative intra-national practice. *International Social Work* 48 (2):161–176.

Abrams, L. S., and Gibson, P. (2007). Reframing multicultural education: Teaching white privilege in the social work curriculum. *Journal of Social Work Education* 43 (1):147–160.

Abrams, L. S., and Jackson, M. (2007). Teaching notes: Reframing multicultural education: Teaching white privilege in the social work curriculum. *Journal of Social Work Education* 43 (1):147–159.

Adams, K. A. (n.d.) What colleges and universities want in new faculty. Washington, D.C.: Preparing Future Faculty Program. Available at http:// www.aacu.org/pff/pdfs/PFF_Adams.pdf (accessed July 13, 2009).

Adkins, L., Williams, C., Vernon, R., Lynch, D., and Gohagan, D. (2002). Developing a tool to review online course content and delivery. Tech presentation at annual meeting of Council on Social Work Education, Nashville, Tenn., February.

Ali, S. R., and Ancis, J. R. (2005). Multicultural education and critical pedagogy approaches. In C. Z. Enns and A. L. Sinacore, eds., *Teaching and social justice: Integrating multicultural and feminist theories in the classroom*, 69–84. Washington, D.C.: American Psychological Association.

American Psychiatric Association. (1999). Position statement on psychiatric treatment and sexual orientation. *American Journal of Psychiatry* 156:1131.

American Psychological Association. (1997). *Resolution: Reparative therapy*. Washington, D.C.: American Psychological Association.

Anastas, J. W. (2006). Employment opportunities in social work education: A study of jobs for doctoral graduates. *Journal of Social Work Education* 42 (2):195–209.

Anastas, J. W. (2007a). Doctoral students in social work: Preliminary report on a North American survey. Manuscript.

Anastas, J. W. (2007b). Guest editorial: Theorizing (in)equity for women in social work. *Affilia: Journal of Women in Social Work* 22 (3):235–239.

Anastas, J. W. (2007c). Initial report on the faculty vacancy survey. Manuscript. Council on Social Work Education, Alexandria, Va.

Anastas, J. W. (2008). Ethics in research. In T. Mizrahi and L. E. Davis, eds., *Encyclopedia of social work*, 20th ed., vol. 2, 151–158. Washington, D.C.: NASW Press; New York: Oxford University Press.

Anastas, J. W., and Kuerbis, A. M. (2009). Doctoral education in social work: What we know and what we need to know. *Social Work* 54 (1):71–81.

Anderson, L. W., and Krathwohl, D. R., eds. (2001). *A taxonomy of learning, teaching, and assessment: A revision of Bloom's taxonomy*. New York: Longman.

Anderson, R. S., and Speck, B. W., eds. (1998). *Changing the way we grade student performance: Classroom assessment and the new learning paradigm*. San Francisco: Jossey-Bass.

Angelo, T. A., and Crossman, K. P. (1993). *Classroom assessment techniques: A handbook for college teachers*. 2nd ed. San Francisco: Jossey-Bass.

Apgar, D. H., and Congress, E. (2005). Authorship credit: A national survey of social work educators' beliefs. *Journal of Social Work Education* 41 (1):135–143.

Applied Presentation Technologies (in Higher Education Project). (2000). Planning a presentation. Available at http://www.umist.ac.uk/apt/prept/index. shtml (accessed August 3, 2001).

Aronowitz, S. (2000). *The knowledge factory: Dismantling the corporate university and creating true higher learning*. Boston: Beacon Press.

Askeland, G. A., and Payne, M. (2006). Social work education's cultural hegemony. *International Social Work* 49 (6):731–743.

Associated Press. (2003). Students called on SMS cheating. Available at http://www .wired.com/culture/education/news/2003/01/57484 (accessed September 2, 2008).

Austin, D. M. (1997). The institutional development of social work education: The first 100 years and beyond. *Journal of Social Work Education* 33 (3):599–612.

Avery, A., Chase, J., Johansson, L., Litvak, S., Montero, D., and Wydra, M. (2007). America's changing attitudes toward homosexuality, civil unions, and same-gender marriage: 1977–2004. *Social Work* 52 (1):71–79.

Aviles, C. B. (2001). Grading with norm-referenced or criterion-referenced measurements: To curve or not to curve, that is the question. *Social Work Education* 20 (5):603–608.

Badger, L. W., and MacNeil, G. (2002). Standardized clients in the classroom: A novel instructional technique for social work educators. *Research on Social Work Practice* 12 (3):364–374.

Baez, A. (2005). Development of an objective structured clinical examination (OSCE) for practicing substance abuse intervention competencies: An application in social work education. *Journal of Social Work Practice in the Addictions* 5 (3):3–20.

Bain, K. (2004). *What the best college teachers do.* Cambridge, Mass.: Harvard University Press.

Baldwin, R. G., and Chronister, J. L. (2001). *Teaching without tenure: Policies and practices for a new era.* Baltimore: Johns Hopkins University Press.

Ballantyne, N., and Knowles, A. (2007). Enhancing student learning with case-based learning objects in a problem-based learning context: The views of social work students in Scotland and Canada. *Journal of Online Teaching and Learning* 3 (4):363–374. Available at http://jolt.merlot.org/vol3no4/knowles.htm (accessed September 4, 2008).

Bandura, A. (1997). *Self-efficacy: The exercise of self-control.* New York: Freeman.

Banner, J. M., and Cannon, H. C. (1997). *The elements of teaching.* New Haven, Conn.: Yale University Press.

Baretti, M. (2004). What do we know about the professional socialization of our students? *Journal of Social Work Education* 40 (2):455–483.

Barnes, D. R. (1992). *From communication to curriculum.* 2nd ed. Portsmouth, N.H.: Boynton/Cook.

Barnett-Queen, T. (1999). Sexual relationships with educators: A national survey of master's level practitioners. *Clinical Supervisor* 18 (1):151–172.

Barretta-Herman, A., and Garrett, K. J. (2000). Faculty–student collaboration: Issues and recommendations. *Advances in Social Work* 1 (2):148–159.

Baskind, F. R., Shank, B. W., and Ferraro, E. K. (2001). Accountability for professional practice: Assessment in social work education. In C. A. Palombo and T. W. Banta, eds., *Assessing student competence in accredited disciplines: Pioneering approaches to assessment in higher education,* 95–120. Sterling, Va.: Stylus.

Belenky, M. F., Clinchy, B. M., Goldberger, N. R., and Tarule, J. M. (1986). *Women's ways of knowing: The development of self, voice, and mind.* New York: Basic Books.

Belenky, M. F., and Stanton, A. V. (2000). Inequality, development, and connected knowing. In J. Mezirow and Associates, eds., *Learning as transformation: Critical perspectives on a theory in progress,* 71–102. San Francisco: Jossey-Bass.

Beless, D. W. (1994). Rank folly. *Social Work Education Reporter* 42 (1):2.

Bennett, L., and Coe, S. (1998). Social work field instructor satisfaction with faculty–field liaisons. *Journal of Social Work Education* 34 (3):345–352.

Berger, R. M. (1990). Getting published: A mentoring program for social work faculty. *Social Work* 35 (1):69–71.

Berkman, C. S., Turner, S. G., Cooper, M., Polnerow, D., and Swartz, M. (2000). Sexual contact with clients: Assessment of social workers' attitudes and educational preparation. *Social Work* 45 (3):223–234.

Bligh, D. A. (2000). *What's the use of lecturing?* San Francisco: Jossey-Bass.

Blonstein, S. (1988). Reconsideration of internships in graduate social work education. *Journal of Teaching in Social Work* 2 (1):91–105.

Bloom, B. S. (1956). *Taxonomy of educational objectives: The classification of educational goals.* New York: McKay.

Bogo, M. (2005). Field instruction in social work: A review of the research literature. *Clinical Supervisor* 24 (1/2):163–193.

Bogo, M., and McKnight, K. (2005). Clinical supervision in social work: A review of the research literature. *Clinical Supervisor* 24 (1/2):49–67.

Bogo, M., Raskin, M., and Wayne, J. (2002). *Thinking out of the box: Developing new approaches for field education.* New York: Field Consortium.

Bogo, M., Regehr, C., Hughes, J., Power, R., and Globerman, J. (2002). Evaluating a measure of student field performance in direct service: Testing reliability and validity of explicit criteria. *Journal of Social Work Education* 38 (3):385–401.

Bogo, M., Regehr, C., Power, R., and Regehr, G. (2007). When values collide: Field instructors' experiences of providing feedback and evaluating competence. *Clinical Supervisor* 26 (1/2):99–117.

Bogo, M., and Vayda, E. (1998). *The practice of field instruction in social work: Theory and process.* 2nd ed. New York: Columbia University Press.

Bourdieu, P. (1988). *Homo academicus.* Stanford, Calif.: Stanford University Press.

Bourdieu, P. (1990). *The logic of practice.* Stanford, Calif.: Stanford University Press.

Bourdieu, P. (1996). *The state nobility: Elite schools in the field of power.* Trans. L. C. Clough. Stanford, Calif.: Stanford University Press.

Bourdieu, P. (2001). *Masculine domination.* Stanford, Calif.: Stanford University Press.

Boyer, E. (1990). *Scholarship reconsidered: Priorities for the professoriate.* Princeton, N.J.: Carnegie Foundation for the Advancement of Teaching.

Boyer Commission on Educating Undergraduates in the Research University. (1998). *Reinventing undergraduate education: A blueprint for America's research universities.* Stony Brook: State University of New York at Stony Brook. Available at http://naples.cc.sunysb.edu/Pres/boyer.nsf/673918d46fbf653e852565ec0056ff3e/d955b61ffddd590a852 (accessed July 4, 2007).

Braxton, J. M., and Bayer, A. E. (1999). *Faculty misconduct in collegiate teaching.* Baltimore: Johns Hopkins University Press.

Braxton, J. M., and Bayer, A. E., eds. (2004). *Addressing faculty and student classroom improprieties.* San Francisco: Jossey-Bass.

Broadband growth. (2001). *PC Magazine,* May 6, 74.

Brookfield, S. D. (1999). *Discussion as a way of teaching: Tools and techniques for democratic classrooms.* San Francisco: Jossey-Bass.

Brookfield, S. D. (2000). Transformative learning as ideology critique. In J. Mezirow and Associates, eds., *Learning as transformation: Critical perspectives on a theory in progress,* 125–148. San Francisco: Jossey-Bass.

Brookfield, S. D., and Preskill, S. (1999). *Discussion as a way of teaching: Tools and techniques for democratic classrooms.* San Francisco: Jossey-Bass.

Brown, A. H., Cervero, R. M., and Johnson-Bailey, J. (2000). Making the invisible visible: Race, gender, and teaching in adult education. *Adult Education Quarterly* 50 (4):273–288.

Brown, G., with Bull, J., and Pendlebury, M. (1997). *Assessing student learning in higher education.* New York: Routledge.

Brownlee, K., Sprakes, A., Saini, M., O'Hare, R., Kortes-Miller, K., and Graham, J. (2005). Heterosexism among social work students. *Social Work Education* 24 (5):485–494.

Brownstein, C., Smith, H. Y., and Faria, G. (1991). The liaison role: A three phase study of the schools, the field, the faculty. In D. Schneck, B. Grossman, and U. Glassman, eds., *Field education in social work: Contemporary issues and trends,* 237–248. Dubuque, Iowa: Kendall/Hunt.

Buchan, V., Hull, G. H., Mather, J., Pike, C., Ray, J., Rodenhiser, R., Rogers, J., and Smith, M. L. (2007). *Baccalaureate education assessment project (BEAP) handbook.* Salt Lake City: Associate of Baccalaureate Social Work Program Directors.

Buchan, V., Rodenheiser, R. W., Hull, G., Rogers, J., Pike, C. K., and Smith, M. L. (2004). Evaluating an assessment tool for undergraduate social work education: Analysis of the Baccalaureate Educational Assessment Package (BEAP). *Journal of Social Work Education* 40 (2):239–253.

Cain, R. (1996). Heterosexism and self-disclosure in the social work classroom. *Journal of Social Work Education* 32 (1):65–76.

Caragata, L., and Sanchez, M. (2002). Globalization and global needs: New imperatives for expanding international social work education in North America. *International Social Work* 45 (2):217–238.

Carnegie Foundation for the Advancement of Teaching. (2006). Basic classification description. Available at http://www.carnegiefoundation.org/classifications (accessed March 14, 2007).

Carter-Black, J. (2007). Teaching cultural competence: An innovative strategy grounded in the universality of storytelling as depicted in African and African-American storytelling traditions. *Journal of Social Work Education* 43 (1):31–49.

Cauble, A. E., and Thurston, L. (2000). Effects of interactive multimedia training on knowledge, attitudes, and self-efficacy of social work students. *Research on Social Work Practice* 10 (4):428–437.

Centre for Curriculum Transfer and Technology. (1999). Report on the online educational resources project. Available at http://www.oer.c2t2.ca/oer-report.pdf (accessed August 6, 2000).

Chambers, R. (2002). Using technology to support student learning styles: A comparison group study. Paper presented at annual meeting of Council on Social Work Education, Nashville, Tenn., February.

Christensen, C. (1995). *The art of discussion leading: A class with Chris Christensen*. Cambridge, Mass.: Derek Bok Center for Teaching and Learning, Harvard University.

Chute, D., and Bliss, M. (1996). *Exploring psychological disorders*. CD-ROM. Florence, Ky.: Wadsworth/Cengage.

Clark, H. G. (2002). A comparison of the critical thinking skills of BSW and MSW students. *Journal of Baccalaureate Social Work* 7 (2):63–75.

Cluse-Tolar, T., Lambert, E. G., Ventura, L. A., and Pasupuleti, S. (2004). The views of social work students toward gay and lesbian persons: Are they different from other undergraduate students? *Journal of Gay and Lesbian Social Services* 17 (3):59–85.

Cole, B. S., and Cain, M. W. (1996). Social work students with disabilities: A proactive approach to accommodation. *Journal of Social Work Education* 32 (3):339–349.

Cole, B. S., and Lewis, R. G. (1993). Gatekeeping through termination of unsuitable social work students: Legal issues and guidelines. *Journal of Social Work Education* 29 (2):150–159.

Collins, M. E., and Amodeo, M. (2005). Responding to plagiarism in schools of social work: Considerations and recommendations. *Journal of Social Work Education* 41 (3):527–543.

Comerford, S. A. (2004). Strengthening the affective and behavioral dimensions of learning about human diversity: Sharing personal narratives on off-site retreats. *Journal of Teaching in Social Work* 24 (3/4):183–200.

Congress, E. (1992). Ethical teaching of multicultural students: Reconsideration of social work values for educators. *Journal of Multicultural Social Work* 2 (2):11–23.

Congress, E. (1996). Dual relationships in academia: Dilemmas for social work educators. *Journal of Social Work Education* 32 (3):329–338.

Congress, E. (2001). Dual relationships in social work education: Report on a national survey. *Journal of Social Work Education* 37 (2):255–266.

Corey, G., Corey, M. S., and Haynes, R. (2003). *Ethics in action CD-ROM*. CD-ROM with manual. Florence, Ky.: Brooks-Cole/Cengage.

Costello, C. Y. (2001). Schooled by the classroom: The (re)production of social stratification in professional school settings. In E. Margolis, ed., *The hidden curriculum in higher education*, 43–59. New York: Routledge.

Costello, C. Y. (2005). *Professional identity crisis: Race, class, gender, and success at professional schools.* Nashville, Tenn.: Vanderbilt University Press.

Cowburn, M., Nelson, P., and Williams, J. (2000). Assessment of social work students: Standpoint and strong objectivity. *Social Work Education* 19 (6): 627–637.

Cramer, E. P., ed. (2002). *Addressing homophobia and heterosexism on college campuses.* Binghamton, N.Y.: Harrington Park Press.

Cranton, P. (1996). *Professional development as transformative learning: New perspectives for teachers of adults.* San Francisco: Jossey-Bass.

Crewe, S. E. (2004). Ethnogerontology: Preparing culturally competent social workers for the diverse face of aging. *Journal of Gerontological Social Work* 43 (4):45–58.

Crisp, B. R., and Lister, P. G. (2002). Assessment methods in social work education: A review of the literature. *Social Work Education* 21 (2):259–269.

Crisp, C. (2006). The Gay Affirmative Practice Scale (GAP): A new measure for assessing cultural competence with gay and lesbian clients. *Social Work* 51 (2):115–126.

Crook, W., and Brady, M. (1998). Computer-assisted instruction in the classroom: Using a Web shell. *Computers in Human Services* 15 (2/3):193–208.

Cross, W. E. (1991). *Shades of black: Diversity in African-American identity.* Philadelphia: Temple University Press.

CSWE Council on Field Education. (n.d.) A Council of the Commission on Curriculum and Educational Innovation. Available at http://www.cswe.org/CSWE/about/governance/councils/Council+on+Field+Education.htm?PF=1.

(CSWE) Council on Social Work Education. (2001). *Educational policy and accreditation standards.* Alexandria, Va.: Council on Social Work Education.

(CSWE) Council on Social Work Education. (2007a). *National statement on research integrity in social work.* Alexandria, Va.: Council on Social Work Education.

(CSWE) Council on Social Work Education. (2007b). Statistics on social work education in the United States: 2004. Alexandria, Va.: Council on Social Work Education.

(CSWE) Council on Social Work Education. (2008). Educational policy and accreditation standards. Available at http://www.cswe.org/NR/rdonlyres/2A81732E-1776–4175-AC42–65974E96BE66/0/2008EducationalPolicyandAccreditationStandards.pdf (accessed July 11, 2008).

CSWE Gero-Ed Center, National Center for Gerontological Social Work Education. (2007). Competencies. Available at http://depts.washington.edu/geroctr/Curriculum3/sub3_3_1Competencies.html (accessed March 8, 2007).

Cummings, S. M., and DeCoster, V. A. (2003). The status of specialized gerontological training in graduate social work education. *Educational Gerontology* 29 (3):235–250.

Daloz, L. A. P. (2000). Transformative learning for the common good. In J. Mezirow and Associates, eds., *Learning as transformation: Critical perspectives on a theory in progress*, 103–123. San Francisco: Jossey-Bass.

Damron-Rodriguez, J., and Corley, C. S. (2002). Social work education for interdisciplinary practice with older adults and their families. *Journal of Gerontological Social Work* 39 (1/2):37–55.

Davis, J. R. (1993). *Better teaching, more learning: Strategies for success in postsecondary settings*. Phoenix: Oryx Press.

Dawes, R. M. (1996). *House of cards: Psychology and psychotherapy built on myth*. New York: Free Press.

Deal, K. H. (2000). The usefulness of developmental stage models for clinical social work students: An exploratory study. *Clinical Supervisor* 19 (1):1–19.

Deal, K. H. (2002). Modifying field instructors' supervisory approach using stage models of student development. *Journal of Teaching in Social Work* 22 (3/4): 121–137.

de Haymes, M. V., and Kitty, K. M. (2007). Latino population growth, characteristics, and settlement trends: Implications for social work education in a dynamic political climate. *Journal of Social Work Education* 43 (1):101–116.

DeLange, J. (1995). Gender and communication in social work education: A cross-cultural perspective. *Journal of Social Work Education* 31 (1):75–81.

Dinerman, M., Feldman, P., and Ello, L. (1999). Preparing practitioners for the professoriate. *Journal of Teaching in Social Work* 18 (1/2):23–32.

Dixon-Reeves, R. (2003). Mentoring as a precursor to incorporation: An assessment of the mentoring experience of recently-minted Ph.D.s. *Journal of Black Studies* 34 (1):12–27.

Dore, M. M. (1994). Feminist pedagogy and the teaching of social work practice. *Journal of Social Work Education* 30 (1):97–106.

Draughn, T., Elkins, B., and Roy, R. (2002). Allies in the struggle: Eradicating homophobia and heterosexism on campus. In E. P. Cramer, ed., *Addressing homophobia and heterosexism on college campuses*, 9–12. Binghamton, N.Y.: Harrington Park Press.

Drisko, J. (1997). Information technologies for social work education. Available at http://sophia.smith.edu/~jdrisko/techslide/index.htm (accessed August 2, 2008).

Drisko, J. (1998). Using qualitative data analysis software: Merits and hazards. *Computers in Human Services* 15 (1):1–19.

Drisko, J. (2000). Computer-aided data analysis. In J. Anastas, *Research design for social work and the human services*, 2nd ed., 503–532. New York: Columbia University Press.

Drucker, D. (2003). Whither international social work? A reflection. *International Social Work* 46 (1):53–81.

Dumbrill, G., and Green, J. (2007). Including indigenous knowledge in Web-based learning. *Journal of Technology in Human Services* 25 (1/2):103–117.

Duncan-Daston, R., and Culver, S. (2005). The disclosure of sensitive student information in social work field placements: When student confidentiality and the code of ethics collide. *Journal of Social Work Values & Ethics* 2 (2).

Eckel, P. D., and King, J. E. 2008. *An overview of higher education in the United States: Diversity, access, and the role of the marketplace.* Washington, D.C.: American Council on Education. Available at http://www.acenet. edu/AM/Template.cfm?Section=Search&section=reports2&template=/CM/ ContentDisplay.cfm&ContentFileID=5100.

E learning. (2001). *PC Magazine*, December 26, ibiz 2.

eMarketer. (2006). *US Internet Users*, September.

Engler, J. N., Landau, J. D., and Enns, C. Z. (2005). Integrating multicultural and feminist pedagogies: Personal perspectives on positionality, challenges, and benefits. In C. Z. Enns and A. L. Sinacore, eds., *Teaching and social justice: Integrating multicultural and feminist theories in the classroom,* 177–196. Washington, D.C.: American Psychological Association.

Engler, J. N., Landau, J. D., and Epstein, M. (2008). Keeping up with the Joneses: Students' perceptions of academically dishonest behavior. *Teaching of Psychology* 35 (2):99–102.

Enns, C. Z., and Sinacore, A. L. (2005). *Teaching and social justice: Integrating multicultural and feminist theories in the classroom.* Washington, D.C.: American Psychological Association.

Erikson, E. H. (1963). *Childhood and society.* 2nd ed. New York: Norton.

Exploring the digital divide. (2001). *Consumer Reports*, February, 6

Falk, D. S. (1999). The virtual community: Computer conferencing for teaching and learning social work. *Journal of Technology in Human Services* 16 (2/3):127–143.

Faria, G., Brownstein, C., and Smith, H. Y. (1988). A survey of field instructors' perceptions of the liaison role. *Journal of Social Work Education* 24 (2):135–150.

Faux, T., and Black-Hughes, C. (2000). A comparison of using the Internet versus lectures to teach social work history. *Research on Social Work Practice* 10 (4):454–466.

Federal Electronics Challenge. (2007). Answers to frequent questions: Total cost of ownership. Available at http://www.federalelectronicschallenge.net/resources/ docs/costofown.pdf (accessed March 2, 2009).

Feld, S. (1988). The academic marketplace in social work. *Journal of Social Work Education* 24 (3):201–210.

Feldman, K. A., and Paulsen, M. B. (1998). *Teaching and learning in the college classroom.* 2nd ed. Needham Heights, Mass.: Simon & Schuster.

Feldman, R. A. (1999). The human resource crisis in social work education. *Journal of Social Work Education* 35 (2):178–181.

Finkelstein, M. J., Seal, R. K., and Schuster, J. H. (1998). *The new academic generation: A professoriate in transformation.* Baltimore: Johns Hopkins University Press.

Finn, J., and Marson, S. M. (2001). Social work programs' use of the World Wide Web to facilitate field instruction. *Advances in Social Work* 2 (1):26–37.

Fitch, D., Peet, M., Reed, B. G., and Tolman, R. (2008). The use of e-portfolios in evaluating the curriculum and student learning. *Journal of Social Work Education*l> 43 (3):37–54.

Formo, D. M., and Reed, C. (1999). *The job search in academe: Strategic rhetorics for faculty job candidates*. Sterling, Va.: Stylus.

Fortune, A. E. (1994). Field education. In F. G. Reamer, ed., *The foundations of social work knowledge*, 151–194. New York: Columbia University Press.

Fortune, A. E. (2003). Comparison of faculty ratings of applicants and background characteristics as predictors of performance in an MSW program. *Journal of Teaching in Social Work* 23 (1/2):35–54.

Fortune, A. E., and Abramson, J. S. (1993). Predictors of satisfaction with field practicum among social work students. *Clinical Supervisor* 11 (1):95–110.

Fortune, A. E., Feathers, C. E., Rook, S. R., Scrimenti, R. M., Smollen, P., Stemerman, B., and Tucker, E. L. (1985). Student satisfaction with field placement. *Journal of Social Work Education* 23 (3):92–104.

Fortune, A. E., Kaye, L. B., Holden, G., and Cavazos, A. (2002). Psychometric properties of the Social Work Skills Self-Efficacy Scale for field education. Paper presented at annual meeting of Council on Social Work Education, Nashville, Tenn., February.

Fortune, A. E., Lee, M., and Cavazos, A. (2005). Achievement motivation and outcome in social work field education. *Journal of Social Work Education* 41 (1):115–129.

Fortune, A. E., McCarthy, M., and Abramson, J. S. (2001). Student learning processes in field education: Relationship of learning activities to quality of field instruction, satisfaction, and performance among MSW students. *Journal of Social Work Education* 37 (1):111–124.

Fortune, A. E., Miller, J., Rosenblum, A. F., Sanchez, B. M., Smith, C. and Reid, W. J. (1995). Further explorations of the liaison role: A view from the field. In G. Rogers, ed., *Social work field education: Views and visions*, 273–293. Dubuque, Iowa: Kendall/Hunt.

Fox, R. (2004). Field instruction and the mature student. *Journal of Teaching in Social Work* 24 (3/4):113–129.

Freddolino, P. P., and Sutherland, C. (2000). Assessing the comparability of classroom environments in graduate social work education delivered via interactive instructional television (IITV). *Journal of Social Work Education* 36 (1):115–129.

Freire, P. (2000). *Pedagogy of the oppressed*. 30th anniversary ed. New York: Continuum.

Friedman, B. D. (2008). *How to teach effectively*. Chicago: Lyceum Books.

Future U. (1999). Comparative features analysis of leading course management software. Available at http://www.futureu.com/cmscomp/cms_comp.html (accessed November 12, 2000).

Gambrill, E. (2001). From the Editor: Social work accreditation standards: Do they work for clients? *Journal of Social Work Education* 37 (2):226.

Gambrill, E. (2002). Evaluating the outcomes of social work practice: A pilot program. *Journal of Social Work Education* 38 (3):355–359.

Gambrill, E. (2006). Evidence-based practice and policy: The choices ahead. *Research on Social Work Practice* 16 (3):338–357.

Gappa, J. M. (1996). *Off the tenure track: Six models for full-time, nontenurable appointments*. Working Paper Series, Inquiry 10. Washington, D.C.: American Association of Higher Education.

Gappa, J. M., Austin, A. E., and Trice, A. G. (2005). Rethinking academic work and workplaces. *Change* 37 (6):32–39.

Garcia, B., and Van Soest, D. (1997). Changing perceptions of diversity and oppression: MSW students discuss the effects of a required course. *Journal of Social Work Education* 33 (1):119–129.

Garcia, B., and Van Soest, D. (2000). Facilitating learning on diversity: Challenges to the professor. *Journal of Ethnic and Cultural Diversity in Social Work* 9 (1/2):21–39.

Garcia, J., and Floyd, C. E. (2002). Addressing evaluative standards related to program assessment: How do we respond? *Journal of Social Work Education* 38 (3):369–382.

Gasker, J. A. (1999). Thoughts on poverty and inequality. *Journal of Poverty* 3 (3):93–96.

Gates, G. J., and Ost, J. (2004). *The gay and lesbian atlas*. Washington, D.C.: Urban Institute Press.

George, A. (1982). A history of social work field instruction: Apprenticeship to instruction. In B. W. Sheafor and L. E. Jenkins, eds., *Quality field instruction in social work: Program development and maintenance*, 37–59. New York: Longman.

Gibbs, L. (2002). *Evidence-based practice for the helping professions: A practical guide with integrated multimedia*. Stamford, Conn.: Brooks-Cole.

Gibbs, L., and Gambrill, E. (1996). *Critical thinking for social workers: A workbook*. Thousand Oaks, Calif.: Pine Forge Press.

Gibbs, L., Gambrill, E., Blakemore, J., Begun, A., Keniston, A., Peden, B., and Lefcowitz, J. (1995). A measure of critical thinking about practice. *Research on Social Work Practice* 5 (2):193–204.

Gibelman, M., and Gelman, S. R. (1999). A quest for citations? An analysis and commentary on the trend toward multiple authorship. *Journal of Social Work Education* 35 (2):203–213.

Gibelman, M., and Gelman, S. R. (2001a). Grading: A problem of credibility. *Areté* 25 (2):1–11.

Gibelman, M., and Gelman, S. R. (2001b). Learning from the mistakes of others: A look at scientific misconduct in research. *Journal of Social Work Education* 37 (2):241–254.

Gigerenzer, G. (2007). *Gut feelings: The intelligence of the unconscious.* New York: Penguin.

Gillespie, D. (2003). The pedagogical value of teaching white privilege through a case study. *Teaching Sociology* 31 (44):469–477.

Gilligan, C. (1982). *In a different voice: Psychological theory and women's development.* Cambridge, Mass.: Harvard University Press.

Gitterman, A., and Gitterman, N. P. (1979). Social work student evaluation: Format and method. *Journal of Education for Social Work* 15 (3):103–108.

Glassick, C., Huber, M., and Maeroff, G. (1997). *Scholarship assessed: Evaluation of the professoriate.* San Francisco: Jossey-Bass.

GlenMaye, L. F., and Bolin, B. (2007). Students with psychiatric disabilities: An exploratory study of program practices. *Journal of Social Work Education* 43 (1):117–131.

GlenMaye, L., and Oakes, M. (2002). Assessing suitability of MSW applicants through objective scoring of personal statements. *Journal of Social Work Education* 38 (1):67–82.

Globerman, J., and Bogo, M. (2000). Strengthening the integration of research, teaching, and practice in graduate programs: An academic field-partnership model. In G. L. Kenyon and R. Power, eds., *No magic: Readings in social work field education,* 115–127. Toronto: Canadian Scholars Press.

Gohagan, D. (2000). Educators, computer facilitated instruction, and the social work curriculum. Paper presented at annual meeting of Council on Social Work Education, New York, February.

Golde, C. M. (1999). After the offer, before the deal: Negotiating a first academic job. *Acacdeme* 85 (1):44–49.

Golde, C. M., and Walker, G. E., eds. (2006). *Envisioning the future of doctoral education.* San Francisco: Jossey-Bass.

Goldstein, H. (2001). *Experiential learning: A foundation for social work education and practice.* Alexandria, Va.: Council on Social Work Education.

Gordon, M., Lewandowski, L., Murphy, K., and Dempsey, K. (2002). ADA-based accommodations in higher education: A survey of clinicians about documentation requirements and diagnostic standards. *Journal of Learning Disabilities* 35 (2):357–363.

Gordon, W. E., and Gordon, M. S. (1982). The role of frames of reference in field education. In B. W. Sheafor and L. E. Jenkins, eds., *Quality field instruction in social work,* 116–135. New York: Longman.

Green, R. G. (1998). Faculty rank, effort, and success: A study of publication in professional journals. *Journal of Social Work Education* 34 (3):415–426.

Green, R. G. (2008). Tenure and promotion decisions: The relative importance of teaching, scholarship, and service. *Journal of Social Work Education* 44 (2):117–127.

Green, R. G., Baskind, F. R., and Bellin, M. H. (2002). Results of the doctoral faculty publication project: Journal article productivity and its correlates in the 1990s. *Journal of Social Work Education* 38 (1):135–152.

Green, R. G., Baskind, F. R., and Conklin, B. (1995). The 1990s publication productivity of schools of social work with doctoral programs: "The times, are they a-changin'"? *Journal of Social Work Education* 31 (3):388–401.

Green, R. G., Baskind, F. R., Fassler, A., and Jordan, A. (2006). The validity of the *U.S. News & World Report*'s rankings of schools of social work. *Journal of Social Work Education* 51 (2):135–145.

Groark, M., Oblinger, D., and Choa, M. (2001). Term paper mills, anti-plagiarism tools, and academic integrity. *Educause Review*, September–October, 40–48.

Grossman, B. (1991). Themes and variations: The political economy of field instruction. In D. Schneck, B. Grossman, and U. Glassman, eds., *Field education in social work: Contemporary issues and trends*, 36–46. Dubuque, Iowa: Kendall/Hunt.

Grunert, J. (1997) *The course syllabus: A learning-centered approach.* Bolton, Mass.: Anker.

Guernsey, L. (2004). When gadgets get in the way. *New York Times*, August 19. Available at http://query.nytimes.com/gst/fullpage.html?res=9B0DE5D7113FF93 AA2575BC0A9629C8B63andscp=1andsq=when%20gadgets%20get%20in%20the %20wayandst=cse (accessed September 2, 2008).

Gustafson, L. (2002). Personal communication, February 27. [There appear to be higher drop-out rates from online BSW courses than in traditional sections at several institutions.]

Gutiérrez, L., Zuñiga, M. E., and Lum, D., eds. (2004). *Education for multi-cultural social work practice: Critical viewpoints and future directions.* Alexandria, Va.: Council on Social Work Education.

Haga, M., and Heitkamp, T. (2000). Bringing social work education to the prairie. *Journal of Social Work Education* 36 (2):309–324.

Hall, J. C. (2008). A practitioner's application and deconstruction of evidence-based practice. *Families in Society* 89 (3):385–393.

Hambridge, S. (1995). Netiquette guidelines (RFC 8155). Intel Corporation. Available at http://www.rfc1855.net/ (accessed September 1, 2008).

Hamilton, N., and Else, J. F. (1983). *Designing field education: Philosophy, structure, and process.* Springfield, Ill.: Thomas.

Harding, S., Ferguson, M., and Radey, M. (2005). Does poverty matter? An analysis of courses on poverty at the top 50 schools of social work. *Areté* 28 (2):39–53.

Harris, D., and Parrish, D. (2006). The art of online teaching: Online instruction versus in-class instruction. *Journal of Technology in Human Services* 24 (2/3):105–117.

Hartman, A. (1990). Education for direct practice. *Families in Society* 71 (1): 44–50.

Helms, J. E., ed. (1990). *Black and white racial identity: Theory, research and practice*. Westport, Conn.: Greenwood.

Hesselbrock, M. (2006). Patterns of doctoral education: Preliminary results of a GADE survey. Paper presented at annual meeting of Society for Social Work and Research, San Francisco, January..

Holden, G., Anastas, J., and Meenaghan, T. (2003). Determining attainment of the EPAS foundation program objectives: Evidence for the use of self-efficacy as an outcome. *Journal of Social Work Education* 39 (3):425–440.

Holden, G., Anastas, J., and Meenaghan, T. (2005). EPAS foundation objectives and foundation practice self-efficacy: A replication. *Journal of Social Work Education* 41 (3):559–570.

Holden, G., Barker, K., Meenaghan, T., and Rosenberg, G. (1999). Research self-efficacy: A new possibility for educational outcomes assessment. *Journal of Social Work Education* 35 (3):463–476.

Holden, G., Barker, K., Rosenberg, G., and Onghena, P. (2007). Assessing progress toward accreditation related objectives: Evidence regarding the use of self-efficacy as an outcome in the advanced concentration curriculum. *Research on Social Work Practice* 17 (4):456–465.

Holden, G., Barker, K., Rosenberg, G., and Onghena, P. (2008). The Evaluation Self-Efficacy Scale for assessing progress toward CSWE accreditation-related objectives. *Research on Social Work Practice* 18 (1):42–46.

Holden, G., Meenaghan, T., Anastas, J., and Metry, G. (2002). Outcomes of social work education: The case for social work self-efficacy. *Journal of Social Work Education* 38 (1):115–133.

Holley, L. C., and Steiner, S. (2005). Safe space: Students' perspectives on classroom environment. *Journal of Social Work Education* 41 (1):49–64.

Holley, L. C., and Young, D. S. (2005). Career decisions and experiences of social work faculty: A gender comparison. *Journal of Social Work Education* 41 (2):297–313.

Hollister, C., and McGee, G. (2000). Delivering substance abuse and child welfare content through interactive television. *Research on Social Work Practice* 10 (4):417–427.

Holloway, S. (n.d.). Some suggestions on educational program assessment and continuous improvement. Manuscript. Council on Social Work Education, Commission on Accreditation, Alexandria, Va.

hooks, b. (1994). *Teaching to transgress: Education as the practice of freedom*. New York: Routledge.

Howe, R.D. (2000). Salary-trend study of faculty in social work for the years 1996–97 and 1999–00. Available at http://www.cupa.org http://depts.washington.edu/geroctr/Curriculum3/sub3_3_1Competencies.html (accessed October 12, 2006).

Hu, S., ed. (2005). *Beyond grade inflation: Grading problems in higher education.* ASHE Higher Education Report, vol. 30, no. 6. San Francisco: Jossey-Bass.

Huff, M. (2000). A comparison study of live instruction versus interactive television for teaching MSW students critical thinking skills. *Research on Social Work Practice* 10 (4):400–416.

Hulette, E. (2009). Students are keeping their attention on the text . . . messages. *The Capital*, March 1. Available at http://www.hometownannapolis.com/news/top/2009/03/01–76/Students-are-keeping-their-attention-on-the-text — messages.html (accessed March 2, 2009).

Hull, G. H. (1991). Supporting BSW faculty scholarship. *Areté* 16 (2):19–27.

Hunter, S., and Hickerson, J. (2003). *Understanding and working with lesbian, gay, bisexual, and transgender persons.* Washington, D.C.: NASW Press.

Hunter College School of Social Work of the City of New York (n.d.). M.S.W. degree pathways. Available at http://www.hunter.cuny.edu/socwork/admissions/pathways.htm (accessed October 6, 2008).

Hyde, C. A., and Ruth, B. J. (2002). Multicultural content and class participation: Do students self-censor? *Journal of Social Work Education* 38 (2):241–256.

Hylton, M. E. (2005). Heteronormativity and the experiences of lesbian and bisexual women as social work students. *Journal of Social Work Education* 41 (1):67–82.

Hylton, M. E. (2006). Online versus classroom-based instruction: A comparative study of learning outcomes in a diversity course. *Journal of Baccalaureate Social Work* 11 (2):102–114.

Ivey, A., and Ivey, M. (2003). *Intentional interviewing and counseling: Facilitating client development in a multicultural society.* 5th ed. Stamford, Conn.: Brooks-Cole.

Jenkins, D., and Johnston, L. (2004). Unethical treatment of gay and lesbian people with conversion therapy. *Families in Society: Journal of Contemporary Social Services* 85 (4):557–561.

Jenkins, L. E., and Sheafor, B. W. (1982). An overview of social work field instruction. In B. W. Sheafor and L. E. Jenkins, eds., *Quality field instruction in social work: Program development and maintenance,* 3–20. New York: Longman.

Jirovec, R. L., Ramanathan, C. S., and Alvarez, A. R. (1998). Course evaluations: What are social work students telling us about teaching effectiveness? *Journal of Social Work Education* 34 (2):229–236.

Johnson, A. K. (2004). Increasing internationalization in social work programs: Healy's continuum as a strategic planning guide. *International Social Work* 47 (1):7–23.

Kadushin, A. E. (1991). Introduction to D. Schneck, B. Grossman, and U. Glassman, eds., *Field education in social work: Contemporary issues and trends,* 11–12. Dubuque, Iowa: Kendall/Hunt.

Kane, M. N. (2004). Predictors for future work with elders. *Journal of Gerontological Social Work* 42 (3/4):61–75.

Karger, H. J., and Stoesz, D. (2003). The growth of social work education programs, 1985–1999: Its impact on economic and education factors relatedto the profession of social work. *Journal of Social Work Education* 39 (2):279–295.

Karrer, T. (2006). LMS dissatisfaction on the rise. *eLearning Technology* (blog). Available at http://elearningtech.blogspot.com/2006/08/lms-dissatisfaction-on-rise.html (accessed September 7, 2008).

Kegan, R. (2000). What "form" transforms? A constructive-developmental approach to transformative learning. In J. Mezirow and Associates, eds., *Learning as transformation: Critical perspectives on a theory in progress*, 35–69. San Francisco: Jossey-Bass.

Keith-Spiegel, P., Tabachnick, B. G., Whitley, B. E., and Washburn, J. (1998). Why professors ignore cheating: Opinions of a national sample of psychology instructors. *Ethics and Behavior* 8 (3):215–227.

Kendall, K. A. (1978). *Reflections on social work education, 1950–1978*. New York: International Association of Schools of Social Work.

Kennedy, D. (1997). *Academic duty*. Cambridge, Mass.: Harvard University Press.

King, M., Smith, G., and Bartlett, A. (2004). Treatments of homosexuality in Britain since the 1950s—An oral history: The experience of professionals. *British Medical Journal* 328 (7437):429.

King, P., and Kitchener, K. S. (1994). *Developing reflective judgment: Understanding and promoting intellectual growth and critical thinking in adolescents and adults*. San Francisco: Jossey-Bass.

Kirk, S. A., and Corcoran, K. (1995). School rankings: Mindless narcissism or do they tell us something? *Journal of Social Work Education* 31 (3):408–414.

Kirk, S. A., Kil, H. J., and Corcoran, K. (2009). Picky, picky, picky: Ranking graduate schools of social work by student selectivity. *Journal of Social Work Education* 45 (1):65–87.

Kisamore, J. L., Stone, T. H., and Jawahar, I. M. (2007). Academic integrity: The relationship between individual and situational factors on misconduct contemplations. *Journal of Business Ethics* 75 (4):381–394.

Kleinpeter, C., and Potts, M. (2002). Teaching practice methods using interactive television: A partial replication study. Paper presented at annual meeting of Council on Social Work Education, Nashville, Tenn., February.

Knight, C. (2000). Engaging the student in the field instructor relationship BSW and MSW students' views. *Journal of Teaching in Social Work* 20 (3/4):173–201.

Knight, C. (2001). The process of field instruction: BSW and MSW students' views of effective field supervision. *Journal of Social Work Education* 37 (2):357–379.

Koerin, B., and Miller, J. (1995). Gatekeeping policies: Terminating students for non-academic reasons. *Journal of Social Work Education* 31 (2):247–260.

Kolb, D. A. (1984). *Experiential learning: Experience as the source of learning and development*. Englewood Cliffs, N.J.: Prentice-Hall.

Kolb, D. A. (1991/1998). Learning styles and disciplinary differences. In A. W. Chickering and Associates, eds., *The modern American college: Responding to the realities of diverse students and a changing society.* San Francisco: Jossey-Bass. Reprinted in K. A. Feldman and M. B. Paulson, eds. (1998). *Teaching and learning in the college classroom,* 2nd ed., 127–137. New York: Simon & Schuster.

Kolodny, A. (2008). Tenure, academic freedom, and the career I once loved. *Academe* 94 (5):22–26.

Koroloff, N. M., and Rhyne, C. (1989). Assessing student performance in field instruction. *Journal of Teaching in Social Work* 3 (2):3–16.

Krentzman, A. R., and Townsend, A. L. (2008). Review of multidisciplinary measures of cultural competence for use in social work education. *Journal of Social Work Education* 44 (2):7–31.

Kreuger, L., and Stretch, J. (2000). How hypermodern technology in social work bites back. *Journal of Social Work Education* 36 (1):103–114.

Krippendorf, K. (1986). *A dictionary of cybernetics.* Norfolk, Va.: American Society for Cybernetics.

Kulik, C., and Kulik, J. (1991). Effectiveness of computer-based instruction: An updated analysis. *Computers in Human Behavior* 7 (1/2):75–94.

Kulkin, H. (2002). The effectiveness of distance education: Comparing apples to oranges. Paper presented at annual meeting of Council on Social Work Education, Nashville, Tenn., February.

LaTerz, J. (2008). Personal communication, July 2. [Smith College SSW has pilot tested thesis advising via videoconferencing for the past two years, nationally and internationally. Student and advisor feedback is quite positive.]

Lazzari, M. M. (1991). Feminism, empowerment and field education. *Affilia: Journal of Women in Social Work* 6 (2):97–114.

LeDoux, C. (1996). Career patterns of African-American and Hispanic social work doctorates and ABDs. *Journal of Social Work Education* 32 (2):217–227.

Leighninger, L. (2000). *Creating a new profession: The beginnings of social work education in the United States.* Alexandria, Va.: Council on Social Work Education.

Lemieux, C. M. (2002). Teaching for professional learning: Peer review, self-evaluation, and the problem of grading. *Areté* 25 (2):58–70.

Lennon, T. M. (2005). *Statistics on social work education in the United States: 2003.* Alexandria, Va.: Council on Social Work Education.

Levine, A. (2007). *Educating researchers.* Washington, D.C.: Education Schools Project.

Levinson, D. L. (1978). *The seasons of a man's life.* New York: Ballantine Books.

Lightfoot, E., and Gibson, P. (2005). Universal instructional design: A new framework for accommodating students in social work courses. *Journal of Social Work Education* 41 (2):269–277.

Lim, D., H., Morris, M. L., and Yoon, S.-W. (2006). Instructional and learner factors influencing outcomes within online learning environments. Paper presented at Academy of Human Resources Development (AHRD) International Conference, Columbus, Ohio, February.

Limb, G. E., and Organista, K. C. (2003). Comparisons between Caucasian students, students of color, and American Indian students on their views on social work's traditional mission, career motivations, and practice preferences. *Journal of Social Work Education* 39 (1):91–109.

Lovaas, K. E., Baroudi, L., and Collins, S. M. (2002). Transcending hetero-normativity in the classroom: Using queer and critical pedagogies to alleviate trans-anxieties. In E. P. Cramer, ed., *Addressing homophobia and heterosexism on college campuses*, 177–189. Binghamton, N.Y.: Harrington Park Press.

Lowman, J. (1995). *Mastering the techniques of teaching.* 2nd ed. San Francisco: Jossey-Bass.

MacFarlane, B. (2004). *Teaching with integrity: The ethics of higher education practice.* New York: RoutledgeFarmer.

Mackleprang, R. W., Ray, J., and Hernandez-Peck, M. (1996). Social work education and sexual orientation: Faculty, student, and curriculum issues. *Journal of Gay and Lesbian Social Services* 5 (4):17–31.

Macy, J. (1999). Exploring the experiences of social work graduate students who have completed their degrees via interactive television. Ph.D. diss., University of Minnesota.

Maddux, C. D., Johnson, D. L., and Willis, J. W. (1997). *Educational computing: Learning with tomorrow's technologies.* Boston: Allyn & Bacon.

Maki, P. L., and Borkowski, N. A., eds. (2006). *The assessment of doctoral education.* Sterling, Va.: Stylus.

Mandel School of Social Services, Case Western University (n.d.) M.S.S.A. overview: Intensive Weekend Program. Available at http://msass.case.edu/academic/mssa/intweek.html (accessed October 6, 2008).

Margolis, E., ed. (2001). *The hidden curriculum in higher education.* New York: Routledge.

Marson, S. M., and Finn, J. (2006). Editorial comment: How far do you go? *Journal of Social Work Values & Ethics* 3 (1).

Martin, J. (1995). Gay and lesbian faculty in social work: Roles and responsibilities. *Journal of Gay and Lesbian Social Services* 3 (4):1–12.

Mason, S. E., and Sanders, G. R. (2004). Social work student attitudes on working with older clients. *Journal of Gerontological Social Work* 42 (3/4):61–75.

McCabe, D. L., Treviño, L. K., and Butterfield, K. D. (2001). Cheating in academic institutions: A decade of research. *Ethics and Behavior* 11 (3):219–232.

McFall, J., and Freddolino, P. P. (2000a). The impact of distance education programs on community agencies. *Research on Social Work Practice* 10 (4): 438–453.

McFall, J., and Freddolino, P. P. (2000b). Quality and comparability in distance field education: Student reports comparing three program sites. *Journal of Social Work Education* 36 (2):293–307.

McGranahan, E. (2008). Shaking the "Magic 8 Ball": Reflections of a first-time teacher. *Journal of Teaching in Social Work* 28 (1/2):19–34.

McIntosh, P. (1988). White privilege and male privilege: A personal account of coming to see correspondences through work in women's studies. Working paper, no. 189. Center for Research on Women, Wellesley College, Wellesley, Mass.

McKeachie, W. J., and Svinicki, M. (1999). *McKeachie's teaching tips: Strategies, research, and theory for college and university teachers.* 11th ed. Boston: Houghton Mifflin.

McKeachie, W. J., and Svinicki, M. (2006). *McKeachie's teaching tips: Strategies, research, and theory for college and university teachers.* 12th ed. Boston: Houghton Mifflin.

McMurtry, S. L., and McClelland, R. W. (1997). Trends in student–faculty ratios and the use of non-tenure-track faculty in MSW programs. *Journal of Social Work Education* 33 (2):293–306.

McPhail, B. A. (2004). Setting the record straight: Social work is not a female-dominated profession. *Social Work* 49 (2):323–326.

McPhail, B. A. (2008). Re-gendering the social work curriculum: New realities and complexities. *Journal of Social Work Education* 44 (2):33–49.

Mehra, B., Merkel, C., and Bishop, A. (2004). The Internet for empowerment of minority and marginalized users. *New Media and Society* 6 (6):781–802.

Melko, M. (1998). *A professor's work.* Lanham, Md.: University Press of America.

Mendenhall, A. N. (2007). Switching hats: Transitioning from the role of clinician to the role of researcher in social work doctoral education. *Journal of Teaching in Social Work* 27 (3/4):273–290.

Menges, R. J., Weimer, M., and Associates. (1996). *Teaching on solid ground: Using scholarship to improve practice.* San Francisco: Jossey-Bass.

Mentokowski, M., and Associates. (2000). *Learning that lasts: Integrating learning, development and performance in college and beyond.* San Francisco: Jossey-Bass.

Merdinger, J. C. (1991). Reaching women students: Their ways of knowing. In R. Middleman and G. C. Woods, eds., *Teaching secrets: The technology in social work education,* 41–51. New York: Haworth Press.

Mesbur, E. S., and Glassman, U. (1991). From commitment to curriculum: The humanistic foundations of field instruction. In D. Schneck, B. Grossman, and U. Glassman, eds., *Field education in social work: Contemporary issues and trends,* 47–55. Dubuque, Iowa: Kendall/Hunt.

Messinger, L. (2004) Out in the field: Gay and lesbian social work students' experiences in field placement. *Journal of Social Work Education* 40 (2): 187–204.

Meyer, I. (2003). Prejudice, social stress, and mental health in lesbian, gay, and bisexual populations: Conceptual issues and research evidence. *Psychological Bulletin* 129 (5):674–697.

Mezirow, J. (2000). Learning to think like an adult: Core concepts of transformation theory. In J. Mezirow and Associates, eds., *Learning as transformation: Critical perspectives on a theory in progress*, 3–33. San Francisco: Jossey-Bass.

Miller, J., and Koerin, B. (1998). Can we assess suitability at admission? A review of MSDW application procedures. *Journal of Social Work Education* 34 (3): 437–453.

Miller, J. B. (1976). *Toward a new psychology of women.* Boston: Beacon Press.

Millstein, K. H. (1997). The taping project: A method for self-evaluation and "informed consciousness" in racism courses. *Journal of Social Work Education* 33 (3):491–506.

Mishna, F., and Bogo, M. (2007). Reflective practice in the social work classroom. *Journal of Social Work Education* 43 (3):529–544.

Monaghan, P. (1998). U[niversity] of Washington professors decry governor's visions for technology. *Chronicle of Higher Education* 44 (41):A23, A26.

Mooradian, J. K. (2007). Simulated family therapy interviews in clinical social work education. *Journal of Teaching in Social Work* 27 (1/2):89–104.

Mooradian, J. K. (2008). Using simulated sessions to enhance clinical social work education. *Journal of Social Work Education* 43 (3):21–35.

Moran, J. J. (1997). *Assessing adult learning: A guide for practitioners.* Malabar, Fla.: Krieger.

Morrow, D. F. (1996). Heterosexism: Hidden discrimination in social work education. *Journal of Gay and Lesbian Social Services* 5 (4):1–16.

Mumm, A. M. (2006). Teaching social work students practice skills. *Journal of Teaching in Social Work* 26 (2/3):71–89.

Munoz, K., and Van Duzer, J. (2005). Blackboard vs. Moodle: A comparison of satisfaction with online teaching and learning tools. Available at http://www.humboldt.edu/~jdv1/moodle/all.htm (accessed March 6, 2007).

Murphy, B. C., and Dillon, C. (1998). *Interviewing in action video.* Stamford, Conn.: Brooks-Cole.

Murphy, B. C., and Dillon, C. (2003). *Interviewing in action: Relationship, process and change.* 2nd ed. Stamford, Conn.: Brooks-Cole.

Murray, H., Gillese, E., Lennon, M., Mercer, P., and Robinson, M. (1996). *Ethical principles in university teaching.* Hamilton, Ont.: Society for Teaching and Learning in Higher Education. Available at http://www.mcmaster.ca/stlhe/documents/Ethical%20Principles%20in%20University%20Teaching.pdf (accessed July 17, 2008).

Myers, L. L., and Thyer, B. A. (1997). Should social work clients have the right to effective treatment? *Social Work* 42 (3):288–298.

(NASW) National Association of Social Workers. (1999). *NASW code of ethics.* Washington, D.C.: NASW Press. Available at http://www.naswdc.org/pubs/code/ default.htm.

(NASW) National Association of Social Workers. (2001). *NASW standards for cultural competence in social work practice.* Washington, D.C.: NASW Press. Available at http://www.socialworkers.org/sections/credentials/cultural_comp.asp (accessed February 2, 2007).

(NASW) National Association of Social Workers. (2005). Social work imperatives for the next decade. Available at http://www.socialworkers.org/congress/ imperatives0605.pdf.

(NASW) National Association of Social Workers. (2007). *Institutional racism and the social work profession: A call to action.* Washington, D.C.: National Association of Social Workers.

National Committee on Gay, Lesbian, and Bisexual Issues. (2000). "Reparative" and "conversion" therapies for lesbians and gay men. Available at: http://www .socialworkers.org/diversity/lgb/reparative.asp (accessed July 9, 2007).

National Gay and Lesbian Task Force (2007). State nondiscrimination laws in the United States. Available at http://www.thetaskforce.org/reports_and_research/ nondiscrimination_laws (accessed July 9, 2007).

Netting, E., and Nichols-Casebolt, A. (1997). Authorship and collaboration: Preparing the next generation of social work scholars. *Journal of Social Work Education* 33:555–564.

Neufeldt, S. A., and Nelson, M. L. (1999). When is counseling an appropriate and ethical supervision function? *Clinical Supervisor* 18 (1):125–135.

Neugarten, B. L. (1976). Adaptation and the life cycle. *Counseling Psychologist* 6 (1):16–20.

Neuman, K. M., and Friedman, B. D. (1997). Process recordings: Fine-tuning an old instrument. *Journal of Social Work Education* 33 (2):237–244.

Newman, B. S., Dannenfelser, P. L., and Benishek, L. (2002). Assessing beginning social work and counseling students' acceptance of lesbians and gay men. *Journal of Social Work Education* 38 (2):273–288.

Newman, P., Bogo, M., and Daley, A. (2009). Breaking the silence: Sexual orientation in social work field education. *Journal of Social Work Education* 45 (1):7–27.

Nilson, L. B. (1998). *Teaching at its best: A research-based resource for college instructors.* Bolton, Mass.: Anker.

Noble, J. H., and Stretch, J. J. (2002). Grade-induced beliefs about under- graduate generalist social work practice competency. *Evaluation Review* 26 (2):213–236.

O'Hare, T., Collins, P., and Walsh, T. (1998). Validating the practice skills inventory with experienced clinical social workers. *Research on Social Work Practice* 8 (5):552–563.

O'Neill, J. V. (2000). Larger doctoral enrollments sought: Few social workers follow path to PhD. *NASW News*, November. Available at http://www.socialworkers.org/pubs/news/2000/11/phd.htm (accessed September 21, 2006).

Opie, A. (2000). *Thinking teams/thinking clients: Knowledge-based teamwork.* New York: Columbia University Press.

Ortiz Hendricks, C. (2003). Learning and teaching cultural competence in the practice of social work. *Journal of Teaching in Social Work* 23 (1/2):73–86.

Ortiz Hendricks, C., Finch, J. B., and Franks, C. L. (2005). *Learning to teach, teaching to learn: A guide for fieldwork education.* Alexandria, Va.: Council on Social Work Education.

Ouellette, P. M. (2002). Moving toward technology-supported instruction in human service practice: The "virtual classroom." *Journal of Technology in Human Services* 16 (2/3):97–111.

Palomba, C. A., and Banta, T. W., eds. (2001). *Assessing student competence in accredited disciplines: Pioneering approaches to assessment in higher education.* Sterling, Va.: Stylus.

Panos, P. T., Panos, A., Cox, S. E., Roby, J. L., and Matheson, K. W. (2002). Ethical issues concerning the use of videoconferencing to supervise international social work field practicum students. *Journal of Social Work Education* 38 (3):421–438.

Papell, C. P., and Skolnik, L. (1992). The reflective practitioner: A contemporary paradigm's relevance for social work education. *Journal of Social Work Education* 28 (1):18–26.

Pardeck, J. T. (1999). Disability discrimination in social work education: Current issues for social work programs and faculty. *Journal of Teaching in Social Work* 19 (1):151–163.

Pardeck, J. T. (2003). Social work admissions and academic accommodations for students with disabilities: An exploratory study. *Journal of Social Work in Disability and Rehabilitation* 2 (1):79–81.

Parnell, S., and Andrews, J. (1994). Complementary principles of social work and feminism. *Areté* 19 (2):60–64.

Payne, M. (2006). *What is professional social work?* Chicago: Lyceum Books.

Pease, B. B. (1988). The ABCs of social work student evaluation. *Journal of Teaching in Social Work* 2 (2):35–50.

Perry, W. G. (1970). *Forms of intellectual and ethical development in the college years: A scheme.* New York: Holt, Rinehart and Winston.

Pescosolido, B. A., and Aminzade, R., eds. (1999). *The social worlds of higher education: Handbook for teaching in a new century.* Thousand Oaks, Calif.: Pine Forge Press.

Petchers, M. K. (1996). Debunking the myth of progress for women social work educators. *Affilia* 11 (1):11–38.

Peterson's Guide to Distance Learning Programs 2001. (2000). Lawrenceville, N.J.: Peterson's.

Petracchi, H. (1999). Using professionally trained actors in social work role-play simulations. *Journal of Sociology and Social Welfare* 26 (4):61–69.

Petracchi, H. (2000). Distance education: What our students tell us. *Research on Social Work Practice* 10:362–376.

Petracchi, H., and Collins, K. (2006). Using actors to simulate clients in social work student role plays: Does this approach have a place in social work education? *Journal of Teaching in Social Work* 26 (1/2):223–233.

Petracchi, H., and Patchner, M. (2000). Social work students and their learning environment: A comparison of interactive television, face-to-face instruction, and the traditional. *Journal of Social Work Education* 36 (2):335–346.

Petracchi, H., and Patchner, M. (2001). A comparison of live instruction and interactive televised teaching: A two year assessment of teaching an MSW research methods course. *Research on Social Work Practice* 11 (1):108–117.

Pew Internet Survey. (2004). The Internet and daily life. Available at http://www.pewinternet.org/pdfs/pip_internet_and_daily_life.pdf (accessed September, 27, 2008).

Pew Internet Survey. (2008a). Home broadband adoption 2008. Available at http://www.pewinternet.org/pdfs/PIP_Broadband_2008.pdf (accessed September, 27, 2008).

Pew Internet Survey. (2008b). Mobile access to data and information. Available at http://www.pewinternet.org/pdfs/PIP_Mobile.Data.Access.pdf (accessed September, 27, 2008).

Pike, C. K. (1998). A validation study of an instrument designed to measure teaching effectiveness. *Journal of Social Work Education* 34 (2):261–271.

Platt, S. C. (1993). The process of learning in clinical social work students. *Dissertation Abstracts International* A: *The Humanities and Social Sciences* 53 (8):2987-A.

Potter, C. C., and East, J. F. (2000). Developing reflective judgment through MSW education. *Journal of Teaching in Social Work* 20 (1/2):21–39.

Quam, J. (1999). Technology and teaching: Searching for the middle ground. *Journal of Social Work Education* 35 (3):322–325.

Quinn, P. (1995). Social work education and disability: Benefiting from the impact of the ADA. *Journal of Teaching in Social Work* 12 (1/2):55–71.

Rai, G. S. (2002). Meeting the educational needs of international students: A perspective from US schools. *International Social Work* 45 (1):21–33.

Raschick, M., Maypole, D. E., and Day, P. (1998). Improving field instruction through Kolb learning theory. *Journal of Social Work Education* 34 (1):31–42.

Raske, M. (1999). Using feminist classroom rules to model empowerment for social work students. *Journal of Teaching in Social Work* 19 (1/2):197–209.

Raskin, M. S. (1994). The Delphi study in field instruction revisited: Expert consensus on issues and research priorities. *Journal of Social Work Education* 30 (1):75–89.

Raskin, M. S., Wayne, J., and Bogo, M. (2008). Revisiting field education standards. *Journal of Social Work Education* 44 (2):173–188.

Rawls, J. (1999). *A theory of justice*. Rev. ed. Cambridge, Mass.: Harvard University Press.

Regehr, C., Regehr, G., Leeson, J., and Fusco, L. (2002). Setting priorities for learning in the field practicum: A comparative study of students and field instructors. *Journal of Social Work Education* 38 (1):55–65.

Reid, W. J., Kenaley, B. D., and Colvin, J. (2004). Do some interventions work better than others? *Social Work Research* 28 (2):71–81.

Resnick, H. (1999). Paraphrase II: A listening skills training program for human service students. *Computers in Human Services* 15 (2/3):89–96.

Reynolds, B. C. (1942/1985). *Learning and teaching in the practice of social work*. New York: Russell and Russell; Silver Spring, Md.: National Association of Social Workers.

Rhodes, R., Ward, J., Ligon, J., and Priddy, P. (1999). Fighting for field: Seven threats to an important component of social work education. *Journal of Baccalaureate Social Work* 5 (1):15–25.

Richardson, V. (2006). Stewards of a field, stewards of an enterprise: The doctorate in education. In C. M. Golde and G. E. Walker, eds., *Envisioning the future of doctoral education*, 245–267. San Francisco: Jossey-Bass.

Richmond, M. E. (1898/2000). The need of a training school in applied philanthropy. In L. Leighninger, ed., *Creating a new profession: The beginnings of social work education in the United States*, 7–12. Alexandria, Va.: Council on Social Work Education.

Risler, E. A. (1999). Student practice portfolios: Integrating diversity and learning in the field experience. *Areté* 23 (1):83–96.

Rittner, B., and Struman, S. (2002). Changing images in distance learning: Integrating film into PowerPoint presentations on CD-ROM. Tech presentation at annual meeting of Council on Social Work Education, Nashville, Tenn., February.

Roberts, T. L., and Smith, L. A. (2002). The illusion of inclusion: An analysis of approaches to diversity within predominantly white schools of social work. *Journal of Teaching in Social Work* 22 (3/4):189–210.

Rompf, E. L. (1995). Student writing in social work: An aggravation or an opportunity for social work educators? *Journal of Teaching in Social Work* 12 (1/2):125–138.

Rosen, A., and Zlotnik, J. L. (2001). Demographics and reality: The "disconnect" in social work education. *Journal of Gerontological Social Work* 36 (3/4):81–97.

Rosen, A., Zlotnik, J. L., Curl, A. L., and Green, R. G. (2000). *CSWE SAGE-SW national competencies survey and report*. Alexandria, Va.: Council on Social Work Education, Gero-Ed Center.

Rosen, A., Zlotnik, J. L., and Singer, T. (2002). Basic gerontological competence for all social workers: The need to "gerontologize" social work education. *Journal of Gerontological Social Work* 39 (1/2):25–36.

Royce, D. (2001). *Teaching tips for college and university instructors: A practical guide.* Boston: Allyn & Bacon.

Rozas, L. W. (2007). Engaging dialogue in our diverse social work student body: A multilevel theoretical process model. *Journal of Social Work Education* 43 (1):5–30.

Saari, C. (1989). The process of learning in clinical social work. *Smith College Studies in Social Work* 60 (1):35–49.

Sakamoto, I., Anastas, J., McPhail, B., and Colarossi, L. (2008). Current status of women in social work education in the U.S. and Canada. *Journal of Social Work Education* 44 (1):37–62.

Sakamoto, I., and Pitner, R. O. (2005). Use of critical consciousness in anti-oppressive social work practice: Disentangled power dynamics at personal and structural levels. *British Journal of Social Work* 35 (4):435–452.

Sansone, F. A., Bedics, B. C., and Rappe, P. T. (2000). BSW faculty workload and scholarship expectations for tenure. *Journal of Baccalaureate Social Work* 5 (2):27–46.

Saulnier, C. (1996). *Feminist theories and social work: Approaches and applications.* Binghamton, N.Y.: Haworth Press.

Saunders, E. J. (1993). Confronting academic dishonesty. *Journal of Social Work Education* 29 (2):224–231.

Scanlon, P. A., and Ford, M. A. (1998). Grading student performance in real world settings. *New Directions for Teaching and Learning* 74:97–105.

Scharlach, A., Damron-Rodriguez, J., Robinson, B., and Feldman, R. (2000). Educating social workers for an aging society: A vision for the 21st century. *Journal of Social Work Education* 36 (3):521–538.

Schatz, M. C. S. (2004). Using portfolios: Integrating learning and promoting for social workers. *Advances in Social Work* 5 (1):105–123.

Schatz, M. C. S., and Simon, S. (1999). The portfolio approach for generalist social work practice: A successful tool for students in field education. *Journal of Baccalaureate Social Work* 5 (1):99–107.

Schiele, J. H. (2007). Implications of the equality-of-oppressions paradigm for curriculum content on people of color. *Journal of Social Work Education* 43 (1):83–100.

Schiele, J. H., and Francis, A. E. (1996). The status of former CSWE ethnic minority fellows in social work academia. *Journal of Social Work Education* 32 (1):31–44.

Schoech, D., and Helton, D. (2002). Qualitative and quantitative analysis of a course taught via classroom and Internet chatroom. *Qualitative Social Work* 1 (1):111–124.

Schön, D. A. (1983). *The reflective practitioner: How professionals think in action.* New York: Basic Books.

Schön, D. A. (1987). *Educating the reflective practitioner: Toward a new design for teaching and learning in the professions.* San Francisco: Jossey-Bass.

Schuster, J. H. (1999). Foreword to *Faculty in new jobs: A guide to settling in, becoming established, and building institutional support,* by R. J. Menges and Associates, xi–xv. San Francisco: Jossey-Bass.

Schutz, M., and Gordon, W. E. (1977). Reallocation of educational responsibility among schools, agencies, students, and NASW. *Journal of Education for Social Work* 13 (2):99–106.

Scriven, M., and Paul, R. (2008). Defining critical thinking. Available at http://www.criticalthinking.org/aboutCT/definingCT.cfm (accessed July 11, 2008).

Seaberg, J. R. (1998). Faculty reports of workload: Results of a national survey. *Journal of Social Work Education* 34 (1):7–19.

Seaberg, J. R. (1999). The virtual classroom: Asynchronous teaching via the Internet. Available at http://www.people.vcu.edu/~jseaberg/virtual_classroom.htm (accessed February 3, 2002).

Seaberg, J. R. (2001). Use of the Internet and other teaching tools in graduate social work education, a national survey. Available at http://www.people.vcu.edu/~jseaberg/teaching_survey.htm (accessed February 3, 2002).

Sears, J. T. (2002). The institutional climate for lesbian, gay, and bisexual faculty: What is the pivotal frame of reference? *Journal of Homosexuality* 43 (1):11–37.

Servon, L. (2002). *Bridging the digital divide: Technology, community, and public policy.* Malden, Mass.: Blackwell.

Shera, W., and Bogo, M. (2001). Social work education and practice: Planning for the future. *International Social Work* 44 (2):197–210.

Shibusawa, T., VanEsselstyn, D., and Oppenheim, S. (2006). Third space: A Web-based learning environment for teaching advanced clinical practice skills. *Journal of Technology in Human Services* 24 (4):21–33.

Shidlo, A., and Schroeder, M. (2002). Changing sexual orientation: A consumer's report. *Professional Psychology: Research and Practice* 33 (3):249–259.

Shulman, L. S. (2005). Signature pedagogies in the professions. *Daedalus* 134 (3):52–59.

Sidell, N. L. (2003). The course portfolio: A valuable teaching tool. *Journal of Teaching in Social Work* 23 (3/4):91–106.

Sikes, A., and Pearlman, E., eds. (2000). *Fast forward: How the Internet is changing your life.* New York: HarperCollins.

Simon, C. A., Carr, J. R., McCullough, S. M., Morgan, S. J., Oleson, T., and Ressel, M. (2003). The other side of academic dishonesty: The relationship between faculty skepticism, gender, and strategies for managing student academic dishonesty cases. *Assessment & Evaluation in Higher Education* 28 (2):193–207.

Singleton, S. M. (1994). Faculty personal comfort and the teaching of content on racial oppression. *Journal of Multicultural Social Work* 3 (1):5–16.

Sowers-Hoag, K., and Harrison, D. F. (1998). *Finding an academic job.* Thousand Oaks, Calif.: Sage.

Spicuzza, F. J. (2000). Portfolio assessment: Meeting the challenge of a self-study. *Journal of Baccalaureate Social Work* 5 (2):113–126.

Spitzer, R. (2003). Can some gay men and lesbians change their sexual orientation? 200 participants report a change from homosexual to heterosexual orientation. *Archives of Sexual Behavior* 32 (5):403–417.

Steele, C. M. (1997). A threat in the air: How stereotypes shape intellectual identity and performance. *American Psychologist* 52 (6):613–629.

Stefkovich, J. A. (2006). *Best interests of the student: Applying ethical constructs to legal cases in education.* Mahwah, N.J.: Erlbaum.

Steiner, S., Stromwall, L. K., Brzuzy, S., and Gerdes, K. (1999). Using cooperative learning strategies in social work education. *Journal of Social Work Education* 35 (2):253–264.

Stewart, D. (2008). Classroom management in the online environment. *Journal of Online Teaching and Learning* 4 (3):371–374. Available at http://jolt.merlot .org/vol4no3/stewart_0908.htm (accessed September 4, 2008).

(STLHE) Society for Teaching and Learning in Higher Education. (1996). Ethical principles in university teaching. Available at http://www.stlhe.ca/pdf/ EthicalPrinciplesInUniversityTeaching.pdf.

Stocks, T. J., and Freddolino, P. P. (1998). Evaluation of a World Wide Web–based graduate social work research methods course. *Computers in Human Services* 15 (2/3):51–69.

Stocks, T. J., and Freddolino, P. P. (2000). Enhancing computer-mediated teaching through interactivity: The second iteration of a World Wide Web–based graduate social work course. *Research on Social Work Practice* 10 (4): 505–518.

Stretch, J., and Kreuger, L. (2002). Hypermodern technology bites back, part II: Predicting acceptance and use. Paper presented at annual meeting of Council on Social Work Education, Nashville, Tenn., February.

Strom-Gottfried, K. (1999a) Professional boundaries: An analysis of violations by social workers. *Families in Society* 80 (5):439–449.

Strom-Gottfried, K. (1999b). When colleague accuses colleague: Adjudicating personnel matters through the filing of ethics complaints. *Administration in Social Work* 23 (2):1–16.

Strom-Gottfried, K. (2000a). Ensuring ethical practice: An examination of NASW code violations, 1986–97. *Social Work* 45 (3):251–261.

Strom-Gottfried, K. (2000b). Ethical vulnerability in social work education: An analysis of NASW complaints. *Journal of Social Work Education* 36 (2): 241–252.

Strom-Gottfried, K., and D'Aprix, A. (2006). Ethics for academics. *Social Work Education* 25 (3):225–244.

Stromwall, L. K. (2002). Is social work's door open to people recovering from psychiatric disabilities? *Social Work* 47 (1):75–83.

Stromwall, L. K., and Hurdle, D. (2003). Psychiatric rehabilitation: An empowerment-based approach to mental health services. *Social Work* 28 (3):206–213.

Strozier, A. L., Barnett-Queen, T., and Bennett, C. K. (2000). Supervision: Critical process and outcome variables. *Clinical Supervisor* 19 (1):21–39.

Sussman, T., Stoddart, K., and Gorman, E, (2004). Reconciling the congruent and contrasting roles of social work teacher, student, and practitioner: An experiential account of three doctoral students. *Journal of Teaching in Social Work* 24 (1/2):161–179.

Swigonski, M. (1993). Feminist standpoint theory and the questions of social work research. *Affilia* 8 (2):171–183.

Tatum, B. D. (1992). Talking about race, learning about racism: The application of racial identity development theory in the classroom. *Harvard Educational Review* 62 (1):1–24.

Tavris, C., and Aronson, E. (2007). *Mistakes were made (but not by me): Why we justify foolish beliefs, bad decisions, and hurtful acts.* Orlando, Fla.: Harcourt.

Tennant, M., and Pogson, P. (1995). *Learning and change in the adult years: A developmental perspective.* San Francisco: Jossey-Bass.

Tesone, D., and Ricci, P. (2008). Student perceptions of Web-based instruction: A comparative analysis. *Journal of Online Teaching and Learning* 4 (3):317–325. Available at http://jolt.merlot.org/vol4no3/tesone_0908.htm (accessed September 4, 2008).

Thomas, S. B. (2000). College students and disability law. *Journal of Special Education* 33 (4):248–257.

Thyer, B. A. (2003). A student portfolio approach to conducting doctoral social work comprehensive examinations. *Journal of Teaching in Social Work* 23 (3/4):117–126.

Thyer, B. A., Polk, G., and Gaudin, J. (1997). Distance learning in social work education: A preliminary evaluation. *Journal of Social Work Education* 33 (2):363–367.

Total cost of PC ownership. (2000). *PC World*, October.

Toth, E. (1997). *Ms. Mentor's impeccable advice for women in academia.* Philadelphia: University of Pennsylvania Press.

Uehara, E. S., Sohng, S. S. L. E., Nagda, B., Erera, P., and Yamashiro, G. (2005). Multiculturalism, social justice, and social inquiry: Issues for social work research education. In L. Gutieerez, M. E. Zuñiga, and D. Lum, eds., *Education for multicultural social work practice: Critical viewpoints and future directions*, 113–124. Alexandria, Va.: Council on Social Work Education.

Urdang, E. (1979) In defense of process recording. *Smith College Studies in Social Work* 50 (1):1–15.

Urwin, C. A., Van Soest, D., and Kretzschmar, J. A. (2006). Key principles for developing gatekeeping standards for working with students with problems. *Journal of Teaching in Social Work* 26 (1/2):163–180.

Valentine, D. P., Edwards, S., Gohagan, D., Huff, M., Pereira, A., and Wilson, P. (1998). Preparing social work doctoral students for teaching: Report of a survey. *Journal of Social Work Education* 34 (2):273–282.

Valian, V. (1998). *Why so slow? The advancement of women.* Cambridge, Mass.: MIT Press.

Valian, V. (2005). Beyond gender schemas: Improving the advancement of women in academia. *Hypatia* 20 (3):198–213.

Vandehey, M. A., Diekoff, G. M., and LaBeff, E. E. (2007). College cheating: A twenty-year follow-up and the addition of an honor code. *Journal of College Student Development* 48 (4):468–480.

Van Soest, D. (1996). The influence of competing ideologies about homosexuality on nondiscrimination policy: Implications for social work education. *Journal of Social Work Education* 32 (1):53–63.

Van Soest, D., and Garcia, B. (2003). *Diversity education for social justice: Mastering teaching skills.* Alexandria, Va.: Council on Social Work Education.

Van Soest, D., and Kruzich, J. (1994). The influence of learning styles on student and field instructor perceptions of field placement success. *Journal of Teaching in Social Work* 9 (1/2):46–69.

Van Voorhis, R., and Wagner, M. (2001). Coverage of gay and lesbian subject matter in social work journals. *Journal of Social Work Education* 37 (1): 147–159.

Vowell, P. R., and Chen, J. (2004). Predicting academic misconduct: A comparative test of four sociological explanations. *Sociological Inquiry* 74 (2):226–249.

Wajda-Johnston, V. A., Handal, P. J., Brawer, P. A., and Fabricatore, A. N. (2001). Academic dishonesty at the graduate level. *Ethics and Behavior* 11 (3):287–305.

Walsh, T. C. (2002). Structured process recording: A comprehensive model that incorporates the strengths perspective. *Social Work Education* 21 (1):23–34.

Washburn, J. J. (2008). Encouraging research collaboration through ethical and fair authorship: A model policy. *Ethics and Behavior* 18 (1):44–58.

Wayne, J., Bogo, M., and Raskin, M. (2006). The need for radical change in field education. *Journal of Social Work Education* 42 (10):161–169.

Weaver, H. N. (2000). Culture and professional education: The experiences of Native American social workers. *Journal of Social Work Education* 36 (3): 415–428.

Weiner, A. (1999). Taking an HIV/AIDS education course to the "Net." *New Technology in Human Services* 12 (3/4):12–16.

Weiner, A. (2002). Evaluating effective use of Internet resources in social work education. Paper presented at annual meeting of Council on Social Work Education, Nashville, Tenn., February.

Wergen, J., ed. (1994). *Analyzing faculty workload*. San Francisco: Jossey-Bass.

Wernet, S., Olliges, R., and Delicath, T. (2000). Postcourse evaluations of WebCT (Web course tools) classes by social work students. *Research on Social Work Practice* 10 (4):487–504.

Wheeler, S. C., and Petty, R. E. (2001). The effects of stereotype activation on behavior: A review of possible mechanisms. *Psychological Bulletin* 127 (6):797–826.

Whitaker, T., Weismiller, T., and Clark, E. (2006). Assuring the sufficiency of a frontline workforce: A national study of licensed social workers. Executive summary. Available at http://workforce.socialworkers.org/studies/nasw_06_execsummary.pdf.

Whitley, B. E. (1998). Factors associated with cheating among college students: A review. *Research in Higher Education* 39 (3):235–274.

Who's online? (2001). *PC Magazine*, February 6.

Wilke, D. J., and Vinton, L. (2003). Domestic violence and aging: Teaching about their intersection. *Journal of Social Work Education* 39 (2):225–235.

Wilson, P. P., Valentine, D., and Pereira, A. (2002). Perceptions of new social work faculty about mentoring experiences. *Journal of Social Work Education* 38 (2):317–333.

Winston, P. H. (1997). *How to speak*. Cambridge, Mass.: Derek Bok Center for Teaching and Learning, Harvard University.

Wodarski, J. S., Feit, M. D., and Green, R. K. (1995). Graduate social work education: A review of 2 decades of empirical research and considerations for the future. *Social Service Review* 69 (1):108–130.

Wolfer, T. A., and Johnson, M. M. (2003). Re-evaluating student evaluation of teaching: The teaching evaluation form. *Journal of Social Work Education* 39 (1):111–121.

Yelloly, M., and Henkel, M., eds. (1995). *Learning and teaching in social work: Toward reflective practice*. London: Jessica Kingsley.

Youn, T. I. K. (2005). The academic job market is bad for all of us. *Academe* 91 (6):27–30.

Young, J. (1997). Rethinking the role of the professor in an age of high-tech tools. *Chronicle of Higher Education* 44 (6):A26–A28.

Young, J. (1998). Skeptical academics see perils in information technology. *Chronicle of Higher Education* 44 (25):A29–A30.

Zastrow, C., and Bremner, J. (2004). Social work education responds to the shortage of persons with both a doctorate degree and a professional social work degree. *Journal of Social Work Education* 40 (2):351–358.

Zhou, Y. R., Knoke, D., and Sakamoto, I. (2005). Rethinking silence in the classroom: Chinese students' experiences of sharing indigenous knowledge. *International Journal of Inclusive Education* 9 (3):287–311.

INDEX

AAUP. *See* American Association of University Professors
abbreviations, used with e-mail, 131
Abrams, L. S., 72
Abramson, J. S., 104, 109
academic approach, to field learning, 96–97, 98, 101
academic dishonesty, 224; reporting students', 228–229
Academic Duty (Kennedy), 253
academic setting, freedom of, 234
academic workplace, social work teaching in, 6. *See also* workplace
academy, citizens of, 234
accountability, 151, 158–159, 258. *See also* assessment
accreditation, 151, 154–155; discipline-specific, 159; and NASW's Code of Ethics, 223–224
accreditation processes, mission-driven models in, 161–162
accreditation standards (EPAS), 5
active learners, 32
adaptation, sink-or-swim, in professional learning, 28–29
Adkins, L., 127
administration, in faculty workload, 190–191, 195
administrators, college and university, 166
admissions: issues of, 153–154; lack of selectivity in, 175

admissions process, and ethical issues, 230
Adobe Acrobat document files, 138
ads, for faculty vacancies, 197
adulthood, 13; early, compared with middle, 15; individual development in, 15–16
adults: learning in, 14, 16–18, 19–20, 21–22; learning theory in, 5, 22, 260; thinking in, 14, 16–18, 19–20, 21–22
advising students, ethics of, 246
affirmative action policies, 72
African Americans: and computer access, 117, 118; identity development of, 70; on social work faculty, 68; in social work programs, 67
ageism, 87
agencies, 4. *See also* social agencies
aging: as academic specialty, 88; of gays and lesbians, 78; and identity, 63; in institutional context, 89–90; and social work profession, 86–87; teaching content for, 88–89
Ali, S. R., 63
Alvarez, A. R., 177
American Association of University Professors (AAUP), 190; on ethical guidelines, 241; standards of, 253; statement of professional ethics of, 236, 237, 248, 249
American Council on Education (ACE), 202

American Psychiatric Association, 78

American Psychological Association, 78

Americans with Disabilities Act (1990), 85

Anastas, J. W., 155

Ancis, J. R., 63

androgogy, 5

application: in job search, 209; scholarship of, 192, 193

apprenticeship approach, to field learning, 96, 97–98, 101

appropriate usage policies, for wireless in classroom, 143

Area Concentration Achievement Test (ACAT), 160–161

articulated approach, to field learning, 97, 98–99, 101

Asian Americans: on social work faculty, 68; in social work programs, 67

assessment, 258; activities for, 184; annual evaluation, 179; audiences for, 159; of cultural competence, 161; definition of, 158; ethics of, 240, 245; of expected learning outcomes, 161–163; and gatekeeping, 175–176; goal of, 162; by graduates, 166; of peers, 165–166; problems in, 185; for promotion, 179; standardized measures for, 159–161; by students, 164–166; of students, 158–159; student satisfaction questionnaires in, 176, 177–178; by teachers, 163–164; of teaching and learning, 58, 152–154, 176–178, 183; teaching portfolios in, 178; and tenure, 179

assessment, of field experience: of instruction, 180; of learning, 174–175

assessment methodology: grading, 173; observation, 168–169; oral performance, 168; paper-and-pencil measures, 167–168; portfolios, 172–173; standardized cases, 169–172

assistant professor, title of, 198

associate professor, rank of, 198

Association of Social Work Boards (ASWB), 156

audience: for educational assessment, 159; for presentation software, 122

audio files, courses available as, 124

Austin, A. E., 196

authority, in effective teaching, 36

authorship: determination of, 242; ethics of, 242–243

autonomy: in faculty work, 220; and professional norms, 240

availability, of field instructors, 183

Aviles, C. B., 174

Baccalaureate Educational Assessment Package (BEAP), 160, 166

Baccalaureate Program Directors (BPD), 205

baccalaureate programs, 1, 189; assessment of, 160; gatekeeping for, 230–231

Baez, A., 171, 172

Bain, K., 68

Baldwin, R. G., 219

Ballantyne, N., 126

Bandura, A., 164, 260

banking model: of education, 24; of teaching and learning, 33

Banner, J. M., 36

Banta, T. W., 158

Barnett-Queen, T., 182

Baskind, F. R., 157

Bayer, A. E., 235, 236, 240, 243, 244

Belenky, M. F., 16, 17, 18, 21, 28, 76

benefits, in job offer, 215–216

Bennett, C. K., 182

Bennett, L., 103, 104

"Bill of Rights, Academic," 251, 252

Bligh, D. A., 38

Bliss, M., 126

block placement model of field education, 99–100

Blonstein, S., 109, 110

Bloom, B. S., 163

Bogo, M., 2, 31, 100, 101, 108, 109, 110, 111, 180, 181, 182

bookmarking, in CMS packages, 133

Borowski, N. A., 152

Bourdieu, P., 74

Boyer, E. L., 35, 192, 193, 194, 257, 258

Boyer Commission, report of, 191, 192, 193

Brady, M., 139

Braxton, J. M., 235, 236, 240, 243, 244

Bremner, J., 199

Brookfield, S. D., 36

Brooks/Cole Publishing, 125

Brown, G., 158

Brownlee, K., 80

Brownstein, C., 101, 103, 104

BSW degree, as hiring qualification, 204

Buchan, V., 160

bulleted style, to "telegraph" content, 123

"buzz group," as lecture technique, 40

Campbell Collaboration, 258

campus visit, during job search, 212–215

Cannon, H. C., 36

Caragata, L., 112, 113

care, ethic of, 240–241

career planning, 8

Carnegie Foundation for the Advancement of Teaching, 191; classification system of, 189

case study, written, 169–170

Case Western Reserve University, 112

Cauble, A. E., 126

Cavazos, A., 182

CDs (compact disks), course material on, 124–126

change, and illusion of inclusion, 62

chat sessions, 139

chauvinism, 42

cheating: deterrent to, 228; factors affecting, 227; forms of, 227; by students, 224, 225–227

Chronicle of Higher Education (American Council on Education), 202

Chronister, J. L., 219

Chute, D., 126

class disparities, and access to technology, 115

class presentations, 168

classroom: assessment techniques in, 259; discussion in, 41; diversity issues in, 90; effective teaching in, 58; electronic devices in, 10–11; electronic technologies in, 260; ethics in, 243–246; ethics outside of, 246–247; field learning integrated in, 99, 106–107; formative feedback in, 176–177; ground rules for interactions in, 43; identity management in, 80–81; instruction in, 6–7; planning for, 56; quality of instruction in, 183–184; silences in, 18; wireless devices in, 143. *See also* discussion; teaching

clinical professor, title of, 198

Cluse-Tolar, T., 79

CMS. *See* course management software

coaching, 59; role of, 50; in teaching, 49

Cochran Collaboration, 258

Code of Ethics. *See* National Association of Social Workers

Coe, S., 103, 104

cognitive development: in adults, 18, 19–20; critical thinking in, 22, 23

cognitive psychology, 38

colleagues: disputes involving, 250; ethical responsibilities to, 249, 250–251; ethics of relationships with, 247–248, 250; evaluation of, 249; impairment of, 250; respect for, 239, 250; unethical conduct of, 251

colleges: and sexual orientation issues, 82; social work programs in, 189

Comerford, S. A., 71

communication: asynchronous, 120, 127, 136; cross-gender, 76; online, 129, 130–132; technology of, 116

compact disks. *See* CDs

computers: access to, 117, 118; costs associated with, 118, 119; environmental impact of, 119; and privacy, 147; rapid obsolescence of, 117

conceptualization, in learning, 24, 25

conferences, annual, 180

conferencing: text-based, 136; video, 140–143

confidentiality: ethics of, 239; NASW Code of Ethics on, 233; protections of, 147

Conklin, B., 157
connected knowing, 18
consciousness raising, process of, 23–24
consultant, faculty–field liaison as, 98
"consultant" teachers, 129
content: in course preparation, 52; diversity
  of, 72–90; for lecture, 41; teaching, 88–89
content areas: choosing, 59; and learning
  tasks, 35
content competence, ethics of, 238
continuing education, 9
contract, in field learning, 107
contract faculty, 198
conversion therapies, 78
copyright permission, 56
Corcoran, K., 157
Costello, C. Y., 73, 74, 75, 261
Council on Social Work Education
  (CSWE), 1, 257; annual conferences
  of, 209; Commission on Accreditation
  of, 154, 155; "cultural competence"
  model adopted by, 62–63; Distance
  Education and Technology Symposia
  of, 143; on diversity, 61; ethical principles
  for research proposed by, 261; on field
  education, 93; model of program
  assessment of, 162; MSW degree
  requirement of, 96; and NASW, 109;
  national conferences of, 205; National
  Statement on Research Integrity in
  Social Work of, 236; newsletters of,
  209; sexual orientation decision of, 82;
  Visiting Scholars Program of, 257
couples therapy, 183
course content, ethical dimensions of, 244
course design: defining goals and outcomes
  in, 53–54; goals and learning outcomes
  in, 55–56; mechanics and materials in,
  56; providing context for, 53; selecting
  course content, 54–55; writing course
  description, 54
course management software (CMS):
  advantages of, 133; availability of, 132;
  choosing product, 136; collaboration
  features of, 135–136; dissatisfaction

with, 120, 137; file management tools
  for, 134–135; group assignments with,
  134; instructor-oriented features of,
  134–135; live chatting sessions with, 136;
  multimedia capabilities of, 135; "plug-in"
  features of, 135; student-oriented features
  of, 133–134; using, 132–133
courses: on CD, 125; CD- or DVD-based
  modules, 126; "computer-based," 137;
  online, 130, 146; portfolios used in,
  172; preparing for, 52; and student
  assessment, 184; Web-enhanced, 127;
  with Web presence, 127. See also
  curriculum
course syllabus, 56; in teaching portfolio,
  57
creativity, collective, 51
credentials, professional, 187
credit, for authorship, 242
criteria, for classroom performance, 175
critical consciousness, 23–24
critical incidents, 90–91
critical thinking, 22–23, 42, 259; and
  independent inquiry and discovery, 47–
  48; in student presentations, 48; and
  transformative learning, 27
critique, ethic of, 240–241
Crook, W., 139
CSWE. See Council on Social Work
  Education
cultural competence: assessment of, 161;
  and faculty recruitment, 69; as hiring
  qualification, 206–207; learning of,
  70–71; model of, 62–63; and practice
  standards, 66
culture: and adult development, 16; in
  course content, 70; and identity, 63; and
  institutional contexts, 72; and learning,
  18; and social work faculty, 68–69; in
  social work profession, 66; of social work
  students, 66–67; teaching about, 71
curriculum: design of, 152; diversity and
  oppression issues in, 65, 260; electronic
  technologies in, 258; horizontal
  integration of, 53; and professional

standards, 154; renewing, 59; and student assessment, 184; "transformative multicultural," 63; vertical integration of, 53

curriculum, social work, 2, 3; aging in, 86–87, 88–89; content on women in, 76; critical thinking in, 22–23; disability content in, 85; diversity content in, 71; gender in, 75; sexual orientation in, 80–81; teaching diversity in, 69

curriculum committee, 54; and field liaisons, 107

curriculum vitae, in job search, 209

Daloz, L. A. P., 27
Davis, J. R., 2, 18
Dawes, R. M., 151
Day, P., 26
Deal, K. H., 30
Defense of Marriage Act (DOMA; 1996), 82
DeLange, J., 76
delivery, varying, 39
demographics, of U.S. society, 260
development: adult, 13; student, 13, 14
Diagnostic and Statistical Manual of Mental Disorders-IV (DSM-IV), 126
different abilities, technology for people with, 150
"differently abled," technology access for, 144
"digital divide," 144, 145; and income, 117–118; at institutional level, 119
digital versatile discs. See DVDs
Dillon, C., 125
disabilities: in institutional context, 85–86; invisible, 85; and social work profession, 82–83; students with, 83–84; teachers with, 84; teaching about, 85; technology for people with, 150
disability status: and identity, 63; and technology access, 144
discovery: in research, 48; scholarship of, 192; in teaching, 47–48
discussion: leading, 42–47; process of, 43

discussion, classroom, 41; principles for, 42–45; small groups for, 45; strategies for, 45–46; teachers' dominance of, 45
dissertation, and job hunting, 204
dissonance, 74–75
"distance" education, 5, 116, 129
diversity: dimensions of, 63; impact of, on social work, 206–207; institutional context for study of, 72; intersectionality of, with identity, 91; issues of, 7; and race, ethnicity, and culture, 66–72; in social work education, 65; teaching content in, 69–72; of U.S. population, 61
diversity content: aging, 86–90; disabilities, 82–86; gender, 72–77; sexual orientation, 77–82
Dixon-Reeves, R., 218
doctoral degree, and job hunting, 204
doctoral education, diversity in, 69
doctoral programs, 1, 192, 261; shortage of, 199
doctorate-granting institutions, classification of, 189, 190
doctorates, shortage of, 199
domination, systems of, and diversity, 63–64
Drisko, J., 7
dropout rates, from online BSW courses, 145–146
dualism: shift out of, 17; truth in, 21
dual relationships, with students, 246
Dumbrill, G., 144
DVDs, course material on, 124

East, J. F., 22, 23
Eckel, P. D., 195
economic conditions, 111
economies, developed, higher education in, 256
education, 13, 93; adult, 6; banking model of, 24; and computer access, 118; continuing, 9; definition of, 116; "distance," 5, 116, 129; international, 9–10; nature of, 4; online, 9, 145–146. See also field education; higher education

education, social work: field instruction in, 105–106; field practicum in, 93; goal of, 2; and transformational learning, 27–28

educational context, 187

educational institutions: e-mail rules of, 138; impact of technology on, 118–119; technology-mediated courses developed by, 146. *See also* institution; institutional context

Educational Planning and Assessment System (EPAS), 5

educators, ethical conduct of, 236. *See also* faculty; teachers

electronic books, 124

electronic technologies, 7. *See also* technological innovations; technology

e-mail: software for, 138–140; text-only format of, 139; use of, 116

emotions, in classroom discussions, 47

employers, 166, 247; commitments to, 247, 248. *See also* institution

empty vessel model, of teaching and learning, 33

English language, 145

Enns, C. Z., 91

EPAS. *See* Educational Planning and Assessment System

Erikson, E., 15, 16

ethical dilemmas, 224; in teaching, 236

ethical issues: academic integrity, 235–241; in field, 231; internship-related, 232–234; "nonacademic" or professional, 229–232

ethics, 7; assessment of, 163; in classroom, 243–246; outside classroom, 246–247; of scholarship, 241–243

ethnicity: in course content, 70; and identity, 63; and institutional contexts, 72; in social work faculty, 68–69; in social work profession, 66; of social work students, 66–67; teaching about, 71. *See also* diversity

ethnocentrism, 42

European Union, social work programs in, 260

evaluation, 58; techniques of, 8. *See also* assessment

evaluation of students, ethics of, 245

evidence-based practice, 234, 258

experience: in learning, 24, 25; reflecting on, 41–42

experimentation, in learning, 24, 25

faculty: adjunct, 188; collaboration of, with field liaison, 99; compensation for, 201–202; contract, 198, 218–219; disabled, 84; diversity in, 68–69; e-mail use by, 139; and ethical issues, 252; in field, 26; and field instructors, 107; in field of aging, 88; gender differences in, 75; impact of technology on, 119–121; individual practice of, 200; Internet resources used by, 128; junior, 201; mentoring of new members, 218; non-tenure-track, full-time, 218–219; and online communications, 130; and online teaching, 130, 146–147; practice competence of, 106; questionable practices of, 224; scholarly activities of, 201; sexual orientation of, 80; social work, 1, 257; teaching experience of, 205–206; tenure-eligible, 114; and tenure requirements, 108; and *U.S. News* rankings, 157; workload of, 200–201. *See also* colleagues

faculty–field liaison, 93–95; academic approach of, 98; in apprenticeship approach, 97–98; purpose of, 97; role of, 101–105, 108; support of, 105

faculty hiring, 197–199, 208; of adjuncts, 207; and cultural competence, 206–207; degrees in, 203–205; and institutional mission, 220; and international interests, 207; and offer of job, 215–216; for part-time teaching, 207–208; research experience in, 206; search committee for, 210; teaching experience in, 205–206. *See also* job search

faculty work, 190–191; administration, 195; advising students, 194; analysis of, 8;

essential elements of, 196; multi-faceted nature of, 220; professional development, 195–196; qualifying for, 197–199; scholarship, 191–193; service, 194–195, 201; in social work, 199–202; teaching, 194

Falk, D. S., 136

Family Educational Rights and Privacy Act (FERPA; 1974), 224

Faria, G., 101, 103, 104

feedback: in classroom, 176–177; in field learning, 174; on process recordings, 169, 183; on teaching, 184

feedback, student, in teaching portfolio, 57

Feit, M. D., 151, 185

feminism: and critical consciousness, 24; and diversity, 64–65

field: electronic technologies in, 260; ethical issues in, 231–234; liaison between faculty and, 101

field director, role of, 106

field education: academic approach to, 96–97, 98, 101; apprenticeship approach to, 96, 97–98, 101; articulated approach to, 97, 98–99, 101; directors, 112; enhancing, 114; future directions for, 107–113; history of, 95–96; individualized approach to, 111; integrated approach to, 108; structure of, 99–101; theory in, 259–260; threats to, 105–106

field forums, 107

field instruction, 2, 6, 21; assessment of, 180; evaluating students' performance in, 180–181; students' satisfaction with, 181–183

field instructors, 26, 104–105, 181; and course content, 107; dual relationships with, 233; ethical conduct of, 236; role of, 108

field learning, 7; assessment of, 174–175; separate from school, 110

field placements, students' satisfaction with, 104–105

field practicum, 93

Finch, J. B., 2, 30, 67, 168

Finn, J., 230

"fishbowl" technique, in classroom discussion, 46

Fitch, D., 172

Formo, D. M., 202

Fortune, A. E., 100, 103, 104, 108, 109, 182

Fox, R., 87

Franks, C. L., 2, 67, 168

Freddolino, P. P., 133

Freire, P., 23, 24, 27

French, C. L., 30

funders, 166

Gappa, J. M., 196

Garcia, B., 63, 71

gatekeeping, in program assessment, 175–176

Gaudin, J., 142

"gay lifestyle," 80

gay people, social workers' attitudes toward, 79

gender: and identity, 63; in social work profession, 72–73; of social work students, 73–75; teaching content in, 75–77

gender differences: in adult development, 16; in classroom discussion, 44; of teachers, 75

gender inequities: in higher education, 73–75; in social work profession, 73

gender theory, 76

George, A., 95

gerontophobia, 87

Gibbs, L., 124

Gibson, P., 72

Gilligan, C., 16

Glassman, U., 97

global education, 9–10

globalization: impact of, on social work, 255–256; of society, 4, 111, 112

Globerman, J., 108, 109, 111

glossary creation, with CMS, 135

goals, defining, 53

Golde, C. M., 215

Goldstein, H., 96, 97

Gordon, M. S., 97, 98
Gordon, W. E., 97, 98, 109
GPA (grade point average), and student self-appraisals, 165
grade inflation, 56
grading: to assess students' learning, 173; ethical aspects of, 245; using portfolios for, 172
grading system, problems in, 173–174
graduate education, 5
graduate programs, *U.S. News* rankings of, 157
graduates, assessment undertaken by, 166
Green, J., 144
Green, R. G., 157, 166
Green, R. K., 151, 185
Grossman, B., 97
group discussion, 43, 45. *See also* discussion
groups, in teaching, 51
"guide on the side," teacher as, 115
Gustafson, L., 145

habitus, Bourdieu's concept of, 74
Haga, M., 142
Harris, D., 142
Harrison, D. F., 202
Hartman, A., 106, 109
Harvard University, 107
HBSE. *See* Human Behavior and Social Environment policy
Heitkamp, T., 142
Henkel, M., 154
Hernandez-Peck, M., 80
heteronormativity, pervasive, 81
heterosexism, in field, 81
higher education, 187; accountability in, 159; assimilative mode of learning in, 25; in developed economies, 256; diversity in, 61; ethical guidelines for, 241; global aspirations of, 259; growth in, 13; inequities in, 74; students with disabilities in, 85–86; types of institutions of, 189–190
HIPPA regulations, 171

Hispanic Americans: and computer access, 118; in social work faculty, 68; in social work programs, 67
Holden, G., 129, 155, 164–165, 258
Holister, C., 142
homophobia, in field, 81
honor boards, 232
honor codes, 227, 252
hooks, b., 24
host setting, example of, 247–248
Howe, R. D., 201
Hu, S., 173
Huff, M., 142
Human Behavior and Social Environment (HBSE) policy, 203
Hunter College, 112
hybrid model, for field education, 110–111
Hylton, M. E., 142

ICQ (American Online), 139
identity, and diversity, 91
identity dissonance, 74–75
identity management, in classroom, 80–81
impropriety, professorial, 235
inclusion, illusion of, 62, 90
income, and computer access, 117, 118
information, evaluating Internet-based, 128
Information for Practice (IP), 258
inquiry: in research, 48; in teaching, 47–48
instant messaging (IM), 116, 131
Instant Messenger (America Online), 139
Institute for the Advancement of Social Work Research (IASWR), 206
institution: ethics of relationships with, 247–248; respect for, 240. *See also* educational institutions
institutional context: aging in, 89–90; disabilities in, 85–86; for diversity, 72; gender differences in, 77; for sexual orientation, 81–82
instruction, 125. *See also* field instruction; programmed instruction
instructor guides, with CMS, 135

instructors, availability of, 56–57. *See also* field instructors

integrated academic partnership, 108–109

integration, scholarship of, 192

intellectual excitement, in effective teaching, 34–35

intensive model, of liaison role, 103. *See also* faculty–field liaison

interactive process, teaching as, 33

interactive television (IT), 140–143; course, preparation for, 146; effectiveness of, 141; multiple microphones in, 140–141; use of, 142

interdisciplinary work, in field of aging, 89

intergroup dialogue (IGD) model, 72

international education, 9–10

international students, 255, 256

Internet: access to, 118; and cheating, 227; and privacy, 147; problems with, 125; teaching with, 127–130

internship: ethical issues in, 232; learning in, 225; model for, 109–110. *See also* field education

interpersonal rapport, in effective teaching, 34–35

intersectionality, of diversity and identity issues, 91

interviews: with faculty, 213–214; inappropriate and illegal questions in, 214–215; in job search, 211–212; on-campus, 212–215

IT. *See* interactive television

Jenkins, L. E., 96, 97, 98

Jirovec, R. L., 177

job ads, for faculty vacancies, 197

job market, for teaching jobs in social work, 202–203

job search, 208, 209; application in, 209–210; first interview in, 211–212; framing expertise and goals for, 209; meeting dean/director in, 214; meeting faculty in, 213–214; on-campus interview in, 212–215; recommendations for, 202–203; references for, 210–211

"job talk," 212–213

John A. Hartford Foundation, 86, 88

Johnson, A. K., 112

Johnson, M. M., 177, 178

journaling, as learning technique, 47

journals: online, 128–129; social work, 12

Kane, M. N., 87

Karrer, T., 120, 137, 147

Kegan, R., 21

Kendall, K. A., 93, 107

Kennedy, D., 49, 253

King, J. D., 195

Kirk, S. A., 157

Knight, C., 169, 183

knowing: connected, 18; subjective, 17; women's ways of, 19–20

knowing-understanding-doing learning paradigm, 97

knowledge: assessing students', 162–163; in learning process, 98; practice, 163; procedural, 17

Knowles, A., 126

Kolb, D. A., 24, 25, 97, 259

Krentzman, A. R., 66, 161

Kretzchmar, J. A., 231

Kreuger, L., 117, 147

Kulkin, H., 145

language: as barrier, 145; proficiency in, 113

leadership, gender differences in, 77

learners: assimilative, 25; convergent, 25

learning: assessment of, 152–154, 183; collaborative, 51; context for, 187, 188; cooperative, 51, 52; defining goals and outcomes for, 53–54; effects of diversity on, 61–63, 64; and electronic technologies, 7; and ethical issues, 224–225; evaluation of, 8; experiential, 97, 111; factors affecting, 2, 3; in field setting, 2, 7, 37, 93–94, 96–97, 260; higher-order, 59; incorporating opportunities for, 58; internship, 225; lessons in, 259–261; lifelong, 21, 42, 259; modes of, 35–36; as personal enterprise, 6; in postgraduate

learning (*continued*)
environment, 14; process of, 32; programmed, 125; social work theory of student, 28–30; stages of, 28–30; to teach, 261; teaching informed by, 32; and technological innovations, 116; technology-mediated, 120; theories of, 259; transformational, 26–28

learning, adult, 14, 15, 16–18, 19–20, 21–22; theories of, 260

learning, modes of: journal keeping, 47; research, 48–49

learning outcomes, and assessments, 184

learning paradigm, knowing-understanding-doing, 97

learning process, in teaching preparation, 41

learning styles, 24–26; and technology, 145

learning tasks and activities, taxonomy of, 35

lectures, CD- or DVD-based, 126. *See also* classroom

lecturing: definition of, 38; framework for, 38–39; suggestions for, 39–41

Lee, M., 182

lesbians, social workers' attitudes toward, 79

Levinson, D. L., 15–16

LGBT issues, 65

liaison, 103. *See also* faculty–field liaison

licensing, 155–156; bodies for, 156; goals of, 156

life expectancy, and adult development, 16

Lim, D. H., 142

linkage, faculty–field liaison as, 102, 103, 104–105

listening, in classroom discussion, 46

list-servs, 136

MacFarlane, B., 236, 243, 246, 249, 252

Mackelprang, R. W., 80

Macy, J., 142, 145

Maki, P. L., 152

Mandel School of Applied Social Sciences, 112

market, for teaching jobs in social work, 202–203

Marson, S. M., 230

Martin, J., 80

master's degree programs, 1, 189; cheating in, 226; gatekeeping for, 230–231

mastery, in professional learning, 29

materials, in teaching portfolio, 57

Maypole, D. E., 26

McGee, G., 142

McGranahan, E., 11

McKeachie, W. J., 47, 52, 234

McKnight, K., 180

McPhail, B. A., 76

"meaning perspectives," 27

mediator, faculty–field liaison as, 102, 103, 104–105

Meenaghan, T., 155

Mentkowski, M., 14

mentoring, 59; of new faculty members, 218; role of, 49

Merdinger, J. C., 18

Mesbur, E. S., 97

Meyer, I., 75

Mezirow, J., 27

micropractice courses, disability content in, 85

Miller, J. B., 16

Millstein, K. H., 71

minorities, in non-tenure-track positions, 219

minority stress model, 75

minority students, 67

misconduct, ethical, 235–236

Mishna, F., 31

modules, CD- or DVD-based, 126

monitor, faculty–field liaison as, 102, 103, 104–105

Mooradian, J. K., 170

Morris, M. L., 142

M.S.S.A. degree, 112

MSW degree, as hiring qualification, 203

MSW programs, gatekeeping for, 230–231

multimedia, interactive, teaching with, 123–127

Mumm, A. M., 169, 182

Murphy, B. C., 125

National Association of Social Workers (NASW): Code of Ethics of, 8, 223–224, 233, 236, 247, 248, 261; and CSWE, 109; on cultural competence, 66; newsletters of, 209

Native Americans: in social work faculty, 68; in social work programs, 67

Naturally Speaking (ScanSoft), 144

netiquette, 120, 143; for appropriate vs. inappropriate content, 139; legal dimensions of, 130; resources for, 131–132, 149

Neugarten, B. L., 16

New York Charity Organization Society, 95, 107

New York School of Philanthropy, 95

Noble, J. H., 161, 165

No Child Left Behind Act (2001), 258

"normative disequilibrium," 16

norms: academic and professional, 234–235; admonitory, 243; inviolable, 243; of scholarship, 241–242

note-taking, encouraging, 39

nursing, student assessment in, 171

objectives, defining, 53

observation, 58; in learning, 24, 25; of peers, 176; "proxy" method of, 168; of students' interactions, 168

Observed Structured Case Evaluation (OSCE), 171–172

offer, job: rank and terms of, 215; salary and benefits of, 215–216; and support for success, 216; and tenure system, 217

one-year residence (OYR) program, 112

online communication, ground rules for, 130–132

online education, 9, 126–127; appropriate marketing for, 145–146; effectiveness of, 136–138

online resources, citing and saving, 129

open-question format, for presentation software, 123

Oppenheim, S., 183

oral presentations, 168

Ortiz Hendricks, C., 2, 30, 67, 70, 168, 182

otherness, constructive engagement with, 27

outcomes: emphasis on, 258–259; measurable, 151

outcomes assessment, accreditation standards in, 155

outline, lecturing from, 39

Pacific Islanders: on social work faculty, 68; in social work programs, 67

Palomba, C. A., 158

Pardeck, J. T., 83

Parrish, D., 142

Patchner, M., 142

Paul, R., 22

pedagogical competence, ethics of, 238

peers: observation of, in classroom, 176; review by, 165–166, 249

Perry, W. G., 17, 18

Peterson, K. J., 2, 7

Petracchi, H., 142

Pew Internet Survey, 118

philosophy of teaching, in teaching portfolio, 57

Pike, C. K., 177

placements: availability of, 100–101; students' satisfaction with, 104–105

plagiarism, 224; methods of detecting, 229. See also cheating

planning, course, 55. See also course design

podcasts, teaching with, 124

Pogson, P., 18, 33

Polk, G., 142

portfolios: to assess learning, 172–173; teaching, 176, 178, 205

posttenure reviews, 217

Potter, C. C., 22, 23

PowerPoint (Microsoft) slides, 138; presentations with, 56, 121

practice: dealing with diversity in, 91; elders in, 87–88; integrating theory with, 183; legal regulation of, 156

practice skills, systematic assessment of, 163

practice wisdom, 1, 28

practicum experience, for reflective practitioner, 31

practitioner, reflective, 30–31

presentation software, 121–122; optimal use of, 122–123; resources for, 148; using, 148–149

privacy: issues of, 147; protections of, 147

problems, to shape discussion, 43–44

problem-solving skills, development of, 47–48

procedural knowledge, 17

process recording, 168–169

professional, requirements of, 200

professional behavior, teaching, 50

professional growth and development, 195–196

professional judgments, and critical thinking, 23

professional standards, ensuring minimum, 154

professions, missions of, 187

professor, rank of, 198

program assessment, accreditation standards for, 155

programmed instruction: advantage of, 124–125; definition of, 124; teaching with, 123–127

programs, social work, national rankings of, 156–158. *See also* master's degree programs

promotion: decisions about, 179; and institutional mission, 220

psychiatric disabilities, students with, 83

public, and social work programs, 166

Quam, J., 142

queer theory, 76

questionnaires: for students' course satisfaction, 176; for students' satisfaction, 176, 177–178; for students' self-assessment, 164, 165

questions: during lectures, 39–41; multiple-choice, 167; to shape discussion, 43–44

Quinn, P., 85

race: and access to technology, 115; in course content, 70; and identity, 63; and institutional contexts, 72; of social work faculty, 68–69; in social work profession, 66; of social work students, 66–67; teaching about, 71

racial identity theory, 7, 70

racism, in social work profession, 66

Rai, G. S., 113

Ramanathan, C. S., 177

rankings, program: assessing students for, 158–159; standardized measures for, 159–161; by *U.S. News*, 156–158

Raschick, M., 26

Raskin, M. S., 100, 101, 105, 108, 110

ratings, students' satisfaction, 176, 177–178. *See also* assessment

rating scales, for field instructors' evaluation of students, 181

Rawls, J., 240

Ray, J., 80

reasoning, inductive, 25

Reed, C., 202

references, in job search, 210–211

reflection, discussion to encourage, 41–42

"reflection-in-action," 30–31

reflective judgment: and critical thinking, 22–23; enhancing, 23; stages of, 19–20

Regehr, C., 181

religion, in social work education, 63

religious identity, self-reported, 79

reorientation therapies, 78

research: on CMS, 137; on effectiveness of educational methods, 151; by faculty, 191–193; on faculty jobs in social work, 196; as hiring qualification, 205, 206; in learning, 48–49; on marketing of online teaching, 146; on online teaching, 141; in standardized outcome measures, 142; teaching supported by, 38; of teaching technologies, 148

research professor, title of, 198

Resnick, H., 125

respect, in classroom discussion, 44

respect for colleagues, 250; ethics of, 239

responsible conduct of research (RCR), 224
retirement policies, 89
Reynolds, B. C., 2, 11, 13, 28, 29, 30, 32, 33, 70, 71, 259, 262
Rhodes, R., 105, 106
Ricci, P., 142
Richardson, V., 192
Richmond, M., 95
Rittner, B., 125
Roberts, T. L., 63, 69
role-modeling, as teaching technique, 50
role-playing: in assessment, 168; traditional in-class, 170
Rosen, A., 88
Royce, D., 36

Saari, C., 28, 30
"sage," teacher as, 115
"sage on the stage" lecture model, 115
salaries, 215–216
Sanchez, M., 112, 113
satisfaction, student: with field instruction, 181–183; questionnaires to assess, 176, 177–178
satisfaction, with faculty work, 220
Scharlach, A., 88
Schiele, J. H., 65, 72
scholarship: of application, 192, 193; of discovery, 192; ethics of, 241–243; in faculty work, 191–193; and teaching, 220; of teaching, 193, 257–258; teaching supported by, 38; typology of, 193
Schön, D. A., 30, 31, 154, 260
schools of social work: evolution of, 96; rankings of, 152
Schutz, M., 109
screen readers: resources for, 150; software for, 144
Scriven, M., 22
Seaberg, J. R., 136, 137, 146, 200, 201
search committee, 208, 210
search engines, optimal use of, 128
self-assessment exercises, online, 134
self-consciousness, acute, in professional learning, 28

self-criticism, encouraging, 183
self-direction, 164; in faculty work, 220
self-efficacy, 260; measures of, 164; scale based on, 181
self-evaluation, 257–258; continual, 59; requiring, 183
self-examination, 91
self-knowledge, 259
self-reflection, 65, 91, 164, 169, 259; continual, 59; in teaching, 37
self-reports, by students, 185
self-study, 257–258
seminar, field, 99
sensitive topics, ethics of dealing with, 238
service, in faculty work, 193–194
service learning, 37, 93
service programs, 10
settings, for social work education, 2, 3, 4
sexual harassment, 250; policies against, 77
sexual identity, 63
sexual orientation: and identity, 63; institutional context for, 81–82; self-reported, 79; of social work faculty, 80; and social work profession, 77–78; of social work students, 78–80; teaching, 80–81
sexual relationships: with colleagues, 250; in field, 233
Sheafor, B. W., 96, 97, 98
Shibusawa, T., 183
Sidell, N. L., 172
"signature pedagogy," 180, 225, 260
Silberman Fund, 257
Simmons College, 107
Sinacore, A. L., 91
Singer, J., 124
Singer, T., 88
site rippers, resources for, 149
skills, in field internship, 231
slide shows, 121; guidelines for, 122–123. *See also* presentation software
Smith, H. Y., 101, 103, 104
Smith, L. A., 63, 69

social agencies: learning in, 4–5; new partnerships with, 110; training programs of, 95

social change, 4

social class, 63

social discourses, dominant, 24

social justice, 23; promotion of, 240–241

social psychology, research on stereotypes in, 68

social work: as calling, 225; faculty jobs in, 190, 196; faculty work in, 199–202; as profession, 187; professional education in, 162

Social Work Congress (2005), 260

social work education programs: abroad, 10; assessment of, 156

social workers: as educators, 223; gerontological, 88

social work programs, evaluation of, 151

Social Work Reinvestment Act (2008), 112

society, and adult development, 16

Society for Social Work and Research (SSWR), 206; annual conferences of, 209

Society for Teaching and Learning in Higher Education (STLHE): Canada's, 241; on dual relationships, 246; on ethical guidelines, 241; ethical principles in university teaching of, 238–240; ethical statements of, 249; standards of, 253

socioeconomic status, 63

software, 121; for Internet-based course management, 132–138; plagiarism detection by, 229; speech-to-text products, 144. See also presentation software

South Carolina, University of, 116

Sowers-Hoag, K., 202

SPSS data files, 138

"spyware," 147

SSWR. See Society for Social Work and Research

standardized cases, evaluating students' performance with, 169–172

standardized measures, to assess educational experiences and outcomes, 159–161

standardized tests, 154

standards, and faculty ethics, 252–253

Stefkovich, J. A., 240, 241

Steiner, S., 52

stereotype threat, concept of, 68

STLHE. See Society for Teaching and Learning in Higher Education

Stocks, T. J., 133

"stress interview" techniques, 214–215

Stretch, J. J., 117, 147, 161, 165

Strozier, A. L., 182

Struman, S., 125

student adviser, 49

student development, ethics of, 238–239

student learning, social work theory of, 28–30

students: as active learners, 32; assessment by, 164; in classroom discussion, 46; doctoral, 261; dual relationships with, 239, 245; and ethical issues, 252; international, 112–113; and issues of authorship, 243; and learning styles, 26; potential ethical problems with, 249, 252; presentations of, 48

students, assessment of, 55, 158, 183, 240; for admission, 153; ethics of, 240, 245; for knowledge, 162

students, in field, 26; performance of, 180–181; satisfaction of, 181–183

students, of color: in institutional context, 72; in social work education programs, 67, 69

students, social work, 5, 31; with disabilities, 83–84; diversity among, 66–68; field experience of, 94; gender differences of, 73–75; older, 87; and sexual orientation issues, 78–80

"subjective knowing," 17

subjectivity, in adult development, 21

subordination, systems of, and diversity, 64

supervision: of field instructors, 183; in professional learning, 30

survey instruments, 167
Sussman, T., 11
Svinicki, M., 47, 52, 234
syllabus, course, 52, 55–57. *See also* curriculum

table of contents creation, with CMS, 135
Tatum, B. D., 70, 71
teachable moments, 90
teacher-in-situation conceptual framework, 2, 11, 259
teachers: academic integrity of, 235–241; assessment by, 163; availability of, 56–57; beginning, 53; "consultant," 129; contact of, with students, 119–120; diversity in, 68–69; as faculty–field liaisons, 102; and gender, 75; and learning styles, 26; portfolios of, 57–58, 176, 178, 205; students' perception of, 50
teaching: assessment of, 152–154, 176–178; "best practice" in, 176; campus-based centers for, 179–180; connected, 76–77; context for, 187, 188; contextual influences on, 37–38; developing philosophy of, 36–37; effective, 34–35; effectiveness of, 179; effects of diversity on, 61–63, 64; and electronic technologies, 7; and ethical issues, 224–225; factors affecting, 2, 3; in faculty work, 194; and feedback, 184; feminist, 77; in field setting, 93–94; informed by learning, 32; with interactive media, 123–127; Internet resources for, 127–130, 149; legitimating scholarship of, 257–258; linked with scholarship, 220; methods of, 33; models for, 33; part-time, 207–208; with programmed instruction, 123–127; scholarship of, 193; successful, 60; teams in, 51; and technology, 116–117, 146, 147–148; using groups and teams in, 51–52
teaching, classroom, 216; ethical issues in, 224; impact of technology on, 120–121
teaching, modes of, 35–36; inquiry and discovery, 47–48; leading discussion, 42–47; lecturing and explaining, 38–41; mentoring, 49–50; reflecting on experience, 41–42; training and coaching, 49; variation in, 58–59
teaching, online, 126–127; advantages of, 129–131; effectiveness of, 136–138; research on, 141
The Teaching Company, 125
teaching experience, as hiring qualification, 205–206
teaching materials, CD- and DVD-based, 123–126
teaching methods, ethics of, 244
teaching modalities, 5, 6–7
teaching portfolio, 176, 178, 205; preparing, 57–58
"teaching tips," learning, 60
teams, in teaching, 51
technological innovations, 148; and educational institutions, 118–119; and faculty roles, 119–121; and teaching and learning, 115
technology: access to, 115, 117, 118, 144; costs of, 117; in economic downturn, 119; and learning styles, 145; and teacher–student interactions, 120; and teaching, 116–117, 147; in teaching, 146; user-friendly, 143–145
Technology in Teaching Conference, 121
television, interactive. *See* interactive television
templates, as CMS feature, 134
Tennant, M., 18, 33
tenure: assessment for, 179; system of, 197, 198, 217
termination, and ethical issues, 231–232
term paper, 48
Tesone, D., 142
text-to-speech software, 144
theories: learning, 259; racial identity, 7; stage, 15
thinking: in adults, 14, 16–18, 19–20, 21–22; higher-order, 59; stimulating during lecturing, 40
thinking skills, teaching, 259
Thurston, L., 126

Thyer, B. A., 142
Townsend, A. L., 66, 161
trainers, ethical conduct of, 236
training: in teaching, 49; for using online
  materials, 129
training, in-service, with CMS, 132
transformational learning, 26–28
translation programs, resources for, 150
translation services, 145
Trice, A. G., 196
trouble-shooting model, of liaison role, 103
truth, dualistic, 21

understanding, in learning process, 29
universities: sexual orientation issues at, 82;
  social work programs in, 189; traditional
  reward systems of, 257
Urwin, C. A., 231
U.S. News & World Report, 156–158

values, assessment of, 163
VanEsselstyn, D., 183
Van Soest, D., 63, 71, 231
Vayda, E., 2
verbatim record, traditional, 168
ViaVoice (IBM), 144
video conferencing, 140–143; limitations of,
  141; traditional and IT classes supported
  by, 141
video files, courses available as, 124
videotapes, in standardized cases, 170–171
violence, and sexual orientation issues, 81
"virtues for university teaching," 252
Visiting Scholars Program, of CSWE, 257
visual aids, during lectures, 39, 40
voice recognition software, resources for, 150

Washburn, J. J., 242
Wayne, J., 100, 101, 110
Web-based materials, evaluating, 121
Web courses, 127
Web pages, student-created, 133
Web search, effective strategies for, 149
Weiner, A., 129, 131, 138
white families, and computer access,
  118
white privilege, teaching, 71–72
whites, identity development of, 70
"Wikis," 128
wireless devices, in classroom, 143
Wodarski, J. S., 151, 185
Wolfer, T. A., 177, 178
women: finding "voice" of, 18; in
  non-tenure-track positions, 219; as
  nontraditional students, 17; in social
  work, 72–75; ways of knowing of, 19–20.
  See also gender
word processing, 122
work. *See* faculty work
work assignments, 216
workplace: academic, 187; discrimination
  based on sexual orientation in, 82
workshops, 107
worldviews, alternative, 91
writing, "low stakes," 47
writing skills, 167–168
written assignments, 167

Yelloly, M., 154
Yoon, S.-W., 142

Zastrow, C., 199
Zlotnik, J. L., 88